THE
DARING
TRADER

THE DARING TRADER

JACOB SMITH IN THE MICHIGAN TERRITORY, 1802–1825

KIM CRAWFORD

Michigan State University Press · *East Lansing*

♾ The paper used in this publication meets the minimum requirements
of ANSI/NISO Z39.48-1992 (R 1997) (Permanence of Paper).

Michigan State University Press
East Lansing, Michigan 48823-5245

Printed and bound in the United States of America.

18 17 16 15 14 13 12   1 2 3 4 5 6 7 8 9 10

LIBRARY OF CONGRESS CATALOGING-IN-PUBLICATION DATA
Crawford, Kim, 1957–
The daring trader : Jacob Smith in the Michigan Territory, 1802–1825 /
Kim Crawford.
p. cm.
Includes bibliographical references and index.
ISBN 978-1-61186-026-9 (pbk. : alk. paper) 1. Smith, Jacob, 1773–1825.
2. Pioneers—Michigan—Biography. 3. Fur traders—Michigan—Biography.
4. Indian agents—Michigan—Biography. 5. Frontier and pioneer
life—Michigan. 6. Indians of North America—Michigan—History—19th
century. 7. Flint Region (Mich.)—History—19th century. 8. Michigan—
History—To 1837. 9. Michigan—History—War of 1812. 10. Michigan—
Biography. I. Title.
F566.S65C73 2012
977.4'03092—dc23
[B]
2011035345

Cover and book design by Charlie Sharp, Sharp Des!gns, Lansing, MI.
Cover art is a detail from a mural painted by Edgar S. Cameron in
1925, located in Circuit Courtroom No. 3, Genesee County Courthouse.
Photograph is by Tom Cheek with photo editing by Charlie Sharp,
Sharp Des!gns, Lansing, MI.

Michigan State University Press is a member of the Green Press
Initiative and is committed to developing and encouraging ecologically
responsible publishing practices. For more information about the Green
Press Initiative and the use of recycled paper in book publishing, please
visit *www.greenpressinitiative.org.*

Visit Michigan State University Press at *www.msupress.org*

CONTENTS

Introduction

"He has been a useful man in this quarter . . ."

On a winter's day in Detroit early in 1816, General Lewis Cass, the federal governor of the Michigan Territory, wrote those words about a local fur trader, Jacob Smith, to the U.S. secretary of the Treasury in Washington, D.C. Smith, then about 42 years old, was in trouble with federal customs authorities in Buffalo, New York, for bringing over from Canada an undeclared shipment of trade goods some weeks earlier. Now Cass felt obligated to put in a good word for Smith, a man who had risked his life and fortune on behalf of his adopted country during the War of 1812—and who would continue to serve Cass and the U.S. government, quietly, sometimes secretly, in the years ahead.

Michigan, at the edge of the country's important geopolitical frontier with the British Empire, had been the scene of an invasion by British forces from Canada during the war; there'd been bloody skirmishes, raids, major battles, and even a massacre of American troops by Indians allied with Britain. Perhaps no federal official in the Old Northwest knew of these strife-filled times better than Cass. He had been a military officer during the war—first a colonel of the Ohio militia and then a brigadier general. He was painfully aware that even after the British soldiers had been driven back into Canada late in 1813, attacks on Detroit area residents by Chippewa raiders had continued for another year.

A true peace treaty with the Indians who lived in Michigan had only been made late in the summer of 1815, just a few months earlier. The tribe that had especially concerned Cass—the powerful and threatening Saginaw Chippewa—had come to the treaty councils because of the influence of this "useful trader," Jacob Smith. Acting on behalf of Cass, Smith had convinced the leaders of the Chippewa to attend and take part in the treaty near Detroit, formally ending the war. The governor knew that peaceful relations were an essential step before settlers from the eastern United States would consider moving to Michigan to build homes and farms in what was still wilderness country north of Detroit. Without Smith, Cass wrote, the presence of those Chippewa chiefs at the 1815 peace treaty "could not have been procured."[1]

Jump forward five years: Governor Cass, explaining to the War Department his expenditures, tells of making payments to that same fur trader, "an influential man among the Indians," in the successful 1819 effort to convince the Chippewa and Ottawa leaders of lower Michigan to cede to the United States what would amount to 4.3 million acres of land.[2] This cession stretched across most of the Lower Peninsula, from just north of the modern-day cities of Jackson and Kalamazoo—towns that did not then exist—north to Lake Huron's Thunder Bay and east to Michigan's Thumb.

From confidential missions on the American frontier near British Canada during the War of 1812 to the exertion of influence on Indians angry about the loss of their lands, Jacob Smith served the federal government in the Michigan Territory early in the nineteenth century, helping to bring about dramatic but mainly peaceful change by the white settlement that would follow him and other traders—a change that was devastating for the Indians and their way of life. In war, Smith posed as a British agent, escaped from British-allied Indians, and was thrown into prison in British Canada; he lost money and property as he worked for his adopted country, the United States, and even reported that British Indian Department officials attempted to recruit him to their side. He would gain the release of white children taken hostage by the Indians. And he would serve as the eyes and ears of Lewis Cass on Michigan's woodland frontier, acting on his authority when necessary.

But Smith, whose work for the government was often confidential and who died in obscurity in 1825, is barely a footnote in Michigan history, even though he traveled and traded around Michigan and was one of the most controversial and influential characters of his time in the territory. Why controversial? Because Smith, Canadian-born, slight of build but "smart as steel," didn't just work for the U.S. government as he dealt with the Indians. At the very same time Smith was also laying the groundwork so that his children would in time gain thousands of acres of land that would become valuable when settlers came from the eastern United States to the Saginaw Valley. This land was at the center of what became Flint, Michigan, and was long the center of legal battles.

Yet this mysterious fur trader was not in favor of the federal government taking away the Indians' land wholesale and leaving them to perish as their hunting, trapping, and trading way of life disappeared. When an influential clergyman and geographer named Jedidiah Morse came to Detroit in the spring of 1820 to assess the state of Indians in the United States, Smith advised him that a large national reservation should be created on what was fertile land along Michigan's Flint and Saginaw rivers. This river valley, Smith told Morse, could be a national homeland for Indians from all over the United States.

In this place, Smith told the Reverend Morse, the Chippewa and other tribes could achieve self-sufficiency and respect, away from the negative effects and influences of the white man. In his subsequent report to the U.S. secretary of war, Morse called Smith "one of their guardians" and recommended he become a government agent to help carry out the plan.[3] Morse, who had the ear of some of the most important officials and leaders of his day, believed that Smith genuinely was concerned about the Chippewa and their future.

Other men of the Michigan frontier, contemporaries of Smith's who worked among the Indians as traders, government agents, and interpreters, agreed with Lewis Cass's appraisal of Smith's power with the tribe. "Smith was a man of great influence with the Saginaw Indians," said James Conner, a veteran scout and interpreter for the United States, "and was active by his exertions and very instrumental in and about the procurement of the treaty stipulations from the Indians."[4]

Charles P. Avery, a mid-nineteenth-century lawyer and amateur Michigan historian, called him "the daring trader, Smith." Avery used that description in mentioning the true story of Jacob Smith's bravely redeeming three children who had been taken captive with their father by Saginaw Chippewa warriors during the War of 1812. Smith was the one and only white U.S. citizen to ride unhindered to the Indian village of Saginaw during the war, to trade goods for the release of the young hostages and return them to their mother in Detroit. The only other white

Americans who went into the Saginaw Valley during that period were themselves prisoners.

But there were also critical words for the fur trader, from those who knew him well. "You know, my Dear Sir, as well as I do that Jacob Smith's character at Detroit was want of *morality and veracity*," wrote James Abbott, a prominent man who'd been in feuds with Smith for years. When Abbott wrote those words in 1813, he had good reason to be angry with Smith: Abbott was then under federal investigation because Smith strongly suggested he had been disloyal to the United States during wartime—an offense for which Abbott could have been executed, had the charge proved true.[5]

Bold and controversial, self-serving and sacrificing, mercenary and patriotic, Jacob Smith served Michigan's first two territorial governors as translator, soldier, courier, and confidential agent among the Saginaw Chippewa and Ottawa Indians. Yet if a person with more than a passing interest in the history of territorial Michigan were to try to find any information about Smith, he or she would be lucky to come up with mere references in state and old county histories. Some of these accounts of Smith, published many decades after his death, are brief, some little better than fiction. For example, Clarence Burton, the Detroit chronicler and author who collected, preserved, and published thousands of historical Michigan documents, described Jacob Smith as "quite a character," but nothing more. Willis F. Dunbar and George S. May, the authors of a standard reference, *Michigan—A History of the Wolverine State,* incorrectly wrote that Smith "was using his influence against" Cass's effort to make a treaty with the Saginaw Chippewa in 1819. In short, Smith, whose important work for the U.S. government was unofficial and confidential, barely achieved a place among the minor figures of the early Michigan Territory— remembered heroically after a fashion in the Saginaw Valley and in Flint, where he was considered the first white American settler, depicted in artists' conceptions as a buckskin-clad frontiersman, but otherwise virtually unknown and only mentioned in a handful of pioneer memoirs.[6]

Yet there were clues about Smith's important role in the Michigan Territory left in the historical record. Dennis Massie, a Lansing college instructor and the first modern researcher to seriously consider Jacob Smith, wrote in the 1960s that the trader "seems to have been as influential as any fur trader in Michigan history." Another historian, who came across Smith's trail as she did research for a U.S.-Indian

Claims Commission and was looking into the federal government's dealings with the Saginaw Chippewa, also recognized Smith as an important figure. "In both the [Detroit] Treaty of 1807 and the [Saginaw] Treaty of 1819, the key figure in dealing with the Chippewa was Jacob Smith, a trader who had a post on the Flint River," wrote historian Helen Hornbeck Tanner. "His services were obviously indispensable at the time of the 1819 treaty."[7]

But how were his services so important? Why did he have such influence? This book attempts to answer these questions, to tell the true story of Michigan's most influential fur trader. From a glance at the information that's been available on Jacob Smith till now, he would seem a romantic figure in a dynamic time. Here was a man born in another place (Quebec, Canada) of foreign stock (German parentage), a tough and clever frontier entrepreneur who lived and traded for months at a time among the Indians in the Michigan wilderness, not just with the Chippewa but also with other Indians in other regions. These accounts say Smith served his newly adopted country as a soldier and give an anecdote or two about his adventures. While some of these stories were based on nuggets of truth, others were not. One such tale by Michigan novelist James Oliver Curwood that had Jacob Smith leading a war party of Indians against another tribe in the rescue of an "Indian princess," was nothing more than fiction. In the 1970s, Ed Love, a popular Michigan novelist, wrote a chapter about Smith in a "picture history" of Flint that also romanticized Smith as a pop history Daniel Boone figure, yet the account is unsupported by real evidence.

Massie's article in *Michigan History* represented the first attempt by a researcher to mine primary sources for information about Smith. Yet Massie relied heavily on the romantic and unsubstantiated accounts written long after the fur trader's time. And none of the references to Smith that were published before Massie's article placed Smith in any sort of historical context, even though he lived and operated in one of the most dramatic periods of change in southeastern Michigan.

Then is Smith a noteworthy figure, enigmatic but nearly lost in the history of Michigan? Or is he a strictly "local hero" for the Saginaw Valley, a footnote on the fringes of the larger story of the Michigan Territory? Consider that Jacob Smith's reports and his actions would come to the attention of Thomas Jefferson and the secretaries of war of Jefferson and James Madison, as well as Madison's postmaster general and secretary of the Treasury. Smith was a familiar figure to various U.S. military commanders in the Old Northwest, and he was even the subject of a complaint by the agents of powerful fur magnate John Jacob Astor.

An examination of primary sources, including records, reports, and letters, as well as reminiscences from Michigan pioneers, reveals that Smith was first and foremost a fur trader, but that he also served in a territorial militia troop for some months at the beginning of the War of 1812. By the end of the war he held the rank of captain. His experiences between those times include the stuff of a frontier adventure, with missions, intrigue, capture, escape, and arrest. These show that Smith was unquestionably part of the U.S. fight against Britain and its Indian allies who had hoped to drive the Americans out of Michigan and the Old Northwest.

Yet in this struggle, Smith was not always a soldier. At times, he acted as a spy or scout and agent of influence. For example, it's well known to Michigan historians that prominent U.S. citizens residing in Detroit were kicked out of occupied Michigan by the much-vilified British commander, Colonel Henry Procter, early in 1813, when Procter suspected them of anti-British activity. But what has been forgotten is evidence that Procter had Jacob Smith arrested and thrown into a prison in Montreal months *before* the exile of those better-known men took place.

Even earlier in the summer of 1812, Smith attempted to reach U.S. authorities at Ft. Michilimackinac on Mackinac Island, to bring them the all-important news that war had been declared with Britain. But Smith, who at one point posed as a British agent in order to travel in Indian country, was too late to warn the U.S. Army outpost. He was captured by British-allied Indians but escaped with the help of other Indians and returned to Detroit. Among those who helped Smith escape was a representative of a local Ottawa chief who was urging the tribes of northern Michigan to stay out of the war. This message caused British officers concern, for a time. Little wonder, then, that Smith was eventually arrested by the British after they occupied Detroit weeks later.

Yet another famous name from the War of 1812 who crossed paths with Jacob Smith was Robert Dickson, the influential British fur trader and Indian agent who rallied warriors from the Upper Mississippi and the Great Lakes to fight against the United States. Here will be recounted Jacob Smith's report of how Dickson tried to recruit Smith as he languished in a Canadian prison, because Dickson wanted him to work for the British, enlisting Indians to fight the Americans on the western frontier.

But Smith did not sign on with the British. He managed to return to the United States, and reported his experiences and the information he'd learned to President James Madison's secretary of war. He rose in the estimation of the commanders of the U.S. Northwestern Army, including a young militia colonel named Lewis Cass. Smith was commissioned lieutenant and then captain in the reorganized Michigan militia when Detroit came back into American hands in the fall of 1813.

Cass, of course, would become the territory's second federally appointed governor and one of the most important figures in Michigan history. Yet Cass required experienced hands when it came to his dealings with the Saginaw Chippewa. Records clearly show that Jacob Smith carried messages to the Indians during times of relative peace when Michigan's territorial governors needed help during treaty talks as early as 1807. Smith was more than just a courier, however, and evidence shows he continued to be employed as an important but unofficial agent among the Chippewa for the U.S. government.

Smith's biggest impact on the history of Michigan—his role in getting the Saginaw Chippewa and Ottawa leaders to agree to a treaty ceding millions of acres of land to the United States in 1819—has not been in dispute by the handful of writers and historians who have considered the treaty over the years. But there has been little or no agreement on the ultimate *nature* of his role and which side he truly represented—the Chippewa or the U.S. government? Did he represent only himself? Here will be presented incontrovertible evidence that Smith acted secretly as an agent for Lewis Cass, with the fur trader exerting his powers on his Indian friends and acquaintances to agree to the treaty with the United States.

But Smith was also working to get land reservations for his white children, and attempted to deceive the federal territorial governor in the process. Although granting land to white individuals by Indian treaty wasn't then considered legal or proper, Smith's heirs would eventually prevail in the divisive question of who was to receive these sections of land along the Flint River at the Saginaw Trail. In death, Smith would leave a legacy of controversy in the legal struggle over these sections set aside by treaty on the Flint River—matters that went to the U.S. Congress and that dragged through Michigan courts for decades. In life, Smith was the subject of numerous lawsuits in territorial Detroit courts, mainly as a result of careless, perhaps even reckless business practices and unpaid debts.

In sum, Smith, among the early immigrants to Michigan after it became U.S. territory, was an important but nearly forgotten figure in the first decades of the nineteenth century—brave and confident on the Saginaw Trail but confounding and aggravating to the businessmen and judges of Detroit. His involvement with the Saginaw Chippewa and the U.S. government in the early 1800s, for good or ill, would help bring about one of the greatest periods of change in Michigan's history.

This is Smith's true story—a narrative that places Smith in his relation to the events of Michigan's territorial period before, during, and after the War of 1812—and one that reveals a new and dramatic picture of his role and his interactions with better-remembered personalities of Michigan's past. It's also the story of U.S.-Indian relations in Michigan during the watershed years when Indian domination over the lands north of Detroit gave way to the coming of American settlers. In following Smith's footsteps to the scenes of events in the fur trade, the War of 1812, and the opening of Michigan to U.S. settlement, the story necessarily takes in his contemporaries—the traders, Indians, scouts, and soldiers with whom he interacted in the Great Lakes woodland frontier two centuries ago.

Witness to Murder:
Saginaw, 1802

The man who would become the most influential fur trader of territorial Michigan for his work among the Saginaw Chippewa and Ottawa began life as the son of German parents in a French city in British Canada, about a hundred miles from the U.S. border in the closing years of the eighteenth century. These circumstances may seem like a dramatic foreshadowing, portending a life of intrigue and adventure, but before Jacob Smith entered the world of the frontier fur trade in Michigan his job in Canada was more mundane: As a young man, Jacob Smith was a merchant butcher in what seems to have been a family business in Quebec.

Jacob Smith was one of the sons of John Rudolf Smith and his wife Elizabeth, born in Quebec in 1773. Quebec town censuses for the early 1790s show there were two different butchers named Smith, both of them Protestants, and there are indications that at least one them, Charles Smith, at 11 rue Notre Dame in 1795, was related to Jacob. These butchers, Charles Smith and one listed or given as "S. Smith," were successful enough that they had servants in their homes and apprentices in their businesses. Biographical notes by a son-in-law of Jacob Smith who didn't actually know him—notes that aren't completely accurate—state that

Smith had a brother Charles who was a banker.[1] There was, however, nothing like a commercial bank in what was then called Upper Canada before the 1820s.

Jacob Smith's name didn't appear in the Quebec census until the spring of 1798, when he was 25 years old and head of his own household, and almost nothing is known about his childhood or youth. But that year Smith was listed as a butcher living in the lower town at the same address on the rue Notre Dame that had been occupied by butcher Charles Smith before him. Jacob Smith's father, a soap-maker, then resided in the Fauxbourg-St. Jean area. After Jacob Smith came to Michigan, he would be described as a slight man, but wiry, agile, and strong—physical attributes that presumably served him well as a butcher but that would be even more important when he lived among the Indians for months at a time. Louis Campau, one of Smith's rivals in the Michigan fur trade, would describe him physically as being "smart as steel"—a testament to Smith's sharpness and speed in a fight.[2]

The summer of 1798 was an eventful time for Jacob Smith, for he was to be married. His bride-to-be was 18-year-old Mary Reed, the daughter of Thomas Reed and Margaret McMaster. Mary's parents had wed in Montreal in 1779 and lived in Quebec afterward. Tom Reed had been a tavern keeper in the lower town; Margaret was an Irish-born immigrant from Killough. Mary was one of three Reed children, and she was about three years old when her father died.

Margaret Reed remarried early in 1784. Her second husband was a local shoemaker named Andrew Doe, born in Maryland when it was an English colony before the American Revolution. The fact that Doe had moved to Canada suggests he may have been a British Loyalist who wanted to remain a citizen of King George III when war broke out, just as thousands of "Tories" in the American colonies did. Andrew Doe took over Tom Reed's inn when he married Margaret and became stepfather to Margaret's three small children. But only Mary survived, with church records showing that her little brother Thomas, age three, and sister Ann, five, died within a week of each other late in the spring of 1786. Andrew and Margaret appear to have had children of their own.[3]

Presumably it was happy day when Jacob Smith and Mary Reed wed on July 25, 1798, in the Holy Trinity Anglican Church in Quebec, with Mary's mother and stepfather and Jacob's parents in attendance. This was the same church where Mary's mother had married her second husband some 14 years earlier. But a state of family peace did not reign over Jacob Smith and his in-laws. Less than three months after Jacob and Mary were married, they sued her stepfather in a local court. In this suit, the Smiths wanted a full accounting of the estate of Mary's father, Tom Reed, since, they claimed, they were entitled to a third of the value of the real estate and property Reed had owned, plus interest, dating from the time Mary had turned 18 earlier that year. The Does eventually provided an extensive listing of the furniture, household goods, and other property that made up Mary's father's estate—it suggests that Tom Reed had been successful, even wealthy. How Jacob and Mary Smith fared in the case isn't reflected in the surviving records, but the suit couldn't have endeared Jacob Smith to his in-laws. The matter may have been the start of a rift between the families that would last for years.[4]

In the meantime the family of Jacob and Mary Smith grew. In the late summer, just over a year after their marriage, Mary gave birth to the first of five surviving children. They named their daughter Harriet Margaretta.[5] These details of Smith's life before he came to Michigan are few, but they place him and his relatives in Quebec, an important fur trade business center, in the years before 1800.

Subsequent evidence Jacob Smith would leave in Quebec and Detroit suggests that he could read and write English and French, and that by 1807 he could also fluently speak the Chippewa-Ottawa dialect of the Algonquin language. As a merchant butcher, he presumably had business experience under his belt. And if he hadn't traveled in the employ of fur-trading merchants in Canada in the years before 1798, he had doubtless heard their talk, surrounded as he was by people involved in the business. Quebec was home to many Great Lakes sailors, frontier soldiers, and trader-merchants. But sometime between 1799 and 1801—the specific date is unknown—Jacob Smith also joined in the fur trade. He and his family left their home in British Canada for Detroit, a frontier town on the edge of the Michigan woodland, just inside of the territory of the young United States.[6]

Although Quebec was an old French settlement and the fur trade had been going on for nearly 200 years, Jacob Smith grew up during the period when the British were in control of most of this trade in the Great Lakes. The most important concern in this region was the North West Company, a loose association of mainly Scottish fur traders. One of this company's strongest incarnations was active and strong and based in nearby Montreal in the 1780s, and was deeply involved in the Great Lakes trade in the 1790s. Closely related to the North West Company was the Mackinac Company, with its field headquarters on Mackinac Island. This outfit was owned by some of the partners of the North West Company. These fur-trading operations were major businesses, and vessels as big as a hundred tons sailed on

Lakes Michigan and Huron, carrying trade goods out to the Indian country far to the west, and bringing pelts back. Smaller shipments for these companies were carried on large canoes and bateauxs, barge-like crafts also sometimes referred to as "Mackinac boats" that could move cargoes of several tons.

Of course, the French explorers, soldiers, and merchants had led the way into Canada and the Great Lakes region back in the 1600s, with the British taking control of the trade after the French and Indian War. By Jacob Smith's time nearly 50 years later, Frenchmen still comprised much of the ranks of the expert traders and the labor force on whom the Scots and English businessmen relied. French and French-Indian voyageurs paddled canoes for endless miles on the lakes and rivers, and they carried huge packs of supplies, goods, and furs at the portages and into forests. Unlicensed traders, rugged men called coureurs de bois, or runners of the woods, knew the Indian trails and winter hunting grounds of the Great Lakes region, and many had Indian wives. Some were themselves the sons of Indian mothers.

But as the nineteenth century dawned, the Scotch-English fur kings of Montreal were worried: The Americans were coming. Merchants and businessmen from New York and Pennsylvania were attempting to break into the Great Lakes trade after the Revolutionary War, into the area the Americans called "the Old Northwest" because it lay northwest of the Ohio River. The British, whose Canadian trading empire spread far across the continent to the west and north, called the Great Lakes area "the Southwest" because of its proximity to Upper Canada, or the southern portion of what was eventually named Ontario.[7]

The growing American presence was one of the developments affecting the fur trade in the Great Lakes region, coming about in part because of John Jay's Treaty, a 1794 agreement between the United States and Britain. This treaty established the boundary between the United States and Canada through the Lakes and it allowed both American and British subjects reciprocal rights to trade and operate across the international border. By the time Smith arrived in Michigan a few years later, there were still few Americans directly involved in the trade; Americans had actually been discouraged, if not prevented, from setting up at Detroit or establishing residence there under British authority.

This was changing, however. Detroit, the largest town on the U.S. frontier on the Great Lakes, had been a fur trading center for a century, having been founded in 1701 by Cadillac in order to expand and preserve French markets and protect them from the British and their Indian allies, the Iroquois. The British had taken over these markets and Detroit, too—right up until 1796, when the Americans took possession of the town. Detroit was located near the straits leading to Lakes Huron, Michigan, and Superior, and it was also accessible from Canada and the Ohio Valley. British officials and businessmen in Canada had groaned when they heard that Detroit and Michigan had been relinquished to the Americans during peace treaty negotiations. Some loyal British merchants moved across the river to Canada so as to remain on "English soil," but some did not. Either way, British subjects still held the upper hand, at least for the moment, in the Michigan fur trade.[8]

It wasn't just the water routes that made Detroit such an important center. Indian trails came from nearly every direction to Detroit and each spring many Ottawa and Chippewa, who wintered in small bands to hunt and trap, made their way to the town to trade their furs and maple sugar for goods; so did Indians from Ohio and areas to the west. Merchants from Quebec and Montreal and their agents had for generations traveled to Detroit or simply set up shop there. By far, the biggest population in Michigan and the Old Northwest was the thousands of Indians who resided in their villages and camps, hunting and fishing, some raising corn, squash, and other produce in fields, clearings, and prairies that dotted the forests of Michigan.[9]

Now as the American age in Detroit was dawning, Jacob Smith was in the vanguard of new traders. He may have had both personal and practical reasons for basing himself in Detroit in order to go into the fur trade. Histories of the North West Company show that family connections were important to its top partners, many of whom were Scotsmen. That meant a man such as Smith, unless he married into one of these families, would likely only be an employee or agent of such a company. Detroit, on the other hand, had long been a center for independent fur traders. It was a logical place for a man to go into business for himself, yet he could still deal with agents of the big company if he wanted or needed to do so.

It is also possible Smith was initially working for or in conjunction with the North West Company—something his heirs believed to be the case. But a letter written by Smith in 1815 suggests that he, like other independent Detroit-based traders of the time, did business individually with Canadian merchants. These were businessmen who extended credit to traders in the form of trade goods; traders used the goods to swap for the pelts of fur-bearing animals the Indians had trapped and hunted.[10]

Finally, there is the matter of a family connection between Jacob Smith and a businessman named William Smith who lived in the Detroit area. A son-in-law of Jacob Smith, Thomas B. W. Stockton, would write that Smith had a brother named

William who was a merchant in Upper Canada with extensive business dealings. These notes also say that one of Smith's brothers lived across the Detroit River in Sandwich in the year 1812. While the accuracy of some of Stockton's information about Smith is open to question, a letter by Jacob Smith's wife in 1817 indicates that he had a relative named William Smith in Upper Canada. It is also a matter of record that a William Smith had lived in Detroit in the 1790s and close by in Canada for years afterward. This man had been active in civic affairs in Detroit, and lived in Amherstburg, a small community about 25 miles south of Sandwich on the Detroit River. Other records reflect that a William Smith resided in Sandwich around 1815. If one of these William Smiths was truly Jacob Smith's brother, perhaps he encouraged Jacob to come to the Detroit area about 1800.[11]

Jacob Smith appears to have left no record reflecting his activities at the turn of the nineteenth century, so there is no indication of what prompted him to make a career change from merchant butcher to fur trader. Was it at the suggestion of a relative? Did Smith lose his lawsuit against his in-laws and feel the need to make a fresh start in a new place? Did he and his wife get a settlement or award in the matter of her father's estate and use the money to buy a stake in the fur trade? Or did Smith long for a venture taking him into a new country? However it happened, evidence shows that Jacob Smith came to Michigan, then part of the Indiana Territory of the United States, by at least the last part of the winter trading season of 1801–1802, at an Indian village on a river called the Saginaw, some 90 miles north-northwest of Detroit.

The Detroit of Jacob Smith's time, though technically in U.S. territory, was a town inhabited by hundreds of French and French-Indian people, a number of Scottish and English merchants and tradesman, some Germans and Dutch, and a garrison of U.S. Army troops. It had narrow streets and rough-hewn, ramshackle houses and buildings for the most part, described by one American as "low and inelegant." Many of the French and English residents were voyageurs and their families, traders, small farmers, and ex-soldiers, some of whom had Indian wives. People from the Ottawa, Pottawatomi, Wyandot, Chippewa, and other nations or tribes of the region came and went from Detroit, trading for manufactured goods and services upon which some were coming to rely.

There were also farms outside of town and a small village called Frenchtown, about 35 miles south of Detroit. This settlement, which would eventually be called

Monroe, was on the River Raisin near its mouth on Lake Erie. Outside of Detroit and Frenchtown, only cabins and farms lined and dotted the eastern coast of Michigan, from the Maumee River (near present-day Toledo) on the south, to the Clinton River, which empties into Lake St. Clair about 20 miles north of Detroit. All told, there were less than 3,800 people living between these rivers, with most of them in the Detroit area, and almost all of them near or along the water.

Again, most of these residents were French and British-Canadians. It was from Detroit that the British military and its agents had encouraged Indian attacks against the American frontier during the Revolutionary War, and Detroit had been an important center for Indian alliances against the United States in the late 1700s. Though Detroit was supposed to be turned over to the United States after the Treaty of Paris in 1783 ended the war between the Americans and Britain, the British had been in no hurry to leave. They only did so 13 years later, when they were increasingly pressured by their involvement in a war in Europe. A contingent of U.S. Army soldiers under Colonel John Hamtramck came in July 1796 to claim the fort at Detroit and raised the American flag over it for the first time.

By the time of Jacob Smith's arrival in Detroit around 1800, the number of U.S. citizen civilians who had come to live there was small. Still, each passing year would see more Americans from the eastern United States arriving at Detroit. There was resentment at these newcomers, from Indians concerned over the Americans' push west and from the British Canadians whose fur trade interests were threatened by U.S. businessmen and settlers. For years settlers from the eastern United States had come over the mountains into the Ohio Valley and Indiana and Illinois to build homes and farms or trade, a tide that represented a virtual invasion to the Indians who lived there. White settlers did this at their own peril, and few had ventured to Michigan. Away from U.S. garrisons at Detroit and Ft. Michilimackinac at the straits between the Upper and Lower Peninsulas of Michigan, a settler had no protection beyond what he could provide for himself.[12]

One American who was very much interested in the fur trade in Michigan and far beyond was John Jacob Astor. A German immigrant who'd come to New York to make his fortune, Astor had established strong links to the Great Lakes through American traders in Albany and the British-Canadian traders in Montreal when Jacob Smith was still young, and he was soon building a massive fortune.[13] The impact Astor would make in the fur business and Michigan was huge. His agents, at a time when they felt a U.S. official in Michigan was being too hard on them after the War of 1812, would point to Smith as an example of someone against whom the federal government should take action, for supplying Saginaw area Indians with alcohol—something Astor's agents also did wherever they traded, on a far greater scale.

These events were still some years off. There was peace between the British and the United States as the new century began, but the Indians of the Great Lakes were aware of the experiences of other tribes as land-hungry Americans came into the region. Raids, murders, massacres, and periodic battles between U.S. soldiers and settlers and Indians in the Ohio Valley had dragged on after the American Revolution, and Indians from Michigan were often participants in these attacks.[14]

This, then, was the situation in Detroit when Jacob Smith moved his family to Michigan around 1800 and began his work there. French and English residents of Detroit and Upper Canada involved in the fur trade usually enjoyed good relations with the Indians of Michigan, but there were violent exceptions. In March 1802, at the Chippewa village called Saginaw, a powerful Indian named Kishkauko stabbed a trader named Antoine Lauzon in the back of his neck with a narrow steel blade. Lauzon, who worked for a fur trade agent named Angus Mackintosh, died two days later. A later grand jury indictment of Kishkauko listed Jacob Smith as a witness in this case.[15]

Lauzon's boss, Mackintosh, was based in the town of Sandwich (now Windsor, Ontario), across the river from Detroit. "Some days ago I received Account of the Man who traded for me at Saginaw, being Killed by an Indian which from information I am able to collect, was done without any provocation on the part of my man, but solely from his refusing to give the Indian liquor," Mackintosh wrote to the partners of the North West Company. Without naming the unfortunate victim, Mackintosh noted that Lauzon's trade goods "were immediately taken charge by two of the engages [*engagees*, or employees] who were there for me." He continued in a rather cold-blooded manner: "The death of this Man will not I suppose occasion me any way considerable loss as I am made to understand he did not indulge the Indians with much credit."[16]

Whether or not Jacob Smith was one of Mackintosh's contract employees, he was later listed at a witness in the U.S. government's case against Kishkauko. The murder of Lauzon at Saginaw appears to have made a significant impression on him, for Smith would not repeat the dead man's mistakes. As an independent trader, Smith would extend thousands of dollars worth of credit to the Indians of the Saginaw region in trade. And like many traders, Smith would certainly trade or otherwise provide his Indian customers with alcohol, in direct violation of U.S. law.

What happened in the wake of Lauzon's murder? A Michigan historian wrote that Kishkauko was arrested, brought down to Detroit, and charged with murder that spring of 1802. He admitted that, while drunk, he had attacked Lauzon. Physically tall and athletic from his youth into middle age, Kishkauko would be remembered later as "one of the most ferocious" chiefs of Michigan's territorial era. But Kishkauko soon escaped from the white authorities, and was later indicted for murder in September 1805 by a Detroit grand jury that heard from Jacob Smith, along with traders Toussaint Campau, Charles Gouin, Pierre Gouin, and Pierre Chovin.[17]

No account of the men's testimony about Kishkauko's attack on Lauzon seems to have survived, but records show that Campau and the Gouins were part of French-Canadian families that had for years been involved in the fur trade. Kishkauko, whose name would take on many different spellings by white men in the years ahead, was also known, according to his indictment, as "the Chippeway Rogue." After Kishkauko's indictment, a federal marshal from Detroit named William McDowell Scott again took him into custody in the summer of 1806, only to see the suspect rescued by his father—a chief named Little Cedar—and other Indians, before Scott could get back to town with his prisoner. Kishkauko's reputation as a dangerous man would go on for two decades, and his path and that of Jacob Smith would often cross in the years ahead.[18]

The murder indictment of Kishkauko, listing Jacob Smith as a witness to the 1802 crime, is the earliest indication of Smith's presence in Michigan in the fur trade. Since traders and their employees sometimes spent the entire winter in Indian country and made their arrangements months in advance of the trading season, this could mean that Smith had been at Saginaw in the fall of 1801 and in the Detroit-Sandwich area before then. Yet it should also be noted that Saginaw was close enough to Detroit that traders could and did travel overland with packhorses during the winter time.

It was also during this period that Smith made Detroit his family's home and his base for trading with the Indians. In 1820 Smith would tell a prominent American clergyman that he had spent "some 20 years" among the Saginaw Indians, clearly dating his dealings with them from about 1800. Similarly, a petition sent to U.S. government officials from Detroit residents shows that Smith was a resident (and presumably, a U.S. citizen) before the spring of 1803. Becoming an American citizen during this time was not difficult for a man who had come from Canada. In 1802 U.S. naturalization law was liberalized, meaning Smith only needed to declare his intent to become a citizen and reside on U.S. soil for a year. While the provisions of naturalization law changed several times during those early years of the nineteenth century, the process of becoming an American citizen may have been as simple as Smith making a declaration and swearing an oath before a federal official.[19]

Records from Wayne County's Court of Common Pleas also indicate that Smith was in business in Detroit. In September 1803, Smith charged in a suit that a man named Peter Swart owed him $80. Smith brought another case in June 1804 in which he claimed that Gabriel Chene, an important property owner, owed him $200. How these suits turned out is unknown, but they are typical of the trade-and-business disputes that were fought in local courts.[20]

Detroit, Wayne County, and Michigan were then part of the Indiana Territory, but that changed when the U.S. government created the Michigan Territory in 1805. Jacob Smith first showed up in the papers of the new territory as part of a property dispute. "In the latter part of the summer of 1805 he [Smith] entered upon building a House in Detroit upon lot 4, in section 2, with Mr. James Dodemead, with whom he then contemplated entering into a general co-partnership in merchandising," this record states.

The background to Smith's complaint was this: On June 11 that year, a devastating fire destroyed most of the homes and buildings of Detroit, just 19 days before the Territory of Michigan came into being by federal law. James Dodemead, 22 years old, was the eldest son of John Dodemead, a prominent tavern keeper and businessman who had lost his property in the fire. James Dodemead was likely trying to get his father back on his feet after the blaze, so he invited Smith into a joint venture, building on property that summer that fronted on Jefferson Avenue, the new main street of Detroit as it was being rebuilt. Smith and young Dodemead worked on the house themselves and also hired laborers or "mechanics." By fall, their building was enclosed and had a chimney. But within several months, this planned merchant partnership between Smith and Dodemead would fall apart.[21]

The reconstruction of Detroit was already under way when the new federally appointed territorial governor, William Hull, arrived from the east to take charge early in July. Soon Jacob Smith was given new responsibilities by the governor. Just two months after Hull arrived in Detroit, he reorganized the local militia and formed companies for a new regiment. As a result, Smith was appointed that September to the post of ensign (roughly the rank of sublieutenant) in a company of men from the town. Other officers in that company were brothers Joseph Campau and James Campau.[22]

The Campaus were part of a sprawling French family that had come from Quebec to Detroit a generation before. Joseph Campau, a merchant, for several years had been training his young nephew, Louis, in the business of buying and selling goods. A photograph taken of Louis Campau late in his life suggests that he was a tall, sturdily built man. Louis Campau was only 14 years old in the fall of 1805, but in a decade's time he would be a fierce rival of Jacob Smith's in the competitive Saginaw Valley fur trade.[23]

Just about the same time that Governor Hull was giving Smith a junior officer's commission in the militia, the trader was called as a witness before the Michigan Territory's grand jury in the Antoine Lauzon murder. By this point, the killing of the trader had gone unpunished for more than three years, and local lawyer Solomon Sibley, who was also U.S. attorney of the territory, renewed criminal proceedings against Kishkauko. An American-born easterner, Sibley had come from Ohio to Detroit about 10 years earlier. He would go on to serve in various governmental posts, including a stint as mayor of the town.

But early in October, not long after Smith and the other traders testified about the Lauzon murder, he resigned from his militia officer's post. This was less than a month after he'd received his commission from Hull. Smith may have done this because he wasn't going to be around Detroit for the winter; like many other Detroit residents involved in the local fur trade, he headed into the Indian country to do business.[24]

On the surface, at least, it seemed an uncomplicated business. Traders and their partners, assistants, or agents would take goods ranging from jewelry and cloth and cooking utensils to ribbons and rum, by canoe, ship, or packhorse, depending on where they set up trading posts in the wilderness. Some traders went directly to Indian villages and encampments, while others set up at forts or outposts. Often trading posts were established near rivers, as were Indian camps.

Fall and winter were the big trapping and hunting seasons for the Indians, when their villages broke up into smaller, family groups, making camps along the rivers and streams of their region, hunting the deer, elk, and even moose that were said to be present in the Lower Peninsula then. During these months they could accumulate hundreds and even thousands of pelts of river otter, muskrat, mink, raccoon, beaver, and other fur-bearing animals, from bears to martens and fishers. These pelts, by the pack, were traded for the white men's goods. When the trader returned from his winter posts, he sold his pelts eastward and paid his creditors. What was left, of course, was his profit.[25]

Jacob Smith had almost certainly been involved in the fur trade before the fall of 1805, but this date represents the first time his name appeared in the licensing records of the new Michigan Territory. Stanley Griswold, a Yale graduate, former Revolutionary War soldier, and Congregational minister, was the new territorial secretary; he recorded that Jacob Smith was the sixth man who came in that fall to get his license to trade at the "Huron."[26]

Records show that traders tended to give the name of the river where they were intended to set up trade when they applied for their licenses, and in 1805 the term "Huron" could mean several different places in Michigan. First, there was the river that is still known as the Huron, which begins in the northwestern corner of Oakland County and runs through Livingston, Washtenaw, and southern Wayne counties into Lake Erie. For years there had been trading going on along this river at what would become the city of Ypsilanti, where a band of the Wyandot lived. But there were also bands of Indians that had camped and hunted near the headwaters of this river, some 30 miles to the north, though whether they were residing there in 1805 is not known. The Saginaw Trail went by good, freshwater springs in this area, locations in what became Springfield and Groveland townships in Oakland County. It could be, therefore, that Smith's trading location at the "Huron" referred to this place, the river headwaters near the overland path between Detroit and the Chippewa community called Saginaw.[27]

But this river was just one of three in Michigan called "Huron" in those days. The second was the river that ultimately became known as the Cass, for Governor Lewis Cass. This river begins in the Thumb and flows southwest to the Saginaw, and Chippewa bands lived along its banks. If Smith wasn't trading on that river in the winter of 1805, he would do so at times in the years ahead, according to his family. This river was accessible from the Saginaw and it was a matter of record that Smith at times traded on the Cass River.[28]

There is, however, another and perhaps better possibility as to the location of

Jacob Smith's Huron. In 1805, "Huron" was also the name of what became known as the Clinton River. It begins in the hills of central northern Oakland County and flows on a winding course to Lake St. Clair. In Jacob Smith's day, the Clinton River was called "the river aux Huron of Lake St. Clair" or "the upper Huron." By the time Smith came to Detroit, French traders had long since established trading posts near the mouth of the Clinton, where Indian bands also lived, in the area that would soon become the town of Mt. Clemens when American settlers came.

If this was the location where Smith traded that winter, the Indians with whom he dealt were again Chippewa and Ottawa. Smith had already been among their people with traders at Saginaw, and he would form bonds with members of the band on Lake St. Clair by fathering a child with a Chippewa woman here. Thus it may be that when Smith noted for licensing records that he was going to trade at the "Huron," he was referring to the part of the Clinton River in today's Macomb County, given the evidence that his daughter of an Indian mother would be born here in 1807.[29]

Wherever Smith set up in 1805, he, like other traders, had to post a $1,000 bond in order to be legally licensed to trade. These bonds were typically put up by businessmen who financed or partnered with fur traders. The bond was, ostensibly, a safeguard held by the territorial government to ensure that the trader followed the law, in particular the prohibition against providing rum or whiskey to Indians. But while every government that ever ruled the Northwest or the Great Lakes had bans on the trading of alcohol to the Native people at one time or another, none ever succeeded. To the Indians, the results were catastrophic and many of them understood that perfectly.

Even when the British had a near total grip on the fur trade with the Indians of Michigan and Ohio in the years preceding Jacob Smith's arrival, some leaders complained about the liquor that was being brought into the Maumee River country south of Detroit. "You advised us some years ago not to permit whisky being brought amongst us," one Indian speaker complained to the British in 1792. "We readily complied with your desire and prohibited that trade with the Americans, hoping you would on your part likewise prevent your people bringing spirituous liquor amongst us."

The complaint had continued: "But Father, we are sorry to observe that this disorder has increased to such a pitch as to threaten our destruction, for whilst the Hatchet is hanging over our heads, our Young Men are kept in continual intoxication parting with everything they have for that pernicious Article."[30]

The use of alcohol in the Indian fur trade of course continued in the American years at Detroit. Father Gabriel Richard, the heroic French priest who was an important leader during the territorial Michigan era, bemoaned in 1800 the drunken state of Indians who visited Detroit. The good father knew that traders were to blame. "No man unacquainted with the trade of our back ward Countryes [*sic*] is able to foretell the cunning means inspired by the exhaustless wish of getting fur," he complained.[31]

By 1801, the approximate time of Smith's arrival in Detroit, the impact of the American fur traders was undeniable to Angus Mackintosh, the veteran British fur trade agent across the river. He wrote that he now needed whiskey, rather than rum, for transacting business with the Indians. "Our chief article will be whiskey, seeing that since the introduction of it into the Indian Country by the Americans, it has become the chief article of trade with the Indians, so much so that West India Rum is now very little in demand with them," Mackintosh wrote to his superiors of the North West Company.[32]

The name of the person who put up Jacob Smith's 1805 trading license bond is impossible to make out in the licensing book of the Michigan Territory. While the entry indicates that Smith probably wasn't heading for the Saginaw Valley during that winter of 1805–1806, at least two of his contemporaries were. One was named William Gourie Watson and the other Charles Girard. Girard also claimed he was going to trade at "the Shiawasa" or Shiawassee River, and this likely meant one or more of three different Saginaw Chippewa communities. It could have meant the "Big Rock" village that would become the site of the town of Chesaning, not far south of Saginaw, or a town near some rapids to the south. Louis Campau, a veteran of the Michigan fur trade, said this village at the rapids was called "Wassau's Village," probably the name of a chief who led this band, though Campau noted the name would evolve when white settlers arrived, turning it into Owosso.[33]

Yet another village on the Shiawassee was just 10 miles or so southeast from the rapids, and this location the Chippewa called Ketchewondaugoning (one of many spellings), which was said to have translated as the "Big Salt Lick." The French traders called it "the Grand Saline." Of course, the traders set up temporary posts at all these locations at various times. A later, local history said the Grand Saline was a favorite spot of a trader named Bolieu or Beaulieu, located near the river in the area of the northwestern corner of Shiawassee County's Burnside Township and the southwestern corner of Vernon Township. Bolieu's first name is given as Henri in some accounts; Louis Campau, who apparently knew Bolieu, described him only as a French trader.[34]

Just as there were Indian communities at points along the Shiawassee River, so were there villages and camps on the Flint, Cass, Tittabawassee, and other creeks and rivers that form the Saginaw, which in turn flows out to the Saginaw Bay of Lake Huron. Chippewa and Ottawa bands, closely related by language, custom, and marriage, utilized all of the rivers of the Saginaw Valley. Smith would variously trade at Indian villages and camps in what would become the towns of Flint, Saginaw, and Montrose and other points, too. In time, trader Charles Girard would aid Jacob Smith when war came to Michigan in the summer of 1812, and he left an account of Smith's first mission of the conflict.

If Smith was working as independent trader in 1805, he may have entered into partnerships or shared arrangements with others. One account claimed it was the French or French-Indian trader Bolieu who brought Smith to the crossing or "Grand Traverse" of the Saginaw Trail at the Flint River during the winter of 1806. This location was where Smith's children would in time claim hundreds of acres of land, and where the city of Flint would grow.[35]

This account of Smith coming to the Grand Traverse was written by Lucius E. Gould of Shiawassee County, an amateur historian of the late nineteenth century who got his information from American settlers who had come there a generation before. These settlers had known a man named Peter Whitmore Knaggs Jr., the son of a longtime Indian interpreter and scout for the U.S. government, Whitmore Knaggs. Both father and son were contemporaries of Jacob Smith, and the older Knaggs probably knew Bolieu. According to a Knaggs genealogy, Peter Knaggs eventually established a trading post at the Grand Saline on the Shiawassee in 1820; Gould wrote that Peter Knaggs passed along stories of the Michigan frontier to those traders and farmers who followed in the late 1820s and 1830s.

Was Gould's information accurate? On one hand, some of Gould's historical writing can be verified by other sources. According to testimony introduced in a Michigan court case, Bolieu truly was a trader, called "Kasegans" by the Indians, who operated in areas that later became Genesee, Lapeer, and Oakland counties. Bolieu had married a woman from a Chippewa band that made its home in the Saginaw Valley along a river they called Pe-wan-a-go-see-ba, the "river of flint," or "river of the fire stones." Bolieu's wife, it was claimed, was related to a local chief called Neome (pronounced *Nay*-ohm), while Bolieu's granddaughter would later say her mother was related to Kishkauko and the chief called Grand Blanc. Regardless of Bolieu's wife's Chippewa relations, Neome would become a close friend of Jacob Smith's in the years ahead. Bolieu established his own home not quite 30 miles south of the Flint River, at the place called Little Springs in what would become Oakland County's Springfield Township, long before any white American settler would do so.[36]

While hardly a trace of Bolieu can be found in territorial Michigan records, later testimony indicated he had fathered several children with his Chippewa wife, including a daughter whose French name was Angelique, perhaps as early as 1780. Bolieu's daughter remained among the Indians in the Saginaw Valley until she was about 12 years old, when she was taken to live with her white relatives in Detroit. Campau remembered Bolieu as one of the early traders, that is, before the War of 1812 and his own time in the fur trade.[37]

Given this historical background about Bolieu, it is possible that he brought Jacob Smith to the Flint River and introduced him to the Chippewa who lived there in the early 1800s. But other claims made in the account written by Lucius Gould cannot be taken too seriously. For example, Gould claimed that Bolieu was "the first white man" to travel the Saginaw Valley. This is simply not the case. By 1806, French traders had been moving throughout this region for more than a century, and British traders for many decades. When Jacob Smith was still young, a fellow by the name of Charles Vallei was bringing pelts from Saginaw to Detroit. Another man who had lived among the Saginaw Chippewa (and who was ending his career as a trader as Smith came on the scene) was James V. S. Ryley. Ryley had three half-Chippewa sons who were also Jacob Smith's contemporaries.[38]

Other accounts of white fur traders in the Saginaw Valley go back even further. Some told of a French trader named Tromble or Trombley who had been among those Indians at Saginaw in the 1690s. Detroit's founder, Cadillac, mentioned that traders were doing business at Saginaw in 1708. And long before Lauzon was murdered by Kishkauko, other French traders had been killed at "Sanguinon," described as an Ottawa village between Detroit and Michilimackinac, during a period of war and unrest between Britain and France in the late 1740s.[39]

In light of this busy history of the Saginaw fur trade, Gould's identification of Bolieu as the first white man to travel through the Saginaw Valley or visit the Flint River can't be accepted as accurate. It is probably more relevant to understand that for the American settlers who followed the fur traders into the Saginaw Valley, Bolieu represented the end of the old French-British era, while Whitmore Knaggs and Jacob Smith were U.S. citizens who served their government and ultimately settled on or claimed land in what was still Indian country after the War of 1812.

Even in those early years of the nineteenth century, Smith and Knaggs aligned themselves with the new U.S. governmental authority in Michigan. Knaggs had worked for the U.S. Army and government as an Indian interpreter and scout as far back as the late 1790s, while Smith was working for Governor Hull in 1807 and perhaps earlier. In later years these men would be remembered by those settlers who followed as heroic American pioneers, though Indians of Michigan would have a view of the men as agents of the federal government's policy of displacing them for their land. Both Smith and Knaggs would risk their lives for the United States when war came to the Great Lakes frontier in 1812.[40]

The Saginaw Trail

I t would be difficult for today's residents of southeastern Michigan, an urban-suburban home to several million people, to imagine the place in the first years of the nineteenth century, the time of Jacob Smith and other traders. To strike out on the Saginaw Trail from Detroit was to venture into a wooded wilderness that was strictly Indian country, where there were no white settlers and where most traders only stayed temporarily. Of course, if a trader and his men were headed for a point on Lake Huron or one of the rivers that emptied into it, he could move his trade goods and supplies by water before the winter freeze. But accounts show that traders used Michigan's Indian trails to get themselves and late season resupplies of goods to where they were needed. An overland journey up the path to Saginaw, or to any point in the Saginaw Valley or southeastern Michigan where Chippewa and Ottawa bands lived, meant a trader moved his goods and provisions by horse and pony.[1]

As one left Detroit, this trail (which would in time evolve into Woodward Avenue) went through flat, wetland forest for several miles, including an area called the Cranberry Marsh that lay between the town and the place that would become known as Royal Oak in Oakland County. Some described this area as scattered woods and very swampy, while others would say that this ground was open and solid underfoot as one left town in the 1820s. Of course, these conditions and descriptions likely reflected specific seasons' precipitation, the expansion of Detroit and the improvement of the trail, and the extent to which trees had been cut and cleared for lumber and firewood by residents year after year. In Smith's time in the early years of the nineteenth century, this area outside of town was more forest than field, with the trail so wet and muddy as to be nearly impassable.[2]

But as the traveler moved farther northwest, the ground slowly rose as the trail went deeper into the woods of what would soon become Oakland County. Now there were periodic clearings or "oak openings" as the terrain became higher, rolling hills. In these clearings, some that stretched for acres, a traveler might see blazes of colorful wildflowers in the summer. Of course, there were no settlers' houses or farms along this trail in 1805; Indian camps were the only signs of human life one might see.

By the point the traveler had gone 30 miles or so from Detroit, he would find himself traveling over ridges, through valleys and hardwood groves, with several springs and lakes close by the trail. From a meadow or opening on these the hillsides, one observer would say he was "presented with the view of the most picturesque and beautifully diversified country." Depending on the time of year, passenger pigeons, ducks, or geese could fill the skies overhead. The traveler might see deer roaming this land anytime of year, and would hear the calls of wolf or the scream of a "panther" or cougar and bobcat, at night. He would necessarily have to be mindful of the presence of venomous massasauga rattlesnakes.

The woods were not thick here, and ferns covered the forest floor. There were bear and beaver and practically every other type of creature, which ranged from the wetlands of the creeks and lakes to the meadows and forest-covered hills. Some miles beyond the crossing of the "Upper Huron," or Clinton River—the future site of the town of Pontiac—a traveler moving off the trail to hunt on a late fall or early winter day may have seen a distant but distinctive crest, topped with evergreen trees and lying to the east, rising over a surprisingly flat plain or plateau. In time, settlers would call this hill the "little pine knob."[3]

As the trail wound into the hills of what would become northern Oakland County or southern Genesee County, several deep marks, several feet apart, were visible in the ground just off the trail. The Indians told a story of these marks having been made by a warrior who had been shot by enemies while standing at the top of the nearby ridge. According to their tale, the marks were left as the warrior leaped down the hillside in an attempt to escape, but, fatally wounded, he had fallen and died. The settlers who came later would call these marks "the Indian nine tracks."[4]

The land over which the trail passed here was "broken," or hilly, rocky, and rough, though there were sometimes areas of open meadow and lightly forested swamps interspersed. Soon the traveler left the Clinton River basin and entered the southern edge of the Saginaw Valley, where the land drained north into winding rivers that formed the Saginaw, the biggest river-drainage system in Michigan and home to various bands of the Saginaw Chippewa. On the way to a northward-flowing creek that would become known as the Thread River, the Saginaw Trail now came to a small Indian village on a hill led by a chief whose skin color was so remarkably light that French traders called him Grand Blanc or "the Big White"; his Native names were recorded as Sawanabenase and Pechegabua. Veteran trader Louis Campau would say Grand Blanc was an Ottawa, though the chief was listed on an 1807 treaty as a Chippewa. Grand Blanc's name became the name for this area near the Thread, and it would live on long after he was gone. Campau would recall that Grand Blanc had a son who would become a chief, too, known as Fisher, and two beautiful daughters. The members of Grand Blanc's band "were great hunters" and regularly transacted business with the trader Bolieu; they also traded with Campau's uncle, Barnaby Campau. Just as Jacob Smith did, this uncle also regularly traded with the Indians about 50 miles to the southeast who lived on Lake St. Clair in the area that would become the town of Mt. Clemens.[5]

Somewhere between Grand Blanc's village and the point several miles north where the trail reached the Flint River was a cleared rise of ground surrounded by wild plum trees, one old ex-fur trader would write. This grassy spot was only about 50 feet in diameter and in the center was a large oddly shaped stone, possibly as high as four feet, which the Indians treated as a kind of deity or spirit they named "Bab-o-quah." "They never allowed themselves to pass this stone without stopping and talking a lingo with their god and having a good smoke from the red pipe of peace and friendship," claimed Ephraim S. Williams, a fur trade veteran who, as a young man, followed in the footsteps of Jacob Smith in the late 1820s. Williams became a businessman, politician, and amateur historian and would leave accounts of Smith and his own time in the fur trade.[6]

The Saginaw Trail continued north through the woods, generally along the Thread, which flowed into a river the Chippewa called Pe-wan-a-go-see-ba, or the Flint River. The French traders called it more simply the "river La Pierre," or the stone river. In time, the pronunciation and spelling evolved into "Lapeer," which would become the name for a town and county settled in the high, rolling country to the east of the Saginaw Trail, where the Flint River begins its westward flow. Hills rose again as the trail approached the Flint River, yet there were also low-lying areas, wet and covered with brush and trees. As the trail reached the point where it intersected a future downtown Flint cross street called Kearsley Street, just a fraction of a mile from the south bank of the river, the ground was swampy, with many alder and black ash trees. The river was not usually deep at this point and could be crossed with reasonable ease. French traders called this place the Grand Traverse.[7]

Looking upstream, to the east, the traveler saw the river gently tumbling over rocks as it descended. In either direction, however, there were higher banks rising above the water. Across the river on the north side, at a point west of the trail, an open, rolling meadow stretched for hundreds of acres. The local bands of the Saginaw Chippewa cultivated their corn on this clearing on the north side of the river, a place they called Muscatawing (also sometimes given as Muscadawin), or the burned-over plain. Indians of Michigan regularly practiced burning to clear areas of trees, opening up places for raising corn and other crops and allowing their hunters clear shots at deer and elk coming to these fields and meadows to graze.[8]

At some point before 1800, the Chippewa had a large village on the Flint River and also on the Saginaw River, Jacob Smith would claim, with 100 to 200 buildings or lodges. However, there is disagreement on that point from other accounts. One witness who actually lived with the Chippewa in Saginaw in 1790, captive John Tanner, described that community as being significantly smaller than Smith indicated. Thus if the Saginaw Indian communities had been as large as Smith was told, it must have been much further back in time.[9]

The traveler going on to Saginaw, had he a canoe, could paddle down the Flint River's winding course west and then northwest, passing along high bluffs and woods that sometimes dropped away into flats or swampy fields of lush grasses along the river. There were more of these flats as one neared the point where the Flint joined others that created the Saginaw River, and a season of drought or light winter snowfall could mean that the traveler had to portage until the river regained depth. Fallen trees might also obstruct this water route to Saginaw.

Along the northern side of the Flint River, the Saginaw Trail led from the Grand Traverse and Muscatawing to a village called Neome's Town, also given in accounts of this time as Reaume's Town. This community was located on a field near today's town of Montrose, just south of a place the Indians called Kishkabawee. According to some accounts, the Flint River band of the Saginaw Chippewa who lived here had periodically shifted their village, historically known as Pewaunaukee (one of many spellings, for "place of fire stones" or "flinty place") to different points up and down the river.[10]

From Neome's Town the trace continued along the river over the last 15 miles to Saginaw. Eventually a shortcut was made to take several miles off the journey from the Grand Traverse to Saginaw by making a more direct, northerly route. Leaving the north bank of the Flint River, this shortcut went into rolling, wooded country that eventually flattened into heavier forests of pine and oak and other hardwoods. At points along this part of the trail, the ground turned to swamp or muck as the traveler pressed northward.

In anything but the most freezing cold or the driest of seasons, traveling this trail was a muddy, sloppy mess; in its worst condition, the trail was very nearly impassable. But the land in the Saginaw Valley was fertile, with so many rivers, creeks, lakes, and wetlands, a productive place to grow crops in the fields that opened in woods and hillsides. When a British commander in northern Michigan had needed supplies to feed his men during the Revolutionary War, he had turned to the Chippewa of this region. "I have sent to Saguina to endeavor to secure six hundred Bushels of Corn from the Indians without which our flour will run short by the fall of year," Major A. S. DePeyster had written in May 1779 from the then-British post at Mackinac.[11]

In Jacob Smith's time, men from the eastern United States would eventually hear about the excellent land of the Saginaw Valley and covet it. But in the first years of the nineteenth century, the region was Indian country. The leaders of the Saginaw Chippewa had no intention of giving it up.

In visualizing this trip from Detroit up the Saginaw Trail in the earlier years of the nineteenth century, one must keep in mind that southeastern Michigan was a very damp, uneven, and forested place, quite different from the paved, drained, leveled, and cleared subdivisions, malls, and developmental sprawl of today. By some estimates, half or more of the wetlands of the Lower Peninsula have been drained over the past 200 years. Therefore, in summer or mild, warm spring or fall, a traveler, unless fortunate enough to have a strong breeze, was beset by swarms of bloodthirsty mosquitoes as he paddled his canoe on a river or guided his horse on the path. "Woods fever," a kind of malaria, was a nearly universal illness for those who went into the Michigan wilds during the warm seasons, and some didn't survive it.

Michigan's winters could be mild or harsh, and the trading season in the wilderness as it then existed could not have been comfortable. Wherever Smith set up his trading post in 1805, he probably constructed a log house or lodge, though Louis Campau said later that Smith lived with Neome while trading after the War of 1812. Eventually Smith had cabins both at the Grand Traverse (Flint) and at Saginaw, accounts show. But some traders, it was said, only built shanties or dugouts in a hillside or on a riverbank. However a trader lived, he and his agents and employees would spend those months trading goods ranging from tools, cloth, weapons, silver jewelry, and alcohol for the pelts of animals trapped and hunted by the Indians.[12]

The French, the British, and the American governments all had regulations aimed at stopping traders from providing alcohol to the Indians, but most accounts say these prohibitions were practically unenforceable and ignored. Traders believed alcohol was a necessary part of their business, giving their customers what they wanted; they felt that if the Indians wanted to trade for whiskey or rum and they didn't provide it, then the Indians would take their pelts to a trader who did.[13]

Although the Michigan traders license record book at the Detroit Public Library does not list the licensees' assistants, most traders did hire employees. On Mackinac Island, for example, the men who would paddle the huge canoes and bateaux out around the Great Lakes for traders and agents of the fur-trading concerns were asked to sign a formal contract for the term of their employment, or, in French, an *engagement*. That gave these men their name, *engagees*. Traders like Smith who were heading into southeastern and central Michigan weren't traveling as far, of course, but they typically had employees, agents, or partners.

An unsigned Detroit document written about events that took place late in 1814, almost certainly authored by Jacob Smith, showed that he considered certain Indians who lived at different locations in the Saginaw Valley as members of what he called "my company." Since the War of 1812 was going on when Smith wrote this, and the fur trade had come to a virtual halt during the conflict, the document indicates he had employed various members of the Chippewa and Ottawa bands in trade before the war. A letter written later by Jacob Smith's oldest son-in-law claimed that the fur trader indeed provided Indians with thousands of dollars of trade goods for them to swap for pelts brought in to Chippewa villages and camps on the Flint, Saginaw, and Cass rivers.[14]

But Smith's use of the word "company" in this particular report could also have a military context. A squad or team of scouts or rangers attached to an army or that reported to a military officer was typically called "a company of spies," and it could be in this sense that the fur trader used the word. Smith, who held the rank of lieutenant and captain in the militia after 1813, may have been referring to Chippewa individuals who provided him information or worked or operated on his behalf. Whether he was using the term in a military or business context, Smith's description of Indians as members of "my company" is strong evidence of close relationships with some of the Chippewa of the Saginaw Valley.

Yet if Smith was cultivating good relations, his government had a more problematic and vexing view of the Indians. Soon, in the fall of 1807, Governor Hull would pass along to the leaders of the Ottawa, Chippewa, and Pottawatomi the stern warning of President Thomas Jefferson, who was concerned about a new war breaking out with Britain. "We have learnt that some tribes are already expressing intentions hostile to the United States," Jefferson wrote in a statement to the chiefs. "We wish them to live in peace with all nations, as well as with us, and we have no intention ever to strike them or to do them an injury of any sort unless first attacked or threatened." But the president continued with a threat: "If ever we are constrained to lift the hatchet against any tribe, we will never lay it down till that tribe is exterminated, or driven beyond the Mississippi." He asked for and pledged friendship, but stressed that those who turned to violence would pay. "In war they will kill some of us; we shall destroy all of them." Jefferson vowed.[15]

When Jacob Smith came back to Detroit after the winter of 1805–1806, he was surprised to find his partner's father, John Dodemead, and his family living in the house Smith and young James Dodemead had built the previous summer. This was a problem. Smith claimed he had put between $500 and $600 into the building. Not only did he need space for his stores, pelts, and other business-related items, his own family was also growing. In February that year, Smith's second daughter, Caroline, was born. But Smith claimed that when he tried to talk to James Dodemead about the matter of the building, the young man would put him off or tell Smith to talk to his father, or offer some other excuse for refusing to deal with him. If Dodemead was going to take possession of the house, then Smith wanted to be paid for his investment in it.[16]

Smith feared that the Dodemeads were out to defraud him by obtaining a deed to the property in which he'd put time and money, and then transferring or selling the building to someone else. Smith had also heard that James Dodemead received a provisional assignment of that property as his "donation lot," or one of the pieces of land given by the federal government to Detroit residents in order to rebuild the town after the disastrous fire of the previous summer. These lots were part of a new and sometimes controversial plan to reconstruct Detroit in a more organized manner.

With the Dodemeads refusing to talk to Smith about the house, the fur trader turned to lawyer Solomon Sibley. Early in 1807 Sibley drew up a petition for a joint deed to the property to be issued to both James Dodemead and Smith. If this petition was accepted by Detroit's land board, it would require that the Dodemeads buy out Smith's interest in the property before they could sell it. How the matter was ultimately settled is unknown. But subsequent land board records show the property was transferred to a relative of the Dodemeads, so it may be that Smith and his family remained renters during their first few years in Detroit before eventually buying a home and property at what would become the corner of Woodward Avenue and Woodbridge Street.[17]

A question that would prove an enduring one regarding Jacob Smith in the pioneer history of the Flint area was whether or not his children were Indian, and the matter was debated by Saginaw Valley amateur historians and buffs for years. The evidence of extracted Canadian church records clearly showed that Smith's wife, Mary Reed, was born in Canada of English-Irish parents, so Smith's children with her were white. But fur traders spent months in the wilderness among the Indians and it was common for a trader to set up households with a woman of the band where he was doing business. Fathering children with an Indian woman helped to cement a trader's relationships with her people, and the "mixed blood" children of traders and Indians were a common result or consequence of the trade.

Witnesses would testify later that Jacob Smith did have such a liaison with a Chippewa woman whose band lived near Lake St. Clair, near the mouth of the Clinton River, and that a daughter, said to have been named Mokitchenoqua (pronounced "Moe-kit-che-no-kwah," but also given as Mokitchewenoqua), was born to this woman, probably in 1807. Louis Beaufait, a veteran interpreter and Indian agent for the U.S. government, would later testify that he knew Smith "lived with an Indian woman and kept her as his wife." Obviously this was not Mary Smith, who was white and lived in Detroit while her husband went off to trade. Beaufait and other interpreters and federal Indian department employees and officials in Michigan later acknowledged that they all knew Smith had a daughter with a Chippewa woman.

Another veteran of the territory's Indian interpreters who knew Smith, a man named Henry Conner, specifically identified Smith's mate as "Now-wa-be-she-koo-qua." No information about this Chippewa woman seems to exist in the historical record, other than that Nowabeshekoqua's mother was named "Qua-Kou." Conner said he thought that Smith's daughter was born "in Mt. Clemens." Of course, there was no town of Mt. Clemens in 1806 or 1807—only a few cabins of French and French-Indian traders in the area near the mouth of the Clinton River and along its banks. But there was an Ottawa-Chippewa community here, and Nowabeshekoqua and her mother seem to have lived in an area where one of the leaders, called The Wing, was friendly to Governor William Hull.[18]

This testimony about Jacob Smith's Indian daughter and her mother from knowledgeable men is evidence that he traded with the band that resided there at this "upper Huron" river as it entered Lake St. Clair. Louis Campau indicated that there were already a few traders who had built cabins in that vicinity, and that it was a jumping-off point or staging area where he, in 1815, took trade goods, transported by horses, northwest into the Saginaw Valley.[19]

What Mary Smith thought of her husband's Indian family is unknown. Where Jacob Smith traded with the Indians in the winter of 1806–1807 is not reflected in the territorial trader licensing book. As noted previously, Lucius Gould later wrote that 1806 was the first time Smith traveled to the Flint River with Henri Bolieu, though other records clearly indicate he'd already traveled to Saginaw previously. And if the birth of Mokitchenoqua, whose English name was Nancy, was truly in June 1807, as her relatives believed, she was conceived in the fall of 1806, probably when her father visited her mother's "Huron" river village.

Smith's name does not appear in territorial records again until the summer of 1807, when he was working for the U.S. territorial government. Governor William Hull was then trying to get Indians from around the region to attend treaty discussions or talks, which were called councils. As was always the case with U.S. officials of that era, Hull wanted to get the Indians to cede territory to the government—Thomas Jefferson hoped he could get land reaching all the way to Saginaw

Bay. But Hull also wanted something even more important: he wanted the Indians of Michigan to remain peaceful in the event of war.

This was a time of uncertainty and fear on the American frontier—the fear of war. A Shawnee healer who called himself the Prophet had emerged in Ohio as an influential spiritual leader among many Indian tribes of the Great Lakes. The Prophet urged Indians to go back to their old ways of life and give up the white man's goods, alcohol, and trade, since many were suffering poverty because of drinking and overhunting for the fur trade. The Prophet's brother, a warrior and chief named Tecumseh, would soon emerge as an even more important leader. He, like other Indians, understood that the United States had pressured, persuaded, or bribed village chiefs in Ohio and Indiana into giving up millions of acres of land—land that he said those chiefs had no authority to bargain away. U.S. officials like William Henry Harrison, governor of the Indiana Territory, also took advantage of the Indian village-political structure as well as tribal rivalries, persuading one group to sign off or trade land out from under their traditional foes or rivals.[20]

While Tecumseh initially did not want war, he knew the growing westward tide of U.S. settlers was the biggest threat to all Indians, regardless of old tribal hostilities and rivalries. He was not alone; other western Indians were also talking about a confederation to oppose the United States. American settlers and officials heard rumors and reports about this and some were convinced that the British were supplying the Indians with weapons, inciting them against the Americans.

In Michigan, members of the Saginaw Chippewa attended councils of Tecumseh and the Prophet or had otherwise heard their messages, and this worried Governor Hull; back during the American Revolution, these Chippewa had allied with the British. Of course, during that conflict American settlers lived nowhere near Michigan, and Detroit had been a British-held fort. Yet Saginaw Chippewa warriors traveled hundreds of miles to attack Americans on the frontier, and they continued to do so as fighting between the United States and the Indians dragged on in the Ohio Valley in the years after the Revolution. "A party of Saginas have just arrived from the Ohio where they intercepted & took the inclosed Paquet of letters, at the same time destroying 11 of the 14 who were conveying them by water from Fort Washington to Fort Pitt," British Indian agent Alexander McKee had reported in 1791 from the Maumee Rapids to Major Smith, then the British commander at Detroit.[21]

Now some 15 years later, Detroit belonged to the United States, but Chippewa antipathy toward the Americans remained strong, and the fur trade was still "largely in control of the British," a Michigan historian noted. Officially, the Indians of the region had ceded to the United States only a six-mile-wide strip of land running along the eastern coast of Michigan from the River Raisin on the south, extending north along the Lake Erie coast and the Detroit River to Lake St. Clair—essentially, the Detroit area. But how long would the Americans be satisfied with this? Throughout the Old Northwest, the U.S. government pushed for more treaties and more land. Even as Jacob Smith had settled into his Detroit business affairs in 1803, President Thomas Jefferson had been working on a plan in which he envisioned moving all of the Indians of the eastern portion of the United States to beyond the Missouri River.[22]

The coming of more traders and white settlers had a powerful impact on Indians, and those living near Detroit may have already felt this or heard about it. Settlers cleared land for farming, taking away lands on which Indians had hunted and lived. In addition, fur prices were often depressed in the early years of the nineteenth century, and that made trading conditions more difficult for Indians who were coming to rely on white men's goods such as cloth, blankets, iron tools, and cooking utensils, and the services of blacksmiths and gunsmiths. Though the U.S. government provided some services under treaties, the Indians' only sources of income to get goods were fur pelts and the land itself, for which they would receive money in the form of annual treaty payments.

Yet when the market for fur was poor and prices were low—and they often were in the late 1790s and early 1800s—traders gave the Indians less for their pelts. That pressured Indians to overhunt their lands to get more furs for the items they needed, but this depressed the value of the pelts further. Of course, this overhunting was no solution, since the Indians also depended on game for food. The coming of more traders and settlers also meant more contact between whites and Indians, and that usually meant that more alcohol was being sold or provided to the Indians, and that more of them were being exposed to the white men's diseases, illnesses to which the Indians were highly susceptible. Jacob Smith would later claim that as these pressures mounted on the Chippewa of the Saginaw Valley, once-large towns on the Flint and Saginaw rivers broke up into smaller bands in order to survive.[23]

Of course, land ceded to the United States by the Indians was a source of funding for the government, which typically had the land surveyed and then sold to settlers and speculators. Though Jefferson didn't think it was wise for Governor Hull to seek a treaty with the Indians of Michigan during the war scare of 1807,

Hull nonetheless planned to try to convince the Indians to sell more land. He wanted to hold a treaty council on July 4. While some tribes were willing to consider the idea of the council, the leaders of the Chippewa insisted they were not. They held a council of their own at Saginaw on June 5, and their message to the territorial governor indicated that they had heard the words of the Prophet. The Chippewa weren't interested in talking to Hull and they told him so bluntly, apparently through Jacob Smith.[24]

"Our Father, we understand that you would buy our Lands at Saguina," the Chippewa council's message stated to Hull. "We will not sell our Lands or give them—We think that you would do better to stay in Detroit and us here, because we love our Women and Children and young men, and if you should come here against the Indians, the young men perhaps kill your cattle, you will put us in jail and that would trouble us and perhaps we will get angry. . . . Never think to come on the Saguina ground because you will make us angry," their warning continued. "Almighty God gave us this Land for us to serve, but not for us to sell—Think never to buy them for it is not of any use. . . . Give us our Answer by the Bearer if it is true that you wish to buy our Lands, or not. You lose your time about thinking of buying our Lands—We never will agree to sell or give them[. You] stay at Detroit and We will stay here."[25]

Hull forwarded this message on to U.S. Secretary of War Henry Dearborn, noting that the principal Saginaw chief had just come from a meeting with the Prophet. Yet Hull was convinced that the wording of the message had been authored by a Canadian trader, rather than the Chippewa themselves. "He [the Saginaw chief] undoubtedly has been advised not to consent to the sale of any lands," Hull wrote. "I am however certain, neither he or any of the chiefs dictated the inclosed [*sic*] speech. It was written by one Gouin, a British Trader, and according to his own wishes. I have sent an interpreter to explain everything to them."

That interpreter sent by Hull was Jacob Smith. No record explains how or why he'd become involved with the federal governor of Michigan in this role—Hull and Smith had first met two years earlier. But Smith went to Saginaw carrying gifts of tobacco and wampum or beaded belt that represented an important message, expressing wishes for peace. Smith also carried Hull's invitation to the Detroit treaty council. The governor went ahead with his plans, inviting the chiefs of the Delaware, Pottawatomi, Shawnee, and other nations. But the Saginaw Chippewa refused, initially.[26]

"Mr. Smith, whom I sent to the Saguina, has this moment returned," Hull wrote, probably to Secretary of War Dearborn, on July 4. The demonstration the Indians put on for Smith to underscore their rejection of Hull's invitation was elaborate and threatening. Three hundred warriors had assembled and 30 of them declared they were in favor of taking up the hatchet, Hull reported about Smith's meeting with the Chippewa; the Indians performed the war dance and brandished the scalp of a white man at Smith. They also complained that their tribe had not been paid the annuities, or annual government payment, as specified in an earlier treaty.[27]

Hull passed all this information on to the U.S. government. Despite that anger and vehemence in the Chippewa rejection, they did come to Detroit when it was time for treaty annuities, or payments, to be made, possibly at the urging of Smith and other American fur traders. By this point, Hull thought Smith's report of the Chippewa threat was exaggerated. But when the Saginaw Indians did arrive, they initially refused to accept their payment—just as Tecumseh's brother, the Prophet, instructed. There was peace now with the Chippewa and other tribes in Michigan after they assembled and approved Hull's treaty in the fall of 1807, but it was an uneasy peace. Jacob Smith's initial assessment of the angry feeling of the Chippewa was more accurate than William Hull or any American settler wanted to believe. The coming War of 1812 would prove this to be correct.

Trouble in Detroit

I f Governor William Hull's relations with the Saginaw Chippewa were rocky in the summer of 1807, his dealings with some of his own people weren't much better. And if Jacob Smith thought he was removed from Hull's conflicts with Detroit residents, he now found out otherwise. Serious rifts had taken place over the past two years between the governor and other officials, particularly with Territorial Secretary Stanley Griswold and also James Abbott, an influential local leader and businessman who held several governmental posts in Detroit.

Years before Hull's arrival, Abbott, the son of a wealthy Canadian trader and merchant, had married the daughter of a U.S. Army officer. Abbott became an American citizen and by 1807 was serving as the public treasurer in Detroit; he was a major in the territorial militia and a member of the Board of Land Commissioners, appointed by the federal government. This important panel investigated and ruled on questions involving Detroit citizens' property, some of which were land grants from Indians or from French authority going back a hundred years or more. Complicating the land board's task was the fact that residents of the town were rebuilding in the wake of the 1805 fire. The board was also making decisions about Detroit's donation lots.[1]

Abbott, well off and respected, had been a Detroit trustee before Governor Hull arrived. Like many or most residents of Detroit, he had strong family connections in Canada. As a result of his business, knowledge, experience, and family history, Abbott had more than a passing resentment of William Hull, the new and intrusive figure of U.S. authority. Hull, as the federal government's man in Detroit, was responsible for gaining more land from the Indians. But many residents of French and British backgrounds, who had lived for years in relative peace with the Indians, didn't approve of the U.S. policies and practices. The fact that the government was pushing for more cessions was increasing tensions with the Indians, and that had the potential to make things dangerous for the people of Detroit, virtually surrounded as they were by Indians and their British allies.

On the evening on July 17, 1807, on the street near Stanley Griswold's home, Jacob Smith stopped to chat with Griswold, James Abbott, and a businessman named John Gentle. Smith had recently returned from Saginaw, having tried on behalf of Governor Hull to get the Chippewa chiefs and leaders or advisors called head men to attend his treaty councils. Gentle, like Abbott and Griswold, was no fan of Hull. A local merchant but a citizen of Canada, Gentle was angry about new U.S. rules and decisions that were adversely affecting his business. In short, Jacob Smith was in the company of three prominent men who had no use for the territorial governor. At that same moment, Abijah Hull, a distant cousin and private secretary to the governor, also walked up. According to Abijah Hull's version of events, James Abbott addressed Smith about his recent trip to the Saginaw Chippewa.

"How much did the Governor give you for going to Saginaw and telling lies to the Indians?" Abbott said sarcastically.

"Five dollars per day," Smith replied.

"Did you tell the Indians all the lies the Governor told you to tell them?" Abbott asked, perhaps to needle Abijah Hull and belittle Smith.

"Yes I did," Smith answered.[2]

Perhaps the other men laughed or chuckled or shook their heads at Abbott's derisive comments about William Hull's dealing with the Chippewa through Smith. But to Abijah Hull, this was dangerous, treasonous talk. He reported the conversation to his relative and employer—and Governor Hull was incensed. Three days later Abijah Hull swore out an affidavit recounting the conversation to the chief district judge of the Michigan Territory, George McDougall, an appointee of the governor. William Hull acted quickly. Though he didn't have the authority to remove James Abbott from all of the public positions to which he'd been appointed by the administration of President Jefferson, the governor did have a say over some of the jobs Abbott held. Hull removed Abbott as major of the militia and as justice of the peace.

There was an immediate reaction on the part of local residents, with hundreds of Detroiters signing a petition protesting the removal of Abbott as militia major. The other men who allegedly had been involved in that controversial conversation of July 17 gave their own depositions in answer to Abijah Hull. Jacob Smith denied that Abbott asked him mocking, seemingly disloyal questions. So did Territorial Secretary Griswold and Gentle.[3]

But Governor Hull had no doubt about Abijah Hull's version of events. To him, Abbott's sarcastic questions to Smith weren't just disrespectful toward his effort on behalf of the U.S. government; Abbott was criticizing his effort to make a treaty with the Saginaw Chippewa. With the threat of war hanging over the Old Northwest, the governor hoped a treaty could get land for the United States while also keeping the Michigan Indians neutral and thereby preventing bloodshed. Yet here was Abbott, an influential community leader and local official, ridiculing the governor's effort as "lies."

Then was James Abbott truly being disloyal to the federal government? Or were his comments simply the expression of his personal disapproval of Hull and what he considered wrongheaded U.S. policy? Even Abbott's defenders at the time admitted there were rumors linking him with pro-British malcontents and locals who didn't approve of what the U.S. government was doing. While this may not have been treason, it put Abbott directly at odds with the Jefferson administration. Other Michigan territorial officials suspected that Abbott's new friend and political ally, Stanley Griswold, was associating with British sympathizers who opposed measures taken by Hull and the United States; word of this reached President Jefferson himself.[4]

The episode must have made for interesting debate in Detroit that summer. If Abijah Hull was telling the truth about what was said that July evening, why didn't Jacob Smith admit that the conversation had taken place? In all likelihood, Smith couldn't afford to admit what had happened. He was indeed acting at least as a translator and probably an agent of influence on the Indians for Hull and the U.S. government at this time—records show this. Simply put, Smith had to protect himself; he traded with these Saginaw Chippewa. While it was one thing to act as the governor's courier or messenger, it was another to admit to acting as his secret agent.

Smith could no more admit to that conversation as sworn to by the governor's aide than could Abbott or Griswold, holders of federal government offices. Smith had been telling the truth when he said he was working for Hull; his name was later listed on Hull's estimates of expenses the governor had incurred in getting the Indians to agree to a treaty. Smith was paid $50 and listed in December 1807 under "persons employed during the treaty and as interpreters and confidential agents."[5] Certainly Jacob Smith was at the very least a trusted messenger for Hull to the Saginaw Chippewa. He had experience dealing with them and knew how to speak their language; his information from and about the Chippewa had gone directly to the U.S. secretary of war. If Abijah Hull's deposition is to be believed, Smith had admitted to being Governor Hull's agent, working to convince the tribe's leaders to take part in treaty councils.

This open conversation on the street about his work for the U.S. government had been a mistake on his part, one he wouldn't make again. Given how the future would turn, it is likely that Jacob Smith understood and maybe agreed with the U.S. policy to try to purchase land from the Chippewa. He had traveled and camped and traded on the land of the Saginaw Valley and may have envisioned a day when white settlers would farm and build on it. As a key figure in the discussions with the Indians, he would ultimately be in a position to take advantage of his relationships with both federal officials in Michigan and the leaders of the Saginaw Chippewa in the not-too-distant future.

Smith's role as a translator and unofficial agent for the governor was little different from several other Detroit-based fur traders who also showed up on Hull's list of Indian interpreters and confidential agents. Of the men on that list, some were paid more than Smith, at least at this stage of Smith's career. That would change, however, in the years ahead. The historical record suggests that Hull understood well, as would Lewis Cass, that fur traders were excellent intelligence operatives. Traders regularly went into Indian country where virtually no other white Americans would or could go. They spoke the languages or dialects of the tribes with whom they traded and they traveled freely to different locations around the region. Hiring a fur trader as a confidential agent was also like hiring a network of spies, since that one trader had partners, employees, contacts, and relatives. Traveling and trading gossip and news, the trader would hear about any information they picked up; being more familiar with the culture and language of the Indians than any other American, the trader was also in a better position than practically anyone else to influence them, especially if he had fathered children with an Indian woman and thereby established family relationships with her band.

As for the other men involved in that incident in June 1807—Territorial Secretary Stanley Griswold and businessman James Abbott—Jacob Smith would get his chance to question their loyalty to the United States in the months and years ahead. Smith and James Abbott would remain at odds for years to come.

Of course, only a portion of Smith's work seems to have been in the area of intelligence gathering or influencing the Chippewa. He was first and foremost a trader and businessman, as well as a father and a husband. In June, he had purchased some Detroit property from James May, an English-born judge of the Court of Common Pleas. The parcel was labeled "lot no. 59 in old plan, and no. 63 of the new plan in Section No. 4." Maps and property records of old Detroit and historical reminiscences by local residents show that this location was at an intersection that was then just a block or so north of the Detroit River. It appears that the 5,000-square-foot lot had at one point been part of what was called the old British "Navy garden" or "military garden" associated with a shipyard that stood at the water's edge, and the few houses and buildings in this area were among the only ones that had survived the 1805 fire. The main avenue along the western edge of Smith's newly purchased property was known as Market Street, but would soon be named Woodward Avenue. The length of Smith's lot fronted on a road that ran roughly parallel to the river, which would soon be called Woodbridge Street.[6]

In terms of today's downtown Detroit, this location would fall roughly in the northeastern corner of Hart Plaza, the open-air amphitheater and park that lies between Cobo Arena and the General Motors Renaissance Center. In early 1800s Detroit, this was a fine location for a fur trader and businessman—it was a stone's throw from the town's two wharfs on the river, the main mercantile highway to the Great Lakes. It was just a block or so from other merchants and businessmen. And if one rode a horse or walked up the street out past the edge of town, he was on the Saginaw Trail to the northwest.

Where Smith and his family had lived since the proposed partnership and building with James Dodemead fell through is not clear. It could be that they had rented this place, a one-story log house at the southeast corner of the Woodward-Woodbridge intersection, before purchasing it from Judge May. But it would be the home of Jacob Smith's family for years to come. In addition to the house, one writer of old-time Detroit would note, Smith also had next door "a dilapidated, weather-beaten building" that he used as a store or warehouse. The deed recorded that Smith paid $150 for his home property in June, but within two months documents filed in Detroit show he mortgaged it for just over $1,300 in a series of bonds or loans from a man named Richard Pattinson, a merchant who lived across the Detroit River in Sandwich, Canada.[7]

Smith also entered into a transaction with a merchant named Eli or Ely Bond that summer. Bond had three barrels of pork and five kettles worth a total of $200; he wanted to trade those items for cider. Smith made a deal with Bond on August 5 for the pork and pots. The merchant soon charged, however, that the fur trader failed to deliver the promised cider. Bond would sue Smith in the local district court.[8]

There were other troubles for Smith as summer turned to fall. In September Smith paid a fine of $20 in Detroit's district court for having attacked Joseph Wilkinson, or more properly, Dr. Joseph Wilkinson Jr. The motive for Smith's assault on Wilkinson isn't spelled out, but Detroit historical accounts suggest two possible motives. First, Wilkinson, a former trustee of Detroit and collector of customs, was suspected of mishandling fees paid to the U.S. government by importers of goods, such as fur traders and merchants. Second, Wilkinson was married to James Dodemead's sister, and Smith had accused Dodemead of trying to defraud him in their building project on Jefferson Avenue a year earlier. Either of those situations might have driven Smith to punch Wilkinson.

A letter written to Solomon Sibley, Smith's attorney, from "W. Park" on the Canadian side of the Detroit River showed, furthermore, that Smith wasn't keeping up his end of another business deal. William Park, a former partner in an important Detroit merchant company, put Sibley on notice that Smith hadn't kept up his part of a transaction. "I shall have to put Jacob Smith to costs which I call upon you," Park noted, "as [he] has not performed his promises."[9]

In the meantime Governor Hull, having been assisted by Jacob Smith and other traders, worked into the fall on his proposed treaty talks with the Indians, and eventually the Chippewa came. Father Gabriel Richard heard about the Indians' antipathy and reluctance to cede more land, as he told his bishop that October. The Indians "have refused to sell any parcel whatsoever, alledging [sic] that they have been cheated already too much," the father wrote; the Indians were aware that while the U.S. government paid the tribes less than pennies per acre of land in treaties, speculators who got the same land from the government turned around and sold the land for as much as $15 an acre.[10]

Certainly Hull wanted the Indians to cede land, but he was also worried about what they would do in case war again broke out with Britain. If conflict erupted, the territorial governor wasn't too concerned about the relatively small number of British army regulars and Canadian militia on the other side of the Detroit River; he was confident the U.S. soldiers at the fort and Michigan militiamen could handle them. But if the Indians joined in the war on the side of the British, well, that was another story.

As the treaty councils were getting under way, a Wyandot chief named Adam Brown, who lived near Detroit (and whose name would be given to his village and the township formed subsequently around it), had a talk with the governor's alcoholic son and aide, Abraham Hull, regarding William Hull's worries about the Chippewa. Brown passed this information along to Thomas McKee, the British Indian agent at Ft. Malden, across the river at Amhertsburg. The British Indian Department, headquartered at the fort, was the liaison between the British government and the Indians, and many of the agents and interpreters had Indian wives and families. McKee and other agents also acted as intelligence officers, gathering information about the U.S. forces on the frontier and keeping tabs on Indian attitudes, encouraging close relationships with Britain and anti-American feelings. "He (Hull's son) said his father always desired the Indians to take no active part on either side; but allow the English & them [the United States] to fight it out by themselves," McKee wrote, passing along Brown's information, "but . . . he was afraid of the Sagana Indians, thinking they would take up the Hatchet against them."[11]

The governor's fears cannot have come as any surprise to the British officers and Indian agents. But with at least 10 different unofficial interpreters and confidential agents working for the United States on the Indians (in addition to official translators and Indian agents), Hull did finally smoke a pipe of peace with Chippewa and other tribal leaders in attendance. In exchange for annual payments and services, the chiefs signed a treaty that the United States maintained ceded some five million acres of land to the government, taking in what today is more than an 11-county area in southeastern Michigan and the Thumb. For this, the Indians, in turn, would receive a payment of $10,000 with a yearly annuity of $2,400.[12]

One of the Indian headmen who spoke at the treaty council was identified as Pooquiboad, a Chippewa chief. "Our solemn determination is, never to raise

the hatchet against the United States," he said. "We too well know the fatal consequences of it. . . . Father: if the war pipe is offered to us to smoke, we will reject it:
we will send from among us all persons who give us bad counsel." Governor Hull
was happy to report these and other such speeches to Secretary of War Dearborn.
"The chiefs of the Ottawa nation, and of the Wyandot nation, have made similar
determinations, and I have great confidence in their sincerity," Hull wrote.[13]

The territorial governor was also glad to see specific Saginaw Chippewa
leaders come in and talk of better relations with the U.S. government. One was
the father of the warrior Kishkauko (Hull spelled the name "Kish-cou-cough")
who had killed Lauzon at Saginaw in 1802 and later escaped from authorities in
Detroit. Kishkauko's father, Meuetugesheck, was a truculent chief whose name
translated into English as "Little Cedar" and he, too, had been involved in attacks
on American settlers in the Ohio Valley. "Until very lately, he [Little Cedar] and
all his tribe have been unfriendly to the U[nited] States," Hull wrote Dearborn.
"This Little Cedar was very influential in preventing the Saguina Chiefs in coming in when I sent for them last summer." Little Cedar had come to Hull's treaty
council and had not been friendly at first, but after much conversation with the
governor he had pledged himself to "throw all his resentments into the River."
The chief asked for a pardon for his son, and Hull promised he would use his
influence with the president to get it. "I believe it would be attended with useful
consequence," Hull wrote of a pardon for Little Cedar's son. "Kish-cou-cough is
himself an influential Man."[14]

Unfortunately for Hull, many of the warriors of the tribes who agreed to that
treaty, including the Saginaw Chippewa, would be at war with the United States
in just a few years. The treaty Hull had signed with them would mean little, except
perhaps that it had bought some time.

Jacob Smith's specific role in these discussions with the Saginaw Chippewa is not
clear, but based on his previous involvement during the summer and the fact he
was listed among the interpreters and confidential agents who worked on the
treaty for Hull, it seems that he used his influence on behalf of the United States.
Smith also showed up in the public record that fall of 1807 when Detroit residents
petitioned the U.S. Congress for aid and a deadline extension so they could apply
for grants of government land after the 1805 fire. Smith signed a version of the
petition that was written in French; he may have put his name on the appeal out

of sympathy and support of his townsmen, but he may have had his own interests regarding a donation lot from the U.S. government.[15]

Smith was also called to jury duty that fall for the Supreme Court of the territory, serving along with traders, merchants, and other prominent men of Detroit. This appears to have been his first time serving as a juror for the court, and the most interesting matter of the docket was when Smith and his fellow jurors had to decide whether a man named Francis DesForges was insane. After considering the matter, the panel decided the poor fellow was "at this time a lunatic and person of unsound mind." In November, probably as Smith prepared to venture into the woods to trade with the Indians, he signed a promissory note, or an agreement for a loan, with local merchants Wiggins, Emerson & Little. This note was for $254.19, with interest, and it was to be paid off by June 1810. Court records indicate Smith did not do so. It would turn out to be just another of the many lawsuits involving the fur trader.[16]

Despite the treaty Hull had signed with the Chippewa and other tribes, Indian war scares continued into 1808. So did Governor Hull's troubles with his territorial secretary, Stanley Griswold. In another controversy even bigger than the previous summer's, Griswold was brought before Detroit's justices of the peace late in January on charges brought by Attorney General Elijah Brush of "enticing militia to desert." One of the key witnesses giving testimony in this "court of inquiry" investigating Griswold was Jacob Smith, member of the Michigan Territorial Militia.

Again some background information is necessary to understand this controversy and its importance in Detroit at that time. First, William Hull's handling of Michigan Territorial Militia volunteers and draftees had gone no more smoothly than many of his other decisions that brought him into conflict with the people he governed. For example, shortly after he arrived at Detroit and reorganized the militia, Hull, a veteran of the American Revolution, announced requirements for new and colorful uniforms for its officers and troops, right down to the color of sashes and plumes, feathers, and capes. These fancy uniforms would have probably been fine in European armies of that Napoleonic era, one writer noted, but they were beyond the budgets of the French laborers and farmers, clerks, and hunters who made up the ranks of the 600-plus militia. The governor's ideas on uniforms and military drill were resented, and his enemies made much of this. Hull's critic John Gentle—another of the men involved in the 1807 controversy with Abbott,

Griswold, and Smith—wrote letters to a Pennsylvania newspaper, accusing the governor of profiting from the sale of uniforms to his militia members.

Hull denied this. In order to calm the situation, Secretary Griswold, serving as acting commander-in-chief during a period when Hull was absent from Detroit, suspended the uniform requirements. At some point, probably to help keep relations between the militia and the governor from deteriorating further, the men were told they would be provided with uniforms from the U.S. government. But by December 1807 some of the militiamen were angry and fearful at Hull's threats that they would be punished if they didn't do their duty as he ordered.[17]

Once again, local officials, community leaders, and residents of Detroit picked sides, and Stanley Griswold, as well as other officials, disagreed with Hull. But this time it seemed that Griswold went too far: In January 1808, he was arrested on a charge that he was undermining the militia, actually encouraging the members to desert. This time, Jacob Smith was among the witnesses making the accusation. Smith told authorities that, early in January, he had been at a home in Detroit where a number of militia members gathered to talk. These militiamen weren't happy with Governor Hull, who had promised them new clothing since they'd been sworn into the service of the United States. But the winter was a cold one and men were fed up. One, a man named James Allard, told Smith they were determined to desert.

Smith did not agree. "Why don't you go at once?" Smith suggested sarcastically to his fellow militiamen. "Perhaps you will be flogged for your trouble."[18]

Allard replied that there were many men who lived south of town—the River Raisin area—who had been drafted for the militia, but who could not be forced to come to Detroit to serve. Besides, Allard claimed, the men couldn't be flogged if they deserted—Mr. Griswold, the territorial secretary who acted as governor and militia commander in Hull's absence, told them so.

Whether Smith showed surprise or anger at this statement by Allard isn't reflected in the surviving record. But minutes later, Allard had second thoughts about what he told Smith. As the fur trader left the house, Allard followed him out and told Smith not to repeat Griswold's name in connection with the matter of the angry militiamen and desertion talk. But Smith did report the conversation. This and other accusations about Griswold's conduct and allegedly disloyal conversations were relayed to Governor Hull, Attorney General Brush, and other federal officials in Detroit. They acted. Within three weeks, Griswold was brought before an investigative panel made up of justices of the peace—Richard Smyth, George McDougall, and James May, men who knew Jacob Smith well.

As the hearing was about to open, a nervous Allard approached Smith and asked him not to testify about what he, Allard, had said regarding Griswold and the would-be militia deserters. "I'm afraid something will happen to me," Allard said, according to Smith's testimony. "I have told you a falsehood—Mr. Griswold never advised me to desert." But Smith went ahead and told of the talk of mutiny and Griswold's alleged support of it. Other Detroit men also gave evidence in the hearing.[19]

Some historians have said the evidence in the case indicated Griswold didn't actually encourage militiamen to desert, but he didn't discourage them from doing so, either. It was clear, however, that Griswold was associating with men who in the eyes of Hull and the U.S. government were malcontents and troublemakers. After hearing the evidence, McDougall and May said they thought Griswold was guilty, over the objection of Richard Smyth. The result of the finding of their court of inquiry, a kind of "probable cause" hearing for Griswold, meant that he would have to stand trial.

But before the Territorial Supreme Court had the chance to hear the case, President Thomas Jefferson intervened. Two months after the court of inquiry ruled that Griswold must stand trial, he was dismissed from his post as territorial secretary by Jefferson, and that ended the matter. The president told a political friend he would have removed Griswold earlier, if he could have found another place to put him.[20]

How much importance was given Jacob Smith's testimony in this matter is hard to tell, but the larger point was that Smith had clearly and openly sided with the U.S. government. He had reported the allegations about Griswold to the federal executive of the Michigan Territory, however unpopular Hull might have been with the populace. Smith felt the residents of Detroit had to do their duty and protect their community and country, and had no right to defy the governor and desert. The case had reached the attention of the president of the United States.

Once removed from Michigan, Stanley Griswold would go on to loyally serve as a senator from Ohio and as a judge in the Illinois Territory. President Jefferson said that he would have liked to replace James Abbott on Detroit's land board also, but the U.S. government needed to have that board functioning to settle property claims and disputes. More clashes between Abbott and Jacob Smith lay ahead.[21]

War Clouds

Despite the treaty between Governor William Hull and Indians of the Michigan Territory, relations remained cool. Colonel William Claus, a key British officer and Indian liaison based at Amherstburg, reported to his superiors early in 1808 about how the chief called Grand Blanc, from the Saginaw Valley, snubbed the federal governor, demonstrating that Grand Blanc considered the king of England his friend and ally, but not the government of the United States.

The incident occurred as Grand Blanc was on his way to Canada to receive presents from the British government. It had been the practice of first the French and then the British government to give presents to the Indians in the Great Lakes and elsewhere in order to cultivate and maintain good relations, and this was continued by the British after Michigan had become U.S. territory. "The Grand Blanc from Saginaw arrived yesterday," Claus wrote in February from the headquarters of the British Indian Department at Ft. Malden. "On passing Detroit, the Gov[ernor] saw him & offered to give him a medal on his neck which he [Grand Blanc] pushed away from him & told him [Hull] that he had one, showing him the King's Medal." It must have heartened British officials to know that an Ottawa/Chippewa chief who lived so close to Hull had no warm regard for the United States.[1]

There was also evidence that warriors in the Great Lakes region were angry with their leaders who had signed the treaty with Hull in Detroit in the previous fall, and that included the Chippewa chiefs and head men. That spring, a U.S. Indian agent in Indiana, William Wells (who would lose his life in the coming War of 1812), warned the secretary of war he had learned there was talk by Indians of murdering those who agreed to the Detroit treaty, and that the Indians were vowing there would be no more cessions of land.[2]

This anxious state of relations between the white Americans and the Indians continued into the spring and summer. In Detroit, Jacob Smith was called again as a juror to the Territorial Supreme Court and heard a few civil suits over business debts late in the summer and into the fall of 1808, and only one criminal matter, *United States v. David Robison.* After hearing the evidence and deliberating, Smith and his fellow jurors found Robison not guilty of assault and battery on James McCloskey, a federal marshal, militia officer, and surveyor later charged himself in a bank embezzlement. Judge Woodward's opinion on the assault verdict wasn't recorded.[3]

The ongoing Indian war scare settled somewhat by the fall of 1808, and Hull sent an American flag to the chiefs of the Chippewa at Saginaw, which he called "a present from your great Father, the P[resident] of the U.S." In this case, it was blacksmith David Henderson who carried the flag to the Indians, bringing his family with him. Records show Henderson had been working for the U.S. government's Indian Department for at least two years. He was one of two blacksmiths paid to make and repair tools and implements for the Saginaw Indians. The assignment of blacksmiths by both the United States and British governments to work for the Indians is indicative of how much they had come to rely on the white man's goods and services, and how the rival governments funded the service to keep good relations with them.

Jacob Smith's name did not appear in Hull's letter to the Chippewa, but one of his important contemporaries did—one of the three half-Indian Ryley brothers. "I am informed a white man has come to trade with you, with whisky and without my permission, and is endeavoring to purchase your lands and injure you," Hull said, not naming the offender. "I have ordered him removed—You must give no encouragement to him. . . . I have sent Mr. Riley, one of your nation, to trade with you—He speaks your language, and, I believe, he will be usefull to you."[4]

Exactly where Smith intended to do his trading that season isn't known—he had been in Detroit for at least part of that October, according to court records.

Within a month's time, his third daughter, Louisa, was born in Detroit.[5] Louisa Smith would eventually marry a jeweler and retailer, Chauncey S. Payne, who would come to Detroit in the years ahead. They would become a wealthy and influential couple and settle in the town of Flint, in part because of her father's dealings with the Chippewa and his work for the U.S. government, and the land they would claim as a result.

Jacob Smith continued to figure in local affairs in the Detroit area. He was sued during the May court term of 1809 by Scottish merchant Robert Smart, who had a store and house on the corner of Woodward and Jefferson avenues, just up the street from Smith. That fall Smith was again called to jury duty before the Supreme Court of the territory. One of the juries he served on acquitted tavern owner Richard Smyth, who'd been a justice of the peace himself, on an assault and battery charge. Soon Smith himself was also in hot water again, this time sued in Detroit's district court for $1,300 by the merchants/trading company Robert Forsyth & William Smith; those men had a complaint issued so that Jacob Smith would be arrested by the U.S. marshal for the district.[6]

One case involving Smith became a focal point in the political-legal struggle between Chief Judge Augustus Woodward and Governor Hull. Relations between these two officials had become so bad that at one point the judge refused to meet with Hull and other territorial judges. This might seem unimportant except for the fact that Hull and a handful of federal judges then made up the Michigan Territory's legislature. As a result of this standoff between the judges and the governor, Hull unilaterally put into effect a law that allowed justices of the peace to impose fines or punishments up to $50 on certain violators without a jury hearing the matter. The governor did this without the approval of a majority of the federal judges who made up the legislature. This was particularly aggravating to Judge Woodward, who was a legislator as well as chief judge of the Territorial Supreme Court. As far as the judge was concerned, Hull's decision to extend the power of the justices of the peace was not legal or binding.[7]

Jacob Smith wound up being the defendant in one of the first test cases for Hull's new law, as was a man named Isaac Burnett. In October 1809 both Smith and Burnett were arrested by the marshal for the "district of Huron & Detroit," seemingly on the grounds of unpaid fines or penalties levied on them under Hull's law. Records don't reflect what it was that Smith and Burnett were alleged to have done, but the men hadn't paid their fines. Both Smith and Burnett applied for writs of habeas corpus, or appeals, which were granted by the court.

Chief Judge Woodward and Judge John Griffin heard the cases and ordered that both Smith and Burnett be released. Of course, this wasn't the first time Smith had found himself in legal trouble and it would not be the last. This time, at least, the judges ruled in his favor. "The bill extending the jurisdiction of magistrates to fifty dollars, without a jury, being signed by the governor alone . . . is not a law obligatory upon the inhabitants of this Territory," Woodward ruled.[8]

Records of the Supreme Court of the territory reflected the fur trader's presence in Saginaw during the spring of 1810, and demonstrated what rogues fur traders could be. Jacob Smith and the blacksmith David Henderson were subpoenaed as witnesses in the matter of *Louis Roi v. Luther Pomeroy and Henry Conner*. In this case, Roi (or Roy) charged the other two men defrauded him of "the value of 550 muskrat skins, four pounds of beaver [pelts] and ten martin skins, the value of $500." According to statements signed by Smith and Henderson, Pomeroy told them that while he was at Saginaw he (Pomeroy) pulled a switch by breaking open a barrel containing Roi's pelts. Pomeroy then replaced the pelts with old deer-skins and corn sacks. He completed this fraud by sealing up the barrel, which was shipped from Saginaw to Detroit on a boat belonging to a trader named Henry Conner. Jacob Smith and Henderson agreed that Conner was "much allarmed and a-feared" when Pomeroy told him about the switch he had pulled on Roi.[9]

Smith also served as a juror in other suits in 1810, and he posted a "special bail" for a defendant named Jeanbaptiste Jubainville in a lawsuit over Jubainville's debts. As noted previously, this was a time when the law allowed for the arrest and jailing of debtors. The posting of special bail meant that if Jubainville lost his case, Smith would be responsible for paying his fines and penalties. But it also indebted Jubainville to Smith, and it is likely the fur trader didn't put up the bail out of the goodness of his heart, but as a business decision.[10]

One of the cases Smith had to decide as a juror would turn out to be an ironic one in a historic sense. A French-Canadian fur trading agent, Toussaint Pothier, sued an American named Michael Dousman who lived and traded on Mackinac Island, or Michilimackinac, as it was then called. What no one could know then was that in just two years' time, Pothier and Dousman would play dramatic roles at Michilimackinac when the War of 1812 came to the straits, close to the U.S.

border with British Canada. Pothier, as a British agent, would carry word that the War of 1812 had been declared to the British commander on St. Joseph's Island, not far from Mackinac Island. Dousman, in turn, an American militia officer, would be sent by the commander of U.S. Army regulars on the island to see what the British were up to. But Dousman was taken prisoner on the waters of the straits by the very British-Indian force he'd been asked to find out about. Topping off this historical irony was the fact that Jacob Smith would also go to warn the U.S. garrison at Michilimackinac, but the U.S. fort was captured before he got there. Smith, too, would be captured, though he would manage to escape from Indians allied with the British.

But all these events lay in the future. On this particular day in court, in September 1810, Jacob Smith and his fellow jurors found for the plaintiff, Pothier. They ruled that Dousman owed him some $443 in damages.[11]

The year 1811 brought Smith new troubles in the form of two lawsuits that both ended up before the Territorial Supreme Court. The first came from a company of merchants, Wiggins, Emerson & Little, the second from Eli Bond. In the first case—the matter of the unpaid promissory note—Smith was accused of fraud because he had refused to pay on his loan. Merchant Robert Forsyth, who sued Jacob Smith in the fall of 1809, kept him out of jail by posting a special bail that made him responsible for the fur trader's potential liabilities and judgments. Of course, this meant that Smith was now supposed to be working to pay off his debts to Forsyth. In the second case, where Smith had not delivered the cider he had promised in exchange for Bond's pork and kettles, the fur trader admitted that he owed $58.08 to Bond. He was ordered by the court to pay it, along with the "costs & charges." That same day, Smith was to appear as a witness in a lawsuit between a man named Henry Berthelet and one Louis Laforge. A jury heard the case and was about to render a verdict, but Berthelet apparently dropped the matter.[12]

Beyond these court cases, little of Smith's activities are reflected in the historical record of the Michigan Territory, other than the fact that a son was born to Jacob and Mary Smith in Detroit in May 1811. They named the boy Albert James, also recorded as Albert Jay. Perhaps Mary had an expectant mother's cravings, or maybe was just baking treats for her family; a month or so before Albert's birth, records show that his mother ordered several pounds of sugar from Detroit merchant Joseph Campau. "Sir," Mary Smith had written to Campau on March 28.

"please let the bearer have eight lbs. of sugar which you will charge to account of Jacob Smith, in doing so you will oblige," she wrote.[13]

The cases in which Smith was sued or testified as a witness during this period indicate that he remained in the fur trade in these years up to the War of 1812, even though his name does not appear again in the Michigan Territorial license book for Indian traders until after the conflict. Of course, this book probably can't be taken as a complete record of such activity. But the absence of Smith's name in the book may indicate that he was working for others, perhaps because of his debts to them.

One of the important local merchant-traders doing business at Saginaw during this time was Conrad TenEyck, who had arrived in Detroit in 1801—just about the same time as Smith. TenEyck was about 30 years old in 1811; he and his brother Jeremiah had come from Albany, New York, an important center of the American fur trade. They would become prominent men in Michigan in the years ahead. The Reverend O. C. Thompson, an amateur historian who later wrote about Detroit, mentioned the connections between the TenEycks, Jacob Smith, and Chauncey Payne, a jeweler and merchant who came to Detroit after the War of 1812 and eventually became Smith's son-in-law in 1824. "The [business] traffic of this family with the Indians was carried on mostly through the house of Conrad & Gerry TenEyck," Thompson wrote about Smith and Payne. Conrad TenEyck had license to trade with the "Saginaw Indians" in February 1811, and documents indicate he would lose more than a thousand dollars worth of property at Saginaw in 1812, taken by the Chippewa when the war came to Michigan.[14]

While Jacob Smith's name dropped from the territorial license book during these years, he continued to trade in the Saginaw Valley at Chippewa settlements along the Flint and Saginaw rivers, continuing to gain familiarity and trust with members and leaders of the tribe, perhaps as an agent of TenEyck and other merchants. Michigan's next territorial governor, Lewis Cass, would send Smith to influence these Indians in the period after the War of 1812, just as Hull had in 1807. And when the commander of U.S. forces in Michigan wanted to talk to a man who knew the Indians and their villages in the Saginaw region in the fall of 1814, he would ask Jacob Smith.

Consider the example of an accounting of deals between Smith and Detroit businessman Richard H. Jones. This record shows Smith remained active in trade with Michigan Indians in the years before the war and even after the war had started. One entry in the document states that the fur trader delivered to Jones packs of fur pelts and barrels of sugar worth more than $2,300 between the late summer of 1811 and September 1812. Of course, by the summer of 1812, war was under way and the British occupied Detroit that August. Yet Smith was having pelts and sugar delivered to a local storehouse for Jones in August and September that year, a time when the rest of the fur trade had virtually ground to a halt.[15]

At some point before the War of 1812 began, Smith made the short journey to the home of his daughter whose name, it was claimed later, was Mokitchenoqua, born to the Chippewa woman called Nowabeshekoqua at the mouth of the Clinton River on Lake St. Clair. Smith's purpose? To remove his young daughter from her mother's people and place her with a white family. Indian interpreter and trader Henry Conner would later testify that Smith did this when the little girl, whose English name was Nancy, was about five years old—an age that would put the approximate time of her removal from her Chippewa family before the war started. Conner said the little girl spent some months at his home, and that she was removed from his care in 1812. Another employee of the U.S. government's Indian Department of the postwar time, Robert A. Forsyth, would testify that Smith indentured the girl to a man named Richard or Rickard—probably correctly spelled "Reichard"—who lived near Meadville, Pennsylvania.[16]

Did Smith place the mixed-blood child first with Conner and then a Pennsylvania family so as not to have to take her back to his wife Mary? Had he removed the girl from her Indian mother because of concerns about the coming war, or simply because he felt an obligation to try to make for her what he considered a better life among whites? How had Nowabeshekoqua felt about the removal of her daughter into the world of the whites? While Smith's motivations are unknown, Forsyth's and Conner's testimony showed Smith sent Nancy to Meadville, where she was indentured to "Rickard" or Reichard. Nancy Smith would spend at least several years in his household. Her relationship with her father and her half-siblings, if indeed she had any, remains a mystery.

If Jacob Smith enjoyed good relations with the Indians in the months before war between the United States and Britain broke out, he may have been among the exceptions to the rule. In the fall of 1811, leaders of Potawatomi, Chippewa, and Wyandot tribes of the Michigan region complained in a message to President

James Madison about being treated unfairly by American traders. "Father, we had had much intercourse with white men and now and then find an honest man," the chiefs said in their message, "but generally speaking white people appear fond of feathering their own nest & often pluck the Red birds for . . . accomplishing their purposes."[17]

By this point, a growing number of American merchants had come from the east, like the TenEyck brothers, to join in the fur trade. That trade had become more and more competitive. As noted earlier, the one American who made the most significant impact on the business was more than just a mere merchant or trader: he was John Jacob Astor, international fur broker and founder of the American Fur Company. The son of a German butcher, Astor had built himself a vast fortune, starting with the fur trade in New York, then in the Great Lakes region and then by going far beyond, diversifying into New York real estate and international trade. In a deal with the fur barons of Montreal, Astor bought from the Mackinac Company what one historian called the American portion of its business. Others say the deal was nonspecific about the territory involved, but that he'd bought into the British-Canadian company in a major way. In either case, Astor was now a businessman with powerful connections in both the United States and Canada. Astor's new acquisition was renamed the South West Company.[18]

Yet while American trade with the Indians had never been greater, tensions were worsening between them and U.S. settlers throughout the Old Northwest. For years, Governor William Henry Harrison of the Indiana Territory, an ambitious young politician and ex-military man, had signed treaties with the Indians of that region, expanding the boundaries of Indiana for the United States. But the charismatic and influential Shawnee leader Tecumseh, working to create a national confederation of tribes, argued that no one tribe or band had the right to cede away land without the approval of all. Though Harrison and Tecumseh mistrusted each other, they agreed on a boundary over which the United States would not advance or seek to gain new land.

Raids on settlers in Indiana continued and Harrison made up his mind to move against Prophet's Town, a large Indian village that had been established by Tecumseh and his brother at the junction of the Tippecanoe and Wabash rivers, some 250 miles southwest of Detroit. In the summer of 1811, Harrison began to pull together an army of regulars and militiamen. With the approval of the federal government, he advanced on the Indians that fall.[19]

Tecumseh was far away on the early morning of November 7 when his brother, the Prophet, decided to attack Harrison's encampment. The battle, which took place near present-day Lafayette, Indiana, was probably a draw in terms of casualties. But to Harrison and the Americans, it was a victory: They turned back the Indian attack. The next day they burned Prophet's Town, which the Indians had fled before the American soldiers got there.[20]

In the meantime, the United States' relations with Great Britain were steadily deteriorating over the "impressment" or kidnapping of American sailors by the Royal Navy at sea (the British claimed they were simply arresting Englishmen who had deserted) and the seizure of American merchant ships. In the Old Northwest, American officials and settlers were convinced that the British were providing weapons to the Indians, as well as inciting them to terrorize American settlers. Of course, the pioneers seemed not to recognize that their buying land and clearing and farming it was increasing the pressure on the Indians who lived there, some of whom had been pushed out years before from areas that now made up the eastern United States. Just three years earlier President Thomas Jefferson had acknowledged the complaints of the chiefs of tribes in Michigan and Ohio that settlers were trespassing and building on their lands, directing the chiefs to complain to their local U.S. Indian agents, who would see to the removal of intruders, at least theoretically.[21]

Hoping to work against British interests during this period of growing tension, the Madison administration banned the import of British goods. Though American and Canadian traders alike smuggled trading stock from Montreal and Quebec into U.S. territory, Indians in Michigan and elsewhere were not happy about the ban, and British agents may have encouraged the notion that Madison's nonimportation act was meant to hurt them. Violence against American settlers and traders continued up and down the frontier.

Because of these grim developments, the news of the battle of Tippecanoe in Indiana hit close to home for those who lived in and around Detroit when it reached them in December. On the edge of the wilderness frontier, with Indians around them and British soldiers across the Detroit River, residents asked the U.S. government for more defensive measures to keep them safe in the event war broke out. War fever was already in the air in many parts of the United States. Early in 1812, the U.S. Congress authorized the raising of more militia soldiers. In Michigan, four new companies were to be created. That spring, Jacob Smith joined a cavalry company serving under Richard Smyth, the Detroit justice of the peace and tavern keeper. Smyth was the company's captain.

This company was part of a defense force called the Michigan Detached Militia; Jacob Smith mustered with the militia troopers of Smyth's company, who were also known as the Detroit Dragoons, on April 21, 1812. Not long after this, Governor Hull's military administrator, Adjutant General George McDougall, appointed Judge James Witherell to command this new militia detachment. Witherell was a former congressman from Vermont and Revolutionary War veteran who had come to Detroit as a territorial judge. He held the rank of major in his new militia command.[22]

These new officers and men of the Michigan Detached Militia drilled and practiced and went on patrols that spring. But some of these citizens-soldiers weren't exactly crackerjack fighting men, and the fact they were led by officers who were also their friends and neighbors made it hard for them to accept orders and maintain discipline. One of Jacob Smith's comrades-in-arms, Private John Andre, refused to go on parade when ordered to do so. He took issue with the warnings he was getting and assaulted Corporal John Palmer; Andre spent a few days in confinement before a court-martial ordered him to apologize to Palmer. Two weeks later, several other members of the company—Joseph Venier, Louis Goddard, Michel Niquot, Joseph Dupley (alias Libland), Jacques Desplanes, and Joseph Bilau—refused to go on patrol and misused their weapons. Captain Richard Smyth found them guilty in the court-martial and sentenced them to 10 days hard labor, attached to ball and chain. Fortunately for them, Major Witherell decided that they had acted from ignorance and remitted their sentence, ordering them to return to duty.[23]

Though Jacob Smith's fellow troopers obviously needed more training and discipline, they were out of time. Less than a month later, on June 18, 1812, the United States declared war on Britain.

One of the first incidents of the war in Michigan, little known and practically forgotten, took place at the Chippewa village and trading center at Saginaw. It involved the family of David Henderson, the blacksmith who worked for the U.S. War Department's Indian Department and who'd been sent to work for the Chippewa by Governor Hull. Henderson was not with his family when word reached the Indians that war had broken out, which probably meant he was back in Detroit to get supplies or to take care of other business. "In the spring of 1812 when information of the declaration of war reached Saginaw, his family was detained by the Indians for some time," wrote James McCloskey, a surveyor and local political figure, "and had it not been for the assistance of some well disposed Indians, who assisted in effecting their escape, could have remained with the Indians during the bad w[eather]."[24]

Henderson's wife and children made it back to Detroit "almost in a situation of nakedness," McCloskey claimed; their household possessions, furniture, and clothing were all lost, taken by the Indians at Saginaw. Who were these friendly Indians who had helped the Hendersons escape? Had they been associated with the Ryleys, who were half Chippewa themselves? Could they have been Indians who worked for Jacob Smith or others in the fur trade? McCloskey did not say.

But a romanticized version of this event, printed in a Saginaw County history many years later, claimed it was Jacob Smith who rode to the rescue of Mrs. Henderson and her children, saving them from Kishkauko, the Saginaw chief who had a record of violence. According to this tale, Smith not only convinced Kishkauko to release the Hendersons, he also got the chief to send an escort of warriors to get Smith and the blacksmith's family safely back to Detroit. Once there, angry Detroiters took the Indians prisoner, but Smith engineered their release and averted violence all around.[25]

Unfortunately, the incorrect date of when this adventure was said to have taken place (off by an entire decade) and circumstances described (with Smith manipulating Kishkauko, rescuing the Hendersons, and preventing bloodshed) open this version of the incident to serious question. No record or report of that specific time substantiates these details, other than the fact that Mrs. Henderson and her children were held as captives but escaped with the help of "well-disposed" Indians.

Yet it is nonetheless true that Jacob Smith actually did go to Saginaw shortly after the War of 1812 began. On top of this, the historical record also reflects that certain Indians working with Smith did indeed help *him* escape from Indians allied with the British in July 1812. Later in the war, Jacob Smith would indeed travel again to Saginaw to trade goods for the release of white captives taken by the Indians. And lastly, Smith would, in the future, certainly manipulate Kishkauko for his own ends.

Thus the tale of the Hendersons' rescue, at least as it appeared in Saginaw County history books, is typical of the tales told about Jacob Smith, some of which have a factual basis. While some of his activities in the War of 1812 have to be pieced together, others are documented in the historical record: A courier mission to Mackinac Island, with a witness testifying that Smith pretended to be a British agent; the capture of Smith by Indians allied with British, but a subsequent escape; the arrest of Smith by British army officers in occupied Detroit; the attempted recruitment of Smith by a top British Indian Department officer; and Smith trading goods for young hostages taken by the Saginaw Indians.

These may sound like the stuff of a James Fenimore Cooper novel, but they are what Jacob Smith would experience in the conflict, risking his life in the frontier woods and on the lakes of the Michigan Territory for the United States in the War of 1812.

War in the Michigan Territory

The beginnings of the War of 1812 in Michigan were inauspicious. First, the U.S. government in Washington, D.C., declared the war, but it didn't hurry to inform its western outposts near the Canadian border of this fact. Detroit area residents figured out for themselves late in June that a state of war probably now existed, based on rumor and what they could see for themselves: excited British and Indian activity across the river at Sandwich and Ft. Malden.[1]

British commanders in Upper Canada actually received word that the war was declared several days before their American counterparts did in Detroit. One particular U.S. officer, Lt. Porter Hanks at Ft. Michilimackinac, never got any official notification, though it was Jacob Smith who tried to deliver the news to that frontier post, a fur trader would testify after the war.

At the time the U.S. Congress declared war on Britain, Governor William Hull of the Michigan Territory, now with the additional appointment of brigadier general, was returning to Detroit from the east. Hull had been given that military commission by the federal government when he'd gone to Washington early in 1812 to consult with President James Madison's War Department about the defense of Detroit in the event of war. Hull then made his way across Ohio, collecting a force of U.S. Army regulars and untrained volunteers to go back with him to the Michigan Territory. This Northwestern Army, as it was called, included the 3rd Ohio Militia Regiment, whose commander was the young prosecuting attorney of Muskingum County. His name was Lewis Cass, an eastern-born American, son of a Revolutionary War soldier, and an aspiring politician. Cass had received an appointment as U.S. marshal during Thomas Jefferson's presidency after his involvement against the Aaron Burr conspiracy; he would figure prominently in the near future in the Michigan Territory and ultimately on the national political stage.

Young Lewis Cass already knew the important figures and leaders in the Northwest, including William Henry Harrison, the governor of the Indiana Territory, and Ohio governor Return J. Meigs. One of Cass's good friends was Solomon Sibley, the lawyer who had moved to Detroit from Ohio and who had represented fur trader Jacob Smith. Sibley was now an officer in the Michigan Detached Militia, the body of men of which Jacob Smith was part. Late in June, these and the other militiamen were put on alert, along with the U.S. Army troops at Detroit's fort. Records suggest Jacob Smith was conducting business as usual, moving fur pelts and Indian maple sugar, as were other merchants and traders. By late June, Hull's Northwestern Army had marched out of the settled portions of Ohio across the great Black Swamp that then stretched for miles from a point north of Urbana up to near present-day Toledo. That city did not exist, of course, though there were small settlements near the rapids of the Maumee River.[2]

Hull and his army were camped near the rapids when, just after midnight on July 2, a rider brought word that the United States and Britain were at war. Historians have concluded Hull didn't hasten to warn the other American forts under his command that war had been declared, and that he did not attempt to warn the U.S. garrison at Ft. Michilimackinac at all. In fact, an American did try to reach Mackinac Island from Detroit, and this messenger was Jacob Smith.

Once the governor was informed that a state of war existed between the United States and Britain, he continued north with his army, arriving in Detroit on July 5. Unfortunately for the Americans, Hull's papers were seized three days earlier when a ship carrying his trunk, along with medical supplies and various American soldiers and officers, was captured by the British as it sailed up the Detroit River by Ft. Malden. On July 6 Hull issued general orders to the commanders of the garrisons at Ft. Wayne, Ft. Dearborn (present-day Chicago), and Michilimackinac to be ready to defend themselves now that war had been declared.[3]

Hull convened a meeting on July 7 with Indians from around the area, urging them to stay out of the war and informing them of another council that was to be held later that month. Many of them, including Ottawa and Chippewa bands that lived near Detroit, said that they would not join the war against the United States, but in fact some if not most of these Indians were ready to join the British and were simply awaiting developments.⁴ Subsequent claims by Jacob Smith indicate it was sometime after this, probably early in that second week of July, that he left for Mackinac Island, but not before clashing with Detroit postmaster James Abbott over who was responsible for paying his expenses for the journey. Within a year Smith would accuse Abbott of delaying his mission, and suggest that perhaps he had done so intentionally. Abbott would deny Smith's mission was government business at all. It would make for a national controversy.

But time had slipped away for the unsuspecting U.S. garrison on the island near the straits. For on the very same day war with Britain had been declared by Congress, businessman John Jacob Astor—more concerned with his company's profits than with the fact that his nation was going to war—sent several letters containing the news to his agents and business partners in Canada. Astor wanted his furs on Mackinac Island and his goods in Upper Canada protected from the ravages of war. The fact that his messages might help the British government and military seems not to have troubled him.

Because Astor was close to U.S. Treasury secretary Albert Gallatin, the millionaire was allowed to send his messages under Gallatin's frank, or official mailing privileges. Incredibly, Astor's letters to his agents in the fur trade in Canada moved faster and more efficiently than the U.S. government's own messages to its officials and military officers in the field. Thus British generals in Canada knew days before Governor Hull that war had been declared. One British general wrote that the news had come by an express from the North West Company—the Canadian fur trade bosses who had allowed Astor to buy into their business. The British officers across the Detroit River at Amherstburg got word about the declaration of war on June 28.⁵

One of the British agents of the South West Company (also called the Michilimackinac Company) was Touissant Pothier, who also happened to be a major in the Canadian militia. Pothier was in the Montreal area when the news of war arrived, and he and his men were said to have hurried into canoes and made their way up to Lake Huron and the British fort on St. Joseph's Island, just 50 miles or less from Ft. Michilimackinac. Pothier arrived at the British fort on July 3. Apprised of the fact that the United States and Great Britain were at war, the commander at St. Joseph's, Captain Charles Roberts, put his redcoats on alert, along with a force of Indians and loyal Canadian traders, voyageurs, and other fur company employees. At the same time, a key leader of the western Indians arrived to help fight the Americans; he was a burly red-haired Scotsman named Robert Dickson, who lived among the Dakota Sioux of the Upper Mississippi as a trader and unofficial British agent.[6]

Twelve days after receiving Pothier's news that the United States and Britain were at war, Captain Roberts got the go-ahead to attack Ft. Michilimackinac. Using a fur-trading ship, several bateaux, and many Indian canoes for transport, Roberts's force reached the island and successfully dragged two cannon to the heights above the vulnerable American fort on the night and early morning of July 16 and 17. It was a bold maneuver, and it worked.

In the meantime, the U.S. commander, Lt. Porter Hanks, noticed that Indians coming to the island seemed secretive and hostile, and he wondered if war was coming. He therefore asked an American resident and militia officer, Michael Dousman, to go over to St. Joseph's Island and find out what the British and Indians were up to (Dousman, it was noted previously, had faced Pothier in court in Detroit, where Jacob Smith had been a juror some months earlier). Dousman agreed to undertake the mission, but he was captured out on the water by the approaching British, Indian, and Canadian militia force.

Though Lieutenant Hanks soon realized that British soldiers had landed on Mackinac Island, the first official word he got about this new war came when he found his enemy had cannon pointed at him from the high ground above on the morning of July 17. Captain Roberts demanded that the American officer surrender; Hanks felt it was useless to try to fight, because he could not win and scores of his men and civilians would die needlessly. He surrendered the fort to the British.[7]

In the meantime Jacob Smith had left Detroit and stopped at Saginaw. Though Smith was ostensibly acting as an express, or courier, his actions indicate he was more than just a mere letter carrier. A communication by the British commander at the straits indicates Smith was traveling in the company of, or in conjunction with, at least three Indians. Who were these men? Captain Roberts of the British Army would write that one was a young Ottawa from the Detroit area who was carrying an important wampum, a beaded belt, that bore a message from his chief, The Wing, whose Native name was given as Ningweegon. The Wing's message advised the northern Indians of Michigan that they should not join the British in the war with the United States.[8]

A veteran fur trader named Charles Girard dit Lavisite was at Saginaw when Jacob Smith arrived. Girard would later testify that Smith hired him the next day to go along with him to Mackinac. Girard had been trading at Saginaw for years; Smith knew him and must have trusted him, for the Frenchman testified that Smith shared with him the fact that he, Smith, was carrying letters for the American authorities on the island.

Of course, the Chippewa and Ottawa of the Saginaw region had known Smith for nearly a decade and he had close associations among them. It could even be that Smith had family connections here, since his daughter called Nancy had been born part of a Chippewa band who lived near the mouth of Clinton River—an area where The Wing was an influential pro-U.S. voice. Accounts suggest that some members of Chippewa families routinely moved between bands at different locations around the region and had relatives at different villages. But even if Smith had friends here, many or most of the Saginaw Chippewa warriors favored the British in this new war. They were immediately suspicious about what the fur trader from Detroit was up to when he arrived at Saginaw.

Smith had guessed that pro-British Indians would search his gear, so he hid the packet of letters he'd been carrying under a hog pen, Girard would later testify. Though suspicious Indian warriors could find no messages in Smith's possessions, they detained him anyway, refusing to allow him to leave Saginaw. Smith understood that he had to have a reason that was acceptable to the anti-U.S. warriors and chiefs, or else he was going nowhere.[9]

But Smith had come prepared. He revealed to the Indians that he had in his possession or was wearing a British gorget, a military breastplate, Girard said. To the Indians, this gorget represented a kind of hidden badge or identity—that Smith was revealing himself to be a British agent. "The Indians detained him at Saguina for a couple days until he shewed them a British Gorget, pretending he was going to an Indian chief at Thunder Bay," Girard testified. In other words, Smith told them he was on some sort of mission going north, with the British army breastplate indicating he was acting on behalf of the British.

This was a dramatic but dangerous game Smith was playing, posing as a British officer—one that could get him executed as a spy. But the Chippewa at Saginaw accepted Smith's explanation, though they did not let him leave unattended. A party of their men started with Smith and Girard for the north up the Lake Huron coast in canoes. Along the way, Smith told Girard that if anything happened to him, Girard was to recover the packet of letters he'd hidden under the hog pen and return them to Postmaster James Abbott in Detroit, according to Girard.[10]

Thus Smith was allowed to continue on his way with a number of Indians from Saginaw. At the same time, the wampum carried by a representative from The Wing was a powerful message to the Indians of northern Michigan, though its effect was strictly short lived. Captain Roberts would report that this wampum had a great impact, until the Indians of the region were assured by British victories that they wouldn't be exterminated by the Americans.[11]

In any event, it was too late for Smith to bring the news of the war's outbreak to Ft. Michilimackinac; the American outpost on the island was by then falling or had already been captured, though the fur trader did not yet know this. Girard testified that he, Smith, and the accompanying Indians, traveling by canoe and now flying a U.S. flag, were "within a half a days march [journey] of Mackinac" when they met another party of warriors coming down from the island. Captain Roberts said this took place "fifteen leagues" from Ft. Michilimackinac.

The confrontation probably happened on July 21 or so on the Lake Huron waters, perhaps off the shore of what is now Cheboygan County. "Our impressions were that they were a war party," Girard said about the downbound Indians. These warriors, coming from Mackinac Island, gave war whoops when they saw Smith's American flag—they had spotted an enemy and were ready to fight. These British-allied warriors, paddling south, were on a mission of their own. This party, which seems to have contained members of the British Indian Department or Canadian militiaman, was an express, carrying messages from the victorious commander at Mackinac, Captain Roberts, to the British military authorities at Amherstburg and beyond. The warriors' canoes bore down on Smith and the Indians from Saginaw and Lake St. Clair, and the American trader was now a prisoner.[12]

Why was Smith openly flying an American flag? The representatives from The Wing had held councils with other Indians, Captain Roberts reported, presenting the wampum and warning that anyone who made war on the Americans would face death. Because of the dramatic effect this message had initially, Smith may have felt that displaying the flag was a bold, confident gesture. But it could also be he raised the flag for the safety of his party as they approached the island, so that U.S. troops would not fire on them in the event that hostilities had commenced at the straits.

Of course, Smith's flying that banner might have been fine if Mackinac hadn't already surrendered to the British and Indians—but it had. The British-allied warriors, who may have been Sioux canoeing down from Mackinac, were not happy to see Smith's U.S. flag. "[They] told him to take down the American flag and asked them where they were going," Girard said.

Someone in Smith's party, probably the fur trader himself, replied: "Mackinac."

Michilimackinac was no longer in American hands, a member of the war party-express replied; it had been taken by the British and Indians only three or four days earlier—these warriors had been there and taken part in it.[13]

There was nothing more to discuss. Someone in a position of authority in that express party decided there was no good reason for Jacob Smith to go on to Mackinac Island. "The Indians near Mackina [sic] took hold of our canoe and requested them [the Indians from Saginaw] to return with them to Detroit as Mackinac was taken," Girard said. Of course, this was really not a request at all, at least not for Smith. As far as the British officers and their Indian allies were concerned, Smith was their prisoner. Nor were these British-allied Indians really going to Detroit; Smith wasn't going to be returning to his home and fellow Americans. British military communications make clear that he was to be taken to Ft. Malden, headquarters of the British Indian Department. There he would at least be questioned, if not imprisoned.[14]

At least one of the British-allied warriors' canoes turned back to inform Captain Roberts of Smith's capture, for the British commander at Mackinac soon reported it to Major John Glegg, aide to General Isaac Brock, the British commander of Upper Canada and Michigan. In the meantime the combined party of anti-U.S. warriors, the party of Saginaw Indians and Smith and Girard stopped at a place called Sandy Creek, where the warriors searched Smith's gear, looking for the U.S. government messages or military dispatches they were sure he was carrying. Then, with Smith in tow, they continued south along the Lake Huron coast.

"One Smith the Bearer of despatches from Detroit was taken [captured] by the Express I sent to Amherstburg about fifteen leagues hence," Roberts wrote from Mackinac on July 29 to the top British commanders in Canada. "I wish he may not prove to cunning, and either make his escape or perhaps carry my despatches to Detroit." The clear implication in Roberts's words was that Smith gave the British officer reason for concern.[15]

Though a prisoner, Smith was apparently not tied up or restrained as the British-allied Indians made their way south. After all, there was nowhere for him to go, surrounded as he was, and hundreds of miles from the nearest U.S. outpost. The warriors searched Smith several more times, Girard later testified.

But Captain Roberts's worries about Smith escaping were well founded. When the party reached the Au Sable River to camp, Smith made his move. Here, Girard said, Jacob Smith "hired three Indians" to get the two of them away from their captors. The identity of these Indians was not discussed by Girard, but another message from the British Captain Roberts did: One of them was the young Ottawa who had been the bearer of the wampum from the pro-American chief, The Wing.

Roberts was initially concerned about the impact this warning message had on the tribes of northern Michigan. "The effect this had on the Indians in general was very perceptible," the British captain reported. A Chippewa chief who had attended a secret council with the northern Ottawa tribe informed Roberts that these Indians talked of begging American forgiveness and even demanding the restoration of Ft. Michimilimackinac back into U.S. hands.[16]

Girard said these three Indians agreed at the camp at the Au Sable to get Smith back to Detroit. They simply but boldly smuggled the two white men out from under the noses of the British-allied Indians. "The [three] Indians on our departure from River Sable got M[r.] Smith help, [telling us] to lay down and hide ourselves in the canoe while they were in sight of the Indians from Mackina," Girard said, "and [they] went all the next night with expectation until they arrived at Detroit."

That was all the detail he provided on Jacob Smith's mission to Michilimackinac and subsequent escape when he gave his testimony. The facts of this matter are confirmed by the letters of Captain Roberts. The British commander at the straits already had sent a message informing his commander that Smith had been captured by the downbound express. Now he had to let his superior officer know that Smith had gotten away.

> You are already acquainted of their having taken prisoner a Man of the [name] of Smith bound here with dispatches from General Hull who was permitted to escape. But what is still worse a young Ottawa, one of the Crew, was the bearer of Wampum from a Chief called the Wing in the River St. Clair to the Ottawas here, telling them they had done wrong in assisting their English Father, that the Americans were as numerous as the Sand and would exterminate them.[17]

In this way Jacob Smith had come to the attention of British army officers in the opening weeks of the War of 1812 in Michigan: An American fur trader who had pretended to be a British agent to the Saginaw Chippewa, carrying messages for the U.S. Army on Mackinac Island, and who had escaped with the help of Indians—one who bore the powerful message from The Wing, warning other Indians not to side with the British.

Smith's mission was audacious but unsuccessful, and it was ultimately forgotten. The only direct references to it were in Captain Roberts' letters, an obscure court record and a wartime letter by James Abbott. Even if Smith had succeeded in warning Lieutenant Hanks about the state of war, Michilimackinac would have been quickly cut off from supply and reinforcement, since the British controlled the Great Lakes, and it would have fallen one way or another. Unfortunately for the Americans, the impact of The Wing's message quickly wore off. After all, the British had taken Michilimackinac and the Americans were powerless to do anything about it. In the days and weeks after the fall of the fort, some of the Indians who had listened fearfully to The Wing's message—that the United States would wipe them out if they joined the British—apologized to Captain Roberts for having doubted the ability of the British to defeat the Americans. Some of these Indians almost certainly joined in the war against the United States. But British officers would not forget this American troublemaker, Smith, in the weeks ahead.

The three Indians who smuggled Jacob Smith and Charles Girard away from the British-allied warriors quickly outdistanced them and stopped at Saginaw, where Smith retrieved the letters he'd hidden. He returned them to Postmaster James Abbott when he made it back to Detroit. Now it was late in July, and it was around this same time that the family of blacksmith David Henderson, taken prisoner by Indians at Saginaw, also escaped back to Detroit. As noted in the previous chapter, David Henderson's friend James McCloskey said it was friendly Indians who aided the escape of Mrs. Henderson and her children. Of course, Indians had also helped Smith escape from what would have been certain detention, if not imprisonment, in Canada.[18]

Furthermore, it was two Chippewa men who brought word to General William Hull at Detroit late in July that Michilimackinac had fallen to the British. Was all this activity by friendly Indians a happy coincidence for Hull and the Americans at Detroit? Or were these Indians friends or operatives working in connection with Jacob Smith, perhaps members of his company? The story that would later appear in histories of Saginaw County would give Jacob Smith credit for rescuing the Henderson family, although details of this account, including the year it supposedly happened, are not accurate. Still, it may be that the tale of the captivity and escape of Mrs. Henderson and her children is based on some truth—and that Smith and his Chippewa allies were part of it in the early weeks of the War of 1812 in Michigan.[19]

Similarly, a story about Jacob Smith in accounts of the history of Flint and Genesee County, Michigan, tell of the fur trader escaping on horseback, riding desperately away from Indian pursuers from Saginaw at the beginning of the War of 1812 after a mission to gather intelligence was exposed. Of course, there is no evidence for that tale, other than it seems to be a romanticized and incorrect version of Smith's real but unsuccessful mission to Michilimackinac.[20]

Given Smith's close relationships with some Chippewa and Ottawa bands and individuals, his presence in Saginaw after the declaration of war and his mission to the straits, the close sequence of these events involving the Henderson family and the reports brought to Hull by Chippewa individuals, there can be little doubt that the fur trader played a role as an unofficial Indian agent, courier, and spy for Hull and the United States government, just as Gov. Lewis Cass would later indicate in communications to officials in Washington. Smith's escape and that of the Hendersons at the same time The Wing was working on behalf of Hull was probably not just a coincidence. One old Michigan pioneer would later write that The Wing's "fidelity to the Americans was so great that he selected eight strong men of his band to man his large birch canoe, with which he passed down Lakes Huron and St. Clair, and gave the information to Governor Hull of the capture of Mackinac."[21]

The fall of the U.S. fort on Mackinac Island was another blow to the American cause in the summer of 1812. It prompted many Indians to join in the war against the United States, and it allowed the British to plant the idea with Governor Hull that their victory at the straits was bringing thousands of hostile Indians from around the region to head for Detroit. In the final analysis, it was a piece of good fortune for the residents of Mackinac Island and the U.S. troops at the fort that Jacob Smith hadn't been able to warn them. Surprised and outgunned, the Americans surrendered without killing or wounding any of the Indians who participated with the British in surrounding the fort. Had a warning reached the Americans in time for them to prepare a resistance, the resulting confrontation may well have resulted in a bloodbath for those U.S. troops and settlers on the island. John

Askin Jr., a British Canadian storekeeper and interpreter for the British Indian Department, stated this convincingly. "It was a fortunate circumstance that the fort capitulated without firing a single gun," Askin wrote from the island, "for had they done so, I firmly believe not a soul of them would have been saved."[22]

The war had started badly for Jacob Smith and the United States in Michigan and the Old Northwest, and now it was about to get worse.

The Arrest of Jacob Smith

While Jacob Smith was gone on his too-late mission to Mackinac Island, General William Hull launched his invasion of Canada on July 12, 1812. The Americans took possession of Sandwich, a small town that would become Windsor, Ontario. Two days later, some of Smith's comrades in Captain Richard Smyth's cavalry company were also sent across the Detroit River to Canada, where they aided other American troopers and a force of infantry under Colonel Duncan McArthur, the commander of the 1st Ohio Militia Regiment. They spent the next few days raiding the Canadian countryside.

These volunteers seized stores of flour, arms, blankets, alcohol, salt, and other supplies, supposedly intended for the Canadian and British military, at points along the Thames River as far as modern-day Chatham, Ontario. Canadian citizens complained the American raiders carried off plenty of their private property, too. Some of this confiscated property was taken to Detroit and placed in Jacob Smith's storehouse. The Americans spread copies of a bombastic proclamation promising that the Americans didn't mean to conquer Canada, but that no mercy would be given to any white man found fighting alongside of the Indians, whom they so feared.

Again some of the Michigan volunteers demonstrated they weren't exactly disciplined soldiers. Members of Capt. Richard Smyth's cavalry company were rowdy and abusive when they were sent on a detail from Detroit to round up some deserters south of town. One officer of the Michigan Detached Militia, Capt. Hubert LaCroix, complained to Major Witherell that Smyth's men "conducted [themselves] with great impropriety" when they arrived at Brownstown by fighting and wrongly taking a couple of horses from an Indian and a local resident.[1]

But this militia misbehavior was strictly a sideshow. More important was the fact that General Hull prepared, planned, and held councils with his impatient officers—but did nothing. No U.S. attack was made on the British at Ft. Malden, which lay on the Canadian side of the Detroit River where it flows into Lake Erie. There were small skirmishes and more raids and seizures of British and Canadian supplies, but no decisive moves were made by Hull to take the fight to the British, even though the American forces greatly outnumbered the redcoats and their Indian allies. Then came the bad news about the U.S. garrison at Mackinac. On July 29, Hull wrote to the Secretary of War William Eustis that he'd learned from "two friendly Indians" that Ft. Michilimackinac had fallen to the British. These were likely men sent by The Wing, possibly the same Indians who had helped Jacob Smith escape and who had spirited away the Hendersons from Saginaw back to Detroit.[2]

The situation for Hull and the Americans in the Detroit area worsened. When a detachment of Ohio volunteers was sent from Detroit south to meet and escort a convoy of supplies, horses, cattle, and reinforcements coming up from Ohio on a bright summer's day, warriors under Tecumseh ambushed Hull's men, who broke and ran. This battle of Brownstown on August 5 left 17 Americans killed and at least 12 wounded. Two prisoners taken by the Indians were murdered in revenge for an Indian killed in the fighting. That same day, the Indians also attacked and killed most of a squad of riders escorting mail coming up to Detroit from Ohio near a place called Swan Creek.[3]

As a result of these defeats, Hull steadily lost what nerve he had. He pulled most of the American force back across the Detroit River, out of Canada. To try to get those U.S. supplies and reinforcements safely to Detroit from the Rapids of the Maumee (an area near present-day Toledo), he sent a force of 600 men, infantry and cavalry, to try again on August 8. Jacob Smith's comrades, the Detroit militia cavalry of Captain Smyth, were part of this mission. At about four o'clock in the afternoon of the next day, the Americans, moving cautiously, reached the vicinity of a recently abandoned Indian village called Maguaga or Monguaga, just a few miles north of Brownstown. Some 400 British soldiers, positioned in a nearby ravine, and a large number of Indians under Tecumseh, hidden in adjacent woods and a cornfield, waited to spring their ambush. As the first Americans came into range, they opened fire.

This time the Americans did not break and run. Unfortunately for the British, some of the redcoats mistakenly fired on their Indian allies, who angrily fired back at them. In the confusion some of the British troops retreated, and so did the Indians. The Americans pursued them, but ultimately their commanders did not press on to reach that convoy of Ohio supplies and reinforcements. The Americans had suffered 18 men killed and 64 wounded, yet they weren't able to break the British-Indian blockade of the road from Ohio. With the British also in control of Lake Erie, Hull, his army, and Detroit were cut off from the rest of the United States. No more help would be coming. Whether Jacob Smith participated in the fighting at Monguaga with Smyth's militia cavalry company is not known. While his military record shows he was on the army payroll for this period, more detailed records of his service don't exist.[4]

The military situation for Americans in the Old Northwest was rapidly dete-riorating and so were relations between Hull and his Ohio colonels, Lewis Cass and Duncan McArthur. Hull didn't trust them—they were aggressive, while he was cautious—and now they had no confidence in him. Eighty men, including Detroit residents and Ohio soldiers, reportedly signed a petition requesting the arrest of Hull or his replacement with Colonel McArthur. This petition is lost to history, but it would be interesting to know if Jacob Smith was one of the signers, as other Michigan militia officers and men supposedly were.[5]

Now came more terrible developments for the Americans. On August 15, a wagon train of 66 U.S. soldiers and militiamen and 27 women and children was overrun by Potawatomi Indians as the Americans abandoned Ft. Dearborn, the site of present-day Chicago. Though the soldiers surrendered on the promise they wouldn't be harmed, half of the women and children were massacred, as were many of the men. Some of the men taken prisoner suffered tortuous, agonizing deaths at the hands of their captors. These Americans had been ordered by Hull to leave the outpost and make their way to Detroit or Ft. Wayne in Indiana. That same day the British began to bombard Detroit. The next day the British launched their invasion from Canada, landing Indians and soldiers on the Michigan shore. One of the Americans killed in the artillery bombardment was Lieutenant Hanks, the unfortunate ex-commander of Ft. Michilimackinac who had been released by the British and sent down to Detroit.[6]

William Hull was in a predicament. Though he was in an adequate fort and decently supplied, he believed that thousands of hostile Indians were just waiting for word to attack with the British. He had about a thousand soldiers to defend Detroit, but hundreds of them were untrained, unreliable militiamen. He had been unable to keep his supply lines open from Ohio, and the British controlled Lake Erie and the Detroit River. The threat of an Indian massacre of hundreds of civilians, including women and children, hung heavily on his mind. In fact, violence against local residents had already taken place. Detroit historian B. F. H. Witherell, the son of Jacob Smith's militia major, later writing under the pen name "Hamtramck," said a family of six named St. Francis, who "took no part in the war," was massacred at their home outside of Detroit by Chippewa who had joined the British. A witness told Witherell he'd seen the Indians proudly displaying the family members' scalps across the river on the Canadian side.[7]

Whether or not Hull knew of the murders of the St. Francis family, he was played brilliantly by British commanders and Tecumseh; he believed he had no option other than to surrender. He had not been a bold leader and soon he would become the scapegoat for President Madison's administration for everything that had gone so badly in the first months of the war. Hull would find himself disgraced nationally and facing court-martial on charges of treason. Though it was fashionable for decades for Michigan residents to curse Hull for his "shameful" surrender to the British, he was probably the wrong man for the job of leading U.S. forces in the Old Northwest. In any event, his position was untenable. Hull thought he was doing the right thing by surrendering and saving the lives of his troops and the civilian population of Detroit; the Ft. Dearborn massacre was a clear and terrible example of what happened to Americans who attempted to surrender to Indians after the shooting had begun. Certainly the British used that real threat of unrestrained Indian violence time and time again to try to induce U.S. commanders to surrender.

One Detroit man who had acted as a scout and agent among local Indians for the Americans—a fellow by the name of Jonathon Pointer—didn't wait around for Detroit's surrender. Whether he was worried about Indian violence or facing the consequences of having been a spy for the United States, he quickly disappeared from the fort when he heard about Hull's decision. "Jonathon Pointer, who was a useful spy or scout, was in Detroit, & said 'I must use my legs' & escaped over the pickets into the woods on the morning of the surrender," said John E. Hunt, a

Detroit resident and witness. "He was tall, strait [*sic*], quick & active & a complete Indian in his habit."[8]

Jacob Smith had also performed as a confidential agent and Indian liaison, but he had a family in Detroit; he stayed and was present when William Hull surrendered on August 16, 1812. The fact Smith was officially a private in the militia meant that he was paroled, or released by the British, shortly after Detroit's surrender, along with the other volunteers from Ohio and Michigan. These terms were spelled out in supplemental articles of the surrender agreed to by Hull and the British commander, General Isaac Brock. "Parole" meant that the Ohio and Michigan militiamen could return to their homes, but in return they agreed not to rejoin the American army. U.S. regulars who were paroled could not reenter their country's armed service until they had been formally processed or "exchanged" for British soldiers taken prisoner by the United States. Smith would later file a claim that he lost his horse, saddle, and bridle in the service of the United States at the surrender of Detroit. Afterward Smith was paid $70 for these when he put in his claim with the government in 1814.[9]

Now that the British and their Indian allies controlled Detroit and the Michigan Territory, Smith and other residents, particularly those who had become United States citizens, lost even more. British officers ordered the confiscation of public stores of food, grain, and other government supplies along with the guns and stores of Hull's soldiers. The Indians were also present, with more soon coming, and they expected to take part in the spoils of Detroit and nearby residents. To them, it was payback time; they helped themselves to what they wanted of the residents' property, taking horses and items of every sort. Some accounts say they also enjoyed burning down barns and outbuildings and even some homes, and that the British commander left in charge of Detroit, Colonel Henry Procter, simply shrugged when citizens appealed to him, for he simply was not in control of the Indians. This was the price of being in U.S. territory that had fallen into their hands. In very short order, Detroit was a difficult place to live for residents who did not leave.[10]

Jacob Smith's store had been used as a repository for supplies and goods seized by Hull's men back during the short-lived U.S. summer incursion into Canada. Now the British and Canadian militiamen and Indians returned the favor, taking back those items and Smith's property, too. His losses, he claimed, were not small.[11]

The loss of Forts Dearborn, Michilimackinac, and Detroit, and other American outposts in the weeks that followed, meant that U.S. authority had been driven out of the upper Old Northwest. American settlements in Ohio, Illinois, and Indiana were vulnerable to Indian attack. British General Brock declared that the Michigan Territory was no longer part of the United States, and he pushed the idea with his superiors that an Indian state should be created in the Old Northwest as a buffer between British Canada and the United States. The idea of such a zone between the two countries was not new, but this represented perhaps the last chance for the British to impose such a change on the young United States.

"The province of Upper Canada (it appears to me) will be of little value to Britain, unless accompanied by the territories of Michigan and Illinois," wrote a British officer, perhaps Procter or Brock, in a paper that was reportedly captured later by U.S. forces. "Because [of] Upper Canada being almost surrounded by the territories of the United States, [the United States] have at all times the opportunity of pouring troops into it on every side, and with a probability of overrunning it."[12]

In time, this British officer predicted, U.S. settlers would populate Michigan and the Old Northwest, cutting off "the most powerful and warlike of the Indians" from Canada. In other words, the tribes of the Great Lakes and the Upper Mississippi, most of whom were hostile to the United States, would be of no help to Britain once Americans had settled and controlled the Michigan Territory. Unless the British and the Indians could defeat the United States or at least fight them to a draw in this region, the Americans would eventually come and get the territory back, this officer understood. But if the British and Indians were successful, Michigan and the Old Northwest could become an Indian territory, with Britain's Native allies driving American settlers entirely out of the region. This, of course, was in Britain's interest, since it would check the western expansion of the United States and keep alive British control in the important Great Lakes fur trade.[13]

Now that the British and their Indian allies had nearly conquered the entire region, this idea of creating a giant Indian zone became soon a matter of the British government's official policy. Major Adam Muir of the British Army's 41st Infantry Regiment made this plain when he tried to talk fur trade clerk Archibald Lyon or Lyons, then working for a Detroit attorney and businessman named John McDonell, into joining the British service. Muir told Lyon the Michigan country was now held by the British "and always would be."[14]

But across the U.S. frontier, white American settlers were outraged—the unilateral cession of Michigan by Britain was considered both arrogant and contrary to international law. The idea of an Indian buffer state was anathema to pioneers who wanted land, especially to those who considered Indians their enemy. As a result, hundreds, even thousands, of Americans flocked to the fight.

Paroled with other Michigan militiamen, Jacob Smith remained in the Detroit area in the weeks after Hull's surrender. First, a simple matter of family biology—the birth of his daughter Maria in June 1813—indicates that Smith was with his wife Mary in the early fall of 1812. His presence is confirmed by Detroit business records that show Smith continued trade-related transactions right up through September.[15]

Of course, the possibility that Smith and other Detroiters acted as spies for the United States is real and likely, though the evidence for Smith's involvement as what would be called a "stay-behind" agent is strictly circumstantial. By early September, William Henry Harrison, the governor of Indiana, was appointed a U.S. brigadier general, and he would soon become commander of all American forces in the Old Northwest. He was then at Piqua, Ohio, some 180 miles south of Detroit. At that time, Harrison was receiving reports about the movement of British troops and Indians from Ft. Malden.[16]

Was Jacob Smith reporting or passing along such intelligence to American military officers? It would seem so, for that fall Smith came to the attention of the British commander, Colonel Henry Procter. Possibly someone in the British military or Indian Department realized that Smith was the man who had attempted to get to Ft. Michilimackinac back in July, and who had escaped. It is also possible that Smith did something that attracted the attention of the British military, their agents, or Indian warrior allies, who kept an eye on Detroit area residents and U.S. military movements south of Detroit.

However it occurred, Smith would state later that Colonel Procter had him arrested. A message forwarded to the U.S. Secretary of War John Armstrong some months later explained, in part, what happened: "Mr. Jacob Smith, Late of Detroit, states that on the 22nd of October last [1812] he was ordered from Detroit by Colonel Proctor [*sic*], then commanding that place, that he [Smith] was sent to Malden, then put in irons and sent to Montreal [and] Was there kept in Prison in Close Confinement."[17]

Though Smith isn't mentioned by name in Colonel Procter's surviving letters, the British commander at Detroit was deeply and correctly suspicious that certain local residents were passing information to the new Northwestern Army of the United States that had been formed after Hull's surrender, or otherwise working against British interests. Also detained that fall was William Walker, a resident of Wayne County who had been raised by Indians and who had worked as an official interpreter and Indian agent for Hull. Walker, like Smith, had tried to encourage Indians to stay out of the war. He was arrested but managed to escape from the British within days of Smith's arrest. Walker made his way to Ohio.[18]

Yet another example of British concern about American spies came a few weeks after Smith's arrest and just before Christmas of 1812. Colonel Procter wanted to deport a group of men from Detroit he also considered American troublemakers. But the ship he wanted to use to exile those Americans, the *Ellenor*, wasn't in any shape to safely sail. He indicated that he had already begun to get rid of these U.S. spies, a reference that almost certainly included Jacob Smith and William Walker. "I could have cleared this territory of Dangerous Characters with whom the Enemy, I believe, correspond," Procter wrote, "but I have not been able to completely effect it. The [sailing vessel] Ellenor, who was to have taken away some of them, has been protested against as not seaworthy. . . . I do not choose to take the responsibility of drowning them tho' they deserve to be hanged."[19]

In the meantime, Jacob Smith was kept in Canadian prison for two months. During this time he was locked up in Montreal, Robert Dickson, the British trader, operative, and friend of the Indians of Upper Canada, arrived there in November 1812. Smith was finally released on January 6, 1813, just after Dickson became his country's official agent for Indians west of Lake Huron. The appointment of Dickson, who had led Sioux and other Indians in the capture of Michilimackinac, meant that he was now the British liaison officer to the tribes of Michigan and the Upper Great Lakes. Dickson either knew of Smith or had heard about his reputation and his influence with the Indians of the Saginaw region. According to Smith, Dickson made him an offer: Come and work for the British against the United States. According to a report to the U.S. secretary of war:

> While [Smith was] in confinement, Captain Robert Dickson call[e]d on him and informed him that said Dickson had superceded Col. Matthew Elliott, Indian Agent at Malden, and requested Said Smith to go with him to Detroit, Lake Superior and Missippi [*sic*], under pay of the British Government in order to bring all the Indians Possible to join with them. In that case he would comply, he [Smith]

should be paid by their Government for all his Losses Sustained in Consequence of the Surrender of Detroit.[20]

Smith reported to U.S. officers that Dickson intended "to get as many men as he could to go into the Indian Country to bring them in, and that he calculated to have at least 3000 Indians by the latter end of June." Not only that, Smith would say, hundreds of additional troops left Montreal for Upper Canada, apparently to reinforce Procter early in 1813.

Then did Smith indicate he would sign on with Dickson and the British so he could get out of prison? Did Dickson release Smith as a goodwill gesture in his effort to get the fur trader's help with Indian recruitment? This is not reflected in Smith's statement, though Smith's family later said they believed he had been released in a prisoner exchange. However it happened, Smith was let out of confinement in Montreal and allowed to go free.

It's unknown what Smith did in the time between his release from Montreal and his showing up at the newly constructed American outpost, Ft. Meigs, on the Maumee River in Ohio, early in 1813. He still had relatives in Quebec; perhaps he was even allowed to return to Detroit. This was, however, the time when Colonel Procter, angry with and suspicious of Michigan residents, was kicking out prominent men who he believed had helped American forces. Proctor referred to Detroit in one letter as "that depot of Treachery," so it seems unlikely Smith could have gone back to his family there.[21]

But when Smith finally reached Cleveland, Ohio, in March 1813, he reported his arrest by Procter, his imprisonment in Canada, and his conversations with Dickson to an American military officer. This information was forwarded to the new U.S. secretary of war, John Armstrong. Smith's report about Dickson's plan was indeed accurate. Other records bear out that in December 1812, Dickson proposed to the British commander in chief that a body of 100 or 200 Englishmen and Canadians in the Indian Country of the Great Lakes and Canada be formed into a unit of rangers "to act with the Indians."

"Twenty young men as Interpreters, and officers, will be wanted," Dickson wrote in his proposal, to gain the cooperation of the Indian tribes as far away as the Mississippi. Though Jacob Smith's name doesn't appear in Dickson's surviving papers, it would make sense that the influential British Indian agent hoped Smith would join him in the effort to recruit the warriors needed to drive the United States out of the Old Northwest. That plan had the support of the Canadian fur bosses, some of whom served with British military officers in a kind of secret service board of directors that was to oversee Dickson's operation. These British-Canadian businessmen supported the idea of regaining control of the fur trade in the Great Lakes region—and pushing the Americans out.[22]

Thus it appears that Jacob Smith knew what he was talking about when he reported to that U.S. Army officer in Cleveland early in 1813—he was providing accurate, important intelligence to the U.S. War Department. In the meantime, the war continued in the Old Northwest. It would be the bloodiest chapter in Michigan's recorded history.

I Pray You Inform Me . . .
the Character of Jacob Smith

O ne of the dramatic stories about Jacob Smith in the War of 1812 that survived over the past 200 years was left in biographical notes written by the man who married Smith's youngest daughter, Maria, and it is an example of how fact and fiction regarding the fur trader became mixed in the years after his death. This anecdote, recorded tersely, was written by Col. Thomas B. W. Stockton, a veteran of the Mexican and Civil wars who settled in Flint with Maria. According to Stockton, who never knew his father-in-law but heard about him from his wife's family, the fur trader tried to approach Indians hostile to the United States "after [the] massacre of Raisin River."[1]

This terrible event took place in January 1813. General James Winchester, one of the key American commanders in the Old Northwest after William Hull's surrender, advanced more than 700 Kentucky militiamen from the area of present-day Toledo. He did this in response to pleas for protection from residents who lived in the community called Frenchtown on the River Raisin, or what is today the city of Monroe. Winchester's men were part of the advance of an army of some 4,000 volunteers under William Henry Harrison. They came from Indiana, Kentucky, Ohio, and elsewhere, many who joined up in the wake of the surrender of Detroit and the British declaration that Michigan was forfeit as U.S. territory. Winchester's force had been getting in position for a new offensive against the British and Indians to retake Detroit when urgent messages reached him from people at Frenchtown, telling him that residents who favored the American cause were being rounded up and taken to Ft. Malden, across the Detroit River.

Though Winchester wasn't supposed to make an advance yet, he did so in order to rescue these pro-U.S. settlers. On January 18, 1813, his Kentuckians attacked, defeated, and drove off a force of 250 Canadian militiamen and Indians, along with some British artillery, in a three-hour battle and pursuit. Then Winchester ordered even more of his troops to come up to the river. Unfortunately for these Americans, Col. Henry Procter, the British commander at Detroit, gathered up more than 1,200 soldiers and Indians and struck back four days later, surprising Winchester's badly deployed troops and capturing the general himself. The Americans surrendered on the promise that they would be protected from the Indians, but that did not happen. At least several men who'd given up were soon after murdered and scalped by the Indians.

Most of surrendered U.S. soldiers and their walking wounded were removed by the British that night and marched as prisoners across the ice of Lake Erie and the Detroit River to Ft. Malden, but scores of other wounded troops remained behind. On the night of January 22 and into the next morning, many of these wounded men were massacred by Indians, and the houses that had been used by the Americans burned. Most of those prisoners who survived were ransomed by the Indians, but some were taken away to their villages throughout the area. The captives could be adopted into tribes and families, but some were tortured to death.[2]

This was the historical background to the notes left by Jacob Smith's son-in-law. It was after the massacre, Thomas Stockton claimed, that Smith was ordered by a "Gen. Butler" to go among the Indians "to find out their design." According to Stockton's brief account, Smith was provided with goods and presents, and he took these to "the Indians," though he didn't specify which tribe or band. These Indians, suspecting Smith was a spy, met in council and determined to kill him, Stockton claimed, but being warned by a friendly Indian, Smith and all but one of his *engagees*, or employees, escaped.[3]

But was this anecdote true? Consider that a variation on this story, as related previously, appeared later in histories of Genesee County, Michigan. That version of a mission by Smith was described as having taken place some months earlier, at the time the war began in the summer of 1812, when Smith had supposedly been sent with a couple of companions on an intelligence mission by Governor Hull to Saginaw, to find out whether the Chippewa would side with the British. As Smith and his companions sat around a campfire with the Indians, this version of the tale goes, the men shared whiskey that was passed around. One of Smith's companions, his inhibitions lowered by alcohol, was said to have "let slip" the party's real intention, and Smith and his friends had to flee for their lives with their cover blown and the Indians in hot pursuit. The men dashed away on horseback, the story continued, but Smith was struck by a branch that injured his eye. One of the other compatriots was said to have been captured and killed by the angry Chippewa warriors.[4]

But there is simply no proof, no report from that time or no later memoir to confirm that anything like this occurred. Of course, records show what really happened—Smith had tried to reach Ft. Michilimackinac in July 1812; he was captured and shortly after escaped by canoe with the help of certain Indians. The deposition of Charles Girard dit Lavisite, who had been with Smith for that real but unsuccessful mission, makes no mention of a chase on horseback or that one of Smith's comrades had been killed.

Nor do the details of the story as told by Thomas Stockton hold up to examination. For the record, there was no "General Butler" in William Henry Harrison's army during the time of the River Raisin battle and massacre. There was a colonel named Anthony Butler in the new Army of the Northwest, but Colonel Butler only had temporary command of U.S. forces in Detroit and Upper Canada for a brief period from December 1813 into the early part of 1814. That was nearly a year *after* the River Raisin massacre.

In truth, there would have been no good reason for an American scout to go among the Indians to "learn the design" of the Indians in the Michigan Territory after the River Raisin massacre. While Smith certainly had friends among the Saginaw Chippewa and Ottawa people, hundreds of warriors had already aligned themselves with the British; others were simply sitting out the war and not involved in it. By the time Anthony Butler was in charge at Detroit late in 1813, an uneasy armistice had been agreed to by some Michigan Indians, including some chiefs of the Saginaw Chippewa. Of course, periodic attacks on Detroit area settlers did continue, and Colonel Butler made it a point to keep tabs on area tribes with spies, continuing a practice carried on by both General Harrison and Lewis Cass. While in command at Detroit, Butler bragged to a British officer who had come under a flag of truce that he knew very well what British Indian agents were up to among the tribes in Michigan.[5]

If this was the point in the war to which Stockton's note referred—the time when Colonel Butler was in command at Detroit—it would tend to reinforce what some records show about Smith's activities as a militia officer who, while working as a fur trader, acted at times as an Indian liaison and intelligence gatherer. It is also true that by the last months of the war in 1814, some Indians in Michigan and elsewhere in the Old Northwest continued to hold American prisoners in the wilderness, and Smith was involved in at least one such mission to trade goods for young hostages held for ransom by the Indians.

What really happened after the River Raisin massacre? Many Detroit residents, fur traders and merchants, and their Canadian neighbors paid ransoms to the Indians for the release of American soldier-hostages and civilian prisoners who hadn't been killed. Indians on many occasions brought their prisoners into Detroit to sell them back to American residents, British officers, and Canadians alike. Was Jacob Smith in any position to help survivors of the massacre in the early months of 1813? According to Smith's own account, he had been released from a Montreal prison just about three weeks before the massacre took place. He said he remained in Montreal into early February 1813—nearly two weeks after the massacre. This would mean Smith couldn't have been directly involved in any immediate trading for the release of hostages until weeks or months later. Nothing in the historical record indicates Smith escaped from unidentified Indians after attempting to carry out a mission in the wake of the River Raisin massacre.[6]

What is true, however, is that in the summer of 1814, Jacob Smith indeed took goods to the Saginaw Chippewa to trade for the release of the children of the Boyer family, who'd been captured and spirited away, along with their father, from their home on the Clinton River. In doing so, Smith would be the only white U.S. citizen to ride into the Saginaw Valley during the War of 1812.

There are two other pieces of historical evidence that fit into this picture of Jacob Smith's mysterious activities in 1813 and 1814. A letter Smith wrote to Michigan territorial governor Lewis Cass in December 1815 shows the fur trader reminding Cass of the missions he'd carried out during the war. Smith, who had been asked by the governor to get Saginaw chiefs to attend a peace treaty that fall, made note of "the trust reposed in me in this instance, as in others of a similar nature previously performed as to your Excellency, and I trust I have proved satisfactory." Those previous missions, Smith reminded the governor, had taken place during "the late war."[7]

Governor Cass acknowledged Smith's work, without going into detail. In a letter the governor wrote to the U.S. secretary of the Treasury, Cass said that Jacob Smith's actions on behalf of the U.S. government "during the recent war have occasioned him much loss."[8] There can be no question, then, that Smith operated on behalf of his country during the War of 1812. The record of the war in the Old Northwest and Upper Canada is filled with references to spies, scouts, and couriers bearing messages and intelligence about the British and hostile Indians. The names of these men didn't often appear in the written record of the war, and with good reason: If army or government communications were captured, the identities of those scouts were revealed to the enemy and their lives jeopardized. British and American commanders alike refrained from naming their scouts and spies in communications, in some cases using codes or ciphers to protect the letters they sent to their superiors.

Of course, like Smith, other fur traders who acted as scouts and spies for the United States didn't get through the war undetected by the British and the Indians. Just as Smith had come to the attention of Colonel Procter in Detroit in the fall of 1812, so too did a Wyandot chief named Roundhead complain to Procter early in 1813 (before the Raisin River battle and massacre) about two Detroit area men suspected of helping the Americans; Procter had them arrested, too. There were also claims that Tecumseh himself complained about a trader named John Kinzie, who was in contact with American forces and working with Indians to oppose the British. Kinzie, who later became a U.S. Indian agent for Governor Cass, was also arrested by the British commandant and sent to Canada.[9]

Consider the case of another of Jacob Smith's contemporaries, trader Whitmore Knaggs. He lived near the River Raisin before the war and had been an Indian interpreter for the U.S. military and government for more than a decade. As a member of the territorial militia when William Hull surrendered Detroit in August 1812, Knaggs, like Smith, was paroled. Of course, a paroled American militia soldier was not supposed to reenter the armed service of his country; a prisoner like Knaggs got his parole, or early release, by swearing to such an agreement. To violate his parole was to risk execution, should the parolee fall into enemy hands again. Yet at the River Raisin battle in early 1813, Knaggs was captured by the Indians and British, less than six months since he'd been paroled at Detroit's surrender.

Procter was furious to find a paroled Michigan militiaman at the scene of that battle with Winchester's army. Despite efforts by Judge Woodward to keep Knaggs out of Canadian dungeons, Procter sent him to prison, referring the matter to his superiors. "The prisoner Knaggs is a violent, dangerous man," Procter warned his commander, General George Prevost. Knaggs, who could have faced the hangman's noose in the spring of 1813, denied he was serving with the U.S. forces when he was captured, unarmed. Why, he only happened to be visiting his family in the area of the River Raisin, he claimed. General James Winchester also insisted Knaggs was in no way associated with his army.

Knaggs was held in prison in Quebec and, luckily for him, the British did not execute him. He was released at some point before the war formally ended. But in an account written many years later, Judge B. F. H. Witherell, an amateur historian and son of a commander of the Michigan Detached Militia, stated that Captain Knaggs really had been serving as "a guide for the division under Gen. Winchester" when he was captured at the River Raisin. In other words, Knaggs indeed violated his parole to work as a scout for the U.S. forces.[10]

The letters written in 1815 and 1816 by Jacob Smith and Lewis Cass clearly indicate that the trader served in similar capacities, as an intelligence gatherer, confidential agent, and Indian interpreter-liaison. This work was unofficial, yet acknowledged by Lewis Cass. Whitmore Knaggs and John Kinzie would go on to serve Cass, the next territorial governor, as appointed interpreters and Indian agents, while Smith would work for him, sometimes officially and sometimes secretly. Not surprisingly, the paths of Knaggs and Jacob Smith would cross in the years ahead.

After Jacob Smith was released from British prison in Canada early in 1813, he soon showed up at the U.S. Army's frontier outpost that was closest to occupied Detroit, just weeks after the River Raisin massacre. Troops under General William Henry Harrison had built a new base, called Ft. Meigs, about 25 miles south of the Raisin and not far from the site of present-day Toledo. Ft. Meigs immediately became the most important American frontline position in the war in the Old Northwest.[11]

General Harrison was himself either at Ft. Meigs or camped in the vicinity from late January to early March, and it was during this time that Jacob Smith arrived. Interestingly, Harrison wrote confidential letters to Secretary of War John Armstrong and Governor Return J. Meigs Jr. of Ohio on February 16, telling them that he had new intelligence that the British were planning an attack on his forces. "Information has been received through various channels that the British have sent a large number of Regulars & British [Indians?] to Malden & that it was their design to attack us on March thither," Harrison wrote to Meigs; he planned to be ready for them. Not long after, Harrison wrote to Armstrong that British emissaries had indeed gone out during the winter among the tribes of the Old Northwest to try to raise a force of 1,000 warriors to go on the offensive against the American forces in Ohio.[12]

Was Jacob Smith one of the sources of this information? The evidence suggests he could have been a source. First, consider a letter written after Harrison sent those communications to Armstrong and Meigs. The writer was a former Detroiter, Capt. Richard Smyth, addressing his brother-in-law, a former Michigan militia officer now serving with the new Northwestern Army in Chillicothe, Ohio: "There is nothing doing here at present," Smyth wrote to Josiah Brady in March. "We have about three thousand men here and the times [enlistments] of two brigades will be out in a few days, which will leave only a force of about five hundred men at this place. And no information of any reinforcement coming and the Indians is [*sic*] seen frequently on the opposite shore [of the Miami or Maumee River] so that I think there will be danger expected without reinforcement."[13]

Smyth went on to tell Brady about what he knew of fellow Detroiters and a Canadian resident named Simon Z. Watson, who had joined Hull's army and the U.S. cause back in the summer. A former U.S. citizen, Canadian surveyor, and justice of the peace who had feuded with British authorities before the war, Watson led some of Jacob Smith's militia cavalry comrades on the raid into Upper Canada in July 1812. Watson escaped the surrender of Detroit, where he might have faced death as a traitor to Britain if he'd been captured. "Simon Watson has arrived safe in camp about eight days since, Jacob Smith has also arrived from Montreal," Smyth wrote. "The British has [*sic*] sent all our citizens from Detroit to Black Rock namely Dr. [William M.] Scott, Capt. Connolly, Doctor [William] Brown, Ja[me]s. Dodmeade, [Conrad] TenEyck, Tremble, [Benjamin] Chittenden, [Elijah] Brush, Judge [Augustus] Woodward and several others."[14]

These prominent citizens were exiled from Detroit by Procter, who saw how settlers at the River Raisin had been quick to help the U.S. forces under Winchester, and how incensed Detroiters were at the massacre of American troops. To keep these angry Americans under control, Procter declared martial law. Though Procter didn't kick Woodward out with the others, the judge, apparently shocked by the murder of Americans at Ft. Dearborn and the River Raisin, left for the east. He had previously tried to cooperate with the British to see that the remaining citizens of Detroit were treated fairly, but no more.

Jacob Smith's name, appearing in Richard Smyth's letter along with those of scout Simon Watson and key U.S. citizens of Detroit considered to be spies and troublemakers by the British commandant, is significant. Smith had traveled to Ft. Meigs and Cleveland, where he gave a statement to U.S. authorities regarding the plan for British reinforcements and Dickson's plan to recruit more Indian warriors—information he probably already gave to William Henry Harrison. In Cleveland, Smith gave a statement to a U.S. officer on March 8, 1813, and from there it was sent to the War Department in Washington. In addition to telling of his arrest by Procter, his imprisonment in Canada, and the attempt by Robert Dickson to recruit him to the British side, Smith reported that "on the 4 of Feb[ruar]y. 500 British soldiers left Montreal for upper Canada in sleighs[, and] that when he [Smith] left Montreal he understood one thousand soldiers & 500 Marines was daily expected at that place from Hallifax [sic]."[15]

Soon enough there was confirmation of part of Smith's warning. British reinforcements did reach Procter that month, and by summertime British Indian agent Dickson indeed had gathered hundreds of western Indians for a new offensive against the US. forces in the Old Northwest.[16] The arrest and detainment by Smith as well as his report to federal officials are strong evidence that he was one of the sources who provided information to the United States about British military plans in the Great Lakes region.

Gen. William Henry Harrison made good use of the intelligence his spies brought him, and he was ready when Procter launched a combined British-Indian attack on Ft. Meigs late in April 1813. Although U.S. casualties were high when hundreds of Kentuckians foolishly charged into a trap set for them by the Indians across the Maumee River, the Americans in Ft. Meigs, well supplied, strengthened, and reinforced, repulsed the British soldiers and warriors who attempted to storm it, inflicting bloody losses on them.[17] Though no one may have realized it at that time, a turning point in the War of 1812 in the Old Northwest had been reached. Slowly the fortunes of war were changing in favor of the United States.

Many Michigan men had long since left their homes in occupied Detroit or been kicked out by the British by the early months of 1813, and they made their way to Ohio or to points east. These included former militia volunteers who had been paroled and officers who had been released from confinement in Canada by the British. Jacob Smith's old friend and company commander, Richard Smyth, was such a man. He was soon given the rank of major with the U.S. forces in Ohio and was made responsible for moving thousands of dollars for the government so Harrison could pay for the war effort.[18]

But if Jacob Smith had old friends like Richard Smyth in Ohio, he had an old enemy there also—James Abbott. By the spring of 1813, Smith and Smyth decided that the blame for the fall of Ft. Michilimackinac in the previous year rested squarely on Abbott, the former Detroit postmaster, since Abbott had refused to pay for Smith's trip to the straits. The men's accusations would trigger an investigation and controversy.

After Hull's surrender of Detroit late in the summer of 1812, James Abbott had left for Washington. Early in 1813, Abbott got a new assignment from the U.S. government: Employed by Postmaster General Gideon Granger, Abbott was made the postal agent overseeing the mail moving between Chillicothe, Ohio, and the U.S. forces in the field under Gen. William Henry Harrison.[19] Chillicothe was a major base of military supplies and communications on the Scioto River, and from here men, materiel, and orders moved to the American armies, detachments, and forts in Ohio and Indiana.

Abbott had reached Chillicothe from Washington after a long, cold, and wet journey of six weeks, only to find himself placed under arrest by U.S. Army officers not long after he arrived. The postmaster general was just as shocked as Abbott; on May 11, 1813, Granger opened his mail to find that his new postal agent at Chillicothe was under investigation. Abbott had been arrested at the direction of Duncan McArthur, one of the former Ohio militia colonels who, like Lewis Cass, was being promoted to brigadier general and who'd gotten to know many of the Americans from Detroit. On what charge was Abbott arrested? On suspicion by certain Michigan men that Abbott was not the helpful and loyal U.S. public servant he'd made himself out to be. Their allegations suggested Abbott was actually a British spy.[20]

On the afternoon that Postmaster General Granger got the news about Abbott, he also found that the denunciations of Abbott had been sent to the secretary of war and to President Madison. The postmaster general quickly began his probe, writing to officials and commanders in Ohio, authorizing them to remove Abbott as postal agent. Granger also wrote to James Witherell, the former Detroit judge and militia major who had gone back to Vermont after Hull's surrender and his release by the British. What, Granger asked, was the nature of Abbott's character? Was he a loyal American? Could he have been a spy who passed information to

British-Canadian officers while he was in Detroit? Granger had reason to ask these questions. Only recently Abbott had asked for permission to leave Ohio and visit his family. Granger gave him permission, so long as it was okay with his commanding general. Of course, Abbott's family included two Canadian in-laws who were high-ranking military officers who resided across from Detroit. A visit by Abbott to his home in Detroit would take him right to the enemy's table.[21]

Abbott had also asked Granger if he could use Canadians to carry U.S. government expresses to Harrison's army, and Granger had said yes, assuming that Abbott meant anti-British Canadians who were working for the United States—men like Simon Watson. But now in light of the accusations, that request by Abbott to employ Canadians didn't seem so innocent. Granger quickly sent a message back to Abbott, removing him from the job of postal agent for the U.S. Army. "Two sources of denounciation [sic] I discovered," Granger informed Abbott:

> First, some officers now stationed at Cleveland & others who claim to have known something against you at Detroit. 2. you are charg'd with having had private conversation with some Canadians when you was lately near the lines from which great suspicion has arisen—here let me remark to you that lately you asked permition [sic] to employ Canadians as riders & I assented to it in case they were persons of approv'd energy & fidelity, but as [of now] the public mind is irritated at the single circumstance of your conversing with a Canadian.

"I think it my duty to advise you against holding any conference in secret with any of them," Granger continued, "& to enjoin it upon you not to employ any of them."[22]

Granger's letters leave no doubt as to the identity of Abbott's accusers. One was Jacob Smith. The other was Smith's former militia captain, now Major Richard Smyth. Colonel John C. Bartlett, a U.S. officer working on army supply and communications in the Chillicothe area, fowarded their charges to Postmaster Granger. Initially, federal authorities didn't tell Abbott the names of his accusers. But Abbott had a pretty good idea who they were. He had taken the position that Jacob Smith's attempt to get to Ft. Michilimackinac in July of the previous year wasn't a mission for the government, but private fur trade business, and he'd refused to pay for the trip. Now, he charged, Smith was trying to get even.

Abbott wrote late that month to lawyer Solomon Sibley, who was now in Marietta, Ohio:

Who my accusers are I know not, but from the information lately received, I have every reason to believe that Jacob Smith is among this number; and that it is in cognizance of my having refused to pay him for his trip to Mackinac on John Jacob Astor's business which you may probably recollect and also for my agency against him in behalf of some persons at Cleveland, in which you was employed as an attorney to conduct the suit.[23]

You know, my Dear Sir, as well as I do that Jacob Smith's character at Detroit was want of *morality and veracity;* and your situation and avocations at that place gave you a complete opportunity of becoming acquainted with it.

You must well recollect," Abbott continued, "his conduct respecting the three *Iron ketels* [kettles] contained in the obligation for which the above suit was brought.

Abbott asked for Sibley to write an endorsement of his character and a denunciation of Smith's. "I know that I am asking of you a very delicate thing; but there is no person at this place, at present, who knows much about him," Abbott wrote. "If my calumnators [*sic*, lying accusers] confine themselves to the truth, I fear not, but if these should be many of Jacob Smith's turn, I know not what the may be the event." For the record, Sibley did write an endorsement for Abbott not long afterward. It doesn't appear, however, that he criticized Smith on Abbott's behalf.[24]

Smith wasn't the only person who suspected Abbott might be a spy—so did some of the U.S. officers, at least initially. These men were suspicious, at first, with how Abbott had handled the army's mail. An aide to General Harrison discovered that a letter he'd sent to Ohio governor Return J. Meigs had been opened—and this about the time that the British and Indians tried unsuccessfully to attack Ft. Meigs. This opened letter seemed more than a coincidence to officers, but Abbott was able to explain to the satisfaction of Harrison that he had the authority to open mail to receive his instructions as local postmaster. There was nothing unusual about this, Abbott insisted, and eventually Harrison agreed.[25]

But most of the accusations were from Jacob Smith. His key charge dealt with the mail Abbott had received at Detroit, allegedly on July 3, 1812. The fur trader stated that this mail contained government dispatches informing the commander of Ft. Michilimackinac that the United States was at war. Smith charged Abbott "detained it [the government mail] for 6 or 7 days" before sending him, Smith, to take the messages to Ft. Michilimackinac, something that would have helped the British get word to their forces first.[26]

In response, Abbott denied he delayed any official government dispatch, but agreed that he had sent Smith as an express to carry two letters to Mackinac Island. The first letter was from fur mogul John Jacob Astor; the second was a letter U.S. Treasury Secretary Albert Gallatin sent to Reuben Attwater, the secretary of the Michigan Territory, who had then been acting governor in Hull's absence. Astor had wanted Gallatin's letter to Attwater also forwarded to Mackinac Island. Abbott insisted that it was Astor—not the U.S. government—who wanted these letters forwarded by express, or courier, to Michilimackinac. As far as Abbott was concerned, the delivery of these letters to Mackinac was John Jacob Astor's responsibility, not official government business. As Detroit postmaster, he refused to pay Smith to carry these messages. Smith was angered by this, Abbott said.[27]

What's odd about this exchange of accusation and response between Smith and Abbott is that Gen. William Hull seems to have had no role or say in this matter of the letters to Ft. Michilimackinac. Hull had arrived in Detroit on July 5, 1812, and during the next two days he had issued orders warning the other American outposts of the war and held a council with local Indians. As U.S. military commander of the Northwest at that time, Hull should have been able to quickly settle this disagreement between Smith and Abbott. He presumably had the authority to send Smith to Mackinac. Yet Hull was not mentioned in the matter of these controversial messages, and whether he believed they were important official notices of the state of war or simply business correspondence for Astor.

Was Jacob Smith a mere carrier of business letters, as James Abbott indicated? Or was he a courier bearing important communications for the U.S. government? Was it just a coincidence that Smith ended up in the company of the Indian messenger bearing the important wampum that warned others not to attack the Americans? Did Smith risk his life traveling through Indian country, initially pretending to be a British agent, all because he only *believed* he was carrying an urgent message to the commander of the American fort at Michilimackinac? Or had he been directed to go to the island at the straits to warn of the state of war between the United States and Britain?

According to the sworn deposition by Smith's companion on that trip, Girard, Smith hid those messages at Saginaw rather than risk carrying them to Mackinac. This means that Smith knew their contents and understood their importance. Historians have noted John Jacob Astor sent communications through both American and Canadian channels to try to protect his furs, goods, and property at Michilimackinac when the war broke out. If Canadian officials understood their significance, why didn't Abbott? Certainly the British commander at the straights believed that Jacob Smith's mission had been to carry dispatches to the commander of the U.S. fort on Mackinac Island, and he was troubled about Smith's escape.

Smith also claimed that once Detroit was surrendered to the British, Abbott had shown his true colors by allowing American property plundered by British subjects to be placed in Smith's own store. In reply to this charge, Abbott claimed the very opposite was true: When Hull had invaded Canada in July 1812 and seized British property and supplies, Abbott said, Hull had made him responsible for storing those items and materials in Detroit. If British and Canadians plundered Smith's store, it was only because they were getting their own property back, Abbott believed.[28]

As these charges and countercharges flew, Postmaster General Granger quickly got the idea that the Abbott controversy was "a petty business" motivated by personal animosity between these Detroit men. By the third week in June 1813, Granger wanted to believe Abbott, but advised him that public sentiment was running against him. "I confess I believe in yr. innocence but should such a charge be established," the postmaster general warned Abbott, "you would merit death."[29]

Yet Abbott was confident that he was going to be cleared of these accusations of wrongdoing. General William Henry Harrison, apparently informed of Jacob Smith's accusations, had been in communication with Granger by then and endorsed the former Detroit postmaster. Though Abbott was sure he would be acquitted, attorney Solomon Sibley warned him that he would probably have to contend with accusations by fellow Detroiters for a long time to come. Both men turned out to be right. General Sam Finley, an Ohio political figure and militia commander asked by federal officials to look into the charges, decided that Abbott should be restored to his post of handling the U.S. Army's mail. "I feel no hesitation, from the weight of testimony adduced in your favor; to say I believe you innocent of the charges exhibited against you," Finley wrote to Abbott in Chillicothe. Abbott, in turn, quickly passed a copy of Finley's letter to officials in Washington.[30]

Still, Abbott was not out of the woods. His other accuser was Richard Smyth, the former justice of the peace from Detroit who would soon be promoted to colonel in the army in Ohio. On July 7, 1813, Smyth swore out an affidavit in Cleveland that for two years, right up until the news of the war had reached Detroit, Abbott was seen in Detroit opening the mail in the company of a local Canadian official, William Hand, the sheriff of Sandwich, just across the river; Hand was one of Abbott's brothers-in-law. Smyth said Abbott's practice of sharing the U.S. mail with his brother-in-law went on right up to the point that Hull's army crossed into Canada. Furthermore, Richard Smyth pointed out, Abbott's other sisters were married to Canadian militia officers, Francois Baby and James Baby (pronounced "Bawbee"), who were posted at Ft. Malden across the Detroit River. Smyth didn't accuse Abbott of passing information outright to his in-laws, but he said he saw Abbott and his brother Samuel travel to the French Ferry house, a building that was only a couple of miles from Detroit and across from Sandwich, while Hull's army was in Canada. Smyth's inference was that there must have been some dark purpose for Abbott's actions.[31]

Smyth said also that he saw Francois Baby in the company of James Abbott after the surrender of Detroit, as the Canadian officer confiscated residents' valuable property and vowing that, he, Baby, "would take as much as he lost by Hull's band of robbers." "He is generally suspected," Smyth said of Abbott, "of being dissaffected to the Government of the United States."

Then was James Abbott a British sympathizer and even a spy, as Jacob Smith and Richard Smyth suggested? One Michigan amateur historian, George Caitlin, wrote that "Abbott was found guilty of treasonable conduct by a court at Cleveland, but nothing serious came of the case except a temporary prejudice against Abbott." The evidence, Caitlin wrote, was "purely circumstantial and more or less prejudiced."[32] If he really was found guilty in Cleveland, it would have placed Abbott in the unenviable position of having been cleared in one investigation yet convicted in another. But ultimately the authority that mattered the most—U.S. officialdom as represented by Gen. William Henry Harrison and Postmaster General Granger—concluded that Abbott was trustworthy.

Of course, the most obvious and perhaps most important witness in the Abbott case should have been William Hull, the former Michigan territorial governor and commander of the first Northwestern Army, now retired to Massachusetts after his release by the British in the fall of 1812. Hull had no warm regard for Abbott. In fact, Granger did write to Hull, asking for his version of events. He also wanted to know about Abbott's main accuser. "I pray you to inform me what you know of these transactions, the true character of Jacob Smith," the postmaster general wrote.[33]

How Hull replied—if he did reply—is unknown. Hull was then under a cloud himself, and he would soon be stained by formal accusations of cowardice and treachery for surrendering Detroit without a fight. Hull would have his hands full dealing with his own troubles. Besides, Hull had no reason to come to the aid of Abbott, who had made so much trouble for him during his time in Michigan. Certainly it would have been interesting to know how the old territorial governor felt about "the true character" of Jacob Smith, but then the whole U.S. conduct of the war had been less than competent up to that time. It could be that no one in the Madison administration wanted to delve too deeply into the question of how the U.S. outposts were notified of the declaration of war, since the federal government had done such a poor job at this, and because Madison and his cabinet were so close to John Jacob Astor.

The postscript to this story of Jacob Smith's accusation against James Abbott was that, eventually, the controversy did fade away. After Detroit came back into U.S. hands in late September 1813, Abbott and other residents who had left during the British-Indian occupation returned to their homes and went about their lives. But lawyer Solomon Sibley was right—Abbott's enemies did continue to question his loyalty to the United States, for a time. In the fall of 1814, about a year after Detroit came back into the hands of U.S. forces, Richard Smyth tried to get a local grand jury to look into the accusations against Abbott. In response, Abbott argued that it wasn't necessary to look into Smyth's charges all over again. Of all the heads of families who were present in Detroit when Hull surrendered, "I venture to say not one will corroborate his statement," Abbott insisted.[34]

James Abbott would go on to again hold several important government posts and a judgeship in Detroit and became a familiar figure in the city. The charges Jacob Smith and Richard Smyth made against him were indeed forgotten. In terms of a lasting historical legacy, Judge Abbott's name would long be fondly remembered in Detroit, while Jacob Smith would be virtually forgotten. The Abbott investigation was a national scandal in 1813, but quickly faded from the public's view as larger and more important crises took center stage. Historians who wrote about the War of 1812 in the Old Northwest don't even acknowledge it, apparently satisfied that the accusation by Abbott's enemies was a matter of wartime hysteria or petty, personal animosity. Yet it serves as another illustration of Jacob Smith's personality and character as a lighting rod, demonstrating his apparent concern for U.S. interests in Michigan, as well as questions about his own motives and controversial reputation.

Abduction to Saginaw

B eyond Jacob Smith's return from arrest and detainment in Canada, his reporting to U.S. authorities, and his controversial accusations against James
Abbott, the fur trader's specific activities in Ohio throughout the rest of
1813 are unknown. The fact that Smith is the most common name in the English
language complicates efforts to track the fur trader, even in the frontier of the
Old Northwest. For example, an army officer named Jacob Smith, acting as the
prosecutor in a court-martial at Ft. Meigs, brought charges against a Lieutenant
Jackson of the 19th U.S. Infantry regiment in July 1813, alleging that Jackson had
called this Smith "a damned rascal," pulled a pistol on him, and then beat and
kicked him. Jackson was acquitted of the overall charges of conduct unbecoming
an officer and a gentleman, but convicted of the specific acts. The commanding
general at the fort, noting the novel verdict by the court-martial, set it aside and
ordered Jackson released from his arrest, despite the fact Jackson had roundly
insulted the general in his statement to the court.[1]

Was the officer who suffered that thrashing the Detroit fur trader, Jacob
Smith? It's impossible to say. Smith had certainly appeared at Ft. Meigs earlier in
the year after his release by the British, and he was likely involved with the U.S.

Army; certainly he had proved himself a controversial figure in other matters. But the larger point is that the name "Jacob Smith" appears more than 15 times in the Ohio rosters of men who served in the War of 1812. Federal pension records from the war show that 21 different men from around the United States had the name Jacob Smith, but available details indicate that none of these was the Detroit-based fur trader. One Jacob Smith, a U.S. Army regular, was even listed in the American prisoner-of-war rosters in Canada, but again, that man was not the trader Smith.

Despite this multiplicity of Jacob Smiths, Ohio was the logical place for the fur trader to operate, what with British and Indian threats against U.S. forts on the frontier in the spring and summer of 1813. The available record, while scant, does suggest the trader remained in the region during this time, when many Detroit area U.S. citizens served in the American army as soldiers, officers, couriers, and rangers, some of them associated with the former Ohio militia colonels, now brigadier generals of U.S. volunteers, Duncan MacArthur and Lewis Cass. For example, Smith would later give a statement on behalf of a man named Joseph Loranger, who had lived near the Rapids of the Maumee (the Miami River) and kept a store near the River Raisin. Smith said that he often visited and stayed at Loranger's house before 1812. The site of this home was near the location on which Ft. Meigs was built early in 1813; Smith testified that when he returned to the Rapids that spring, he saw that the house had been burned to its foundation. Another witness agreed, stating that the house was destroyed by British-allied Indians in September 1812.[2]

Then there is the possibility that Smith was involved in intelligence-gathering or Indian liaison work. The diary and orderly book of Capt. Daniel Cushing and the papers of William Henry Harrison show many instances where Frenchmen who lived in the vicinity of the Maumee River and other men from Detroit came and went from Ft. Meigs as spies, just as the U.S. Army sent out its own scouts, spies, and rangers from the fort. Any of these missions would have been the kind that could have been taken on by Jacob Smith, fur trader. When a history was published about the Saginaw area decades later, some old-timers who misunderstood Smith's circumstances would wrongly state that he came to Michigan from the Ohio Valley after the War of 1812; another local historian thought Smith had come to Detroit around 1810, which was also incorrect.

Of course, the facts show that Smith's home base had been in Detroit for a decade by the time of the war, and that he'd been working for the United States in Michigan for several years, in peace as well as in the War of 1812. But even flawed local history places Smith in Ohio during the war. The historical record is also clear that the American commander, General Harrison, was a firm believer in the use of spies and scouts to know what his enemy was doing. Even before hostilities reopened in March 1813, he had received $600 from the army's deputy quartermaster general, a fund to pay for "secret service."[3]

In the meantime Jacob Smith's family grew. While he was in Ohio, his wife Mary gave birth to their last child, Maria, on June 19, 1813. A family birth registry states that Maria was born in Detroit, which would mean she came into the world during the British occupation.[4] Was Smith able to see his baby daughter before that fall, when the British were forced to withdraw from Detroit? There is nothing in the available record that gives an indication. But occupied Detroit was said to have been a hard place for residents during the time it was in possession of the British. With crops confiscated and no fur trade or commerce to speak of, it was a lean and fearful year. Perhaps Jacob Smith was satisfied that, based on his previous relations with some of the Indians, no harm would come to his family in Detroit. Though he was probably powerless to do anything for them personally, both Smith and his wife had relatives in Canada who may have been able to help their family.

The war continued. Though the British and Indians had been unsuccessful in their siege of Ft. Meigs, they were far from finished in their war against the United States in the Old Northwest. "Every Indian that can bear arms along Lake Michigan and Huron from Saginau Bay to Matchedash are going to exert themselves in driving away, if possible, these scoundrels that have harassed them so long," wrote John Askin Jr., the Canadian trader and Indian interpreter, about the conflict with the Americans. Askin, who also worked as a clerk for the British government, wrote those words on Mackinac Island in late spring of 1813.[5]

He was correct. That summer the British and their Indian allies did attack the American forces in Ohio, but those forts did not fall. In the meantime U.S. military efforts grew, though they weren't always successful. In areas of Indiana, Illinois, Ohio, and southwestern Michigan, Indian villages and crops were destroyed by American soldiers and militia, forcing thousands of Indians to retire from the war to try to provide for their families or to turn to the British, making them dependent on British supplies for their survival. Of course, some of the destroyed crops and villages belonged to Indians who were neutral or had no part in the war, but to vengeful American militia and frontier soldiers, that made no difference. Most of the Old Northwest would soon be under U.S. control for settlement by whites.

Again, records from this time reflect the existence of a kind of American "underground" organization in the Detroit area that kept U.S. commanders informed about British-Indian intentions and helped at least one American soldier escape to Ohio. A letter written by General Green Clay to the governor of Ohio told of how a young militiaman from Kentucky, who had been captured in Ohio in May and taken to Saginaw as a prisoner with others, managed to get back to the U.S. Army with the help of Detroit residents.

This soldier, whose name was given as Thomason, was being held with two other captives when the men decided to try to escape. But they were discovered, the Indians opened fire on them, and they scattered in different directions into the Michigan forest. The young Kentuckian evaded recapture and made his way to occupied Detroit, where he contacted a Frenchman who agreed to escort him down to Ft. Meigs. Incredibly, another Detroit man caught up with Thomason's French guide as they made their way south, and this man passed along information for U.S. officers: The pro-British Indians were urging General Procter to renew attacks on the American forts.[6]

The identities of these Detroit men were not given in Clay's letter, but their information was correct. The British and Indians did launch more attacks, but these failed and the Americans under William Henry Harrison prepared for the push north to recapture Detroit. Just as importantly, a young U.S. Navy officer, Lt. Oliver Hazzard Perry, had arrived at Presque Isle (later Erie), Pennsylvania and supervised the construction of five new ships on the southern shore of Lake Erie. In September Perry sailed his small American fleet into the western end of the lake and defeated the British fleet off the island of Put-in-Bay in a dramatic, thunderous, and bloody naval battle, the first and only one of its kind in the history of the Great Lakes.[7]

Perry's victory was decisive for the United States in regaining Detroit. With the Americans now in control of Lake Erie and the Detroit River, it was impossible for the British to hold the town; for the redcoats to stay in Detroit was to risk defeat and capture. Henry Procter, the British commander who'd since been promoted to brigadier general, was running low on supplies and confidence in his Indian allies and the local Canadian population. To the dismay of his Indian allies, he withdrew his forces back to the Canadian side of the river.

Hard on his heels came the Americans. U.S. forces under Brigadier General Duncan McArthur swept into Detroit, while General Harrison and the rest of his army landed on the opposite shore, pursuing the retreating British and Indians into Upper Canada. The lore that grew up around Jacob Smith in later years, when his family members appear to have talked with late-nineteenth-century writers of Flint-Genesee County history, was that he was with Harrison's army in the battle of the Thames River on October 5, 1813, where Tecumseh was killed and the British and Indians were defeated. While it is true that Smith and other Detroiters such as George McDougall and Richard Smyth were associated with Brigadier General Lewis Cass during the war, and Cass was present at the battle, there is no evidence that Smith was. It is a matter of record that Cass acted as an aide to Harrison, but Jacob Smith's name doesn't appear in the various accounts and records of the battle.[8]

Accounts do show that other men from the Michigan Territory, such as Whitmore Knaggs's brother James Knaggs and the half-Chippewa Ryley brothers, were present and in the fight as U.S. officers aiding the Kentucky soldiers and troopers. It could be that Smith, along with other members of the reformed Michigan Militia, stayed in Detroit with troops under General McArthur to protect the town from rumored Indian attacks; the warriors who hadn't gone with Tecumseh for Canada had only left Detroit reluctantly. One witness, John Hunt, was a boy at the time the Americans took possession of Detroit. He would write that there were Saginaw Chippewa warriors in the town right up until the time the American troops reclaimed it. Thus it may have been the case that Jacob Smith's services were needed more in Detroit at that moment than they were with Harrison's army pursuing Procter.[9]

And records show that Jacob Smith was definitely back in Detroit for a time in the fall and winter of 1813. According to a list of officers' commissions issued by Governor Cass on December 18 for the territorial militia, Smith was made a lieutenant under Lt. Col. Richard Smyth's new "Legionary Corps." Smith also signed a petition with 31 others recommending that his onetime lawyer, Solomon Sibley, be made a judge of the general territorial court. This petition circulated late in 1813, after U.S. forces moved back into Detroit.[10]

Back in Quebec, on December 7, Smith's father, John Rudolph Smith, died at the age of 81 and was buried three days later. How or when Jacob Smith got the news of his father's death is not clear. The witnesses who signed the register of St. Andrew's Presbyterian Church in Quebec after the old man's burial were men named Franz Vogeler and William Lang. Though the burial records don't reflect whether these men were related to Smith or simply friends, it could be that these names support the claim of Smith descendants who said that Jacob Smith's parents were German.[11]

The death of Tecumseh and the defeat at the Thames were serious blows to the British-Indian alliance, and some Michigan Indians, including Chippewa bands, quickly sued for peace with the United States. On October 14, chiefs and head men from several tribes, including 15 different Ottawa and Chippewa leaders, signed an armistice with Harrison that called for them to return their prisoners. But Harrison was under no illusion that the armistice meant real peace had returned to the Michigan Territory. "The Chippewa mentioned in the Armistice are those only who reside with the Tawas [Ottawas] in this country," he wrote to the governor of Ohio. "Those more remote as well as the Tribes West of Lake Michigan may also continue the war until reduced."[12] Indian warriors who remained intransigent included some of the Saginaw Chippewa. More than 40 years later, a woman named Cecilia Boyer Campau told Judge Witherell, who published accounts of the War of 1812 in the *Detroit Free Press,* about what happened to her family that fall.[13]

French residents of Michigan had for the most part been left alone by the Indians during war, but there were exceptions. The incident described by Mrs. Campau came after the battle at the Thames and around the time of the Indian armistice with the United States. Cecilia was 12 years old in October 1813, living with her parents, Mr. and Mrs. Nicholas Boyer, and three siblings. They resided on the Clinton River, not far from Lake St. Clair, in what would soon become Macomb County. Nick Boyer had traded and spent time among the Indians, for other records indicate he also had an older son, Francis, with a Chippewa woman, something that was not unusual for men who lived with the Indians in the fur trade, like Jacob Smith. But according to Louis Campau, who knew the family, Nick Boyer's younger children, Cecilia and her siblings, were white; Cecilia said her mother was related to the Trombleys, a French family that had been involved in the fur trade for generations.

On this particular fall day in 1813, Nick Boyer's young daughter Cecilia was dangerously sick in bed with a fever. An Indian named Tickesho, a family friend, was visiting the Boyer home on the river, just a few miles upstream from the mouth of the river, where the town of Mt. Clemens would grow. Cecilia's mother had gone outside when she saw that warriors were approaching though the woods, stealthily, toward her house. Realizing that something bad was about to happen, and seeing that her family couldn't possibly escape, Mrs. Boyer hid. The approaching Indians didn't notice her; they came on and burst into the home, surprising Nick Boyer, his children, and their guest Tickesho.

There were five raiders in all—the Saginaw chief Kishkauko; another chief called Chemokamun or "Big Knife"; a warrior named Pocomigon; and two other warriors. They herded Boyer, Tickesho, and Cecilia's siblings together and went through the house, taking what they could use and carry and vandalizing the rest; they also searched for Mrs. Boyer, but missed her hiding place. The Indians enjoyed slitting open the family's beds, watching as feathers erupted into the air and floated on the breeze, according to Cecilia's account.[14]

But what would they do with the sick little girl, Cecilia? Chemokamun and one of the other warriors stood in the room with the child, debating whether it was better to kill her quickly or leave her, perhaps to die of illness and hunger. The girl knew what they were saying, so she begged for them to leave her alone. "Che-mo-ka-mun drew his tomahawk, and suddenly sprang to her, flourishing the weapon over her head, then raising it up for a final blow. . . . But ere the blow of the tomahawk fell, the other Indian called out: "Stop, Che-mo-ka-mun! Stop! Don't kill the child; she is very sick and will soon die; let us leave her here."

Then they were gone, following the other warriors and their prisoners into the forest. Cecilia felt she couldn't risk the Indians changing their minds about sparing her life, so she dragged herself from the house and crossed the Clinton River on logs. Then she lay down, exhausted, and slept. When the girl awoke a few hours later, she saw her family's guest, Tickesho, following her track, looking for her. He'd managed to quietly escape his captors when they stopped to camp for the night, but before he did so, he heard the others talking: They had agreed it was a mistake to allow the sick Boyer girl to live, Tickesho said; one of them was going to return to the house to kill Cecilia.[15]

Now Tickesho carried Cecilia to the relative safety of the nearby home of her uncle, Michael Tromble or Trombley. Not long after they got there, Cecilia's mother, who had hidden in the woods overnight, also appeared at Trombley's house. Soon they went to stay in the comparative safety of Detroit, which was back in U.S. hands. What happened to Nicholas Boyer and the three other children taken by the warriors? Although Mrs. Boyer and Cecilia would not know the answer for many months, the children were taken to the Indian village of Saginaw, while Mr. Boyer was led across Michigan to the mouth of the Grand River on the western side of the Lower Peninsula. When the release of the Boyer children would come, several months after their abduction by Kishkauko and his comrades, it would be because of Captain Jacob Smith, fur trader and territorial militia officer, riding into the Indian country of the Saginaw Valley to buy their release.[16]

Even as winter came on in 1813, Lewis Cass had already dispatched a small party of friendly Indians and Canadians to Lake Michigan to bring back prisoners held by hostile natives.[17] Though the Americans living in Detroit and the Michigan Territory still had to worry about raids, and times were still dangerous, the days of the threat of Indian war were coming to a close. Jacob Smith would have a direct and major role in the coming peace with the Saginaw Chippewa.

The Return of the Boyer Children

S hortly after Detroit was back in the hands of the U.S. forces and the British had retreated into Canada, General William Henry Harrison turned command of his army over to Lewis Cass, the Ohio lawyer and politician turned brigadier, and left for the east. Soon after, Cass was formally appointed territorial governor of Michigan. With illness spreading among his troops and the destitute civilian population of Detroit, Cass had his hands full. "No man who has not seen the country can form an adequate idea of the distressed situation of the people, or the outrages committed upon their persons and property," he wrote to U.S. Secretary of War John Armstrong.

There was still danger from hostile Indians, despite the truce that most of the chiefs and head men of the bands of the region had agreed to that fall. Just as chiefs couldn't require warriors to go to war, neither could chiefs stop members of their villages and bands from conducting attacks. Indian leaders could only advise their people on a course of action, but that was all. Chiefs were not kings or dictators, and their words were only suggestions and didn't have the force of law. Some warriors continued to periodically raid and kill, their method of warfare since long before contact with whites. Just weeks after the new territorial Michigan

Militia was formed, Cass asked permission from Secretary of War Armstrong for the hiring of five or six Indian "interpreters."[1]

What was the purpose of these so-called interpreters? Counterintelligence. Cass said he would "send them into Indian country, to watch their movements to give us notice of their intentions and to counter the secret intrigues of the enemy." Cass said that British agents were still active among Michigan's Indians, and that the funding for his interpreter/spies, "a small sum for secret service money," should be placed in his Indian department budget, where it wouldn't arouse undue suspicion. In addition, Cass also reported he was using spies in Upper Canada to keep an eye on things there.

Jacob Smith's name doesn't appear on this list of interpreters mentioned in the territorial governor's letters of this time, yet Smith clearly had worked as an unofficial agent for Hull in dealing with the Ottawa and Chippewa. Events would soon prove he also did such work for Cass. Much was at stake, after all. The Michigan-Canadian frontier continued to be an important area for both sides during the War of 1812, and driving the British and their Indian allies out of Detroit had been a major objective for the United States. Though Michigan and the rest of the Old Northwest was U.S. territory, if only on paper and in a legalistic sense, the British had hoped to retain control of the fur trade by forming alliances with the Indians and establishing an Indian territory and buffer zone north of the Ohio River. Indians had come for hundreds of miles to aid Tecumseh and fight alongside of the British and to share in the plunder; there were still hundreds if not thousands of hostile or potentially hostile warriors in the Michigan Territory. With the continued British presence at Michilimackinac and in Upper Canada (including British Indian Department agents and Canadian fur traders), Cass understood he would need spies and "interpreters" to monitor Indians and counter British influence.

"I would merely observe," Cass wrote to Armstrong in the summer of 1814 from Greenville, Ohio, "that every white man who can speak one of the Indian languages ought to be taken into pay. The stated compensation of one of them does not equal the amount expended for the pay and support of two private soldiers, and there can be no comparison between the services to be rendered by them." Cass repeated these circumstances to John C. Calhoun, another secretary of war, in just a few years' time, to explain the expenses for his Indian department. "During the years I have specified [1814, 1815, and 1816], Detroit was, emphatically, Indian head-quarters," he wrote. "The eyes of all the Indians north of the Ohio and east of the Mississippi, together with many of those west of that river, were fixed upon that place. Either as actors or as anxious spectators, their attention was directed to Detroit and to Malden." Fort Malden, of course, had been the location headquarters of the British Indian Department and its agents. Given the serious-ness of this situation, it would have made sense for Cass and other U.S. officials and commanders to employ Jacob Smith as a scout or confidential agent, even if he was not on the governor's list of interpreters.[2]

Cass would make clear that Smith worked on behalf of the United States dur-ing the war in a letter to the U.S. secretary of the Treasury. After Detroit was back into U.S. hands, Smith was given an officer's commission in the militia, so it may be that Cass paid for Smith's special skills and knowledge in that manner.[3] Smith's fur trading and business dealings still provided him with cover for any mission he might take on in Indian country or Canada. And Smith *was* a businessman. One of the contracts he got during that winter of 1813–1814 was with the U.S. Army for building materials. Smith delivered two tons of stone on January 1 for the use of the 28th Infantry Regiment, apparently for the construction of "hutts." These may have been part of the new U.S. fort at Detroit, called Ft. Shelby, which was built in the fall. The stone probably came from a nearby island in the Detroit River. An officer wrote Smith a receipt that stated the United States owed him $60 for the two tons of stone, but when the government finally got around to paying Smith's bill five years later, a Treasury Department officer decided that price was too high; instead they paid him $50.[4]

Though these records place Smith in Detroit up to the beginning of 1814, he was also involved in some activity or business in Chillicothe, Ohio, still an important U.S. Army depot and center. At that place, Smith wrote to a man named Isaac Morris, who was then in Wood County, Virginia, living near the mouth of the Little Kanawha River. Eventually, this region of country would be part of the state of West Virginia; the Little Kanawha enters the Ohio River at the town of Parkersburg.

At this time, Smith was sending Morris money—$200 in "Xenia green backs." Smith described this money has being "recovered of a Mr. Hugh Phelps, due me on a note." Colonel Hugh Phelps, for the record, was an important local official, mili-tia officer, and political figure in his region of southeastern Ohio. Smith instructed Isaac Morris to take a fee out of the money "for your servis [sic]," and deliver the rest of it to William Woodbridge, an Ohio politician and lawyer in Marietta. Once

Morris turned the money over to Woodbridge, Smith asked that Woodbridge send him a draft, or check, drawn upon a Chillicothe bank. "This will be a great favor to me," Smith wrote.[5]

Nothing in Smith's letter indicates whether this was strictly a matter of private business or if it had to do with matters of a military nature. The movement and transfer of this money may not be of great importance, for Woodbridge handled scores of similar transactions for others during this time. But Woodbridge was a close friend of Lewis Cass and he would soon be appointed Michigan's territorial secretary and tax collector. Col. Hugh Phelps, like Cass, had figured in the federal government's case against Aaron Burr, the controversial American patriot and vice president who had achieved infamy in the so-called Burr Conspiracy to conquer Spanish territory in North America during the Jefferson administration. If nothing else, Jacob Smith's brief letter is indicative of his continued association or involvement with men of influence and leadership in the Old Northwest during the war, despite the fact that men like James Abbott believed Smith was a disreputable and untrustworthy character.

Smith was back in Detroit by the spring of 1814, when he served as a member of a federal grand jury that looked into the death of Private James Davis of the U.S. Army's 19th Regiment. Davis had been killed on January 25 of that year by "violent blows on his Head." But a hostile Indian or British solider hadn't killed Davis, the grand jury decided. After hearing testimony, the members ruled the victim had been done in by a fellow American soldier. In April, the grand jury, which included Smith's friend and sometimes business associate Conrad TenEyck, indicted a man from the 27th Infantry Regiment for the murder.[6]

Though Tecumseh's dream of a great Indian confederation was dead and the British position in the Old Northwest diminished, many Indians in Michigan were still hoping to renew the battle against the United States and the Americans in Detroit. Captain Richard Bullock of the British Army's 41st Infantry Regiment had taken over command at Mackinac Island, and a report he made early in 1814 showed that while most warriors remained allied with Britain, some from Saginaw, the area where Jacob Smith had influence, did not. The Indians of northern Michigan, Bullock wrote late in February to his superiors, were "well disposed" toward the British fight against the Americans "except a few of the Saguinas, Residing at Saguina Bay on the south side of the Huron."[7]

But there were still Chippewa and Ottawa warriors in the area ready to attack Detroit. One British Indian Department officer's report, made that spring, passed along information brought from Indians from "Naywash's band" who encamped at the Flint River during the winter. This message told British commanders that hundreds of warriors who had gathered nearby at Saginaw were hoping to fight alongside the British and attack Detroit.[8]

The more accepted spelling of the name of this particular Ottawa chief was "Naiwash." He had fought alongside of Tecumseh and had been considered his second-in-command of those British-allied Indians. Naiwash appealed to the British governor general of Canada, George Prevost, for more guns and supplies so that Indians could continue their war against the Americans. "These Indians report that there are about 500 men at Saguinaw, who were ready to show their attachment to their Great Father [the king of England], whenever his troops shall return," the British officer wrote.[9]

Although there were rumors of a new attack on Detroit that summer and British agents remained in communication with the Chippewa and Ottawa, the redcoats would not be returning to threaten the town again. The British continued to hold Mackinac Island and other points in the far reaches of American territory, but the vast majority of British troops in Upper Canada had been pulled east. In Ohio and Indiana, leaders of some tribes that had been at war with the United States were ready to talk peace. Small-scale military action continued on the Detroit front as American rangers made patrols into Upper Canada (what today is southwest Ontario) and skirmished with the British and Canadian forces. Warriors from the Saginaw Chippewa and other hostile tribes also made hit-and-run attacks on Detroiters, killing or taking prisoners and disappearing into the wilderness.

Judge James Witherell, who returned to Detroit that summer from the east (and who was the father of historian Judge B. F. H. Witherell), wrote that at least four local men, some of them French, had been killed in the area shortly before his arrival. Lewis Cass stressed this to the War Department. "The northern Indians are almost intangible," he warned in the late summer of 1814. "If they are disposed to attack you, they do, when you are unprepared, or when the advantage of position is theirs, and if hard pressed they disperse and are lost in the immensity of their forests. This post [Detroit] in peace or war is the most important point so far as respects the Indians in the Union."[10]

Though war was still ongoing, Jacob Smith borrowed $630 in August from a man named John Rodgers or Rogers, who later moved to Washington, D.C. While trade and business with the Indians and British Canadians hadn't officially resumed, many Indians and whites, both U.S. and Canadian, were anxious to resume the fur trade, so it may be that Smith used this money to buy trade goods. As was his typical practice, Smith was negligent in making payments to Rodgers over the next few years, so Rodgers would later file suit against the fur trader, requesting damages of $1,000.[11] But there's another possible explanation for Smith's taking out that loan—a more humanitarian reason. He may have needed that money to pay a ransom for the Boyer children.

When Smith's name appears again in the historical record of 1814, it was with the rank of captain with the Michigan Territorial Militia, a promotion that could not have happened without the approval of and commission from Governor Cass. According to Benjamin F. H. Witherell, a friendly Indian came into Detroit sometime that year and told Mrs. Nicholas Boyer, whose husband and three children had been abducted in October 1813, that her family was still alive, prisoners of the Chippewa. "About a year after they were captured," Witherell wrote of the Boyer youngsters, "the late Capt. Jacob Smith, whom all our old residents remember—a brave, generous, warm-hearted man—took a couple of pack horses, loaded with goods, through the wilderness to Saginaw, redeemed the children and brought them in to their mother."[12]

Though Witherell used the phrase "about a year" to describe the time that passed between the capture of the Boyers and Smith's rescue of the children, evidence shows that their release from the Indians took place in the summer of 1814, around the same time Smith signed the note for the loan from John Rodgers. At a time when Indians were still killing and abducting white settlers around Detroit, it was no small risk for an American to loiter unguarded at the edge of town, let alone leave it and ride into the Saginaw Indian country. "There are but few people who dare to be found singly far from the settlement," Judge James Witherell wrote to a friend.[13]

Smith was one of those few. With the fur trade all but halted and the British military having virtually stopped major offensive operations in the region, many Indians were in a bad way. They had come to depend on firearms to get the game and the pelts they needed to survive. That meant they also needed the white men's services, such as gunsmithing, to keep their firearms working. Some accounts say they needed other supplies, such as blankets, flour and grain, and cooking utensils, almost as badly. But without trade or regular shipments of British supplies, they had to go without these things. Even Indians who wanted to carry on the fight against the United States probably had to admit that Jacob Smith was familiar to them and that he held the respect of certain Ottawa and Chippewa leaders and warriors. Thus the fur trader was not harmed when he rode to Saginaw with the trade goods. The exchange for the hostages was transacted, and Smith returned the children to Mrs. Boyer in Detroit.

In the meantime the veteran Canadian fur trader and merchant John Askin, who lived just across the Detroit River, also pitched in by paying for the release of Nicholas Boyer, the children's father, B. F. H. Witherell wrote. Askin had a canoe full of goods taken up Lake Huron, around the straits, and down Lake Michigan to the Grand River, where Boyer was being held. Nick Boyer was released and transported to Ft. Michilimackinac, which was still under British control, and he spent the winter there. When the ice broke in the spring of 1815, Boyer finally made it back to his family in the Detroit area, Witherell said.[14]

Jacob Smith's rescue of the Boyer children, purchasing their freedom with goods, was appreciated by those who knew of it, but it was overshadowed by other events and only mentions of it appeared later in a couple of Michigan county histories. When a lawyer and amateur historian named Charles P. Avery wrote an article he called "The Indian and Pioneer History of the Saginaw Valley" decades later, he referred to the Boyer children being brought from captivity, calling their rescuer "the daring trader, Smith." Avery noted that Smith was the only white American citizen to venture into the Indian country of Saginaw during the War of 1812.[15]

That the Boyers were actually kidnapped by the Indians there is no doubt. A postscript to this story was that about 25 years later, Nicholas Boyer made a claim against the Saginaw Chippewa for the destruction of his property and the abduction of him and his children. Under the terms of a treaty between the tribe and the United States in the 1830s, a fund was set up with proceeds from the sale of Indian land in order to pay damages to Michigan citizens whose property they destroyed during the war. Boyer asked for $3,000 for the loss of his furniture and crops, and he also wanted reparations for what was described as "the captivity of (the) claimant and his whole family and their detention for nine months."[16]

Unfortunately for Boyer, he couldn't provide ironclad proof of the destruction of his property so many years later. While the treaty commissioner for the U.S. government was satisfied that Nicholas Boyer and his family had indeed been captured and held by the Saginaw Chippewa, an official in the Indian Affairs office of the War Department noted there was no provision in the treaty that provided for reparations to people who'd been taken prisoner. The recommendation to the secretary of war, J. R. Poinsett, was that Boyer's claim be denied, and it was.

Another incident of marauding Indians in the fall of 1814 overshadowed Jacob Smith's rescue of the Boyer children. On September 15, a Detroit man named Ananias McMillan who served in a local cavalry/scouting company was shot and scalped after he and his young son Archie had walked to the edge of a town pasture to retrieve their cows. As horrified witnesses looked on, a warrior chased the fleeing boy down and carried him off. In the meantime, another part of the Indian raider band shot and killed a second man working at a nearby farm.[17]

A company of Smith's contemporaries, including the Ryley brothers, under the command of Lewis Cass, gave chase. In a woodland rifle skirmish, the Detroiters killed or wounded several Indians. But other warriors fled with their young captive. Archie McMillan was released four months later after Captain Whitmore Knaggs, by this time released from Canadian prison, seized three Chippewa who were relatives of those who had taken part in the attack. These prisoners were exchanged for the McMillan boy on January 15, 1815. Because of the prominence of the violent attack on McMillan in Detroit and the involvement of Governor Cass in the dramatic pursuit and firefight with the Indians—and because Jacob Smith would end up with a poor reputation for his business dealings among local merchants—this incident was better remembered than Smith's peaceful return of the Boyer children in the goods-for-hostages trade.

There was still danger on the Michigan frontier as 1814 ended and 1815 began—the record of a council held by pro-British Indians from around the Great Lakes and Ohio with British officers on Michilimackinac in late October showed that Saginaw Chippewa chiefs and warriors were among them. Yet Capt. Jacob Smith reestablished his presence in the Saginaw Valley during this time. Though Cass had Indian interpreters acting as his spies, Smith would also serve as the government's agent and officer on the Saginaw Trail in the Indian territory north of Detroit, as his rival Louis Campau would soon learn.

Jacob Smith versus Louis Campau, 1815

By October 1814, the Territorial Supreme Court was back in session and Jacob Smith served on two juries that acquitted two different men in criminal cases. That month, his mother, Elizabeth Smith, died back in Quebec. She was about 80 years old, according to church records.[1] There was still a war on, however, and the United States had been faring poorly in the main theater of the conflict, back in the east. President James Madison needed his forces in the Old Northwest to conduct diversionary action to take the pressure off. At the same time, tensions were again high in Detroit because of the attacks by Indians on area residents. Even though some of the chiefs and head men of the region had agreed to a general armistice a year previously, Cass and other Americans wanted to strike back at those Indians who remained hostile.

General Duncan McArthur, the latest commander of federal forces in the Old Northwest, now returned to Detroit to mount a large-scale raid into Canada. But there were few secrets in Detroit. Between the small-town gossip, pro-British residents, and family connections between people on the U.S. and Canadian sides of the river, McArthur knew it would be impossible to keep plans of his raid under wraps. Therefore he engaged in his own campaign of "disinformation" by letting it be known that his new operation was going to be mounted against the Indians of the Saginaw area. This was strictly a deception, but it was completely believable and accepted, given the Chippewa attacks that occurred that fall.[2] To further his ruse about the real target of the U.S. raid, McArthur used Jacob Smith to lend credence to the notion that the mission was to attack the Indians in villages and camps of the Saginaw Valley.

McArthur made his preparations and asked for local volunteers. With the American forces that would make this raid was Col. George McDougall of Detroit and about 20 Michigan Militia and local volunteers serving under his command. Notes taken by someone in the expedition, perhaps McDougall himself, show that directly beneath McDougall in the chain of command was Capt. Jacob Smith, the highest ranking field officer of the Michigan volunteers on the mission.[3] And though no name appeared on an account of this raid that was written in Detroit after the fact, there can be little doubt that it was authored or dictated by Jacob Smith. It states:

> I was called upon by Col. McDougall on the Sixteenth day of October last [1814] to accompany him as a Volunteer under General McArthur to Saguina; he desired me to give him what information I was possessed of regarding that country; we fell to work and sketched out a Map of the various Routs thither, the different villages around, distances and number of those warriors of my company likely to be found there in each; he remarked that the General, finding I was so well acquainted in that quarter, wished me particularly to join him.
>
> On the 17th I waited on the General; he remarked that he was desirous of obtaining ten or fifteen young men who knew the country, for the space of eight or ten days, to go to Saguina. I then volunteered my services and assisted in procuring a dozen of active woodmen and faithfully promised them that they should be detained no longer than the time mentioned, relying on the General's word. No compensation was offered or was any expected. We volunteered with our horses, from the purest motives and zeal, to render service to our country, and I am well convinced that if the General had gone to the place he mentioned, that we would have acquitted ourselves with honor.[4]

Smith, because of his knowledge of the Saginaw Chippewa, unknowingly became part of McArthur's effort to deceive British and Indian sympathizers as to the true objective of the raid. The general issued orders implying that the mission on which he was about to embark would be "a short, rapid, and it is believed, a brilliant expedition," and the men were urged to take special care of their horses.

A few days after consulting with Smith—or at least, making a show of consulting with Smith—McArthur gathered his officers and troopers and began moving out on October 22 and 23, riding along the river toward the western shore of Lake St. Clair. John Askin, that important Canadian merchant and trader who lived across the river from the Detroit, saw the mounted soldiers moving north. "This day [I have] seen 150 American Horsemen around riding past Mr. Meldrum's upward on some Expedition," Askin wrote in his diary. His entry shows that, just as McArthur had hoped, the rumor had spread that the U.S. troopers were on their way to the Clinton River, to follow the trail along it west and then move north into the Saginaw Valley, to punish the Chippewa for their raids on Detroit citizens.[5]

Actually the total American force was composed of several hundred troopers and militia as well as some Indians who had come over to the U.S. side of the conflict. Well after the horsemen were on their way, General McArthur told Jacob Smith the truth: They were not really going to attack the Indians of the Saginaw Valley at all. Smith related his reaction:

> To my utter astonishment, the General mentioned to me that he was going to River Thames and not to Saginau; wished me to mention the circumstance to my Command and expressed a desire that they should cross the river with him, to which they agreed, expecting that there would be no difficulty in returning from the Thames; we continued for two days and a half up Big Bear Creek and across towards Moravian Town, always in our station in advance of the Detachment, when within about eight miles of the latter place, I received orders from Adjt. Woods to take my men in the rear of the Detachment, which we obeyed with great reluctance and surprise.[6]

Soon the Michigan men got an explanation of why they had been pulled from the advance of the cavalry raid. It turned out that some rangers under an officer named Captain McCormick were jealous of the fact that the Michigan volunteers had been given the lead position. The problem was that more than 20 of McCormick's men had fulfilled the term of their enlistment; if they didn't get to ride at the head of the column, these men threatened, they would quit and go home. Jacob Smith's men were not happy when they heard this was the reason they'd been ordered to the rear. Smith's account continued:

On the evening of our arrival at the Moravian Town, my men assembled and requested I should make a representation to the General that their time was nearly
expired and if he would not give them their former station, they asked for permission to return home. I accordingly sent him a note that evening which he did not
answer, but he came to our tent next morning accompanied with Dr. Turner, and
in a violent passion, remarked that my men should not be allowed to return and if
they deserted to Detroit, that he would send the Indians after them. He said that
the citizens of Detroit, to the exception of perhaps a dozen, were Traitors and as
ready to send information to the enemy as the people of Sandwich, that the Territory was not worthy of our Government's protection.[7]

Moments after insulting the Detroiters, McArthur realized he'd gone too far.
He added that he didn't include the Michigan volunteers among those he thought
were disloyal. But the damage had been done; the Michigan militiamen were furious. When McArthur's troopers camped that night at Westminster, several of
Smith's company came straggling in late, ate some dinner, and then started back
toward Detroit, unimpressed and unintimidated by the general's threat that he
would send warriors after them. McArthur soon after dismissed Smith and the
rest of the Michigan men, allowing them to go home. Smith said he thought this
was proper, since none of them had been provided with suitable warm clothes for a
late fall raid into Canada, nor had they been paid so that they could buy what they
needed. After all, they'd been told to prepare for a brief raid of a few days, while
this foray by McArthur took more than three weeks.[8]

McArthur's raiders, without the Michigan men, pressed on toward the Canadian town of Burford. By now the British had organized some defenses, but
the American horsemen twice successfully engaged and defeated battalions of
British troops and militia. These U.S. raiders successfully destroyed most of the
flour mills in that portion of Upper Canada. This would make it a difficult winter
for the British military and the civilians who lived there, but it would also mean
Detroit was safe from British attack, a big disappointment to the Indians who
remained hostile to the Americans. John Askin, the old Canadian businessman
who lived near Sandwich, saw the Michigan men returning to Detroit. The rest
of McArthur's force returned about a week later. "I think the 10th [of November]
Mr. George McDougall with Jacob Smith & the Detroit Volentiers who had went
with General McArthur left him & returned back by this route," Askin wrote in his
diary on November 17.[9]

Duncan McArthur's destructive raid into Upper Canada lasted 24 days. He wrote an extensive report about his mission for the War Department, but said nothing about insulting the Michigan men and instead complained that "not more than twenty" of the local militia had accepted his invitation to go on the expedition in the first place.[10] But it also seems that some Detroiters were not happy with McArthur's disparaging remarks, which was probably why an officer who had gone on the raid—Capt. Jacob Smith—was asked to provide his account of what happened to a committee of citizens. While Smith's name doesn't appear on the report, dated February 16, 1815, the words could only have been his. First, the narrator of the account described being recruited by Colonel McDougall for a raid to Saginaw, and being specifically asked about his knowledge of the region and the Indian villages.

Second, the narrator of this report noted that he'd told McDougall about "the number of those warriors in my company"—clearly a reference by Smith to his dealing with them for many years. Lastly, Smith was the only Michigan Territorial Militia officer other than McDougall listed as having taken part in the raid. There can be little doubt, therefore, that Jacob Smith gave the account of the Michigan volunteers' experience on that raid into Upper Canada. Though the record suggests that Smith was sometimes shrewd and manipulative in his dealings, clearly he resented being misled and used for deception by General McArthur in the affair of the raid in the fall of 1814.

In the meantime Governor Lewis Cass organized his company of "interpreters" or spies to keep tabs on the Indians of the Michigan Territory, and many of Jacob Smith's fur-trading colleagues were among them. At the top of the list were Cass's trusted agents, Gabriel Godfroy and Whitmore Knaggs, old hands at speaking Native dialects, scouting for the military, and dealing with the Indians. Both had years of militia, U.S. Army, and other government service under their belts. The 20-odd interpreters, along with the Indian agents, were to cover the Chippewa, Pottawatomi, Ottawa, Delaware, and even the Shawnee, from the River Raisin to the St. Joseph, from Saginaw and Michigan's Thumb to the lower Huron River of what would become Washtenaw County. They got a dollar a day for their service. The Saginaw Indians would be observed and monitored by three fur-trading brothers, James, John, and Peter Ryley, sons of a white fur trader, now retired, and a Chippewa mother.[11]

Although Detroit's residents had been impoverished by the war, men of business like Jacob Smith started back about their affairs. That included taking one's debtors to court, now that U.S. authority had been reestablished. Not long after he'd returned from McArthur's raid into Canada, Smith took action against a man named Charles Labadie, who owed Smith $100. How Smith fared in the case against Labadie is unknown, but he was not the only person who owed Smith money. Just a month later, Smith was one of several creditors notified in the case of a man named Louis Soyer, who was arrested and jailed in Detroit for debt.

Smith himself was in sufficient financial shape to advance funds for the purchase of a horse, saddle, and bridle for a Detroit volunteer who joined an Army ranger company. Documents reflect that one Francois Gobeille or Gobey, along with his commanding officer, Captain Audrain, signed agreements that Smith would be reimbursed $70 when the soldiers got their pay.[12]

Finally, early in 1815, word arrived that the war with Britain was over. These were hard times in Detroit, what with the destruction and seizure of crops and goods that had gone on under the British and their Indian allies previously. Illness took the lives of hundreds of soldiers and civilians that year. These were also fearful times, with continued reports of British intrigue and agitation and Indian violence that spring. The son and daughter-in-law of the pro-U.S. Ottawa chief named The Wing, of the St. Clair River area, were reported to have been murdered by Indians hostile to the United States. On May 10, 1815, William Woodbridge, the territorial secretary, warned officials in Ohio and Washington that war parties from Saginaw were afoot in Michigan.[13]

"A man some time since sent by me to Saguina, returned last evening," Woodbridge wrote. "He was so fortunate as to cause a war party to be stopped, who were on their way to strike at the Rapids of the Miami." That last reference—the Rapids of the Miami, or the Maumee River—referred to the American settlement and garrison near present-day Toledo. Who was Woodbridge's agent? One of Cass's interpreters or agents, such as Whitmore Knaggs or one of the Ryley brothers? Could it have been Jacob Smith—the same man who had gone to Saginaw to rescue the Boyer children only months before? There is no definite answer, but Smith had long since returned to the Saginaw Valley, where he was going back to trade as well as acting as the eyes and ears of the U.S. government in Michigan.[14]

The territorial governor had learned during the War of 1812 of the need for agents who could communicate with the Indians and had their trust. Now Cass understood that even with the war over between Britian and the United States, he would need to utilize these agents in times of peace as well. "It is the result of my deliberate judgment that the peace of the frontier cannot be so easily and cheaply secured as by the employment of young men who speak the Indian tongue and are connected with them," Cass wrote to the War Department. "Their fidelity is unquestionable and independent of their own strength, they are always attended by a party of friends and relatives ready to receive impressions from them."[15]

The fur traders went back to work in the wilderness. In an autobiographical statement given when he was 72, Louis Campau indicated that both he and Jacob Smith quickly headed to Indian country at the conclusion of the war early in 1815—Campau to Saginaw and Smith back to the Grand Traverse of the Flint River, a location that would in time become the center of the city of Flint. But according to Campau, Captain Jacob Smith was also acting as a one-man listening post and agent for Governor Cass at his cabin on the Saginaw Trail.[16]

Young Louis Campau knew his business. A clerk in his family's trade-mercantile operation, he had also served in the territorial militia in a company that had been under the command of attorney Solomon Sibley back when the war began in the summer of 1812. After Hull's surrender of Detroit, Louis Campau got his parole and eventually made his way to the Clinton River, to the location near the river's mouth on Lake St. Clair. There was a small cluster of French families there and Campau's mother was one of the residents, though not his father, who was also named Louis. The elder Louis Campau, once a local justice of the peace and major in the territorial militia, had clashed with Governor William Hull over his pay just before the war broke out and went back to Canada, leaving his wife in Michigan.

Young Louis Campau was under suspicion when William Henry Harrison's forces came back to Michigan in the fall of 1813—there'd been talk that he had remained in touch with his father in Canada and that he was being protected by a large body of Indians. Although young Campau was arrested and his house searched when an American force of hundreds of men descended on him, Cass's men found no evidence to show Campau was disloyal to the United States.[17]

In February 1815, on the heels of the news that the war between the United States and Britain was over, a visitor with an important message arrived at Campau's door. "A man in the employ of Conrad TenEyck and others came to my mother's . . . and engaged me to go to Saginaw and make a sale of goods, remains of army goods," Campau said. TenEyck, of course, was one of the veteran merchant traders who had done business with John Jacob Astor's agents as well as with Jacob Smith and other Detroiters. TenEyck's man brought three sleighs full of goods to Campau, to make the point that this was a serious proposal and that TenEyck was ready to get back to business.

The notion that there were legally obtained "surplus" army goods somehow available to fur traders in a destitute frontier town ravaged by war, hunger, and disease was clearly a stretch, since this was a time when Governor Cass was using government rations to keep Detroiters from starving. But Louis Campau agreed to take the goods to trade. He would undertake the venture—an illegal one, since peace hadn't been secured with the Indians—as long as those proposing it would provide help. TenEyck's agent agreed with the condition. Campau had himself a deal.[18]

A young fellow named Francis Boyer would act as guide, Campau said. This Boyer was the older, half-Indian brother of the Boyer children who had been taken captive and then ransomed by the Chippewa warriors, redeemed by Jacob Smith in the goods-for-hostages deal at Saginaw in the summer of 1814. Francis Boyer knew the Indians of the region and he knew the territory.

Campau didn't name the other merchants and backers who were involved in this shady trading mission, other than TenEyck. As for the identity of the person or persons who ultimately set in motion and backed this deal, a good bet would have to include representatives of Astor's American Fur Company. Astor and his men were in a hurry to reopen the fur trade, so even though many Detroit residents were sick and hungry, these ostensibly surplus army supplies were being taken into the wilderness for the Indian fur trade for someone else's private profit. TenEyck, it should be noted, had been an officer during the war, and he had handled government funds for supplies while in Ohio. Though Detroit traders and merchants were wily characters, one has to wonder if they alone were powerful enough to acquire U.S. Army goods and trade them to the Indians, or whether they had the backing of even more influential individuals. For the record, Smith's old nemesis, James Abbott, was the American Fur Company's agent in Detroit in 1815, and he may have been one of the parties whom Louis Campau declined to name.

In any case, Campau's underlings transferred the army supplies and goods from the sleighs and packed them onto ponies. They headed northwest along the Clinton River, spending the first night in an Indian camp and then traveling north for what the French traders called the "River La Peer" (more properly, "La Pierre" or "the Stone River," or as it was called in English, the Flint River). But as the column of packhorses reached the Flint somewhere east of the Saginaw Trail, one of General Cass's Indian interpreters, the part-Chippewa James Ryley, rode up with two men and demanded they stop.[19]

It was a dramatic confrontation. Ryley told Campau that he had an order from the territorial governor: Campau and his party must go back on the grounds they were carrying contraband goods. But Campau refused. He said he "got rid of him [Ryley] by firmness and resolution." Of course, it may be that Campau's "firmness" was backed up with the threat of violence, since his party almost certainly outnumbered and outgunned Ryley's and included some Indians in Campau's pay. Campau, however, admitted nothing like that when he told the story decades later.

Although he had gotten rid of the governor's agents for the moment, Campau intended to cross the river at the Grand Traverse—the domain of Captain Jacob Smith. The implication in Campau's statement was that although he'd been able to bluff or intimidate his way past young James Ryley, he knew he would not be able to pull the same on Smith. Campau decided that his party would have to split up. He therefore "distributed the goods to reliable Indians for them to take up the Cass River, the Tittabawassee and other rivers," telling his men to trade the goods for fur and to meet him later at Saginaw. Then Campau continued on his way to the Grand Traverse. In the meantime Jacob Smith had been informed of Campau's illegal trading mission and was watching for him. As a man who had served the U.S. government, risked his life, and spent time in a Canadian prison during the war, Smith was probably well aware of the suspicions about Campau's loyalty. Of course, Campau was also a competitor of Smith's in the fur trade.

Campau said he indeed "was arrested by Capt. Smith" when he got to the Flint River. But Campau had no trade goods with him, so there was no evidence that he was committing a crime. There was nothing Smith could do but release him. A gleeful Campau went on to Saginaw, where members of his party who had the goods rendezvoused and where, he bragged, the "almost naked" Chippewa "bought with great largesse, giving the finest furs at my own price."[20]

Only 23 years old when he pulled off this coup—defying the territorial governor and going scot-free after being arrested by Capt. Jacob Smith of the Michigan Territorial Militia—Louis Campau was proud that he was the first trader to get back to Saginaw once the war was over, even if he had thumbed his nose at the highest U.S. authority in Michigan. His connections must have been powerful enough to keep him from any further legal trouble or prosecution, for Campau suffered no fallout from this "unlawful" trading mission. This fact alone may be suggestive of the involvement of Astor's agents as the ultimate backers of the deal, since Astor was extremely influential. Some historians and writers believed Astor paid off Cass and other government officials in order to do as he pleased in the fur trade. Even if this particular charge is false, Astor had at least the tacit support of President Madison and his Cabinet members, to whom Astor had made large loans of cash.[21]

Jacob Smith may or may not have been trading himself at the Grand Traverse early in 1815 when Campau went up to Saginaw, but records show he was legally licensed to trade that spring. On April 3, Smith received his license to trade at "Saguina" when his $1,000 bond or security was posted by a "W.M. Scott." This was Dr. William McDowell Scott, a Detroit resident who held various local offices and who lived around the corner from Smith's home at Woodward and Woodbridge. Louis Campau clearly remembered that his rival Smith was one of the traders who was located at Saginaw that season. "Captain Smith came also that spring then to trade," he said. "He lived mostly with Neome at his [Neome's] village." This was the Chippewa community located on the Flint River, in modern-day Montrose Township in Genesee County, near the Saginaw County line.[22]

But Jacob Smith's work for Cass and the U.S. government was not over, nor was his feud with Louis Campau. Smith's battle with his old foe James Abbott also continued, with Smith filing suit against the Detroit businessman, justice of the peace, and postmaster, in a case that would reach the Territorial Supreme Court by the fall. In his complaint, Smith charged that Abbott owed him $200 for his expenses and labor in the ill-fated mission to Michilimackinac in July 1812 when word had reached Detroit about the declaration of war with Britain. On July 11, 1815, Charles Girard dit Lavisite gave his deposition before Justice of the Peace George McDougall about Smith's unsuccessful attempt to reach the U.S. fort three years earlier. The Frenchman, whom Smith had hired to go with him to Mackinac, said he and Smith had never actually agreed on a price, but that when they had returned to Detroit after their adventure, the fur trader had paid him a dollar a day for 12 or 15 days.[23]

Girard's deposition may be the only surviving account ever given of Smith's attempt to get to the U.S. fort on Mackinac Island in the days after the declaration of the War of 1812, with the letters of British Captain Charles Roberts confirming that Smith had indeed been captured and suspected of carrying dispatches, and then escaped from the British-allied Indian warriors. Girard's testimony was enough to prompt an out-of-court settlement by Abbott, who presumably didn't want those old accusations of disloyalty brought up again. While the amount of the settlement isn't recorded, notes in the case file suggest Smith eventually accepted $150 from Abbott to end the matter.

Smith remained in Detroit into August, when he signed a petition in appreciation of Major William H. Puthuff, commander of the U.S. Army's 2nd Rifle Regiment, which was stationed in Detroit. Puthuff, who'd earlier been an adjutant to Duncan MacArthur back in the early days of the war, was retiring from the army, and Smith was one of the many Detroit traders, businessmen, militiamen, scouts, and veterans who signed the address praising him.[24]

Later that month, while Smith was traveling on business, his wife, Mary, wrote a winsome letter to her sister, or more accurately, her younger half-sister, Peggy, in Canada:

Detroit Aug. 22, 1815

Dear sister—with what heartfelt satisfaction I received your inestimable Letter. Words are unable to express my feelings, a pleasure so little expected for so long. Often it was to me one of the great blessings I could expect, particularly at the moment I received it. My husband, my child, my dearest Harriet [far] from home yet let me not say from home for she is gone to my home, where my dearest relatives dwell, and I hope long ere this you have seen her as well as my husband.

This is the first time she has ever been from under the maternal eye and no doubt you will find her but an awkward little girl, however you must make some little allowance for the little advantage she may have had. But she has had as much as the country could afford and that you will say & may with a great deal of propriety, that it is nothing at all. However I hope you will look on her as the child of your sister and that in that case I shall be well satisfied.

Another & the greatest wish of my heart is that you will take her to my dearest mother & I could have no objection if your father could see her likewise. He surely would not hate the child for the sins of its father. O my dear sister when I think of the time past & never to be recalled, it makes me at times unhappy to be separated from friends and relatives who ever were & ever will be dear to my heart as yet I will not despair. A Day may come when I may again embrace you all. Give my love to my dear mother & tell her to look on Harriet as if it were her own Mary. . . .

You have never my dear told me the difficulty existing between our father & your better half. Yet he visits you and adores your children. That my dear Peggy is one happyness you have over me, none of mine has been clasped in his or my mother's embraces. Oh he surely cannot have entirely forgot me. I never can forget him.

I have talked too much about self. I must alter the subject if I do not wish to tire you. I hope you are not determined of going to England, as you mentioned in your last for I really do not know what your father & mother should do if you were to leave them for you are their only consolation & in fact [likely] their only treasure remaining. As to myself you know that I am an outcast, at least from their society. Yet my heart is as much theirs as ever.

Have you seen William Smith? I should like to know how you like them. They have no doubt informed you how we were situated, our wishes & our prospects in this country. I had not time to write you by Jacob when he went down. I hope you will excuse but a favorable opportunity offers at this moment that I cannot slip. I think that I wrote a very long letter, I hope you will do the same when Jacob & Harriet returns. I do not fail for I shall be very much disappointed in you if you do. Kiss your dear children for me, tell them they have an aunt who will always love them & give my love & affection to your Moschana & if you please you may kiss him in my name.

Adieu dearest sister & believe me to be your affectionate sister till death

M. Smith
Once more love to dear Mother[25]

Because Mary Smith's biological father, Thomas Reed, died in 1783, her references to "your father" and "our father" are to her stepfather, Andrew Doe, the Quebec shoemaker who had married her mother, Margaret. Had Doe shunned Jacob and Mary Smith because of their lawsuit against him back in 1798? Was it because of Jacob's decision to become a citizen to United States, rather than remain a subject of the king of England? Could it have been because Smith had fathered a child with an Indian woman? Certainly the War of 1812 had divided families who had members on both the U.S. and Canadian sides of the Detroit River, just as families (including those of Jacob Smith's daughters and granddaughters) were divided, North and South, during the Civil War. Any one or combination of these factors certainly could have been the reason for the split between the Does and Jacob Smith.

Whatever the reason for the unhappy estrangement from her stepfather, Mary Smith did not have long to live after she wrote that letter to her half-sister. Within two years, she was dead. As for Mary Smith's hint about an opportunity that had presented itself to Jacob Smith, records suggest two possibilities: First, Smith had acquired the deed of sale and power of attorney to collect the estate of a Quebec man named Daniel McNeal (sometimes given "McNiel" and more properly, "McNeil"). In this particular case, McNeal's estate was property he owned in Detroit. Smith made this deal with McNeal's son, John, who lived in Detroit and was seemingly in debt to the fur trader. The legal agreement for the property, written in French, was dated "Sept. 7, 1815 Provenc Bar Canada, district of Quebec." It was recorded at the register's office of the Michigan Territory in February 1816, and it conveyed to Smith a lot on Woodward Avenue, next door to his own property, along with one other "donation lot" parcel.[26]

But there was also another, more important job Smith was being asked to undertake—one that was very sensitive, and one that Mary Smith couldn't discuss in her letter. On July 25, 1815, Governor Cass learned that a treaty council was going to be held at Spring Wells, located just south of Detroit, with U.S. generals William Henry Harrison and Duncan McArthur and a government official named James Graham, all of whom had been designated U.S. treaty commissioners. This would be a full-fledged peace treaty, to arrange formal terms with the Indians of Michigan and other parts of the Old Northwest.

Of course, someone would have to convince the leaders of the proud and stubborn Saginaw Chippewa to attend. That someone, Cass knew, was Jacob Smith. The fur trader claimed he was "strongly solicited" by Cass to undertake the mission to get the Indians to the treaty. Smith, however, said he had his own concerns to worry about. "I had made arrangements to visit Montreal with a small lot of furs and peltries, the remains of my property saved from the ravages of the late war," Smith wrote about his plans for the late summer of 1815. He said that he knew Cass's assignment could be trouble.[27]

"It would be prejudicial to my private concerns, and might eventually involve me in difficulties, by the delay it would occasion as well as the prejudice it would create in the minds of my creditors in Canada," Smith continued. But Smith made clear that although the assignment was risky, he had carried out such jobs for Cass before on behalf of the U.S. government. Smith referred to "the trust reposed in me in this instance, as in others of a similar nature previously performed as to your Excellency, and I trust I have proved satisfactory."

Smith accepted the mission and accomplished it. That August and September, in councils held at Spring Wells, Indians from all over Michigan and the Great Lakes, the Saginaw Chippewa included, came and agreed to peace terms with Harrison. Cass would later give Smith credit for getting hostile chiefs to attend. Though many of these Indians were resentful and unhappy with the fact that the war had ended without victory over the Americans, they were in fairly desperate circumstances late that summer, as a British Indian Department officer at Amhertsburg indicated in a letter to his superior. "Crowds of Sagunau Indians flock in upon us making out demands," wrote the officer, "but we having nothing to give them, they must wait untill the stores arrive—which I hope only too soon."[28]

The postwar peace made between the Saginaw Chippewa and the United States, an effort aided in no small part by Jacob Smith, was uneasy, but it was the start of great changes. In the years ahead Smith would be called on again by the federal government to influence the Chippewa and Ottawa of the Michigan Territory in the forested regions that lay to the north of Detroit, to Saginaw Bay and beyond.

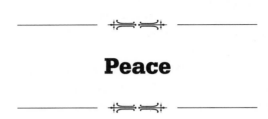

Peace

Despite the terrible outbreak of illness and other hardships they faced, life for the residents of Detroit slowly returned to normal after the attacks by Indians subsided. In the months following the end of the war, Nicholas Boyer, the man who had been kidnapped along with his children from their home on the Clinton River, was walking on Jefferson Avenue across from Governor Cass's residence when he saw the Chippewa named Chemokamun, or Big Knife, one of the Saginaw warriors who had abducted them and, according to his daughter Cecilia, had come a hair's breadth of murdering her. Nick Boyer had spent months as a captive until he was ransomed, just as his three other chilren did until Jacob Smith redeemed them.

In a testament to how the situation had changed, Boyer, enraged at the sight of one of the warriors who had tormented his family, swiftly unslung his rifle from his shoulder, raised it and cocked it, levelling it at Big Knife. The surprised warrior begged for his life, admitting he had done wrong. The moments must have seemed like hours with the Frenchman's weapon pointed at his heart, but Nick Boyer finally took his finger from the trigger and lowered the rifle, sparing Big Knife.

Though the confrontation was a personal one, it was nonetheless emblematic of the shifting balance of power in Michigan.[1]

Jacob Smith was in a hurry to get back to trading after successfully urging the Saginaw Chippewa and Ottawa, at the request of Lewis Cass, to attend the councils with William Henry Harrison to formally end the state of war. These councils in August and September 1815 resulted in the Treaty of Spring Wells.[2] By November, Smith was late in getting ready for the trading season. One of the Detroit businessmen with whom he was dealing was Dennis Campau, who entered into an agreement that called for Smith to deliver him "187 prime raccoon skins."[3] But now a run of bad luck befell Smith when he headed to Canada for trade merchandise. While Smith already was in debt to Montreal businessmen, he blamed his misfortune on the fact that word of his work for the U.S. government had reached the ears of Canadian parties who disapproved.

"The first opportunity after my return from the Indian country I embarked for Montreal, where after a tedious passage I arrived, disposed of my peltry and with the proceed purchased a small cargo of goods suited to the Indian trade which I had intended to prosecute at Saginau the ensuing winter, calculating thereon as the means of supporting a numerous family of small children," Smith wrote, describing to Governor Lewis Cass the events of that fall. "As I had anticipated," he continued, "the information of what I had done in bringing the Indians to attend the treaty was communicated to my creditors in Canada which produced my arrest and confinement in Montreal, where I was detained until my brother living at Quebec liberated me by the assumption of my debt."[4]

Though he was now free to go with a quantity of trade goods, Smith's troubles with his creditors in Canada left him broke by the time he arrived at Ft. Erie, a British military post on the Niagara River at the eastern end of Lake Erie. From this point, he had to ship his goods over to the U.S. side. "Here I was seriously embarrassed as I was out of money & had no friends either at Lake Erie or Buffaloe [*sic*] to whom I could apply for assistance," Smith complained. "I had neither money nor credit to enable me to meet the duties on my goods."

Smith crossed to the New York side of the river, where ships bound for Detroit were docked and waiting to take on cargo. He told his hard-luck story to someone—Smith didn't identify this man, though it was apparently a person who claimed knowledge about duties that had to be paid on goods from Canada. Smith claimed this man advised him to go ahead and bring his goods over and load them on a Detroit-bound ship, without entering them at the U.S. customs house at Buffalo. After all, the man supposedly advised Smith, it didn't matter to the federal government whether Smith paid the duty on his goods in Buffalo or in Detroit.[5]

The fur trader said he was relieved and pleased to hear this. Yes, Smith had resources and credit in Detroit; he would pay his duties there. He therefore brought his goods across from Canada to the U.S. side. Unfortunately, Smith said, he "was in the act of shipping them when a seizure was made of the whole" by U.S. officers. "I have reason to suspect that the seizure was made under information given the collector by the person who advised me to bring my goods across & ship them as above stated," Smith complained. He insisted that he had not been trying to get out of paying duty on his goods—he had only acted in good faith, believing, as he had been told, that he could pay the U.S. duty in Detroit. But he'd been set up.

Smith made it back to Detroit and early in December appealed to Cass, asking the territorial governor of Michigan to write up a statement for U.S. Treasury officials "of such facts as have come under your observation, relating to me & my conduct thro' the last war." After all, he claimed, he'd gotten into all this trouble as a result of helping Cass and the U.S. government. "If I eventually loose my property seized at Buffalo, I shall always attribute that loss to the delay resulting from my journey into the Indian country at your request," Smith wrote.[6]

It was two months before Cass responded to Smith's request for help with the Treasury Department. Perhaps the governor was busy or out of town, but it is also possible that he wanted to look into the matter himself before taking up Smith's case. Early in 1816, Cass wrote to Alexander J. Dallas, secretary of the U.S. Treasury under President James Madison. The governor outlined what had happened to Smith and the seizure of his goods by the federal customs house at Buffalo. "He was sent at my urgent solicitation to bring to the treaty at this place certain influential Chiefs whose presence it was important to procure and which without him could not have been procured," Cass wrote of Smith and his successful effort to get Saginaw Chippewa leaders to the peace treaty council. "He accomplished the object with much zeal and fidelity. And I have reason to believe it materially interfered with his proposed journey to Montreal and finally led to the seizure of his property.

"He has been a useful man in this quarter and his exertions during the recent war have occasioned him much loss. How far considerations like these can enter into the decision of his case is not for me to determine. It was due to his zeal and his misfortune that I should state them."[7]

These words from Cass are the strongest pronouncement made by a government official as to Smith's work for the United States during the War of 1812. Cass didn't go into any more detail than this, and with reason. Jacob Smith would continue to work for him, usually in a confidential manner. He would still have a major impact in Michigan in the years ahead. Unfortunately for Smith, Treasury Secretary Dallas seems to have been unimpressed with Cass's appeal on the fur trader's behalf. The war had left the United States deeply in debt, and the idea that Smith should be given a break for not paying the required duty on his imported goods in a timely fashion may have fallen on deaf ears, regardless of Smith's loyalty and work for the federal government. According to an 1820 letter written by Albert H. Tracy, a Buffalo attorney, not only were Smith's goods seized, but the fur trader was also sued by the U.S. government for the penalty, or fine, for his violation of U.S. customs law.

"I defended the suits for this penalty and succeeded in getting him clear of it," Tracy wrote later to William Woodbridge about representing Smith that winter of 1815–1816. But the Buffalo lawyer was apparently unable to beat the government's forfeiture case, and Smith lost his goods. Unfortunately for Tracy, just as Smith neglected to pay his other bills in the years ahead, he also failed to pay his attorney. Tracy would go on to succeed in politics as well as law, eventually becoming a U.S. senator, while Smith would die in obscurity and debt.[8]

After that season of trouble in Canada and the loss of his goods in New York, Smith made a change from his usual routine. Instead of heading back to Saginaw, in February 1816 he posted his bond, put up by his old acquaintance and militia colonel, George McDougall, a prominent Detroiter and official. Territorial licensing records show that Smith said he would trade with Indians at Lake Michigan and the Grand River during that period. That location may have been near present-day Grand Haven, about 125 miles west of where Smith usually traded on the Flint or Saginaw River.[9]

He also transacted some real estate business with McDougall. For the sum of $80, McDougall transferred title to Smith of a piece of property described as "Lot numbered forty-two in the old plan of the City of Detroit and being lot numbered one hundred and seven on the new plan in section number three." This property, a donation lot that dated back several years and had had various owners, was located in an area across Woodward Avenue from Smith's home and store.[10] These dealings in the fur trade and city property were probably linked, perhaps with the two men entering into some kind of partnership or with Smith working to pay a debt to McDougall.

Sometime before the 1815–1816 trading season, Smith also entered into a deal with a businessman named DeGarmo Jones—probably a matter of Jones covering one of the debts Smith owed, or otherwise loaning him money. By spring Smith had paid part of this debt, though Jones expected the fur trader make good on the balance when he returned to Detroit from the wilderness. "Enclosed you have the Bill of Sales of the Furs belonging to Jacob Smith which he is to have credit for on his note," Jones, then in Pittsburgh, wrote to attorney Solomon Sibley. "Should he return from the Indian Country, I will pay the balance of his note in fur at current price. If not, please bring suit."[11]

Smith did eventually return from the Indian country of western Michigan, but he apparently didn't pay that balance. Jones, who would go on to be a Detroit mayor, filed suit and probably won in a local court, for the case was on the Territorial Supreme Court's docket in September. Since these were times when a debtor could be jailed, Smith needed someone to post his "special bail," and that was provided by his old friend Conrad TenEyck. In addition, Smith went into debt to Dennis Campau again in November when he was advanced $1,000 worth of trade goods.

Three years later Smith would settle the DeGarmo Jones case out of court, apparently with a payment of $1,372, but he would be sued for his debt to Dennis Campau. Probably because he also owed money to TenEyck, and because they were often associated in the fur trade, TenEyck posted Smith's trader's bond early in 1817. Fur trade license records show that Smith returned to trade "at Saguinaw and its vicinity" as well as the Grand River and another location.[12]

But if Smith was returning to his old stomping grounds on the Flint and Saginaw rivers for part of the new year, other changes were now coming into his life and that of his family. On September 22, 1816, Smith's teenaged daughter, Harriet, married a promising young U.S. Army officer from Virginia, one John Garland, who had been stationed at Detroit with the 3rd Infantry Regiment, and who was promoted from first lieutenant to captain during this time. Garland was from a prominent Lynchburg family and had been a soldier since the War of 1812. Soon the couple moved west, for a time, when Garland was reassigned to Wisconsin, which was then still part of the Michigan Territory. One acquaintance playfully described Harriet in 1819, then about 20 and living with her husband at the frontier fort at Green Bay, as "a pretty neat *raly* [really] Butiful [beautiful] still pitty-patty doll of a thing." Many decades later, Harriet's youngest sister, Maria, would be remembered as having also been a physically small woman, and her portrait would indicate she was dark-haired and attractive. The future husband of yet another of Smith's daughters, Louisa, had also come to Detroit from the east to make his fortune shortly after the war. His name was Chauncey S. Payne and he'd gone into business as a jeweler and merchant with a man named Levi Brown, who had married Payne's sister.[13]

Several months after Jacob Smith's oldest daughter was married, his wife Mary died in Detroit on April 11, 1817, leaving four children at home. Mary Reed Smith was 37 years old at the time of her death. Judge Augustus Woodward, the chief judge of the Michigan Territory and old friend of Thomas Jefferson, was one of the people whom the Smith family invited to attend Mary's funeral "from her late dwelling on Monday, 14th Inst. [April] at 3 O'clock P.M." It is not certain whether the judge attended, but his invitation was written in a neat hand, unsigned, and dated "Sunday Morning, April 13, 1817." The procession presumably made its way northwest up what is now known as Woodward Avenue, and it may be that Mary Smith was buried on the east side of the avenue between what would become Larned and Congress streets. This was called "the English burial ground."[14]

A widower with young children, Jacob Smith at some point placed his youngest daughter, Maria (who was not quite five years old when her mother died) with Harriet and John Garland. There are also indications that the Garlands also took care of son Albert. Yet the 1820 census suggests that Smith tried to keep his younger children together in Detroit, at least for a time. A later account written in a Genesee County history about Smith claimed, incorrectly, it was at the point after his wife's death that he began to spend more time at his post on the Flint River and among the Indians and less time in Detroit. Smith's daughter and son-in-law Louisa and Chauncey Payne may have been a source of this information. Smith's son, Albert, giving a deposition in an 1855 lawsuit, gave credence to the claim that Jacob Smith primarily lived in the wilderness after the death of his wife. "My father had made Flint his home for several years," Albert Smith testified after telling of the death of his mother. "After three or four years, he lived there all the time." This would mean that from 1821 or 1822 on, the fur trader no longer resided in Detroit, and that he considered his place at the Flint River his home.[15]

But that was simply not the case. Records show that Smith kept a house in Detroit until he lost it to his creditors in 1824. In fact, Smith moved back and forth between his two homes in these years as his business demanded or as his debts and legal problems would dictate. As for these children of Jacob Smith, in the years ahead Harriet Garland, after a lifetime as an army wife, would die suddenly in Saratoga, New York, on August 31, 1860, at the age of 62, perhaps from a heart attack as she walked with one of her daughters, Mrs. Bessie Deas. Harriet's husband, John Garland, by then a retired brigadier general, would follow her less than a year later, dying in New York about six weeks after the start of the Civil War.[16]

Jacob Smith's youngest daughter, Maria Smith, when grown, would marry a U.S. Army officer of her own, a Lt. Thomas B. W. Stockton. Stockton would serve on the Minnesota frontier and work as a civilian engineering agent for the War Department in the Great Lakes region; be appointed colonel commanding a Michigan volunteer regiment in the Mexican War and another regiment in the Civil War; and end his days in Flint with his wife after a career as a businessman. Maria Stockton would help found the local library. "Maria (Mrs. T. B. W. Stockton) . . . I remember very well," one resident of Flint would recall. "She was a tiny old lady, very refined, and well educated. She always wore old fashioned silk dresses and looked as if she had just stepped from one of the old frames on the wall of her home." Of the other white children of Jacob and Mary Smith children, daughter Caroline would die after reaching adulthood, while brother Albert would grow up, marry, and eventually reside in South America and New York City. And as noted previously, his sister Louisa married silversmith-merchant Chauncey Payne; they would eventually settle in Flint and live out their days there with the Stocktons nearby.[17]

These developments, however, were years off. Whatever the living arrangements were for Jacob Smith's young children after the death of their mother in 1817, certainly there were changes. The reminiscence of a man who had been a schoolboy in Detroit after the War of 1812 confirms that around this time Smith had room he no longer needed in Detroit. "[In] 1816, or possibly 1817, Mr. William Brookfield and his wife kept an excellent school for more advanced scholars, in the house of Mr. Jacob Smith, standing on the corner of Woodward Avenue and Woodbridge street," Benjamin O. Williams would recall.[18]

Perhaps with Mary gone and his younger children being cared for by others during the trading season, Smith decided to rent his house to those teachers. Young Ben Williams only attended school in Smith's building briefly, for he would soon after move with his father Oliver Williams and their large family, including

Benjamin's brothers Ephraim and Gardiner, north to the vicinity of the newly established village north of Detroit named for the great Indian chief Pontiac. Slowly, inexorably, these American settlers would move up the Saginaw Trail to an area where no white family had previously attempted to put down roots.

Three months after the death of his wife, Jacob Smith quit his post as an officer with the local defense force. "Your resignation of the office of Captain with the first regiment of Michigan Militia is accepted," Cass wrote to the fur trader in the summer of 1817.[19]

The fact that Smith had held the post of captain in the territorial militia for the past three or more years was likely the direct result of the trust Cass and/ or William Henry Harrison had in him. Harrison had personally reorganized the Michigan Territorial Militia back during the war in the fall of 1813, and it was about this time that Smith was listed as a lieutenant. Cass's correspondence showed that as a military commander, he maintained it was his prerogative to appoint officers who served under him. Thus, if Harrison hadn't given Jacob Smith an officer's commission in the reorganized militia of Michigan, then Cass did. Certainly the governor had trusted Smith, for he had made Smith a captain within less than a year.

Records reveal only small details about Jacob Smith in 1817. First, about the same time his wife died, the U.S. government reimbursed him for the loss of his horse, saddle, and other items at the surrender of Detroit back in August 1812. Smith also failed to show up for grand jury duty in September that year, as did three other men, including James Dodemead, Smith's onetime business partner. The Supreme Court judges of the territory weren't happy that they didn't appear and ordered that they be brought before the court "at the next term to show cause, if any they have, why they should not be fined for their non-attendance." The court journal didn't say whether or not Smith was found in contempt for not showing up for grand jury duty.[20]

The postwar recovery of Detroit and the Michigan Territory continued. There was a newspaper in Michigan now, the *Detroit Gazette,* and new Protestant churches. There were also plans for a University of Michigan, a bank, and an agricultural society. Fur business giant John Jacob Astor consolidated his vast control over the trade on the American side of the Great Lakes, buying out his Canadian partners. One writer claimed that Astor also bribed Governor Lewis Cass himself with a payment of as much as $35,000 in May 1817, though other historians have taken pains to point out that no one else has ever seen evidence that the governor actually received a payoff. Cass also signed another treaty with the Indians, one that extended land cession boundaries set up by Hull's 1807 treaty and added hundreds of square miles to U.S. territory in southeastern Michigan. Whether Smith had a hand in this treaty is not reflected in records.[21]

Some men who had come from Kentucky and southern Ohio and other parts of the country during the war had seen some of Michigan and liked it, and there were new businesses and industries under way around Detroit. But Michigan had gotten bad publicity because of Ohio surveyors who had run into wet weather, low-lying land, and unfriendly Indians, so settlers were not exactly hurrying to the territory. If that weren't difficulty enough for Michigan officials, the British military and Indian agents continued to make trouble, Cass and others believed. But this was probably of little consequence to the men who went among the Indians to trade. Jacob Smith continued to travel between Detroit and Saginaw, trading at the Chippewa villages on the rivers of the Saginaw Valley. Since the early 1800s, Smith had often traded at the Grand Traverse crossing of the Saginaw Trail at the Flint River, or at Neome's village, also on the river about 15 miles to the northwest. Louis Campau would later point out that Jacob Smith also spent much time at Neome's village.[22]

This Chippewa chief was one of Smith's close friends, and it is probably significant that Neome's name doesn't appear in accounts about Michigan Indians who fought alongside the British and Tecumseh. While some Indians who lived in the region had made war against the United States, some did not participate and it appears that Neome was one of them. Charles P. Avery, a Flint lawyer and amateur historian who represented Smith's heirs, described Neome as "honest and simple-minded," and "short and heavily molded."[23]

Louis Campau, who was trading at Saginaw after the War of 1812 and dealt with Neome on a regular basis, testified that the chief was "very ignorant, but he was very good, honest and kind," which may have been Campau's way of suggesting that Smith could manipulate the chief.[24] Attorney Avery's account reflected less cynicism; he wrote that Smith and Neome called themselves brothers and that the chief's family members, in speaking of them, "would bring their hands together, pressing the two index fingers closely to each other, as the Indian symbol of brotherhood and warm attachment."

Were Smith and Neome truly this close? Smith's son Albert, giving a deposition years later at the age of 44, would say that as a small child he'd been actually "adopted" by Neome as a kind of grandson to the chief in a ceremony held in Jacob Smith's Detroit home that included the attending Chippewa wearing painted faces and smoking a ritual pipe with the boy.[25] It was a relationship Smith cultivated while living and trading among the Saginaw Chippewa bands for weeks and months at a time.

"By long residence among the Indians he [Smith] had assimilated his habits and ways of living to that of the natives, even to the adoption of their modes of dress," Avery wrote about the trader. "He spoke their language fluently and correctly; he was generous to them, warm-hearted and intrepid." The Chippewa gave Smith an Indian name: they called him Wabesins or Wahbesins, which was said to mean "Young Swan." It was in this account of Avery's that the only physical description of Jacob Smith was given: "Though small in stature and light in weight, he was powerful as well as agile."[26]

Avery's article also went on to note that Smith also had had an Indian family, something that Governor Cass's agents said they knew. "Like most men living upon our Indian frontiers, he had become the father of a half-breed family, one of whom, a daughter, Mo-kitch-e-no-qua, was then living," Avery wrote. "Skilled in woodcraft, sagacious and adroit, he may be said to have equaled, if not excelled, the natives in many of those qualities which, as forest heroes, they most admire." By this time, of course, Smith's half-Indian daughter Nancy (whose Indian name was also given as "Mo-kitch-e-wee-no-qua") was living in Meadville, Pennsylvania.[27]

All in all, Jacob Smith had over the course of the past 17 years or so become a well-known and influential man among the Saginaw Chippewa. Over the next two years, he would exert this influence to benefit his family as well as the federal government.

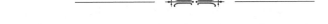

Conclude a Treaty for the Country upon the Saginac Bay

B y now some settlers from the eastern United States were coming to southeastern Michigan, though not in large numbers. Plans were also under way by a company of investors to build the village of Pontiac on the Saginaw Trail at the Clinton River crossing, a point about midway between Detroit and the Flint River. These developments would cause the wilderness to recede even further and bring more newcomers into contact with the Indians. Territorial officials wanted to prevent hostile incidents from occurring, since bloodshed would hurt the expansion of white settlements and towns; it could require tough and expensive military responses against the Indians, and that would be bad for the business of selling land to settlers. Of course, the issue of alcohol was a concern because of its devastating effects on the Indians and the possibility it would fuel violence.[1]

As noted previously, traders like Jacob Smith weren't supposed to trade or give alcohol to the Indians with whom they were doing business, but American traders, like others, ignored the prohibitions. There had been a long history of traders routinely dealing or providing rum or brandy or whiskey in their transactions with the Chippewa and other tribes. But since the fur trade was a highly competitive business, it was perhaps inevitable that agents of the powerful American Fur

Company, based at the company's Great Lakes headquarters on Mackinac Island, learned from their traders in Saginaw that Smith was doing just that.

Astor's agents, Ramsay Crooks and Robert Stuart, had for months been feuding with Major William Puthuff, the veteran U.S. Army officer who was given the job of federal Indian agent at Michilimackinac by Gov. Lewis Cass. Puthuff knew many independent fur traders from his time in Detroit, and he had the authority to regulate and penalize traders. He didn't like Astor's powerful company, which had bought out all of the South West Company's interests. Crooks and Stuart charged that Puthuff was a despotic and perhaps corrupt bureaucrat who improperly seized their traders' boats, property and possessions; they said he wrongly charged their traders for licenses and banned Astor's Canadian traders and their employees from taking part in the fur trade in U.S. territory. Crooks and Stuart maintained this was unfair.[2]

The complaint by Astor's men centered on a federal law that made it illegal for anyone but American citizens to be in the fur trade on U.S. territory. While the law was aimed at creating and preserving American control of the trade in the U.S. territories of the Great Lakes and the West, the reality was that Astor needed Canadian employees to carry on his trade far and wide. With his strong connections and influence on the Monroe administration and Lewis Cass, Astor expected that his agents in Michigan should be granted special exceptions so they could continue to use Canadian employees and traders. Major Puthuff, however, knew American traders such as Jacob Smith from his time in Detroit. He insisted he was only doing his job, enforcing U.S. law and trying his best to oppose the interests of the hated Astor.

Crooks and Stuart, back in New York early in 1818, charged that Puthuff employed a double standard: While he enforced rules that made things difficult for John Jacob Astor's men, he allowed other fur traders who broke the law to go unpunished. Jacob Smith, they claimed, was one of these scofflaws whom Puthuff ignored. "The first thing we learned on arriving at Mackinaw last June, was the injury of our outfits had sustained at Sagina Bay on Lake Huron, and at Grand River, of Lake Michigan; from the clandestine introduction of Spirituous liquors; at the first place by Jacob Smith from Detroit," the American Fur Company agents complained. "These acts were made known to Major Puthuff, and evidence offered in support; but we are not aware that he ever took the trouble to investigate their merits."[3]

Jacob Smith, of course, was doing what every other fur trader had done, including those who worked for Astor's company, one of the biggest and most powerful fur-trading concerns that ever existed. The complaint about Smith was just one of many that Crooks and Stewart outlined in their long letter. In response to Astor, the administration of President James Monroe decided that Puthuff had gone too far—the major was removed from his job that spring. In passing along the bad news, Cass told Puthuff that he'd been fired by U.S. Secretary of War John C. Calhoun.[4]

Astor's influence on the federal government and Cass can hardly be overstated. Whether or not one accepts or believes the allegation by the provocative writer Gustavus Myers that Astor paid a bribe to Cass, Astor had indeed made personal loans to President Monroe and other officials. And his company was growing larger and stronger—by this time he controlled most of the trade on the U.S. side of the Great Lakes. But the complaint by Astor's agent about Jacob Smith's using alcohol in the fur trade did not result in the government taking action against him. Not long after Astor shared his men's complaints with the Monroe administration, Cass heard from the secretary of war in a letter dated March 2. In it, Calhoun asked Cass to report on a letter he'd received from Astor. Unfortunately, that enclosure from Astor was not found by archivists who compiled Michigan Territorial papers. There is no way of knowing whether Astor specifically complained about Smith or whether he simply demanded Puthuff's removal.

In any event, Smith continued to work for Cass in various capacities. As a small independent trader, Smith was no real threat to the American Fur Company, yet it is clear that Astor's managers in Michigan wanted him shut down for violations that their own agents and traders practiced day in, day out on a vastly larger scale. What is also noteworthy about this episode is the fact that Astor's men often bought out men such as Smith or drove them out of business by purchasing trade goods cheaper and trading them at lower rates than an independent trader could afford.

This was the time, historians say, when Mackinac Island was the most important center for the Michigan fur trade because of Astor's business. Thousands of Indians, trappers, traders, clerks, and boatmen gathered at the company's large buildings, with ships, canoes, and barges coming and going. By comparison, an independent trader's cabin store or post on the Flint or Saginaw River must have been small potatoes. Yet Astor's men apparently did not or could not drive Smith out of the fur trade. That Smith would do to himself.

Only bits and pieces in the historical record reflect the doings of Smith during this time. A news item in the *Detroit Gazette* during the late summer of 1818 suggests that Smith, at least for a period of time, owned a dock on the river from which ships could take on and unload cargo. This was just a block or so south of his buildings at the corner of Woodbridge and Woodward.

Father Gabriel Richard, Detroit's energetic and community-minded Catholic priest, put a notice in the paper that he needed 200 tons of large stone from "Stoney Island" in the Detroit River for the building of a new St. Anne's Church; this masonry needed to be "delivered to the wharf of Jacob Smith." The good father would pay $200 for the stone to be brought to Smith's dock, but $240 if it was delivered to the church grounds. Smith's ownership of this dock cannot have lasted long, for there is no other reference to this "wharf of Jacob Smith." Perhaps like other Detroit property, he had this for a time and then lost it.[5]

Yet another lawsuit was filed against Smith, this time by George Bellows and David Stone, businessmen who'd been partners with another Detroit merchant named Richard Hall Jones. Jones had died late in 1813, but Bellows and Stone claimed Smith still owed Jones hundreds of dollars. Now that money was due them. This case also went before the Territorial Supreme Court, though Smith asked that it be delayed until the court's next term.[6]

That fall in 1818, Smith purchased goods from his longtime associates Conrad and Jeremiah V. R. TenEyck for the coming season's Indian fur trade. An important item all traders needed to have for business with the Indians was silver jewelry—ornamental pieces that they prized highly. In discussions with Smith, the TenEycks proposed to get their jewelry for the trade from either Chauncey Payne—a skilled jeweler, artisan, and future Smith son-in-law—or from a man identified in court documents as "Mr. Riopelle."[7]

Smith, however, had a different metalworker in mind. His subsequent deposition about the silver jewelry provides an interesting view of an important part of the fur trade—the Indians' love for silver work and the great profits this jewelry generated for traders. For while the TenEycks wanted to contract for jewelry from Payne or Riopelle, Jacob Smith said he preferred the less expensive jewelry of a man named Joseph Andre dit Clark. The TenEyck brothers agreed that they should consider Smith's proposal, so Smith went to talk to Andre. Andre said, yes, he could make Indian ornaments, if he was supplied the silver. Smith then took Andre to talk with the TenEycks, where they made a deal for the ornaments.

Smith said that one month later he received jewelry worth about $350 from Andre, which the fur trader packed in his saddlebags. According to Smith's deposition, Andre was to deliver another batch of jewelry to Conrad TenEyck, who in turn would meet Smith at a place called Ft. Harrison so that Smith could use the pieces in trade. For the record, Ft. Harrison had been built on the Wabash River in the Indiana Territory in 1811—further proof that Smith didn't just operate in Michigan's Saginaw Valley.[8]

When asked by attorneys if he got the balance of jewelry as he had expected on January 1, 1819, Smith replied that he did not. "The want of the silver work was an injury to me," the fur trader testified, "because I could have disposed of them at a hundred percent profit." Smith explained that large pieces of silver, such as armbands and breastplates and gorgets were sold or traded with the Indians by the weight of the piece, while other, presumably smaller articles were sold by the dozen or even by the hundred.

When Jacob Smith returned to Detroit that winter, he sold off some of his property holdings—specifically, the lots and buildings that had been a part of the estate of Daniel McNeal, real estate he had received back in 1815. For $1,647.50, Smith turned over the deed to that property on December 18, 1818, to Detroit businessmen and merchants Robert Smart and James Abbott—the man whom he'd practically accused of being a British spy. For his part, Abbott, now a Wayne County judge, was still concerned with Smith's "veracity and morality." Only a few days after the sale, an item in the newspaper suggested that Abbott didn't trust Smith with the note of the indebtedness that he and Smart had written out. "Persons are warned against purchasing a bond drawn by James Abbott and Robert Smart in favor of Jacob Smith, for $1647," the item in the *Gazette* said. "Payments have been made on account of that bond." But the sale of Smith's land to Abbott must have gone smoothly, for in the coming months, the trader would sell other pieces of his Detroit property to his old foe.[9]

Another note in the newspaper, printed soon after, confirmed that Smith indeed wasn't using all of the building space he owned in town, and that he had rented rooms to a newspaper proprietor who was now subleasing them. That man who had rented from Smith was the owner and editor of the *Detroit Gazette*. "James P. Sheldon has two rooms in the building of Mr. Jacob Smith, on the corner of Woodward Avenue and Woodbridge Street, nearly opposite the post office," Sheldon's paper reported. "He desires to lease the rooms."[10]

Jacob Smith appeared before Justice of the Peace Thomas Rowland in Detroit just a month later in February 1819, but not because he was in any legal hot water this time. Smith swore out an affidavit for one Joseph LaPlante, asserting that LaPlante had served under him, "aforesaid Capt. Jacob Smith, late commanding a company of volunteers in the service of the United States." LaPlante, Smith swore, had been a volunteer during the late war between the United States and Britain and "performed the duty of a faithful and intrepid soldier until honourably discharged."[11]

Records also show that at some point during 1819, Smith also carried a message from Detroit to Piqua, Ohio, for the government. According to Governor Cass's expense/disbursement reports, he paid the fur trader $45 for what the governor described as an "express to Piqua." In this mission, Smith was paid for "15 days at $3/day," the entry reads, though neither the date nor the nature of the message he carried is reflected in the record.[12]

Smith continued to attract troubles big and small with various government authorities. Wayne County records show that at some point after July 1818, Smith was fined $7 for an unspecified offense or violation of local law.[13] Much more potentially serious for him was that by the summer of 1819, he had become the target of an investigation by the U.S. Indian Department's new agent on Mackinac Island.

The island, of course, was where John Jacob Astor's American Fur Company agents commanded their Great Lakes empire. Indian agent George Boyd—a former Detroit judge and official and friend of Lewis Cass—had taken the place of Major William Puthuff. Boyd wrote to Cass that summer that he'd been collecting evidence about Smith's providing alcohol to Indians. "I hope to be able to forward by the next vessel the statement required of the probable number of Indians belonging to this agency," wrote Boyd, "also all the evidence within our power at this late date touching the illicit introduction of ardent spirits within the Indian Country by Mr. Smith."[14]

Between Astor's men and their new federal Indian agent at Mackinac, allegations about Smith providing alcohol to the Indians had been hanging around for a year and a half by this point. It would seem that if Governor Cass wanted to look into the matter and charge Smith with a violation of the law, it would have been more easily and readily investigated from Detroit than from Astor's headquarters at the Straits of Mackinac. It can probably be inferred that Boyd was investigating Smith not because Cass wanted it, but because Astor's men wanted it. The language employed by Boyd in his letter describing Smith's violation was practically the same that Astor's agents had used.

Though various accounts relate that Cass heartily disapproved of traders giving or selling alcohol to the Indians, there is nothing in his papers to suggest that he took any action against Smith. Of course, Cass had a good reason to look the other way when it came to accusations against Smith. For although no one other than the territorial governor knew it, Smith was already working on another important assignment for the U.S. government.

Detroit and southeastern Michigan continued to change in 1818 and 1819. The territory had sent William Woodbridge to Congress as a nonvoting member of the U.S. House of Representatives. The government had a land sales office in Detroit now and the steamboat *Walk-in-the-Water* arrived late that summer on her maiden voyage. The population of Michigan was growing, and roads, transportation, bridges, and settlements were being built or improved. It was slowly getting easier and cheaper, therefore, to move goods and people back and forth between Michigan and the eastern United States.

The government's point man in the development of Michigan, naturally, was Governor Cass, the eastern-born Jeffersonian Democrat who had been a brigadier general over Ohio troops during the war and a vehement critic of William Hull's performance in the opening months of the war. As territorial governor, Cass had to try to maintain peace with the Indians while promoting the settlement and development of the territory. Of course, these were incompatible if not irreconcilable ideas, since turning Michigan into farmland necessarily meant diminished hunting and trapping for the Indians. Cass hoped that the growth of settler's farms and towns would force them to leave Michigan for the West—a continuation of the policy favored by Thomas Jefferson nearly 20 years previously. But could this be done without bloodshed? The fact that settlements were expanding out of the Detroit area to Mt. Clemens and Pontiac meant that the Indians were seeing that land they ceded previously (land they had still been able to use) now forever lost as it was surveyed and sold. Of course, there were some incidents of violence, theft, and robbery by Indians against settlers at intervals during these years after the War of 1812, probably as a result of the increasing pressure on the tribes and the expansion of white settlements and farms.

Furthermore, north and west of land the U.S. government already claimed under prewar treaties was even more land, millions of acres of forests and hills, flatlands and meadows, rivers and lakes. Beginning in about 1817, small expeditions of Detroit residents, U.S. military officers, and officials began to explore the land between Detroit and the Saginaw Bay, making them some of the first U.S. citizens who were not fur traders, missionaries, or prisoners of the Indians to see it. Fur traders who worked and traveled these woods to the Grand, Flint, Saginaw, and Shiawassee rivers and their tributaries reportedly tried to discourage settlers in this region by telling stories of swamps and beasts and dangers, but Cass knew that these lands would soon be desirable. This was Chippewa-Ottawa country, and the Indians had formally ceded only some of this land to the United States in 1807. Practically no white American settler lived in this area—yet.

By early 1819 the territorial governor had learned that the Indians, or at least certain Indians, might be willing to sell more land. "Information, which has recently reached me from different quarters, induces me to believe, that an attempt to procure from the Chippeways a cession of the Country upon the Saginaw bay in the territory would be successful," Cass wrote to Secretary of War John C. Calhoun. This was the time to act, the governor believed. Americans who'd fought in the War of 1812 in the Old Northwest or who had lived on the western frontier in Ohio had witnessed or experienced raids by Indians from Michigan; now it was believed the United States should do whatever it could to gain this land and to either move the Indians west of the Mississippi River or to "confine them within reasonable limits" by obtaining their land. Cass thought so, and he expressed no sympathy for the Chippewa. "Those Indians have always been troublesome and discontented and even now commit almost daily depredations on the exposed settlements of this territory," he complained.[15]

Whether Jacob Smith was one of the sources of the information about the Chippewa and Ottawa allegedly being willing to cede land in the Saginaw Valley is not certain, though it is clear that Smith was active in that area during 1818 and 1819. Cass pressed the federal government in Washington, D.C., for approval to convene treaty talks with the Indians. So did William Woodbridge, Cass's old friend and Michigan's delegate to the U.S. Congress. Woodbridge "conversed with the President [James Monroe] on the subject of the value to our Country of the lands possessed by the Saguina Indians & the probability of being able by treaty to procure those lands." Monroe recommended that Woodbridge raise the subject with Secretary of War Calhoun, head of the branch of government that then dealt with the Indians.

Several weeks after Cass proposed that 1819 was the year to convene a treaty council for the purpose of getting land from the Saginaw Indians, he repeated his recommendation to Washington. "From information that has recently reached me, there is reason to believe, that the cession of a considerable portion of it may be obtained from the Indians," he wrote. Cass admitted that it was impossible to judge how much land he might be able to gain from the Chippewa. "Much depends upon the temper of the Indians at the time, and much upon circumstances, which cannot be foreseen. But I should think it improper to make the effort without a strong probability of success."[16]

To anyone who knew anything about the history of the often-hostile nature of Chippewa-U.S. relations, this must have been considered an ambitious plan. But Calhoun agreed that Cass should call for a treaty council. On March 6, 1819, President Monroe issued Cass the authority "to conclude and sign a treaty or treaties with the Chippeway Nation of Indians, with the Territory of Michigan for the accession of the country upon the Saginac Bay."[17]

"Every confidence is reposed in your judgment and discretion," Secretary of War Calhoun advised Cass, "not only to obtain the lands on the most favorable terms, but that you will incur no expense that will not be necessary to the success of the negociation [sic]."[18] And that was why in that summer of 1819, Jacob Smith was quietly working in the Indian country northwest of Detroit, the Saginaw Valley, on behalf of the government.

To those who traded with the Indians, treaty talks represented an important opportunity to do business. Hundreds, perhaps thousands of Native people would come to the councils. Not only would the Indians bring pelts to trade, there was a good chance they might have money to spend as well, since the successful conclusion of a treaty typically meant that their tribe would receive a payment from the government. Cass would also need translators and contractors for supplies, provisions, and gifts. Word of the proposed treaty council at Saginaw, to be held in the fall, spread through the territory.

"Supposing there would be goods wanting, I take the liberty of requesting and hope you will consider me an applicant to furnish a part or the whole of those goods which may be wanted for the Indians," wrote Abraham Wendell, a merchant who had come from New York state to Detroit some years before. "You will confer a particular favor by informing me what amounts will be agreeable to you for me to furnish so that I can make my arrangements to transport my goods from New York."[19]

Other contemporaries of Jacob Smith were interested in getting on Cass's payroll. Joseph Marsac, a military officer who had much experience dealing with Indians, was recommended by General Alexander Macomb, retired from the U.S. Army, to work as an interpreter. Marsac was hired and accompanied the governor's party to Saginaw. Many years later Marsac would give testimony about Smith's role in the treaty, particularly regarding the fur trader's influence in determining how reservations of land along the Flint River were made for certain individuals.[20]

John Ryley, one of the part-Chippewa brothers, applied to Cass for a license to "dispose of merchandise at Saginau at the insuing [*sic*] Indian treaty." The treaty council was more than just a matter of a trading opportunity for John Ryley and his brothers Peter and James Jr. This would be the chance for them, as mixed-blood men who had served Cass and the federal army as interpreters and scouts, to get large pieces of land. Nor did their father, Judge James V. S. Ryley, intend to be left out. The senior Ryley was a former fur trader who spent about 15 years among the Indians of the Saginaw region. He had retired from the trade about 1800 and now lived in Schenectady, New York. But upon hearing of the planned treaty council at Saginaw, Ryley insisted that the Indians still owed him over $6,000. He figured at 3½ percent interest over the past 19 years, the local Chippewa were indebted to him for just over $10,000.[21]

Of course, the Indians didn't actually have money to reimburse Judge Ryley. But they did have land—fertile land along rivers that would in the near future be valuable to American settlers. Ryley therefore decided to return to Detroit; he told one of Cass's aides that he had important connections and sources of information and could be of great help to the governor at the upcoming treaty council. "I added that if I did go, the Government would have to pay me well," Judge Ryley declared later.

Cass agreed that the senior Ryley could accompany him to Saginaw, but stressed that Ryley wouldn't be allowed to make a claim in the treaty talks with the Indians. "To avoid these embarrassments, I determined to prohibit the attendance at Saginaw of any person who had previously [been] concerned in the Indian trade, and who would not engage to withhold any demands," Cass insisted.[22]

The governor also turned to Louis Campau, the young trader who had established himself at Saginaw during the winter trading seasons since 1815. Clearly, the
governor wasn't holding against Campau the fact he'd led an illegal trading mission to Saginaw at the close of the war in direct violation of the governor's order.
Campau, who was working closely with Astor's American Fur Company, had built
a trading post at Saginaw in 1816, added on to it in 1818, and built a nearby blockhouse in 1819. Many years later, Campau recounted that during that summer of
1819, Colonel Louis Beaufait of the territorial government's Indian Department
showed up at Saginaw with a message: Governor Cass wanted to meet with him.
Campau did as requested this time and journeyed back to Detroit. "He [Cass]
asked me how Indians would feel about a treaty," Campau recounted. "I told him
they were not pleased about it."[23]

Cass conceded that he would have to bring troops with him to Saginaw, and he
mentioned that his Indian interpreters Henry Conner and Beaufait had given him
the idea for a treaty. Campau recognized an opportunity when he saw one; this was
a chance to act as a government contractor as well as an Indian trader. He agreed to
erect buildings for the governor and his men at Saginaw, and also to supply them
with provisions. While in Detroit, Campau also made arrangements to ship a large
quantity of trade goods that he could sell to the hundreds of Indians who would
assemble for the treaty talks.[24]

Cass naturally counted on his own men—that is, fur traders who worked as interpreters, scouts, and soldiers during the war—to act as translators. These included
Conner, a veteran interpreter, and Whitmore Knaggs, the former militiaman and
scout. Conner, who with his brother James had been taken captive while young
and raised by Chippewa, was one of the "interpreters and confidential agents" who
had worked for Governor William Hull back during the 1807 treaty in Detroit.
Whitmore Knaggs's brother, Thomas, had also been one of these interpreter-agents
at that treaty, as was Jacob Smith.[25]

Certainly Cass intended to use every possible influence that he could muster
on the Indians to get a favorable treaty for the United States. But Jacob Smith, who
was still actively trading with the Saginaw area Indians and present at the councils,
had no official job at the proceedings. Was that because Cass and Smith had had
a falling out? Or was it because Smith almost never had an "official" role as he
worked for the United States?

Charles P. Avery, an amateur historian who would write the only major account
of the treaty, but who was not actually there, believed that Governor Cass didn't

completely trust Smith. Avery thought, therefore, that Smith was there strictly as an outsider.[26] Of course, this doesn't jibe with Cass's previous comments about Smith and his abilities in dealing with and influencing the Saginaw Chippewa.

A historian named Edwin Wood, writing in a Genesee County history, believed Smith must have attended the council as a secret agent of influence on the Indians, working once again for the territorial governor. By this reasoning, Smith couldn't influence the Indians from the governor's side of the negotiating table, sitting beside Whitmore Knaggs, James V. S. Ryely, and others who were with Cass in official capacities. Smith could, however, have an impact on the Chippewa if he acted independently of the governor and his aides, counseling the Indians as their friend and advisor. Louis Campau would testify some 40 years later that "the government had a number of men here to influence the Indians outside, but they were not sworn as interpreters." Campau did not name names, but certainly Jacob Smith fit that description.[27]

In any event, Smith was there and his presence would have a major impact on the outcome of the treaty councils.

The Treaty Councils Begin

The invitations to the Indians were made by Cass, and other arrangements for the treaty were set in motion. But complaints about thefts by Indians and incidents of violence on settlers continued around Detroit. By May, the territorial governor was complaining that he needed more soldiers to help keep the peace, and he had roads improved so as to be able to move troops over southeastern Michigan.

The treaty plans went forward, though not always smoothly. Cass worried that summer when the U.S. bank in Chillicothe initially refused to honor a check for over $10,000 for silver he needed for payments due under terms of earlier treaties to Indians of southeastern Michigan. "This draft was destined to pay the annuities due to the Ottawas, Chippeway and Potawatomy Indians which by our treaty stipulations are to be paid in silver," the governor explained to Secretary of War Calhoun. "The failure of payment will injure the publick interest and may affect the result of the proposed treaty at Saginaw." As it turned out, Cass had to raise the money himself from the bank that had been established in Detroit, just a couple of weeks before he was to leave for Saginaw that fall. Eventually the federal government paid for his treaty expenditures.

Other arrangements for the treaty talks were handled by Louis Campau, who left for Saginaw shortly after his meeting with the governor in Detoit. "I went across the country," the ex-trader recalled many years later, "built the council house, rolled in logs for seats, crossed it over with elm and cedar bark [and] built a *crotche* of trees." In court testimony given years afterward, Campau was even more specific about the features of his buildings near the Saginaw River. "I was requested by Cass to come on ahead and make suitable provisions for a store-house and dining room and council room," he said. "There was a long table in the dining room, and the private council was held there—the office and the log buildings were all together, end to end. These were six to eight rods from the room where the grand council room was."[1]

Amateur historian and lawyer Charles P. Avery, who apparently spoke to people like Campau who attended the treaty, described this room as a large, open-sided log structure built along the river. The roof was made of boughs and branches woven together. A foot-high, stage-like platform allowed Cass and his officials to sit on benches above the earthen floor in the center of this hall, while the assembled chiefs and warriors sat on the logs rolled in by Campau's men.

With the buildings completed, Campau went back to Detroit to get goods and supplies. Jacob Smith also had responsibilities in advance of the treaty, including building a bridge over the Cranberry Marsh—Louis Campau said this was the swampy area that lay between Detroit and Royal Oak—so that the governor's party and their packhorses could move more easily through on the way to Saginaw. Smith also rented his trading post/house at Saginaw for the governor's purposes, and the use of his boat to move supplies to the council site.[2]

As the time drew nearer, two ships carrying supplies and a company of soldiers from the U.S. Army's 3rd Infantry Regiment under the governor's brother, Captain Charles L. Cass, left Detroit and sailed to Saginaw Bay. To get to the site of the treaty (now part of the city of Saginaw), the soldiers rowed boats from the bay near the mouth of the Saginaw River, landed on a beach near what is now Essexville in Bay County, and marched along the river more than 10 miles south. They were, of course, present to protect the territorial governor and his party and serve as a living embodiment of U.S. authority.

Even as the traders and soldiers and government aides prepared for the treaty, there was no letup in the rivalry between Jacob Smith and Louis Campau. When two large Mackinac boats bearing Campau's goods arrived at the mouth of the Saginaw River, Smith told the commander of the U.S. revenue schooner *Porcupine*, a man named Captain Keiff, that Campau's shipments were illegal. Smith's word was enough for the officer. "My boats were seized by Keiff as contrary contraband [on] the complaint and interference of Captain Smith at the mouth of the river," Campau said, describing events decades later. The crews tied Campau's hired boats to the schooner *Savage*. Archibald Lyon, a trader who was working for Campau at Saginaw, sent a runner to give their boss the bad news. Campau, who was then at the fledgling community of Pontiac, where a handful of houses had been built on the Saginaw Trail, scrambled to undo Smith's damage.

"I was making the trip [to Saginaw] with Col. Beaufait and the latter [the runner] found me in camp near Pontiac," Campau recounted. "I went back to Detroit, obtained proof of my innocence, came back to Saginaw and demanded the surrender of my goods and they were given up."[3] Letters in the papers of William Woodbridge, the territorial secretary of Michigan, confirm Louis Campau's story. On September 9, 1819, Woodbridge sent a note to Captain Keiff stating that the trader indeed had proper invoices to show his goods were legally imported. A postscript on Woodbridge's note also shows that he did not want trouble for Jacob Smith, perhaps figuring that Campau might strike back at him by making a similar accusation: "P.S. Mr. Jacob Smith has sent up his boat & has himself remained to go by land & has his clearance with him. You will please respect this, not to consider his having no duplicate manifests as sufficient cause of detention, as Mr. Smith has regularly cleared."[4]

The people of Detroit understood as well as fur traders and merchants that if a successful conclusion of a treaty was made between Cass and the Chippewa and Ottawa, the Indians would receive cash and the government would receive land. Some of them had claims of their own and appealed to the governor not to forget them. Dave Henderson, the blacksmith who had worked among the Indians of Saginaw for many years, was now ill. He had his friend, a longtime local officeholder named James McCloskey (also given as McClosky), write a letter to Cass on the day of the governor's departure, outlining how the Chippewa had captured Henderson's family and taken their property at Saginaw back when the War of 1812 began. If the Indians were going to answer for their past actions, then his claim for damages should be among the first considered, Henderson felt. Cass, however, maintained that the treaty talks were no place for such issues to be raised, since land cessions were strictly matters between the tribes and the U.S. government, and not individual whites with claims.[5]

In the meantime, Judge James V. S. Ryley, the former Saginaw fur trader who had three mixed-blood sons of a Saginaw Chippewa woman named Menaw-cumgoqua, left his home in New York state late that summer, making a 10-day trip to Detroit to join Cass and his party. As the preparations for the treaty were being finished at Saginaw, the governor and his men left Detroit on Monday, September 13, heading up the trail on what has been described in some accounts as a three-day journey, first by horseback to the Flint River and then by canoe to Saginaw. Smith, who was also in Detroit, made the trip by the overland route, though whether he traveled with the governor's party or separately isn't known. Judge Ryley, who later made much of his own contribution to the treaty, claimed that he received warm greetings from his old friends, the Chippewa, when the party reached the Flint River and again when they reached Saginaw. Hundreds of Indians were present as the treaty councils were about to begin, with hundreds more arriving as the proceedings got under way. These were Chippewa and their close relatives and cousins, the Ottawa. Cass and his party arrived in Saginaw on what presumably was the afternoon of September 16. He sent his Indian agents to gather at the new council house at 10:00 A.M. the next morning, Louis Campau remembered.[6]

One of the Indians who recognized Judge Ryley was Kishkauko or "the Crow," the Indian leader who lived at Saginaw and had a notorious reputation as a dangerous man who drank too much and had killed the trader Lauzon nearly 20 years before; he had been part of the group that took the Boyer family hostage. "That *Murderer Keis cau kow* told me that he had sent for me and expected that I would aid them in the negotiations," Ryley wrote to Cass, recounting their meeting at Saginaw. "I told him in particular I would see about that, but that he should always consider you as being at the head and that you would do them justice."[7] Now after months of planning by the governor and his men, the treaty councils began.

"The next morning they met at the Council house," Louis Campau testified years later, referring to the assembled Indian leaders and Cass. "The first council was to let them know that he [Cass] was sent by the great father to make a treaty with them, that he wanted to buy their lands, stating the points, and for them to go back and smoke and think about it." The governor did this through his interpreters, though Judge Ryley claimed that he himself "opened the treaty" at the urging of Cass's agents.[8]

It had been a year of some tension and unrest between the parties, and everyone present knew it as the governor's men spoke. Cass and others were sure that British agents across the river from Detroit had been liberally giving presents to the Indians, and U.S. government surveying parties and settlers in Michigan had been threatened by Chippewa men. The Indians knew that American settlers were moving up the Saginaw Trail to the Pontiac area, closer and closer, and that white men had come to see the Saginaw Valley. Though the Indians probably didn't know it at that time, the government's survey of the 1807 cession would ultimately show that the Chippewa leaders had already sold off the southern portion of the Saginaw Valley, in the area of the Flint River and the Grand Traverse.

Campau told interviewer Lyman Draper in 1864 that before Cass arrived at Saginaw, the Chippewa had chosen a chief named Mickchemenequet (also given in the record as "Misheneanonquet" or Black Bird) to speak for the tribe, and also a man Campau said was named "Wen-di-go-insh" or possibly "Nea-di-go-ush." This individual was deaf, the old trader said, "very rough, coarse [and] big, but a good man" who lived on the Tittabawassee River halfway between "the forks" of that river and Saginaw (probably near or in what is Freeland Township). Draper's notes on his interview with Campau indicate it was this man who answered Lewis Cass. But if Campau's memory was correct, then it appears that this chief apparently never signed the resulting treaty, as did scores of other chiefs and head men. Of course, it is possible that Campau was wrong about the name, or that the chief had more than one name, as did some Indians. In any event, this particular name or even an approximation of it doesn't appear among the treaty signers.[9]

"[He] said their great Father the English King had never asked for their lands," the trader said, paraphrasing the speaker's words to Cass. "He [the king of England] has treated us better than you [Americans] have." In response, Campau said, Cass stood up. "Stop that language," the governor admonished the chief; the President of the United States had whipped the English king and he had whipped the Indians, too, Cass reminded them. From the viewpoint of the victor, the Indians' claim on the land was forfeit. Because the United States had beaten them, Cass said, it was entitled to take their land without paying anything at all. While this statement was probably more a bold opening for the U.S. negotiators than it was a direct threat to the Indians, his point was that the British were gone from

Michigan, and that it was generous of the U.S. government to pay for Chippewa land, given the war's outcome.[10]

A moderate chief from the Mt. Clemens area then spoke, Louis Campau remembered, and though he could not recall the chief's name, he was probably referring to The Wing, who had been friendly to the United States. This chief's rhetoric was softer, Campau said.[11] Perhaps the most eloquent answer to Cass came from a young chief speaker named Ogemawkeketo. He was not yet 25, handsome, and about five feet, ten inches tall. His band lived at the place where the Pine River joined the Chippewa and Tittabawassee rivers, Ephraim Williams later claimed, near present-day Midland. It is not clear whether Ogemawkeketo spoke immediately at the conclusion of Cass's opening or one or two days later, after discussions with other chiefs. But at some point he rose and replied to Cass with a speech that could be considered a classic of Native American history.

"Your people trespass upon our hunting grounds," the young leader reportedly said. "You flock to our shores. Our waters grow warm; our land melts like a cake of ice; our possessions grow smaller and smaller; the warm wave of the white man rolls in upon us and melts us away. Our women reproach us. Our children want homes: shall we sell from under them the spot where they spread their blankets? We have not called you here. We smoke with you the pipe of peace." Cass answered Ogemawkeketo: What their women and children needed, the governor replied, was enough land where they could live unbothered by their white neighbors, where they could receive aid and learn how to farm.[12]

Wherever the first break in the talks came, this had not been a promising start for a new treaty, though some of Cass's party apparently sent back letters with a courier to Detroit that made no mention of this. The proprietor of the *Detroit Gazette,* who was sympathetic to Cass and his goals, took these letters as good news and commented on the land the men had seen on their way to Saginaw. "The country, generally, is represented to be delightful, having a first rate soil and possessing a pleasing variety of hill and dale," the journal reported late that month.[13]

A day or so after the start of the talks, Cass also sent a note to Territorial Secretary Woodbridge, expressing confidence. "Our business here has not assumed a shape that will enable me to predict with certainty [the] result. My own opinion however is that it will terminate successfully. The quantity of land which we shall oblige and the amount of the annuity which we shall engage to pay are yet uncertain," the governor wrote. "I trust we shall hear the answer of the Indians tomorrow and close our business in a very few days."[14]

But other accounts say that the developments at Saginaw were far from positive at this point—that they turned ugly and dangerous. According to Louis Campau, the principal Chippewa chiefs were in favor of an agreement with Cass after holding talks amongst themselves, but not all of the leaders known as head men felt the same way; the division ran deep and bitter. Some were extremely angry and vehemently opposed to giving up more land. The next session with Cass and his party, which probably took place on September 19 or 20, was filled with tension and even menace, as those Indians who didn't want to give up more land made their feelings known. "At the second Council there was great difficulty, hard words," Louis Campau later testified. "They threatened General Cass among the rest." Another transcriber of Campau's testimony believed that the old trader said that "all [of the governor's party were] frightened; Gen. Cass among the rest." Either way it was clear that some Chippewa were angry and threatened violence.[15] Judge Ryley claimed that Kishkauko would have probably killed the pro-U.S. chief, The Wing, who was agreeable to the governor's proposals, "had I not prevented it." As this portion of the treaty talks broke up, "the Indians replyed [sic] they would not cede any part of their Territory," Judge Ryley wrote.[16]

This was the low point of the treaty talks, from the view of the representatives of the United States, with negotiations at a standstill and the threat of violence hanging over Saginaw. Campau said there were no more councils for another few days, though it was probably only two or three days at the most, given that the treaty was over by September 24. It was at this deadlock in the talks, according to the account by lawyer-historian Charles Avery, that Jacob Smith entered the picture. Avery believed that Smith "had no position at the treaty, either as an interpreter for, or agent of, Gen. Cass."[17] While there is no record of the discussion or arguments among the Saginaw Chippewa and Ottawa leaders, there were basic factors they probably had to consider. First, the hardliners who threatened violence to Cass and his men may have been confronted with a tough new reality. Yes, there would be no further cession of Chippewa-Ottawa lands in Michigan if they killed the Americans or pro-United States chiefs like The Wing. But harming the governor could also bring a new war, misery, and hardships for their people.

Every chief and warrior there, whether or not he had taken up arms against the United States in the War of 1812, remembered that the curtailing of the fur trade had left their people destitute, as Louis Campau had seen when reopening the Saginaw trade, and as British officers had reported from Malden.[18] Their people had suffered, even though U.S. troops had never set foot in the Saginaw Valley during the war and had not attacked a single encampment or set fire to a village or cornfield. If the warriors at Saginaw overwhelmed the company of soldiers and the governor's men there at the treaty, it would be just the beginning of a new round of bloodshed and hardship for the Chippewa. Perhaps one of the chiefs in favor of a deal with the United States reminded the others that Americans had destroyed crops and burned Indian villages to the ground during the war in the Great Lakes region, and Tecumseh and the British hadn't been able to stop them. To kill or to threaten Cass now was to invite the destruction of the Saginaw tribe.

The British in Canada might wish the United States nothing but bad luck in the Michigan Territory, but there was peace between the war-weary countries now and the redcoats would not be coming back to fight alongside the Indians. While other tribes of the Old Northwest were no more happy about the coming of the American settlers, the Indian confederation put together by Tecumseh had long since broken apart. At the same time, it may have been pointed out to those Chippewa who threatened Cass that Detroit was gaining in population and the military roads from Ohio into Michigan had been improved and so had the Saginaw Road from Detroit, to a point several miles north of Pontiac; American ships could bring cannon and soldiers right to the doorstep of Saginaw itself. It would only be inconvenient, but not impossible, for the United States to make a terrible war on the Chippewa if Cass was harmed.

Those who wanted to sell more land to the United States may have pointed out that although they ceded some territory south of Saginaw, lands along the Flint and Shiawassee rivers remained as of yet unsold, unsurveyed, and unoccupied by American settlers. The nearest white settlement to Saginaw was the fledgling town of Pontiac, some 60 miles away. Those chiefs in favor of selling land may have asked: Were the wishes of those favoring a treaty with Cass to be ignored?

Of course, not all the Indians were warlike or threatening. Neome, a chief of the Flint River band and friend of Jacob Smith, was described in Charles Avery's account as being a key leader in these talks. Neome, he wrote, was "honest and simple-minded . . . by no means astute, firm in his friendships, easy to be persuaded by any benefactor." Only when Smith joined in the discussions that were going on between the governor's agents and Indians did the talks move toward a deal with the United States. "There was a power behind the throne greater than the throne itself," Avery wrote of this moment. "That power rested in the hands of . . . Jacob Smith."[19]

Smith was not mentioned as having a part in the first two council meetings. An Indian named Naugunnee, who witnessed the council talks as a lad but who would testify in court 40 years later, said Smith wasn't even trading there at Saginaw in the fall of 1819. "We-ba-zince [Smith's Indian name, usually spelled as Wabesins or Wahbesins] was a man who had no particular occupation at the treaty," Naugunnee would recall. "He had been an Indian trader, but was not trading at the treaty . . . We-ba-zince was very friendly with Neome."[20]

Though Naugunnee was just a boy then, he was in a position to know about Smith's relationship with Neome since, he said, he was Neome's grandson. A chief described as Neome's younger brother, a leader named Kawgagezhic (also written in court records as Kaukokesik), also testified that Jacob Smith acted as Neome's interpreter. But according to the grandson Naugunee, Smith did more than just interpret for the chief.[21]

Neome, a short, stocky, good-natured man, was probably between 45 and 55 years old at the time of the treaty and slightly stooped with age, Louis Campau recalled. Another who claimed to have been at the treaty was a Chippewa woman named Wabeshewaqua. She would testify years later that Neome had two wives, one named Mutwabuhge and another named Mishquakquahnoquah. This witness said that Neome was "not a great chief," perhaps inferring that he was not fierce or powerful like Kishkauko, but possibly because she understood, so many years later, that the treaty had not been a good thing for the tribe and marked the end for her people's domination of the land.[22]

Neome's grandson Naugunnee, who had lived in what became Lapeer County and then on the Shiawassee River at the time of the treaty, recounted that the Indians did not know how to respond to Cass:

> While Smith and Neome were talking in the evening or in the night at Neome's tent, Smith said to Neome, it will be difficult to secure any place or future home for your children, and Neome said, "I know not what to do in the case," and Neome requested Smith to assist him in trying to get a reservation for his children, and Smith agreed. Smith said that reservations had been made for the band generally, and it would better for him [Neome] to get a special reservation for his children.[23]

Thus Naugunnee, who claimed to be an eyewitness, stated in sworn testimony that he heard Neome asking for Smith's help to get land for his (Neome's) children. Avery's romanticized account claimed, incorrectly, that a proposal for individual reservations, conceived by Smith and requested by Neome, was presented to Whitmore Knaggs and other aides to Governor Cass:

> Not a step of progress was made until Mr. Knaggs and other agents . . . had promised the faithful Neome that, in addition to various and ample reservations for the different bands of several thousand acres each, there should be reserved as requested by Wahbesins (Smith) eleven sections of land of six hundred and forty acres each, to be located at or near the Grand Traverse of the Flint. Eleven names as such reserves, all Indian names, were passed over to Mr. Knaggs on a slip of paper in his tent.[24]

Avery's version of events was accepted in the later nineteenth century histories written about the Saginaw treaty by whites who were not present. But accounts by actual eyewitnesses and participants suggest this matter of reservations on the Flint River wasn't resolved quite so simply and congenially. In reality, witnesses said, it was Smith himself who angrily intervened in the Indians' discussions about these individual sections of land and who should get them.

The incident occurred after the Chippewa and Ottawa leaders had generally agreed to sell land to the government, if their people were guaranteed reservations. Robert A. Forsyth, an aide and private secretary to Governor Cass, about 20 years old at the time of the treaty, later testified that the chiefs met, with no white men present, to discuss which members of their tribe should get individual square-mile reservations, or 640-acre parcels of land. Louis Beaufait, who was an interpreter for Cass, agreed. He said the chiefs specifically called him to their council and "pointed out some of the half breeds"—the children of Chippewa women and fur traders—and instructed him to write their names on a piece of paper.

These mixed-blood individuals were the ones the chiefs wanted to have their own personal reservations of land that fronted on the Flint River in the area of the Grand Traverse, Beaufait said. In essence, the chiefs had made their decision without outsiders present to influence them. One of those reservations was for Francis Boyer, the Indian son of Nicholas Boyer (the man who'd been taken captive with his younger white children back during the war). Three other reservations were for members of a family Beaufait said was named "Sponyard," and one was for the family of a person named "Lapat," who was one-quarter Indian. The name Mokitchenoqua, however—the name that was said to be that of Jacob Smith's Chippewa daughter—was not on that list, the interpreter said.[25]

Louis Beaufait left the chiefs and went back to the cabin that served as the governor's office, where he wrote out the list of these five and other names the Indians had given him. Joseph Marsac, another Indian translator working for the government, would later testify that Beaufait said Jacob Smith entered the room and picked up Beaufait's list, which also included the name of the daughter of the fur trader Bolieu.

Smith noted that his own daughter's name—that is, his half-Chippewa daughter Nancy—wasn't on the list, Forsyth and Beaufait agreed. Forsyth said Smith "seemed dissatisfied and angry" about the fact his daughter had not been included. Marsac, retelling the story as he heard it from Beaufait, said Governor Cass stated that Smith's Indian daughter "ought to have land." The angry Smith then left the governor and his men and headed to the spot where the assembled chiefs were still seated.[26]

Did Smith remind the assembled chiefs of the gifts and favors he had given them, the credit he had extended to them? Did he remind them of promises or agreements they had made with him? Did he bully or threaten them or influence them in some way? There is no record of that. But what happened next is clear: Beaufait and other witnesses said that the names of the individuals who were to receive reservations of land on the Flint River changed. The list that made it into the treaty language—Smith's list—was different from those names first written down by Beaufait at the direction of the assembled Chippewa chiefs.

Forsyth, the private secretary to the governor, later testified in an 1843 lawsuit that Cass's aides and interpreters, Louis Beaufait and Henry Conner, had definitely prepared a list of names of the individuals who were to receive reservations. But the second list of names—the list that Cass accepted—was written by Smith himself. "Jacob Smith handed to the commissioner [Cass] the names of certain persons for whom reservations were to be made," Forsyth said. Others working for Cass and the U.S. government agreed that Smith had taken a direct hand in determining the names on the list. Translator Joseph Marsac said he had heard this directly from Beaufait: It was the names on the second list—Smith's—that were written into in the treaty language as it was approved by the U.S. Congress. What happened to that first list of names, written out by Beaufait? Marsac, testifying decades afterward, said that "the recommendations had got lost during the treaty."[27]

But the lawyer who asked Marsac the question was not satisfied with that answer when the matter went to trial. He asked: "Did Colonel Beaufait at any time state that Jacob Smith stole that first list?"

Marsac did not answer that question with a direct yes or no, but related the circumstances at the treaty as he had heard them from Beaufait: The first list must have been "mislaid or lost," he said. Despite Marsac's careful answer, the lawyer's implication was that Smith had pulled a switch, replacing Beaufait's list from the chiefs with his own.[28] In other words, Smith had taken control of the names of individuals who would receive reservations on the Flint River under the terms of the treaty between the Saginaw Chippewa and the United States.

This would, in the long run, benefit Smith's white children and their spouses. Beaufait would testify in 1845 that a few months after the treaty, Smith showed him a list of at least five names or more, and one of those names was Mo-kitch-e-wee-no-qua (a variation of the name Mo-kitch-e-no-qua). Smith, Beaufait testified, said "that he had done pretty well, at the treaty, or words to that effect;—that he got five sections of land." Beaufait wasn't completely sure of the number, but of course it was known that Smith had five white children. Forsyth agreed that the Indian name of Smith's daughter with a Chippewa woman was on the list of those persons who were to receive a section of land.[29]

Other accounts about Jacob Smith's role at the Saginaw treaty also say he acted as translator for certain chiefs. Neome's younger brother, Kawgagezhic, testified that Neome and two other chiefs, Mixenene and Tondogane, went into Cass's room to speak with him, with Jacob Smith translating for them. "They each stated to Smith what they wanted, and Smith interpreted it to General Cass," Kawgagezhic testified years later. Once the momentum of the talks shifted to striking a deal with the governor and the United States, even the fierce and intimidating Kish-kauko wanted a deal. Kawgagezhic testified that "Kishkauko went, in the night, to the tent without the knowledge of other Indians, to cede the land." In the resulting treaty, Kishkauko would be given 640 acres of land on the east side of the Saginaw River, nearly across from the place where the talks were being held, as well as a nearby island.[30]

Smith wasn't just translating for the chiefs—he was also carefully stage-managing events. The testimony of Chippewa witnesses indicates Smith led these chiefs to believe that he was securing individual sections of land for their full-blooded Indian children, when in the practice of that time, such reservations were typically made for the mixed-blood children—offspring like Smith's daughter Nancy or the Ryley brothers. This controversial question of who was actually supposed to receive individual sections of land by treaty lingered on—it would go to the heart of disputes lasting for decades over land along the Flint River.

Who, then, were the rightful recipients? Were they the full-blooded sons and daughters of the Chippewa chiefs, as some Indians later insisted? Or were they mixed-blood individuals, as Louis Beaufait and other Indian translators testified? Lewis Cass, Louis Campau, and other white men who attended the treaty said individual reservations were never intended for full-blooded Indian children at all, but for the sons and daughters of fur traders and Chippewa women. Cass would inform Secretary of War John C. Calhoun of this fact after the conclusion of the treaty: While the Indians would keep large tracts of thousands of acres of land for tribal reservations, most of the individual reservations of one-square-mile sections were made for the half-Indian offspring of traders and interpreters, such as the children of Colonel Beaufait and Judge Ryley. Ryley's sons each received 640 acres along the Saginaw River. "I do recollect that your Excellency called them in and told them to make the first choice in the *Saginaw* country, of a section of land each," James V. S. Ryley wrote later about his sons.[31]

Decades later, other white witnesses in a lawsuit over one of these sections of land on the Flint also testified that the individual reservations were intended for mixed-blood children of white traders. One witness, John B. Truedell (whose name is also given in records as Jean Baptiste Truedell), said that he learned this from both Jacob Smith and Louis Campau after the treaty. "They told me that all the half breeds got each a section of land," Truedell said.[32]

Yet Chippewa individuals who were at the treaty understood these sections of lands were being reserved for specific Indian children, including the daughters of Mixenene and Neome. One witness was Kawgagezhic (or, as it was alternately spelled, Kaukokesik), who said he was Neome's brother. He testified that Neome specifically requested reservations for his children and that these children, and other full-blooded Indian children, were presented to Cass.

Another of the witnesses, George Wainjegezhic, believed that he had been around 10 to 12 years old at the time of the Saginaw treaty. "I remember there was a great reserve made at Mus-ca-da-wain [also given as Muscatawing] for the children," Wainjegezhic said, "and one at Pe-wa-na-go-wink for the band." Muscatawing, it will be recalled, was a place on the Flint River, not far from where Jacob Smith set up one of his trading posts at the Grand Traverse; Pewaunaukee was the Chippewa village sometimes called Neome's town, located down the river near modern Montrose, where Smith also traded. And Sagosequa, Neome's youngest daughter, testified that she heard her father request reservations of land at Musca-tawing for herself, her two siblings, and other Indian children.[33]

Governor Cass apparently wanted some sort of proof of the identities of these individuals whose names were to be written into the treaty to receive section-sized reservations of land. There was good reason for this. Cass "suggested that the children should be brought forward to whom the land was being reserved, that he should see them," Naugunnee testified in 1860. "The crowd made room for the children to come in, and the children came forward and their names were taken; the names were given in and Neome and Jacob Smith stood together and gave in Ah-won-non-wa-to-qua and Taw-cum-e-go-qua and the others."[34] Ahwononwa-toqua, whose name was also given as Annonketoqua or Annokitoqua, was the eldest of Neome's daughters, while the Tawcumegoqua was described as a young daughter of Mixenene.

Cass would later testify that he didn't recollect being introduced to a group of Native children during the treaty talks, though at least one letter from the government's land office in Detroit indicates that Cass acknowledged this hap-pened.[35] But at least several Indians who said they were at the treaty gave testimony similar to Naugunnee—that a group of children was definitely presented to Cass as Jacob Smith and Neome looked on. One of the witnesses, a woman named Kazheobeonoqua, testified years later that Smith took one of Neome's children, a son, and led him forward to meet Cass. Smith, she said, described the boy as his own child.

Kazheobeonoqua, who said she was about 17, of mixed blood, and lived at Saginaw at the time of the treaty, claimed that Smith was "not a great favorite with the Indians" and that he "took not much part" in the proceedings. Of course, there is plenty of evidence to the contrary and it should be noted that Kazheobeonoqua at one time was married to fur trader Archibald Lyon, who worked for Smith's arch-rival, Louis Campau. But Kazheobeonoqua did say that Smith lived in a tent during the treaty sessions and that she saw him there each day. She also described how Smith brought Mixenene's young daughter Tawcumegoqua into the council during the discussions "to get land."[36]

Tawcumegoqua was dressed in calico, "a long dress and pantalets and smoked skin for moccasins" for presentation to the governor, the witness remembered. "Neome's children were dressed the same way, and Smith took the whole of them forward to Gen. Cass and tried to get land for them and the boy," Kazheobeonoqua said. "And the boy was taken forward, and Smith said *this is my boy*" (emphasis added). Other Indian witnesses confirmed this. One account was given in a deposition, from a woman named Nowchigoma. "For what reason was land reserved for Mixene's child when the band they belonged to had a general reservation?" an attorney asked her. "*Because Jacob Smith borrowed and adopted the child as his child and asked for land,*" Nowchigoma replied. "*Jacob Smith borrowed the child and said this is my child.*"[37]

Louis Campau's later testimony indicates he heard that four or five Indian children were introduced as Jacob Smith's, and that he knew Smith paid Indian women for the use of their names so that they could be written into the treaty terms for Smith's white children. Campau, like other white witnesses who were present, thought the sections of land were truly intended for mixed-blood individuals. Thus the totality of the testimony of the Chippewa witnesses showed that Jacob Smith presented Indian children to the governor, declaring some of them his own son and daughters, and this version of events was supported by Louis Campau. The Indians who testified about it later said they believed Smith was lining up individual reservations for specific full-blooded Chippewa children, including Neome's two daughters, his son named Ogibwok, about 15, and a grandson named Metawanene.[38]

Smith had effectively taken control of the list of individuals who would receive reservations on the Flint River. Then he had brought forth for Cass a number of Indian children, introducing them as the individuals who were to receive these reservations, calling some of them his own children, as if they were mixed-blood offspring. But these were strictly deceptions on Smith's part. The fur trader had even more tricks up his sleeve as the council continued.

Saginaw
1819

Influenced and advised by fur trader Jacob Smith, who was working secretly for Michigan Territorial Governor Lewis Cass, Chippewa and Ottawa leaders in the fall of 1819 ceded 4.3 million acres of land stretching from a corner of Kalamazoo County north to the headwaters of the Thunder Bay River, and across south central Michigan to the tip of the Thumb. This cession included the sites of the future cities of Lansing, Saginaw, Midland, Bay City, Mt. Pleasant, Frankenmuth, Chesaning, Alpena, Richland, Hastings, Eaton Rapids, Ionia, Alma, St. Johns, Clare, Montrose, Tawas, Oscoda, Vassar, and Bad Axe. In time, Smith's children would also win for themselves and their spouses individual sections of land along the Flint River that they said tribal leaders wanted them to have.

According to Flint courthouse lore, fur trader Jacob Smith and his son Albert are depicted in this imaginative scene, as they visit the local chief, Neome, at the crossing, or "Grand Traverse," of the Saginaw Trail at the Flint River. In fact, Neome's village was located several miles to the northwest, near the Genesee-Saginaw County line, though the Chippewa had for years set up camps, raised corn, and buried their dead near the ford, where Smith built a trading post. Albert visited the crossing with his father in the early 1820s, when he was nine or ten years old. Detail from a mural painted by Edgar S. Cameron in 1925, Circuit Courtroom No. 3, Genesee County Courthouse, Flint.

Heroic community leader and educator in Detroit during Jacob Smith's lifetime, Catholic priest Father Gabriel Richard was concerned about the terrible effect on Indians of alcohol they received in the fur trade. He knew the Indians resented that land purchased from them at low prices by the government was in turn sold at much higher prices to settlers and speculators.

The first federal governor of the Michigan Territory, William Hull employed Jacob Smith as an emissary, courier, and agent of influence on the Saginaw Chippewa up to the start of the War of 1812, including the effort that resulted in the 1807 Treaty of Detroit. This picture is based on a formal oil portrait by Gilbert Stuart.

A judge of Detroit's court of common pleas, English-born James May sold Jacob Smith the property which was his family's home and his base of operations for years to come. The house was located at the intersection of what would become Woodward Avenue and Woodbridge Street, and the transaction was recorded in June 1807.

Arriving in Detroit in 1805, eccentric federal judge Augustus Woodward heard the first of many lawsuits involving Jacob Smith and other fur traders. Smith was sometimes a juror in Woodward's court, but he also was often witness and party in lawsuits.

Michigan's second territorial governor, Lewis Cass continued to employ Jacob Smith as a soldier and unofficial agent to influence the Chippewa to end hostilities in the War of 1812 and to cede more than four million acres of land in the 1819 Treaty of Saginaw. This portrait shows Cass in the 1820s.

A rival of Jacob Smith's in the fur trade, Louis Campau was only 23 when he was arrested by Smith, then a captain of the territorial militia, as Campau headed a legally suspect trading mission to Saginaw early in 1815. Since Campau was not carrying any contraband when he reached the Flint River (his party had divided the contraband goods among themselves rather than leave any with him), Smith had to let Campau go free. They remained at odds for years.

Another of the federal judges for the Michigan Territory sent from the East, James Witherell also heard many cases involving Jacob Smith. Witherell was a commander in the territorial militia in which Smith served in the War of 1812. His son, B. F. H. Witherell, wrote historical articles about Michigan residents and their experiences, including the account of Smith's riding to Saginaw to redeem children taken for ransom by Chippewa warriors.

Chief of an Ottawa-Chippewa band that lived on the Red Cedar River, Okemos attended the councils at Saginaw in 1819 and was a signer of the resulting treaty with Lewis Cass. He later testified that his home was then a few miles from what became the city of Lansing, and that he was "about 50" at the time of the treaty.

An imaginative scene by artist Percy Ives depicted Governor Lewis Cass addressing the Chippewa in a treaty council in the fall of 1819, with an American soldier, the flag, and a seemingly buckskin-clad white man standing next to him. Ives's portrayal of the governor appears to be based on a portrait of Cass painted later in his life. Of course, Cass addressed the Indians through translators who spoke the Chippewa dialect.

In a bold script and again with a lighter touch, the controversial fur trader signed his name twice on the title page of a book of which only a fragment remains. It is one of a few surviving artifacts and documents that Jacob Smith's heirs retained before donating these items to a local museum.

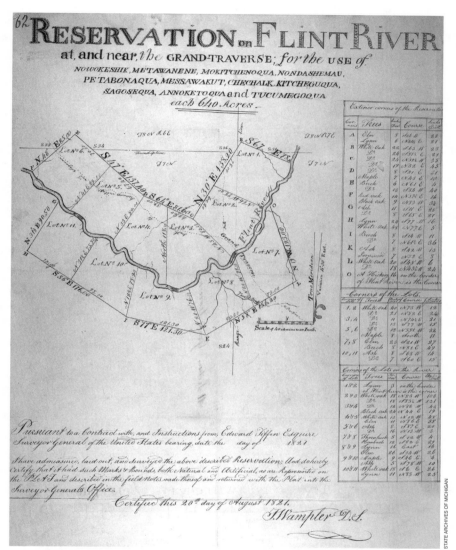

In the summer of 1821 government surveyors went to Jacob Smith's trading post at the Grand Traverse to mark off the individual sections of the "Smith Reservation," and other parts of the Saginaw Valley. Notes by surveyors show they thought the land was good, though that fall the Chippewa chiefs briefly blocked the surveyors when they tried to cross to the west side of the Saginaw River. Smith acted as their guide and interpreter, and helped resolve the confrontation.

LYNCHBURG MUSEUM SYSTEM

Career U.S. Army officer, Virginia native, and husband of Jacob Smith's oldest daughter Harriet, John Garland started the effort by the Smith heirs to claim sections of land along the Flint River—land they said had been granted to them by the Chippewa chiefs. Garland served at different army outposts over the course of his career, including Detroit and Saginaw.

SLOAN MUSEUM

SLOAN MUSEUM

Jacob Smith's daughter Louisa was a teenager in 1824 when she married merchant and jeweler Chauncey Payne, who had arrived in Detroit after the War of 1812. Louisa, her siblings, and their spouses maintained they had been granted land under their Chippewa names in the Treaty of Saginaw and they ultimately won the long legal battle for those sections of land they claimed.

After the death of Jacob Smith's wife in 1817, Smith's youngest daughter, Maria, was raised by her oldest sister, Harriet, and Harriet's husband John Garland. Maria eventually married Thomas B. W. Stockton, who with his brothers-in-law, Garland and Chauncey Payne, carried on the Smith heirs' political and legal fight for the land they said had been granted them in the 1819 treaty. Stockton was an army officer, engineer, and businessman. This portrait of him was made during the Civil War.

Businessman and politician Ephraim Williams went into the fur trade as a young man, and with his brother influenced, or pressured, Chippewa chiefs in 1835 to support the claims of Smith's white children—that they were named in the Saginaw treaty to get sections of land on the Flint River. Williams helped pave the way for Congress to change the law on the Smith heirs' behalf. Williams and his brother changed their position on the matter after they went unpaid for their efforts, and they challenged the legitimacy of the claims of Smith's children for years afterward.

Traveling up the Saginaw Trail in the summer of 1831, Alexis de Tocqueville and his friend Beaumont, guided by a local Indian youth, stopped to rest on their way from the Flint River to the Chippewa community and trading center, Saginaw. Beaumont sketched the scene and created this picture from his sketch, depicting a time when practically no white settlers had yet penetrated this wilderness.

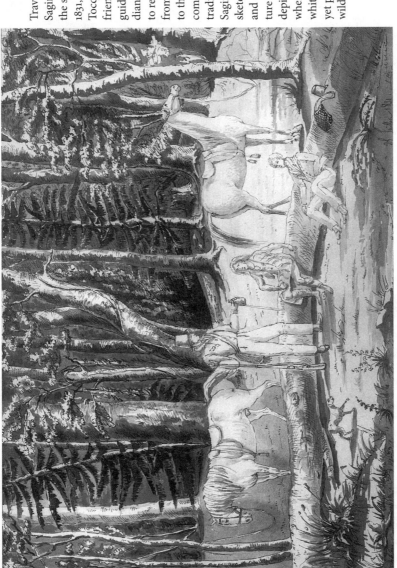

He Was Smart as Steel

I t didn't take long for the interpreters and aides of Gov. Lewis Cass to realize what Jacob Smith was up to by the time the final treaty council was held at Saginaw. Smith, they warned, was trying to have Indian names for his white children written into the treaty provisions that granted section of land for individuals.[1]

Smith's intervention on the question of who was to receive reservations on the Flint River probably seemed reasonable at first, for the governor's men knew Smith had a daughter, Nancy, with a Chippewa woman who had lived near the mouth of the Clinton River at Lake St. Clair; Smith had objected, in the presence of Cass, when he saw she wasn't on the chiefs' list of mixed-blood individuals who were to receive a section of land. Witnesses said that Cass himself agreed that Smith's Indian daughter should get land, as certain other sons and daughters of white fathers and Chippewa women had been picked to receive sections.

Of course, the governor's men also understood that Smith took charge of the list of those who were to receive individual reservations. Chippewa witnesses said Smith introduced to Cass several Indian children as the persons who were to get that land, apparently to allay any suspicions on the part of the governor and the

Indians, too, about what he was up to. And Smith had met with Chippewa chiefs and the governor, apparently to translate their requests and demands in the negotiations.

In reality, Smith was maneuvering to get what would become valuable riverfront land for his *white* children. Cass later wrote that his aides brought the matter to his attention: While Smith did indeed have a half-Chippewa daughter, his other children in Detroit—his son and daughters with Mary Smith—were white. Cass had met Mrs. Smith before she died, and he had been introduced to her children, so he knew this was true and he would testify to it years later. But these white children had been given Indian names by their father's Chippewa friends, the governor's men said. They warned Cass that Smith was attempting to have Indian names of his white children written into the treaty provisions so they could, in time, claim reservations of land on the Flint River.[2]

Did the chiefs of the Saginaw Chippewa truly want Smith's white children to receive reservations? Did they watch Smith introduce several Indian children to the governor and understand this was just a deception so Cass would think that they were Smith's mixed-blood sons and daughters? A government official in Detroit maintained in 1822 that Cass wrote a letter in which he called this action "fraud." Yet, in time, the governor and his men also stated that the chiefs really did intend for Smith's white children to get land.[3]

"I have been requested to state the facts connected with the reservation of eleven sections of land at Flint River, made under the treaty of Saginaw, so far as respects any interest held therein by the children of Jacob Smith," Cass later wrote in a letter from Detroit, dated June 22, 1831, to the Indian Department in Washington. "At the time this reservation was made, I understood that the Indians intended that a number of the sections—I believe five or six—should be granted to the children of Smith, and the names given by them as the grantees were said to be his children."

"From circumstances not necessary to detail here," he continued, "I was led to suspect that Smith designed [i.e., planned to get] the land for his white children, and that most of the names purporting to be those of his Indian children were, in fact, the names of his white children, which the Indians—who were in the habit of frequenting his house—had given to them."[4] In referring to "his house," Cass meant Smith's home in Detroit at the corner of Woodbridge and Woodward.

Louis Campau agreed that Smith was trying to get land for his white children, and that he understood Smith had brought forward Chippewa children in order to accomplish this. He testified in later years that he heard "four or five little Indian children mentioned, who were intended [presented] as Jacob Smith's legitimate children" at the treaty. Campau, too, felt that the individual reserves called for at the treaty were actually intended for the mixed-blood sons and daughters of fur traders and Indian women. "I understood they were for half-breeds," Campau said of the reservations, "but there were three or four Indian women who lent their names to Jacob Smith."⁵ Here was another witness testifying that Smith used Chippewa children and names to show the governor the individuals who should get land, but that this was just a ruse so that Smith's white children could claim land.

Of course, Lewis Cass knew in 1819 that, according to the U.S. policy, Indian treaties could not grant reservations of land to individual whites, but only sell their land to the government and the government alone. The governor therefore had a simple solution to deal with Smith's scheme. "To guard against the consequences of this attempt, I therefore inserted into the article providing for these reservations a clause confining them to persons of Indian descent," Cass wrote. "I have an indistinct recollection that one young girl was spoken of as the Indian daughter of Smith, but cannot remember her name." That girl, of course, was Nancy, who some said had the Native name of Mokitchenoqua. By writing those words into the treaty—that the Flint River land was to be reserved for individuals who were "all Indians by descent"—Cass believed he had made sure Jacob Smith's white children in Detroit couldn't claim any of these reservations.⁶

Article 3 of the treaty is where those 11 Indian names Smith had written out appeared, with the provision that each of the people listed was to receive 640 acres of land "to be located at and near the grand traverse of the Flint River in such matter as the President of the United States may direct." Those names were Nowokeshik; Metawanene; Mokitchenoqua; Nonda-Shemau; Petabonaqua; Messawwakut; Checbalk; Kitchegeequa; Sago-sequa; Annonketoqua, and Tawcumegoqua. The land set aside and marked off along the river near the Grand Traverse would collectively become known as "the Smith Reservation."⁷

Jacob Smith probably didn't know that Cass inserted those qualifying words "all Indians by descent" into the text of Article 3, for the fur trader was sure he succeeded in getting reservations for his five white children, Harriet, Caroline, Louisa, Albert, and Maria. Only two years or so after the treaty was approved by Congress, 11 sections for the individuals with those Indian names were laid out by government surveyors along the Flint River, extending west and slightly east from the Grand Traverse. Smith would tell friends and acquaintances that his children's land lay on the north side of the river, the side where his trading post–cabin was located.

Louis Beaufait, the veteran interpreter and officer who worked on the treaty for Cass, said that Smith showed him a list of at least five names a few months after the treaty; Smith said that he had "got a section of land for each [of his children], and that he had done pretty well at the treaty, or words to that effect." Other Saginaw traders, like John B. Truedell, agreed that Smith believed he had managed to get a section of land for each of his white children. Smith also discussed the identities of some of the others who were supposed to receive the other six sections on the river, these witnesses would state.[8]

Years later, in making their claims to five sections on the Flint River, Jacob Smith's white children would insist that the Indians at the Saginaw treaty council fully intended and understood that these reservations were for them. These heirs would say that Metawanene was Albert Smith; Messawwakut was Harriet Garland; that Annokitoqua (or Annonketoqua) was Louisa Payne; that Nondashemau was Maria Stockton; and that Sagosequa was Caroline Smith, who would die before 1835. The Chippewa, they would argue, had asked for these reservations for them as a favor to their father.[9]

Yet the author could find no evidence in the surviving Michigan land records, court records, and depositions about the Saginaw treaty to support this claim— no place where individual, identified Chippewa chiefs or head men flatly stated on the record or testified, "Yes, I wanted Jacob Smith's white children to receive reservations of land." Some officials would write that chiefs with whom they met in groups later maintained this was the case, but these statements were recorded indirectly and generally by white U.S. government officials, without specific, direct attribution to tribal leaders. In the mid-1830s, a group of Chippewa leaders did sign a statement at Saginaw saying it was the intention of the chiefs in 1819 to grant sections of land to Smith's white children, but this was a statement the Indians were pressured to make, an old fur trader named Ephraim Williams would admit decades later; the leaders of Chippewa bands at other villages throughout the area then followed suit, agreeing that it had been their intention to grant land to Smith's children.[10]

Of course, the other view of what happened at the 1819 treaty in regard to these reservations came from multiple Chippewa individuals who lived long enough to give testimony in lawsuits that followed. They told of witnessing Jacob Smith introducing full-blooded Chippewa children at the treaty, and that they believed these were individuals who would receive sections of land. Consider that Smith's friend, Neome, actually had daughters named Annonketoqua, who was grown, and Sagosequa, 10 or 12 years old—the same names that had supposedly been given to Smith's daughters Louisa and Caroline. Did Neome really intend for two of Smith's white children to have sections of land, rather than his own daughters? Had Jacob Smith manipulated the Indians, specifically his friend Neome, even as he tried to trick the governor? That scenario can't be discounted. Yet years later— after settlers had come to the Flint River and settled a town and established farms and mills—some of the governor's men such as Forsyth and Marsac testified that the Indians truly wanted Smith's white children to have land.

Was this strictly a coverup, a *fait accompli?* Consider that Judge James V. S. Ryley, who had his own axe to grind about his failed plan to get a large grant of land, claimed that the vast majority of Indians attending the councils had no idea what was spelled out in the provisions of the treaty. He said that his sons were very unhappy with the terms, though they themselves were granted sections along the Saginaw River in the treaty. "The meaning of the different articles in said Treaty was hard for the most part of the people present to understand," Judge Ryley insisted. "I knew that not one out of fifty of the natives understood the meaning and after the treaty was signed there was contentions [sic] about the meaning. . . ." Ryley claimed that there was discontent when the Indians finally understood the terms of the treaty.[11]

Another of the veteran interpreters for the government, Joseph Marsac, ad- mitted later that he heard about the controversy over the Flint River reservations, something clearly reflected in government documents in the 1820s. "Afterwards I heard there was trouble about it and they got somebody to make an investigation," he said. Who conducted the investigation he didn't say, but nothing seems to have come of it, other than the insistence by federal land officials, initially, that patents for those sections couldn't be issued to white individuals.[12] By 1835 Marsac acted as an interpreter at meetings where head men and chiefs were asked to confirm the claims of Smith's white children that they were the rightful recipients of five of the sections.

Cass himself wrote a letter in 1822 to the U.S. Treasury Department where he explained that he was concerned about what had happened at the treaty. Though that specific document apparently doesn't survive in federal records, the governor's feelings were repeated in a letter written by John Biddle, the register of the federal land office in Detroit, to his superiors in Washington, D.C. Biddle wrote that Cass had "suspicions of fraud haveing [sic] been practised at the Treaty by attributing to certain white persons Indian names & producing Indian children as the persons in whose favour the grants or reservations were made."[13] Of course, the court records and transcriptions of the testimony of Chippewa witnesses who were at the treaty show only one man introduced Indian children to Cass, and that was Jacob Smith.

Still, for all these statements and concerns about fraud, in the years after the 1819 treaty, when men like Cass and Marsac and others were questioned about what had happened, they would routinely reply that Smith was "a man of influence over the Indians." A Detroit attorney who worked closely with the Saginaw Chippewa on the matter of their outstanding debts wrote in the late 1830s that the head men of the tribe told him that the reason for the grants of land to Smith's children "was on account of their friendship for Smith, and his kinship to them, and particularly to one of the principal chiefs of the tribe."[14]

That chief, of course, was Neome. Had Neome been Smith's unwitting dupe, or was he the close friend and confidant in this effort by Smith to get land for his heirs? Even those who would choose to take the position that Neome must have intended Jacob Smith's white children to get land still have to admit that the fur trader had schemed, deceived, and manipulated people and events to get his way. Even as the talks wrapped up that fall in 1819, Smith wasn't yet finished with his machinations.

Some eight days after the first council began at Saginaw, the terms, wording, and boundaries of the new treaty were finalized by Cass's aides. Surveys would show that the southwestern edge of the Indians' land cession took in the northeast corner of present-day Kalamazoo County. From there, the cession's western boundary line ran at a slight northeasterly angle across most of the Lower Peninsula to the headwaters of the Thunder Bay River and along the river to Lake Huron. That marked the northern limit of the cession. The lower eastern edge of this huge tract was a line running north from the area of present-day Jackson on through Ingham County, and then at an angle across Shiawassee County to Lake Huron, to a point in the upper portion of the Thumb. In terms of modern Michigan, this cession included all of 12 counties; more than half of eight more counties; and parts of nine other counties. It included half or more of the Lake Huron coastline and the sites of what would become the cities of Lansing, Saginaw, Midland, Bay City, Mt. Pleasant, Frankenmuth, Chesaning, Alpena, Richland, Hastings, Eaton Rapids, Ionia, Alma, St. Johns, Clare, Montrose, Tawas and Oscoda, Vassar, and Bad Axe. Cass estimated this land at six million acres but a more accurate and modern calculation said the cession amounted to 4,321,280 acres.[15]

For this the Indians were to receive an annual payment of $1,000 into perpetuity; they were also to receive the services of a blacksmith, and also cattle, farming equipment, and teachers to show them the white men's ways of agriculture. Just how much was to be spent on these things was left up to the president of the United States. Cass estimated in a letter to Secretary of War John C. Calhoun that providing these items and services to the Indians would cost between $1,500 and $2,500 a year.[16] The Indians would be entitled to hunt on the cession as long as it remained public land, and the treaty spelled out over 100,000 acres in various reservations around the region for the tribes, including many of their existing villages and camping places, such as Neome's Town and Kishkabawee on the Flint River, Big Rock and Ketchewondaugoning ("the Grand Saline") on the Shiawassee, and other tracts from the Saginaw and Tittabawassee to the Au Sable. Though the government hoped Cass could convince the Indians to move out of Michigan, the Chippewa weren't interested in going to the west. They had long-standing tribal enemies there, and Cass did not press the matter. Kishkauko (given as "Kawkawiskous, or the Crow") was written into the treaty terms to receive a section of land on the east side of the Saginaw River.[17]

Late in the afternoon of September 24, 114 chiefs and head men signed, or more properly, affixed to the treaty their signature-clan symbols, or totems, or made an X by their names as written out by the governor's men. William Webber, an attorney practicing law in Michigan about the time of the Civil War, thought this explained why the name of Smith's close friend, Neome, didn't appear as a signer of the treaty. The name "'Reaume' signed to the treaty [was] doubtless intended for 'Neome,'" Webber wrote.[18]

The Flint River village called Pewaunaukee or Neome's Town, was therefore misspelled "Reaum's Village." It was an easy mistake for the governor's men to make, since there had been a family by that name in the region at that time, some of whom were traders and one who was a U.S. Indian agent. Smith's friend Neome put an X by his misspelled name. Ogemawkeketo and Kawgagezhic, said to be Neome's brother, appeared as signatories, their names spelled slightly differently from those given here. The names of other chiefs who had dealings with Smith at the treaty, Mixenene and Tondogane, appear as "Mixabee" and "Fonegawne." These men also made their marks on the document.

Now it was time for the Indians to receive their first payment from the U.S. government. "After the treaty was signed, the silver was counted out upon the table in front of Cass for distribution," Louis Campau would recount. In court testimony, he recalled that this money was half-dollar coins, an initial payment, according to some accounts, of $3,000. It was probably everything Campau could do to keep from grinning at the sight of the stacks of silver, for the Indians owed him for supplying them with food and other items. "All the chiefs had given me their word . . . that I should get $1,500," Campau said.[19]

Yet that "agreement" was neither settled nor certain. Cass addressed the chiefs and the head men directly: "The money is for you," the governor said to the Indians, according to Campau, "but if you want to pay the trader that amount, then say so and it's all right." Unfortunately for Campau, there were other traders there, including Conrad TenEyck, John Truedell, Jacques Godfroy, and of course his old rival, Jacob Smith. "It did not please them to see so much money go to me," Campau said. "They crowded around Jake Smith to get him to work the Indians to object."[20]

Smith spoke to Kishkauko, the troublesome chief who allegedly had been drunk and uninvolved in the previous treaty councils, yet who was to receive his own personal section of land in the treaty terms. Now prompted by Smith, Kishkauko stood and said he was speaking on behalf of his fellow Indians. "They want their money in hand," Kishkauko said to Cass. "They are your children."

Louis Campau watched the money the chiefs had promised him disappear as Cass announced that the silver would go directly to the Indians. Campau, who was physically large and probably much bigger than the slight Jacob Smith, was furious. "I got out of temper when the Governor said it would be paid to them," Campau said later. "I jumped over a log and struck Smith two blows. He was smart as steel and I was not slow." But others jumped up and stopped this from turning into a brawl. Barney Campau grabbed his nephew while Cass's men, Beaufait and Conner, separated the rival traders. "The money went to the Indians," Louis Campau said. "They did not hand any to me." Perhaps Smith's pain was lessened by the satisfaction of having just cost Campau the sum of $1,500.[21]

Despite the fact he had punched Smith, Campau's anger was not allayed and was still smoldering. "Five barrels of whiskey were opened by the United States Quartermaster for the Indians," Campau said. Though certainly destructive to them individually and as a community, the alcohol was a kind of payoff, a token or reward of the government's appreciation for the treaty agreement. Campau claimed he got even with Cass for allowing the Indians to get their money without paying him by giving the governor a tremendous scare that night by making this drunken party even worse. "I ordered ten of mine opened and two men to stand with dippers at the open barrels." He told his men to charge the Chippewa a dollar per gallon of whiskey yet, he said, "they got awful drunk."

At 10:00 P.M., the first of three aides to the governor appeared—Robert A. Forsyth, who was acting as one of the U.S. treaty commissioners, came to Campau. "Gen. Cass says stop the liquor," Forsyth ordered. "I shall not," Campau curtly replied. "He commenced it." As the drinking continued, Indian subagent Gabriel Godfroy appeared on the scene and then interpreter Louis Beaufait, bringing soldiers to surround Campau's post. The merchant trader decided then to change to cost of the whiskey, possibly lowering the charge for the alcohol to aggravate Cass. Campau said he "told Jim Riley give notice it was 44 [cents?] per gallon." He continued:

> Soon after some of the Indians from the Bay were coming to my shanty. A soldier pointed his bayonet and in the scuffle the Indian was stabbed in the thigh. He gave the war-whoop & in fifteen minutes the quarters were surrounded by excited Indians. They came in from all quarters.[22]

Campau said Cass appeared—in a published account he described the governor as "looking very grotesque with a red bandana handkerchief tied about his head," though that description didn't appear in his 1864 account to Lyman Draper. Cass reportedly shouted, "Louis, Louis, we shall all be killed! Stop the liquor, Louis!" Draper's notes from his interview reflect that Campau replied that the governor had started it, and that he told the governor and his men that they had "plundered" him. But in Charles Avery's version of the same event, Campau specifically blamed Jacob Smith. Avery quoted Campau: "I said to him, General, you commenced it; you let Smith plunder and rob me but I will stand between you and harm."[23]

The trader and the governor's men managed to calm the excited warriors. "I lost my money; I lost my fight; I lost my liquor," Campau said after the fact. "But I got good satisfaction." James V. S. Ryley also mentioned in his summation of events at the treaty that the Indians got drunk that night. Before the sun was up the next morning, the governor and his men were on their way back to Detroit.[24]

Five days later, on September 30, Cass wrote to Secretary of War Calhoun, informing him of the conclusion of the treaty with the Chippewa and its terms. The governor claimed he had tried to strike a fair deal rather than simply get lots of land at the lowest possible cost, and he felt sure the president and Calhoun would agree. "The great moral debt, which we owe them, can only be discharged by patient forbearance, and by rigid adherence to that system of improvement, which we have adopted, and the effects of which are already felt in this quarter," Cass wrote, referring to efforts to teach Indians the settlers' way of farming. Yet Cass was sure that as more white settlers came, the Indians would not remain in Michigan. "When they are surrounded by our settlements and brought in contact with our people," the governor noted, "they will be more disposed to migrate."[25]

Cass made no mention of the tense and threatening deadlock in negotiations with the Chippewa and Ottawa, or how it was finally broken; he said nothing at all about Jacob Smith. He did mention the land that had been set aside for the Indians. "Reservations have also been made for a few half breeds," the governor wrote. "It was absolutely necessary to our success, that these should be admitted into the treaty."

A supplementary article to the treaty requested by the Chippewa granted land to Dr. William Brown of Detroit, who had always provided medical service to Indians, and five other white people, including former captives (now translators and scouts) Henry and James Conner, to whom the Indians wanted to also provide reservations.[26] But this supplementary article was rejected by Congress when the Saginaw treaty came before it for approval in 1820, on the grounds that an Indian treaty could not reserve land for individual whites. Yet because of the actions of Jacob Smith, his heirs would manage to create for themselves a controversial exception to this rule in the years ahead.

Then was Smith really the ace up Lewis Cass's sleeve, the man who counseled, suggested, influenced, and even manipulated his friends among the Chippewa to make this treaty with the U.S. government? The answer is yes, and the proof of it rests in Cass's record of his expenditures for the Treaty of Saginaw. In a careful description to the U.S. government about his expenses and disbursements in relation to Indian affairs, the territorial governor recorded the payments, or vouchers, he made to tradesmen, interpreters, Indian agents, and for the purchase of gifts given to certain Indians.

Of course, Jacob Smith's name appears as having been paid for doing different sorts of routine work. For example, Cass paid Smith $28 for transporting provisions by boat for the councils and $30 for building that bridge over the Cranberry Marsh. Smith received $40 "for a horse delivered to an Indian," a present from Cass to one of the Chippewa—one of many such gifts made to smooth the way for the treaty. But the single biggest payment Jacob Smith received from Cass was $500 "for services during the summer, in relation to the treaty at Saginaw." The governor would follow that payment to Smith in less than three weeks with another payment of $104. Cass entered this payment under the heading "For treaty at Saginaw" and described the payment as being "for services in the Indian country, ninety-four days, 94.00; use of his house for the Indians, 10.00." In sum, Smith, who was neither an official government interpreter nor Indian agent, received nearly $600 for his "unofficial" work on behalf of the treaty.[27] That is roughly the equivalent of more than $10,000 today.

That was not all Cass had to say about his payments for Smith's services. In a message dated November 9, 1821, in which he explained certain expenditures and payments made for the treaty, the territorial governor revealed that Smith had been working on the Indians for weeks if not months before the treaty "This charge is for the sum of $500 paid Jacob Smith," Cass wrote, "an influential man among the Indians, for his services in the summer of 1819, in relation to the Saginaw treaty."[28] Here, then, is the proof that Smith was working, again, as a confidential agent of influence for the U.S. government.

Did Smith simply give the Indians presents and generously see to their needs so that they were in his debt when he counseled them to accept a deal to give up land for the government? Had he quietly bribed key Chippewa and Ottawa leaders to look favorably on a cession of land? Had he tricked them so that his white children would be written into the treaty as recipients of property that would in time become valuable? The answers to the questions may be more complicated than one might suppose. Richard White, author of *The Middle Ground* about relations between whites and Algonquin peoples in the Great Lakes region up until the time of the War of 1812, noted that the giving and sharing of presents was expected and practiced in Indian communities, and that various officials of the French and British governments and armies had been surprised to find that gift-giving didn't necessarily buy or compel loyalty or obedience from Indian individuals or leaders. To the Indians, a gift was a gift, a favor, but not a bribe. Whether white or Indian, a man who was considered by the Algonquin people to be a friend or a good leader was expected to be generous, liberal, giving, and forgiving; those who had the good fortune to come into plenty were expected to share with others in their community.

Smith seems to have understood this, and he had long been trusted and accepted by them, or at least by some of the Saginaw Chippewa leaders. He was said to have provided them with presents and favors, and he had become respected and influential by doing so. At the same time it was also true that fur traders, whether French or British or American, had long since tried to impress on the Indians the ideas of credit and debt, that favors could be called in, and debts had to be paid. Did Smith demand these Chippewa leaders repay his favors to them by providing land for his children and looking favorably on a deal with Cass? Another possibility is that Smith simply deceived many or most of the Indians, taking advantage of their trust and their lack of understanding of what was in the treaty language. Historians have pointed out that fur traders and interpreters, the so-called "culture brokers" like Smith who moved between the worlds of the Indians and whites, regularly benefited from their knowledge and position throughout the history of relations between whites and Indians. These fur traders and Indian agents took their chances and risked their lives on the frontier, so they reasoned that they would reap rewards when they could take them.

Yet despite all of Smith's manipulations and trickery at Saginaw, he had most importantly delivered for his employer, the government of the United States. The one outright complaint by Governor Cass about having to pay someone off during the treaty councils in order to advance the government's agenda involved one of his own interpreter-agents, Peter Ryley. In this case, Cass recorded on his books a voucher for this Ryley brother in the amount of $300 "for services on account of the Saginaw treaty."[29] Although Ryley had initially worked on behalf of the government in influencing the Indians, a letter written by Cass shows that he ultimately paid Peter Ryley off, in essence buying his silence when Ryley didn't like what was happening. In this letter, Cass doubled the cash amount he said he paid the young interpreter.

"I was compelled to grant Peter Ryley a gratuity of $600 on account of his objections to the nature of their [the treaty's] terms and that his father was the medium through which his participation was removed," Cass later explained to his friend William Woodbridge. Peter Ryley and his brothers, whose mother was Indian, also received land. What those terms were that Ryley didn't like weren't specified, but Cass had to pay him to keep him from making trouble.[30]

The governor's words and records reflect that if any one man was responsible for getting the Chippewa to approve the treaty, it was Jacob Smith. How influential was Smith among the Indians at the treaty council at Saginaw? The statement was made in the Avery/Williams articles that "it is safe to say, that of the 114 chiefs and head men of the Chippewa nation, whose totems were affixed to the treaty, there was not one with whom he had not dealt and to whom he had not extended some act of friendship, either dispensing the rights of hospitality at his trading post, or in substantial advances to them of bread or blankets, as their necessity may have required."[31]

The audacity of Jacob Smith at the Treaty of Saginaw was truly impressive. On one hand, he was acting as a secret agent on behalf of Cass to get the Chippewa and Ottawa to approve the cession of a huge portion of Michigan's Lower Peninsula. At the same time, he was also laying the groundwork for his children to claim and eventually receive thousands of acres of land by getting Indian names for them into the treaty—something Governor Cass tried to stop.

Cass made it clear to the Chippewa and Ottawa leaders that the government previously rejected attempts by Indians to grant land via treaty to white friends like Dr. Brown of Detroit, even though they wanted him to have land as a reward for the medical attention he'd given them.[32] Jacob Smith would have known this, too, since he had worked for Governor Hull in the 1807 treaty and had been dealing with the Indians in the fur trade for so many years.

Smith, one can imagine, must have been a fearsome opponent in a poker game. In the signing of the 1819 treaty by the Chippewa and Ottawa, he had earned himself several hundreds of dollars in payment from the government for his secret work, while also quietly sowing the seeds for his white children to each receive hundreds of acres of desirable property where white settlement would almost certainly take place and a town would grow. While skillfully juggling these tasks, Smith established a cover so strong that no one seems to have suspected he'd been working on the governor's behalf.

Others were sure that Cass didn't trust Smith in these treaty discussions and indeed, on a certain level, the governor had not. Cass's men had warned him that Smith was trying to have his white children written into the treaty. If the Chippewa had picked up on any tension between Smith and the governor's aides, it probably only strengthened the notion that Smith was on their side. On top of this, Smith had cost Louis Campau dearly by urging the Chippewa and Ottawa to demand their money up front. By manipulating Kishkauko and derailing the payment of the Indians' silver to Campau, Smith benefited other traders who had goods to sell the Indians; he also got a measure of revenge on his rival.

Among the Chippewa who attended the treaty and owed Louis Campau were almost undoubtedly some of the same people of whom Campau had taken such advantage after the War of 1812, when they had, out of desperation, paid incredibly high prices in pelts for those contraband trade goods. The fact that Jacob Smith got Kishkauko to step forward and take payment from the United States without paying Campau may have convinced any doubting Indian leaders that Smith was indeed a friend.

Still, the Indians did regret that they hadn't paid their debts to one of the Campau family traders, and that was Louis Campau's uncle, Barnabas Campau, who was also called Barnaby and Barney. In one of the supplemental articles to the treaty, the Indians asked that "$1600 be paid, in five equal annual installments, to Barnabas Campau" out of the money they were to receive each year. Of course, those supplemental articles were not approved by Congress, and years later, Barney Campau applied for reimbursement from the federal government.[33]

Louis Campau, who'd been hired by Cass as a supplier of provisions, goods, and other services, may have lost the $1,500 payment he expected from the Indians because of Jacob Smith, but he didn't walk away from the treaty empty-handed. He was paid more than $1,000 shortly afterward for provisions, brandy and other alcohol, writing paper, and other items he supplied to Cass, as well as the work of his employees and payments he'd made to Indians at the direction of the governor.[34] Campau would eventually send fur-trading agents out around the state; he would outlive his rival Jacob Smith by decades; gain credit for founding the Michigan cities of Saginaw and Grand Rapids, and die a wealthy man. Smith would be called the first settler of Flint and die penniless.

If Lewis Cass was perturbed at the attempt by Jacob Smith to have reservations made for his white children written into the provisions of the Saginaw treaty, he did not express it in his explanation to Secretary of War John C. Calhoun. Of course, that was probably something better left unsaid, since he would soon be paying Smith several hundred dollars for his efforts. Besides, the governor was delighted to have the treaty signed and he was probably the person who informed the newspaper, the weekly *Detroit Gazette*.

Some of the wording in the paper's report of October 1, 1819, matches the language the governor used to inform the secretary of war. It is likely Cass himself was the author, or at least that he'd written to the proprietor of the newspaper, who used the governor's words in the press. "We anticipate a speedy migration to this tract and a great increase of population and wealth to the territory," the *Gazette* concluded about the treaty with the Chippewa. Three months later, in January 1820, according to government records, Lewis Cass wrote out Jacob Smith's payments, including some $600 for his "services . . . in relation to the treaty at Saginaw."[35]

Cass was very pleased with the outcome of the treaty council with the Indians of Saginaw and proudly wrote of it to another United States Indian agent as the year came to a close. "I succeeded at Saginaw beyond all my expectations," he bragged.

In the months after the treaty council, former trader James V. S. Ryley complained to Cass, William Woodbridge and Secretary of War Calhoun that he'd been badly treated by the government, since he hadn't been able to get a grant of land in Saginaw that he felt he was owed by the Chippewa. Unfortunately for Ryley, these officials said there was nothing they could do. Cass took a dim view of fur traders and former fur traders and the claims they tried to make for Indian land cessions at the treaty:

> The greatest difficulties which the negotiators of Indian treaties have now to encounter result from the interested views of those who are or have been engaged in the Indian trade, and who attend for the purpose of prevailing upon the Indians to urge a grant of money or of land in payment of their debts. . . .
>
> To avoid these embarrassments, I determined to prohibit the attendance at Saginaw of any person who had been previously concerned in the Indian trade, and who would not engage to withhold any demands.[36]

Of course, that last statement wasn't true at all. Fur traders *were* in attendance at the Saginaw treaty, some of whom were hoping to get paid by the Indians or to get land. But none of them ultimately succeeded in this regard as did Jacob Smith. Years later, Cass would give a deposition in a lawsuit between feuding Flint property owners over who was the rightful recipient of a section of land set aside in the Treaty of Saginaw. Though the former Michigan territorial governor left much unsaid, his few words spoke volumes: "He was a very shrewd man," Cass said of Jacob Smith, "who had great influence over the Indians."[37]

Mounting Trouble, Mounting Debt

A s the year of the Saginaw treaty came to an end, the white population of Michigan was nearly 9,000 people, with most of these living in and around Detroit. The town itself now had 1,442 residents, and settlers were coming into the newly created Oakland County. Jacob Smith returned to Detroit after helping Cass secure the treaty, and late in 1819 or early in 1820, he was the third person to sign a petition to the U.S. Congress for reimbursement for Detroiters and residents of the Michigan Territory who had suffered economic losses and property damage during the War of 1812.[1]

Many residents of Detroit, Frenchtown and surrounding hamlets, and the farms along water from Lake St. Clair down to the Maumee, had been robbed, vandalized, or otherwise victimized—not just at the hands of Indians allied with the British, but also by U.S. troops who had been quartered in area houses and farms, and who thought nothing of taking a farmer's chickens or fence rails. The citizens of the territory also asked that they be reimbursed for paying for the release of hostages taken by the Indians.

Dr. William Brown signed this petition first, followed by Conrad TenEyck, who had lost goods seized by the Indians when the war had broken out. (In the supplemental article to the 1819 Saginaw treaty, the Chippewa had asked that TenEyck receive $1,298.20 in installments from their yearly treaty payments, "as compensation for the property taken by them at Saginaw, in the year 1812." But as noted previously, that article was not approved by Congress. It would take years for TenEyck to get a reimbursement from the federal government.)

It probably is significant that Jacob Smith was the third signer of the petition for payment of war damages. Lewis Cass had written that Smith had been useful in dealing with the Indians and that Smith's work in the war had cost him personally. This petition to Congress, along with Smith's rescue of the Boyer children by paying the ransom, and the governor's words about Smith's work on behalf of his country, are indications of his service to the United States. Yet no direct reimbursement to Jacob Smith seems to have been made by the federal government except that for the loss of his horse at the surrender of Detroit in August 1812, payments that other militiamen also received.[2]

It was almost a matter of routine by now that Jacob Smith was back in court that fall of 1819, both as a juror and a party to lawsuits before the Territorial Supreme Court. In September, Smith and a merchant who had once sued him, Robert Smart, joined together to post the bond for a man named Oliver Miller, who had been charged by the United States for assaulting a fellow named Terrence Smith. Miller was found guilty, however, so it would seem unlikely Jacob Smith and Robert Smart benefitted from backing the defendant. On October 16 Smith settled his four-year-old lawsuit against James Abbott over his wartime mission to Ft. Michilimackinac out of court.[3] Three days later Smith was called to court and served on a jury hearing another case. But not enough jurors showed up, so the Wayne County sheriff grabbed a bystander who was quickly impaneled. Unfortunately for the plaintiffs in this case, Smith and his fellow jurors decided that the defendant, a man named John Connelly, only owed the plaintiffs $5. Plaintiffs' attorney Solomon Sibley moved that the verdict be set aside and a new trial be granted, presumably hoping for a more favorable decision with a larger judgment.

As the month of October was ending, Smith agreed to arbitration in the old case brought by merchants Josiah Bellows and David Stone, the partners of the late Richard Hall Jones. Lawyer and businessman Henry J. Hunt, merchant Abraham Wendell, and Antoine DeQuindre served as the referees who would consider the evidence and even take testimony; then they would make a recommendation to

Judge Woodward. The referees didn't see things Smith's way. They ruled that he should pay Bellows and Stone $332.57¾. As Judge Woodward entered the award into the record on December 21, he also instructed both sides pay each of the referees $8 a piece for their work.[4]

Not all of the fur trader's legal appearances were because of problems of his own making. On November 19, Smith gave a sworn statement to a public notary dealing with the destruction of the home of Joseph Loranger at the Rapids of the Maumee during the war. In what may be a glimpse into the way Smith thought liberally about claims and financial dealings, he estimated that the value of Loranger's home was between $1,600 and $1,800; Loranger himself thought his home was worth a more modest $1,200.[5]

As was usual by this time, Smith didn't have just one or two legal matters or financial problems pending. On December 8, his home and outbuildings and property on the corner of Woodbridge and Woodward were seized—or as certain lawyers would argue later, those friendly to Smith "pretended" to seize the property. In reality, Smith was allowed to retain possession of this home and land. This confiscation-on-paper was done in connection with debts Smith owed. Yet at the same time, Smith entered into a $580 bond with businessman DeGarmo Jones, borrowing more money to keep from losing this property outright. Smith's deal with Jones was just one of what had become a continuing and confusing series of mortgages, notes, and loans that Smith took out on his debt-plagued home. Some of these notes on which Smith owed had been sold or transferred to other persons with the expectation that Smith would, at some point, actually begin to pay them off, with interest.[6]

But he did not. It appears from the number of transactions involving the property that Detroit area businessmen were aware that Smith could not or would not make payments and that Smith's notes were proverbial hot potatoes, the holders simply passing them off to others. Within just two years, Jacob Smith had debts in excess of $3,000 on these notes. This would eventually anger two Pennsylvania men who believed they were taking ownership of Smith's buildings and lot, since Smith didn't pay off his debt. They would in time charge that Smith and others were actually defrauding them, since none of the people who held Smith's notes or mortgages ever actually moved against him when he didn't make his payments.[7]

Of course, in December 1819, when Smith entered into that bond with DeGarmo Jones, he was about to come into several hundred dollars from the U.S. government—Smith's pay for his work among the Indians in their approval of the

Saginaw treaty. With this money it would seem that Smith could have easily paid the judgment in the Richard Hall Jones case and other debts. He didn't do this, however, and his troubles continued growing. One such suit was filed in Wayne County Circuit Court by attorneys for John Rogers or Rodgers, the man who'd loaned Smith more than $600 back in the summer of 1814. By the time this suit went to trial in early January 1820 in Detroit, Rogers wanted $1,000 in unpaid principal, interest, and damages. It may be that Smith paid at least some of what he owed Rogers, for the case wasn't appealed to the Territorial Supreme Court as so many of his other cases were.[8]

But if Smith truly made good on his debt or otherwise settled with Rogers, then this case was truly an exception. In the months ahead, authorities in Wayne County and the newly formed Oakland County would seize Jacob Smith's possessions and even his livestock in order to pay the judgment in the Richard Hall Jones case. In what was undoubtedly the first legal seizure of property on the Flint River, Oakland County Sheriff William Morris rode up to Smith's post to take possession of 14 head of cattle in the spring of 1820. In Wayne County, Sheriff Austin E. Wing confiscated from Smith's Detroit home a cart, two carriages, a clock, a looking glass, three tables, a sofa, a stove, 12 chairs, a liquor case or cabinet with four bottles in it, a mahogany card table, and a china tea set. These items were advertised and sold in May 1820 per the order of Judge Woodward. But Smith's friend and associate Conrad TenEyck again came to the rescue, stepping in to pay for the items and allowing Smith to keep them.[9]

What was happening to Jacob Smith's finances, that his obligations were going unpaid even as he borrowed money? Smith's son-in-law, John Garland, a U.S. Army officer, would later claim that Smith, for several years by the early 1820s, had been extending thousands of dollars worth of trade good to Chippewa acquaintances. This was not unusual, for other fur traders extended credit to Indians and also employed trusted individuals to act as agents to trade goods for pelts. Unfortunately for Smith, the Indians with whom he was dealing were not returning with fur or otherwise paying for the goods the fur trader was advancing them, Garland claimed.

"I recollect to have summed up the balances due to Mr. Smith from each Indian who had failed to pay up his credits and I am sure it exceeded five thousand dollars," Garland wrote late in 1843 about Smith's accounts during this time. "The amount was so large as to have made a strong impression on my mind."[10] If Garland was telling the truth, it meant Smith was mortgaging his property so he could buy thousands of dollars of goods to virtually give away without getting any furs in return. This was a recipe for financial disaster, since Smith's credit was drying up and he would be unable to purchase more trade goods. Of course, he was also risking arrest and imprisonment on the complaints of his creditors.

Smith had been at the height of his influence and power with his secret work for Lewis Cass in 1819 with the successful Saginaw treaty. But now in his business matters he was sliding into a sea of red ink from which he would never emerge. How could an experienced fur trader allow this to happen? Was he already chronically sick or drunk, as Ephraim Williams would observe when he visited Smith's trading post on the Flint River in 1822? If Smith had betrayed the trust of his Indian friends during the treaty councils at Saginaw, might he have suffered a guilty conscience? While this is of course only speculation, Smith certainly understood the Chippewa would be forced to leave when the government surveys of what had been their land were completed, when that land was sold, and when American settlers came up the Saginaw Trail from Pontiac. Knowing this, could he not demand payment for the goods he turned over to them? Or did he believe the land on the Flint River in his children's Indian names would soon make him rich, and that his money troubles would soon disappear?

While these questions cannot be answered, the writings of one of the most important clergymen in the United States at that time give a view of Smith's statements about the Chippewa and their future. These statements by the fur trader were quoted by the Reverend Jedidiah Morse, who today is remembered as the father of telegraph inventor Samuel Morse. In the Reverend Morse's day, however, he was known as an important geographer and educator deeply concerned about the fate of the American Indians. As Jacob Smith's Detroit property and possessions were being sold off at the order of Judge Woodward, Morse was on his way from the eastern United States to Michigan, where he would investigate the condition of the Indians there for the federal government. Once he got to Detroit, the information and opinions on which Morse would most depend were those of Jacob Smith.

The territory continued to grow slowly, with fears of "unhealthful" swamps and Indian depredations still making Michigan an undesirable place to settle in the minds of many Easterners. Though the approval of the treaty at Saginaw seemed like a hopeful development for white settlement along the Saginaw Trail, it was followed by yet another period of Indian unrest. The governor's records and letters reflect concern over the fact that hundreds if not thousands of Indians were still making their way through Michigan to go to Ft. Malden to receive British presents. There were also reports, false but terrifying to white settlers, that Tecumseh's brother, the Prophet, was hoping to revive the idea of an Indian confederation against the United States, and that an Indian was killed early in January 1820 in an incident at Detroit.[11]

Despite these problems, Lewis Cass was sure that more settlers would eventually come, and he followed up the Saginaw treaty with another coup—an exploratory expedition along the southern shore of Lake Superior with geologist Henry R. Schoolcraft and geographer Capt. David B. Douglass. The men hoped to find the source of the Mississippi River, but at the same time Cass tried to convince the Indians they came across that the United States government's intentions were peaceful but determined. Of course, the government also wanted more and more land from the tribes of northern Michigan and the Upper Great Lakes.[12]

There is no record that Jacob Smith was asked to participate in this exploratory mission—it may be that Cass had had enough of the fur trader's scheming after the Saginaw treaty, and Smith did not have the same kind of influence with the Chippewa who lived so far north and west of the Saginaw Valley. While the 1820 expedition was historic, it was also another boon to Detroit vendors who had supplies or services to sell to the governor and his men. But the governor did need good canoes to make the trip, and "orders were placed with the Saginaw Indians, with whom he had made friends in 1819, for three large birch canoes." The members of the governor's expedition were waiting anxiously for the delivery of their canoes on May 24, the date of the party's departure from Detroit. Just as they made alternative arrangements and began to load replacement canoes, "those from Sagina came down," wrote James D. Doty. Not surprisingly, it was Jacob Smith who acted as the vendor or middleman for the mission's canoes.

The day before Cass's expedition left Detroit in May 1820, the record of expenditures for the mission shows Jacob Smith was paid $226.62½ for "three birch bark canoes, $135.00; eight bundles of bark, 16.00; forty paddles, 10.00; three masts, 75 cents; twelve poles, 3.00; thirty-five bundles of watap, 4.37½; one hundred and forty pounds of gum; 17.50; four fish nets, 40.00." If the bundles of bark and watap and the amount of gum seems high in relation to the cost of the canoes, it was probably because those were necessary supplies for fixing the light but thin-skinned vessels. Cass later purchased two more canoes when his party reached Mackinac Island.[13]

The sale of the three big birch canoes and related items to the expedition seems to have ended Smith's involvement in the famous exploration mission. James Ryley, one of the half-Chippewa sons of Judge James V. S. Ryely, acted as the governor's interpreter, as did the mission's guide, a man named Joseph Parks who had been a longtime captive of the Shawnee. One of Jacob Smith's future sons-in-law, Chauncey S. Payne, profited even more from the governor's mission than Smith. Payne, the jeweler and retailer who'd come to Detroit after the war, had for years been making Indian jewelry. Payne received a check for just over $1,400 from the territorial governor for gorgets, armbands, brooches, "earwheels" and "earbobs," and wristbands. These, Cass reported later, were "delivered to Indians at the treaty of Sault de St. Marie, and upon the northwestern expedition."[14]

The sale of supplies to Cass shows that Smith was still doing business as a merchant and a trader and had money coming in, even as he borrowed and failed to pay creditors. Just weeks after Smith sold those canoes to the Cass-Schoolcraft-Douglass mission, Buffalo attorney Albert Tracy sent a letter complaining to Territorial Secretary William Woodbridge about Smith's unpaid legal bill from the fur trader's troubles with the U.S. customs officers during the winter of 1815–1816. "The costs in the penalty suit were . . . at $26.70," Tracy explained. "He owes my charge in the other business which ought to be 20 dolls. more at least. The business has now been sleeping 3 or 4 years and I have not at any time received one cent from him." The Buffalo attorney appealed to the territorial secretary to try to get Smith to pay his legal bill. Whether or not Woodbridge succeeded in getting the trader to settle up with Tracy is not reflected in his letters.[15]

Early in 1820 the Reverend Jedidiah Morse, a nationally known geographer, author, and educator then living in New Haven, Connecticut, proposed to the secretary of war, John C. Calhoun, that he go on an extended mission to visit Indian tribes around the United States and its territories, to study their condition and to "devise the most suitable plan to advance their civilization and happiness." Though this sounds patronizing and racist by today's standards for sensitivity and respect for other cultures, at the time many white Americans, including religious leaders, believed the only way for the Indians to survive the rapid westward movement of land-hungry settlers and development was for them to give up their old ways of life, in essence, to stop being Indians. Morse, a Congregational minister, was considered a distinguished scholar and he was secretary of the Society for the Propagation of the Gospel (for Indians). He and others, such as the New York–based

Northern Missionary Society, believed the Indians should become Christians and farmers. Otherwise, they felt, the tribes would suffer war and virtual extinction as the expansion of American settlements robbed the Indians of their hunting and trapping grounds.[16]

Calhoun presented Morse's proposal for a nationwide Indian survey to President James Monroe, and Monroe approved. That spring, Morse and his youngest son, Richard, journeyed from their home across New York, arriving in Detroit on June 2. Governor Cass had already left on his expedition bound for the Upper Mississippi, so Morse was assisted by William Woodbridge, territorial secretary and now acting governor. Woodbridge saw to it that the clergyman was introduced to "many other respectable gentlemen of this city." In the 12 days Morse spent in Detroit he found "a variety and abundance of valuable information concerning the Indians."[17]

The opinion that mattered most to Morse, at least in terms of the matter of the Chippewa and Ottawa tribes, was that of Jacob Smith. "The following information concerning the Indians of the Michigan Territory, particularly the Chippawas [*sic*], I received for substance from Mr. Jacob Smith, who has resided among these Indians more than twenty years; and at the treaty of Saganau, of 1819, was appointed by the government one of their guardians," Morse wrote.[18]

Of course, the last part of that statement was simply not true. There had been nothing official about Smith's presence at the treaty—he'd been there as Cass's confidential agent, and the Chippewa and Ottawa chiefs had turned to him for advice. Smith may have considered himself a guardian to the tribe; it is possible that he was now an "Indian farmer" who was instructing local Indians on the white men's way of agriculture. If Smith made the claim that he was a Chippewa "guardian" appointed by the United States, then he was certainly bragging, since there is no record of him in Cass's papers as being appointed an agent for the tribe.

Even so, Smith's other comments reflected a concern over the future of the Chippewa and other Indians of Michigan and the United States. As the tribes of the eastern United States had ceded land at giveaway prices, the Indians' own small reservations had increasingly come into contact with white settlers, Morse wrote of Smith's observation. In Michigan, game had diminished and tribes that once lived in large towns with as many as 200 dwellings were now dispersed into small bands, he reported. Those once-large Indian towns had been located on rivers such as Ohio's Sandusky and Maumee and Michigan's St. Joseph, Saginaw, and Flint, and also at L'Arbre Croche, Morse wrote; some bands had left for Canada. "Now, their game having year after year become more and more scarce, and no substitute yet provided, and no corresponding change in their education and habits takes place, they are becoming spiritless, poor objects of commiseration and charity," Morse continued.[19]

Quoting Jacob Smith, Morse went on to write that if the government could teach them to grow their own food, "civilization would gradually follow, and they would become a happy, and useful people to the United States—whereas if they remain in their present deplorable state, in twenty or thirty years, they must become extinct." Smith believed that Indians throughout the United States could be saved by taking the small reservations that were now homes to small bands and tribes in the eastern part of the country and trading them for much larger tracts of government land, "say on the Flint River, near Saganau, a tract selected for a like purpose by Gov. Hull during his administration."[20]

Again, this statement appears unsupported by the records of Hull's time in Michigan. In reality, there was nothing in Hull's 1807 treaty that designated a place on the Flint River for Indian farming; Saginaw Chippewa bands had lived and raised corn along that river for decades, perhaps for as much as a century or more. Yet Smith's recommendation was reported in good faith by Morse: The Saginaw Valley, especially the Flint River portion, could be turned into a district that would serve not just the Chippewa, but Indians from all over Michigan and beyond, as many as 30,000 or more.

"This spot is admirably suited to this purpose," the clergyman wrote of his talk with Smith. "The land is excellent for cultivation; and that which the Indians would give in exchange for white settlements. The exchange would be reciprocally advantageous." This would remove small bands of Indians from small pockets around the eastern United States, and the men believed, benefit the tribes. "By being placed together, the Indians would be strengthened and animated, they would feel more their own importance," Morse continued.[21]

Of course, Smith's own children possessed by treaty, or at least so Smith thought, thousands of acres along the Flint River. Perhaps Smith believed that if the government pursued this idea of turning the basin of the Flint River into a large reservation, his children's land would be bought out or exchanged for small but valuable Indian reservations that had been enveloped by white American towns and farms back east. But Smith apparently said nothing to Morse about this. "To this spot [on the Flint River], so strongly recommended by Mr. Smith, for the purposed mentioned, I would turn the attention of the government, as being probably next to the vicinity of Green Bay, the best situation for colonizing the Indians," Morse wrote. Of course, he added that if the Flint River was chosen for such a purpose, Smith should be appointed the government's man there. "Mr. Smith, who has resided among the Indians here for twenty years successively, is familiarly acquainted with their language, has their confidence, is one of their guardians, and anxious for their improvement, might be an important an efficient Agent."[22]

Smith told Morse that based on what he'd seen at the Flint River, the Indians were "ingenious and susceptible of improvement, as were the uncultivated nations of former ages." Smith claimed he was more impressed with the Flint River band (where he had such influence) than those who lived at Saginaw. "The Indians (Chippewas) on Saganau river, about six hundred in number, are a mixed body, strollers, the refuse of other tribes," Smith said to the clergyman. "Of those there is less hope, than those on Flint river, who are of a different and better character." Of course, the trader did not say that he was very close to the chief of the Flint River band, Neome, let alone that he manipulated or conspired with Neome in order for Smith's children to claim sections of land under the terms of the 1819 treaty.

Morse pressed on with his research. With the help of a merchant-trader named John Williams, a member of the Campau family, Morse conducted an interview with an Indian leader he called "Keesh-kah-ko-ne," which someone translated as meaning "Bears den." Whether Keeshkahkone was Kishkauko ("the Crow") is an open question. Morse described this man as appearing to be about 60, "of ferocious aspect, sensible, stout and of commanding figure." Keeshkahkone told the clergyman that he was not interested in living as white people did, but he admitted it was possible to teach the young to do so. Would Keeshkahkone allow the whites to send teachers to the Chippewa to instruct the children? Yes, the chief replied, so long as the teachers "don't deceive us, will learn our language and teach our children English."[23]

Morse's report reflected further discussions with Jacob Smith. Smith told him that British presents to the Indians of Michigan were helping to alienate them from the United States. Nor did it help that the Indians traveled as much as 200 or 300 miles to come to Detroit to be paid their treaty annuities, Smith said. By traveling so far a distance, the Indians would expend most if not all of what they were given.[24] Of course, like any trader in the wilderness, Smith would benefit if the Indians were paid their annuities at the place where they lived, a place where he would have less competition for their business.

Morse may have been naive and his judgment clouded by his desire to convert the Indians to Christianity, but he clearly didn't consider Smith to be a charlatan or a rogue in his assessment of the condition of the Chippewa of Lower Michigan and the proposal for the Flint River area to become a national Indian colony. By the time Morse's report was published in 1822, he had more than enough time to check on Smith's reputation and bona fides and could have excluded Smith's comments in the presentation to the secretary of war. The clergymen recommended that missionary families be posted at the Flint River and on the Saginaw Bay (among other places), where Indians would learn Christianity and agriculture.

But Smith's suggestion that a giant national Indian district be created in the Saginaw Valley of Michigan wasn't taken seriously by the U.S. government, for the idea was directly opposed to what officials hoped to accomplish going back to the Jefferson administration. Early in 1819, Secretary of War John C. Calhoun had urged Lewis Cass to get the Saginaw Indians to agree to leave Michigan entirely, since they were viewed as a threat to the United States and because of their proximity to British Canada and the influence of British agents. "The rapid and dense settlement of the Peninsula of Michigan is considered important in a material view," Calhoun had stressed. Populating the territory with settlers would ensure that U.S. territory wouldn't again be invaded by British troops from Canada, and that the settlers of Old Northwest couldn't be threatened by the Chippewa or any other tribes.[25]

The next generation of farmers coming to the fertile land of the Saginaw Valley in the 1830s and 1840s would mainly be settlers from New York and immigrants from places like Germany and Ireland. Smith's proposal to turn the Flint River region into a national Indian district or homeland may have appealed to Jedidiah Morse, but it was the last thing the United States government wanted for Michigan in the 1820s. The next decade would see federal officials pressing the Saginaw Chippewa to give up more land.

After spending about two weeks in Detroit, the Reverend Morse—dressed in what was even then considered the "old school" fashion in black clothing, silk stockings, a wide-brimmed hat, and white neckcloth—went on his way to Mackinac. Smith resumed his fight with rival Louis Campau, appearing before Justice of the Peace Thomas Rowland and swearing an affidavit that more than a year earlier, back in September or October 1819, he had heard a man named Charles Gendre say, in the presence of two other witnesses, that "Campau had purchased his goods at auction in Canada and smuggled them over the river." These goods undoubtedly were for the Indian fur trade. Smith's accusation meant that Campau hadn't paid duties and had therefore broken the law. Smith said that Gendre told the men that Campau had taken his goods "to his uncle, Jaques [*sic*] Campau." What Smith expected the territorial officers to do with this information nearly a year after the alleged smuggling took place is not clear, and there is no evidence of any action taken against Louis Campau.[26]

The day after he swore out that affidavit, business matters were on his agenda. He entered into a bond for $163.94 along with businessmen Warren Howard and David McKinstry. Why they would need to borrow slightly more than $50 each from Peter Godfroy isn't reflected in the record, but once again, this debt was apparently not paid in a timely manner. Godfroy would in two and a half years' time sue the men for repayment and damages of $300 in a Wayne County court.

Smith also got his own legal licks in that spring and summer, suing John Connelly (sometimes given as Connolly) for just under $25 and a man named I. Solomon for the larger sum of $500. Smith's lawyer charged that the fur trader had in August 1819 provided Solomon with "a keg of whiskey and barrels of tools" to sell to others. This alcohol and merchandise had been worth $500, Smith claimed. Smith seems to have won both cases, for both defendants indicated they would appeal. Ultimately, Smith probably got some of his money since there is no record of these cases at the Supreme Court of the territory. Whatever settlement Smith reached with the men, it was just a drop in the bucket when compared to the thousands of dollars he owed others.[27]

If Smith still harbored ill feelings that summer toward Louis Campau, he had no problems with selling more of his Detroit property to the man he had once accused of being disloyal to the United States. On September 8, 1820, Smith received $50, perhaps a down payment, from James Abbott and Robert Smart for a 1,500-square-foot lot bounded in part by Woodward Avenue and, on the southeast side, by Atwater Street. This property was a stone's throw from Smith's home. The deed recorded this as being the southeast half of Lot 66 in Section 4. Just a week or so later, Smith sold another piece of property (one he'd received from George McDougall in 1816) to Abbott for $300. These were rock bottom prices on property that should have been increasing in value, perhaps reflecting that Smith badly needed the money.[28]

Smith voted in Detroit shortly thereafter in the election held September 21 for the territory's delegate to the U.S. Congress, and was called to jury duty for the Territorial Supreme Court early in October. Not long after this he headed back up into Indian country, probably to one of his trading posts on the north side of the Flint River or at Saginaw.[29] Along the way, he heard complaints from settlers in Oakland County about the problems they were having with Indians who demanded food as they passed up and down the Saginaw Trail to Detroit or Amherstburg.

One of the settlers affected by the passing Indians was Oliver Williams, who had settled on a place he called Silver Lake in modern-day Waterford Township, and who was the father of a son named Ephraim. Oliver Williams wrote to Lewis Cass that fall, saying that while he had tried to be patient with the Indians, "it is impossible for me to support my family." Williams pointed out that a man named Mr. Buffet and Jacob Smith had "the last season witnessed my situation and in part what I have suffered."

That fall, the Saginaw chief Kishkauko had traveled down to receive his portion of the yearly treaty payment from the government; Smith had been there also. Cass apparently provided the Indians with food while they were in the Detroit area, but gave them no provisions to take with them. This was why, Kishkauko told Williams, the Indians needed food for their return trip. Buffet, who was present when the Indians arrived at Williams's farm, said he would do what he could to convince Cass to reimburse Williams for his lost crops. "I can only say that the Indians have this season taken from me at least thirty bushels of corn and as many potatoes and more pumpkins than two yoak [sic] of Oxen would draw at twice or thrice and as many other times too tedious to mention," Oliver Williams complained.[30]

Smith probably couldn't have done anything for Williams other than listen sympathetically. Cass and other officials, of course, thought they knew what they needed: more soldiers, both in Detroit and at forts around the region, to project U.S. power and encourage more settlers and more farmers. They knew full well that would hasten the Indians to move or bring to an end their previous way of life. The world of Kishkauko and the Saginaw Chippewa was changing fast, never to be the same.

U.S. vs. Jacob Smith

When the federal census takers made their count in Detroit in 1820, one recorded that the household of Jacob Smith was comprised of one white male under the age of 10 (presumably son Albert), two white females between the age of 10 and 15 (likely daughters Caroline and Louisa), and at least one white male aged 45 and older. If 1773 was the year of Smith's birth, as evidence indicates, he would have turned 47 sometime in 1820, so that entry almost certainly indicated the presence of Smith himself.

But different transcribers of this census don't agree about the data from Smith's household. One transcription indicated that there were two men living there. If this was correct, it may reflect the presence of a man named "Doane" who was recorded as working with or for Smith in 1821. A member of the government surveying team that traveled to the Flint River that year would remember Doane helping Smith cultivate crops planted near his cabin–trading post–farm on the Flint River. Whether Doane was a friend, partner, or hired man isn't clear, but that 1820 census noted that one person in the home was "engaged in agriculture." This indicates Smith was farming near his Flint River trading post, possibly because he had received an appointment as a government-paid instructor to teach white men's farming practices to local Indians.[1]

Jacob Smith was due back in Wayne County court early in January 1821 in the lawsuit brought by Joseph Campau. This was the matter of the estate of another member of that clan, Dennis Campau, who had committed suicide in December 1818. Joseph Campau charged that Smith had owed Dennis Campau money going back as far as 1815; Joe Campau wanted that money and damages, for a total of $500. The jury hearing the case agreed, but only to a point. "Detroit, 4 January 1821," wrote jury foreman William Brewster on a slip of paper that recorded their decision. "The jurors find a verdict for the plaintiff for $320.19." Smith made plain he would appeal the case to the Supreme Court of the territory.[2]

Smith continued to work for or supply Governor Cass in one way or another, and that month he was paid $25 "for 1 cwt. tobacco issued to Indians previous to Saginaw treaty." This referred to the first annual payment to the Indians, made under the treaty terms, in the fall of 1820. Smith received that check just two days before he began acting as an interpreter for nearly two months, from January 20 through March 21 of 1821. For this service he was paid $64.[3]

A young surveyor who met Jacob Smith that summer and who experienced frontier Michigan for himself was Harvey Parke (also given as Hervey Parke). He had been raised in Connecticut and was teaching in Camden, New York, early in 1821 when he decided to join government surveyors under Joseph Wampler of Ohio. Wampler had teams running township lines in the regions that would become Oakland, Lapeer, and Genesee counties, and early in May, Governor Cass instructed Smith to aid Wampler and act as liaison between the Indians and the government surveyors. Parke would write in later years that he set off with others in the surveying team on June 13 of that year from the town of Pontiac and found the Flint River so swollen by heavy rains that they could not ford it.

"We started up the river to the Kearsley [Creek], where we felled a suitable pine, about sixteen feet of which we removed from the main body of the tree and shaped it canoe-like, digging out the same, so far as could be done with axes," he wrote. The men floated down the river to "where the city of Flint is now located. Here we found Jake Smith, called 'Wabeseis' [Wabesins] by the Indians, who had been [an] Indian trader for several years, and who had recently received the appointment of Indian farmer," Parke recounted. "He had built a comfortable log house a few rods below the present railroad bridge," the surveyor wrote about Smith's wilderness home, referring to a mid-nineteenth-century trestle to indicate where the cabin stood, just a city block or so north of the Flint River. "This was occupied by Smith, a white man, with his mother and sister. Also by a man by the name of Doane. The two men at this time (the middle of June) were hoeing corn, with veiled faces on account of the mosquitoes."[4]

This description of Smith having his mother and his sister with him is remarkable, since other records indicated Smith's mother had died in the fall of 1814 and there is no mention in the available family record of Smith having a sister. Perhaps these women were related to Smith, but given Smith's propensity to bend, break, or ignore the rules, it is possible the fur trader explained their presence to the surveyors by saying they were family. Detroit, like any community with a military post, had its prostitutes, and the frontier was often a place for criminals and others who needed to make a fresh start or to lose themselves beyond the reach of the law.

In the meantime Parke said he and the other surveyors, after waiting at Smith's post for about a week, received their instructions and set to work. That effort didn't last long—it was only about another week before Wampler and the others returned to Smith's, "refusing to continue longer on account of the suffering they had endured from the mosquitoes, both men and horses being weak from loss of blood and want of rest." Despite the terrible mosquitoes, undated field notes in a small booklet taken by one of the surveying team, perhaps Parke or Wampler, show that the man jotting down measurements on the north side of the Flint, upriver from Smith's post, was impressed by the country. "Good land," the surveyor noted. Similar comments followed as the work continued in the laying out of the 11 reservations: "Good well-timbered land."[5] In short order, this land would be settled. In less than a few years, a small community of French-Indian families would exist here, neighbors to Smith, followed by white Americans from the east in the 1830s. The town would be known as the Flint River Settlement at first, and then Flint.

Although Jacob Smith seems to have spent much of the year of 1821 at the Flint River and elsewhere in the Saginaw Valley, his legal cases were back on the Territorial Supreme Court's docket that fall. Smith had appealed Joseph Campau's lawsuit in the matter of Dennis Campau's estate, and on October 8, 1821, the case went to trial before Judge James Witherell. The jury ruled that Smith owed Campau damages of $285.79½. With costs, this judgment rose to $323.23½—almost the same amount that the Wayne County jury had decided back in January. But as with other fines and penalties, Smith did not pay. Twelve days later he was arrested and taken to jail by a Wayne County deputy sheriff named Samuel Sherwood.

Smith turned to local businessmen David C. McKinstry and Johnsy McCarthy for his bond, and he was soon released. But as was often the case with Smith's legal affairs, the matter turned into a complicated and controversial mess. Joseph Campau's lawyers would soon charge that Smith violated the terms of his bond by leaving Wayne County after his release from jail. That meant McKinstry and McCarthy had to pay Campau twice the amount of the judgment Smith owed, or about $650. McKinstry would claim later that Deputy Sherwood, as a favor to Smith, helped draft that bond so that he could release the fur trader from jail. Because of this, McKinstry argued, he couldn't be held responsible for what the deputy had done.[6] A series of charges and pleas in the matter of Smith's bond in this case would go on for years. But in late October 1821 it was just another of Smith's mounting legal and financial difficulties. The trader went back to the Flint River.

So, too, did the government surveyors. Joseph Wampler's team returned to finish their job, but again conditions proved harsh and uncomfortable for the ill-equipped surveyors. During the two months surveyor Harvey Parke and his comrades went into the field to work, aided by Smith, they suffered from hunger and cold. When finally finished at sunset of their last day, somewhere northwest of the Grand Traverse, the team followed "up the river, forcing our way through thick beds of rushes knee high, at about nine o'clock we reached Smith's trading-house, so hungry from several days' short allowance that we took potatoes from the kettle half-boiled."[7]

What Parke did not mention in his memoir was that the settlers' nemesis, Kishkauko, blocked the surveyors, refusing to allow them over to the west side of the Saginaw River that fall. Their supervisor, Joseph Wampler, complained to William Woodbridge, then acting governor, and the incident was also reported in the newspaper. According to the *Detroit Gazette,* the Saginaw Indians "interfered with the surveying being done by Mr. Wampler." The Chippewa chiefs were then awaiting their treaty payment, and Kishkauko maintained that the government hadn't delivered all the agricultural supplies the Chippewa were due under treaty terms. Wampler argued he needed to survey the area so as to specifically mark their own reservation, but there was an ugly confrontation between him and the chief.

Colonel Beaufait, Cass's trusted Indian agent, quickly arrived at Saginaw with the treaty payment, and the surveyors were allowed to proceed. Incredibly, Smith, who had been counseling patience and calm, was soon discussing with forty tribal leaders the notion that they should give up their Saginaw reservation entirely and move to locations on Saginaw Bay. Wampler was impressed with Smith's influence, and enthralled with the idea that the United States could gain that Saginaw reservation land. "If so, Smith has accomplished a great thing for [the] government," Wampler wrote, since he believed the soil of Saginaw was better and worth "many thousands of dollars" more than land along the bay.

Cass endorsed Smith heartily. "I am glad to hear that Smith conducts himself so entirely to your satisfaction," he replied to Wampler. "I have no doubt of his fidelity & his wish to promote the public interest." The governor, however, did not want Smith to go too far. "I do not wish to have the Indians pushed on the subject of their reservation," Cass wrote. He told the survey chief to "let them decide freely."[8]

If the Chippewa had briefly blocked the surveyors in 1821, they sent packing other white Americans who tried to set up shop at Saginaw. That same year, the group called the Northern Missionary Society, after consulting with fur traders and Cass's Indian agents, tried to establish a school at Saginaw. This was the same group with whom the Reverend Jedidiah Morse had worked on the idea that Indians could be turned into Christian farmers. The missionaries were unsuccessful. "A total stop was put to the progress of the building and the workmen were prevented from proceeding with their labor in consequence of the threat and lawless interference of the Indians," Woodbridge complained to the secretary of war, passing along the news of the failed attempt by the missionaries.

"The Indians who have so long resided in the Saguina country evidently feel the most poignant regret at the rapid advance toward them of the white population," he continued. Woodbridge felt the answer to this was simple. He suggested "the expediency of establishing in the vicinity of the Saginau Bay a small garrison and military force." He repeated the idea to Major Jonathan Kearsley, a U.S. Army officer then in Pennsylvania but who would soon come to Michigan to serve as an official in the courts and territorial government. "Two companies of men stationed at the head of the Saginau Bay would give a certainty to our remote settlers and at once put down the lawless temper among the Indians," Woodbridge wrote.[9]

Robert A. Forsyth, who had served Lewis Cass as an aide, would later testify that he was returning to Detroit by ship from Buffalo across Lake Erie during that fall of 1821 when he struck up a conversation with a man named "Rickard" from Meadville, Pennsylvania. This was probably Henry Reichard, an early Meadville settler and family man who had first come to the New World as a Hessian soldier to fight for Britain in the Revolutionary War. Forsyth said they talked about a subject that would later be the source of a major legal battle in Michigan—the Indian daughter of Jacob Smith.

Forsyth knew something of Reichard and Smith's daughter; Smith had told him two years earlier at the Saginaw treaty that he had placed or "indentured" his half-Chippewa child, Nancy, with this very fellow. Why was Reichard making the journey to Detroit? Reichard said he had been providing a home for Nancy Smith for several years, and he had learned that a reservation of land had been made for her in Michigan. "[Reichard] was fearful that Smith would not do her justice," Forsyth testified. Reichard told Forsyth that he had brought Nancy up "in a Christian like manner" and that he had taught her how to use a spinning wheel to make woolens.[10]

In time, the husbands of Nancy's white half-sisters would buy out her interest in the section of land that they maintained was set aside for her on the Flint River, in what became the city of Flint. Nancy would eventually marry a young man who had come to Michigan named Alexander Crane, and they would settle near Ann Arbor. But there would be a long legal battle for Jacob Smith's white heirs in trying to prove that Nancy was the "Mokitchenoqua" named in the Saginaw treaty, and some would maintain that the real Mokitchenoqua was not Nancy Smith Crane at all.

During this period in 1821, Jacob Smith was paid by the United States at the rate of about a dollar a day for six months. Under Governor Cass's "ordinary expenditures," a Detroit area man named Peter J. Desnoyer was given a check for $180 for "the amt. of Jacob Smith's account for Smiths services from the 1st May 1821 to the 31st October 1821."[11] What Smith's services were and why Desnoyer was paying for them and then being reimbursed by Cass isn't clear, but it probably reflects Smith's work with the government surveyors and as an Indian farmer. Other expenses recorded by the governor during this time reflect the usual payments for Indian agents, interpreters, blacksmith services for Indians, and for the transporting of goods for Cass's Indian department.

While Kishkauko and some of his followers had blocked surveyors (temporarily) and missionaries in the Saginaw region, they continued to allow Jacob Smith to do as he pleased. Smith therefore went into the business of leasing some land for growing crops. On December 1, 1821, a man named David E. W. Corbin entered into an agreement to rent land from Smith. This farming seems to have taken place in the area where Smith had built his cabin–trading post on the north side of the Flint River, perhaps at a location nearby where the Indians grew corn and had done so for years.[12]

Corbin was described in historical accounts as an ex-soldier who had worked for Oliver Williams, the settler who hailed from the east and was now farming north of Pontiac. Corbin was one of four men who Governor Cass said had been selected by the Indians and employed by the government in 1822 to aid them in farming at the Flint and Saginaw rivers. Albert J. Smith, son of Jacob Smith, would years later claim that it was in 1821 or 1822 he visited his father at the Flint River trading post. "My father had made Flint his home for several years and for three or four years he lived there all the time," Albert Smith said in an 1855 deposition. "I do not know of his ever having an Indian wife at Flint, or of his having an Indian family. I heard of his having one Indian child, a daughter of about my age. [But] I never knew of his having a wife or family, after my mother died."[13]

While it was true that Smith didn't have an Indian wife at the Flint River—he had actually fathered the girl called Nancy with a Chippewa woman from the band on Lake St. Clair years before—this statement by Smith's son is contradicted by records that show Jacob Smith continued to make trips between the Flint River and Detroit in the early 1820s. Albert Smith, who was only 9 or 10 years old when this visit took place, said there were two houses "a few rods apart" (probably 100 feet or less) on the north side of the Flint River, and it was not clear whether both of these were his father's buildings or if one belonged to someone else. Smith's dwelling was a small log house "five or six rods from the bank of the river," or about 90 feet from the water. It stood on a clearing of several acres that had been fenced; there were also some Indian graves close by, Albert Smith remembered.

Other accounts of those who crossed the river at the Grand Traverse or who saw what remained of Smith's buildings in later years agreed substantially with this description of Smith's Flint home. Alvah Brainerd, who was a young man when he came to Grand Blanc in the fall of 1832, saw Smith's cabin after the fur trader had been dead for several years. He remembered it as "a very coarse log house" or "shanty" near the river ford, where Flint's First Baptist Church would be built decades later. The remnants of that cabin were visible for years. "A portion of [Smith's] old house still remains upon the bank of the river," noted an account published in 1858.[14]

By the early 1820s then, Jacob Smith was more than just a transient fur trader at the Flint River. Though Smith continued to have a house in Detroit and was perhaps not a frontier settler in the conventional sense, he was farming, leasing land, trading, and residing there at least some of the time. He was also working, in some capacities, for the U.S. government. Nor was Smith the only person living at the Flint River by this period. When a settler named Jacob Stevens brought his family in 1823 to the area called Grand Blanc, several miles south of the river, he would note in a letter in 1825 that there were "some French families seven miles northwest of us." Businessman and ex-fur trader Ephraim Williams would later explain that this "French settlement" at the Flint River in the early 1820s included the part-Chippewa Edouard Campau and the Lyon brothers, George and Archibald, the fur trader.[15]

These men, like Smith, were keeping an eye on land they or their Indian relatives had been granted under the terms of the 1819 Saginaw treaty, and with good reason. According to the *Detroit Gazette,* groups of U.S. citizens were now regularly leaving town to explore the Flint, Shiawassee, and Cass river areas, all the way up to Saginaw. Positive stories about these lands (with no mention of the swarms of bloodthirsty mosquitoes) appeared in the Detroit paper.

One writer who visited the Saginaw Valley blamed local fur traders for spreading earlier stories that each year there was flooding of the rivers—something that would-be farmers and settlers would find discouraging. That writer called these tales of floods "misrepresentation and deception" by fur traders who didn't want settlers coming in and spoiling things by driving away Indians and fur-bearing animals. Whether Smith was one of those traders who had spread these sorts of stories is unknown. On one hand, he had been a competitive fur trader. But given that he felt his children had a claim on thousands of acres of land on the Flint, he may have encouraged the more positive view of the Saginaw Valley in order to promote settlement and improve the property's value.[16]

Controversy was never far from Jacob Smith, of course. In the spring of 1822, a trader named John Grant swore out a complaint before a justice of the peace in the town of Pontiac that, sometime between April 22 and April 30, someone had broken into his Saginaw store and taken silver Indian jewelry, a calico shirt decorated with silver, skeins of thread, and some furs. All told, he estimated the value of the stolen goods and pelts at about $26. Grant went on to claim that on May 10, slightly more than a week after he had discovered the burglary of his trading post, he found some of the stolen items—in Smith's post on the Flint River! There was no doubt in Grant's mind as to what had happened: The jewelry and other goods and skins, he swore, "I do [believe] Jacob Smith to have taken." Smith was arrested and then released after signing a statement or surety that he would show up for proceedings on the matter in the July term of the Oakland County court. If he didn't, Smith promised, he would forfeit $200 in goods and property. Interestingly, Grant, as the complaining witness, also had to pledge a bond of $100, just in case he failed to show up to prosecute his complaint, set for trial in July.[17]

Smith was back at the Flint River crossing later in May when a man named J. L. Cole took a walking tour with some acquaintances from Detroit up to Saginaw. Cole kept a diary of his trip, and his comments make him sound like a land speculator looking for an investment. He left from Detroit at 8:00 A.M. on May 24 and described in some detail the sights and conditions of the land, the forest, and the clearings along the way. He and his companions reached Pontiac, "a promising country town," by evening. The next day, after touring the village and getting a late start, they made only several miles before stopping at another home for the night, probably in the Waterford Township area with one of the Williams family settlers. They continued on May 26 into the hills and by the lakes of northern Oakland County, halting near the place the traders called Grand Blanc, by what Cole described as "the remains of an Indian village." The party walked along the Thread to the Flint River, and following it for about a mile, "we put up at one Smith's (an Indian trader) for the night."[18]

Cole made no comment on Smith, who by then had been accused by Grant of burglary, but he did describe the location. "Many mill privileges might be found on the Thread river, and some on the Flint river, near Mr. Smith's, of the most advantageous situations," Cole noted. He thought the land was probably productive. The water was clear and excellent and the woods thin and scattered, with large stands of hickory and pine. The next day, May 27, Cole's party left at sunrise and took what he described as "the new trail, due north" to Saginaw. Whether Smith had been an obnoxious or disagreeable host—whether he had even been present—is not clear. But Cole and the guests who had stayed overnight at his abode on the Flint River did not bathe or breakfast there. Instead, they walked five miles that morning before stopping for a bath and refreshments; then they continued on to Saginaw.

Cole and his comrades were shown around the Saginaw area by one of the Campau family traders, probably Louis Campau. They returned to Smith's late at night on June 1, having come down the trail along the Flint River that afternoon from Pewaunaukee, Neome's Town. "Arrived at Smith's not far from midnight," Cole wrote, "nearly exhausted with fatigue and hunger." Cole said nothing more about Smith or his place, but he returned to Detroit for the most part favorably impressed by what he'd seen.[19]

While Cole and others believed the land of Saginaw Valley held opportunity for settlement and investment, it was nonetheless true that the only whites in the area were still traders, visitors, and people who had Indian relatives. Only those accepted by and known to the Indians could even consider living in this area. Governor Lewis Cass added his important and influential voice to those who'd been expressing the need for the presence of U.S. troops at Saginaw. A military post in the trading community would help to ensure "a strong and speedy settlement" of the region; it was needed, if only temporarily, to make an impression on the Chippewa, whom the federal governor described as "notorious for their disaffection" and "hostility" to the United States.[20] Within months, Cass would get his wish.

Jacob Smith had a date in criminal court that summer. When July came, Daniel LeRoy, a New York lawyer who'd come to Michigan to participate in the company that founded the town of Pontiac, acted as the government prosecutor, representing the people in John Grant's complaint against Jacob Smith. LeRoy presented the case to a grand jury composed of Oakland County residents, and they indicted Smith on a charge that, on April 30, while at Saginaw, the fur trader had broken into Grant's house and had taken

> two pairs of Indian arm bands made with Silver of the value of five Dollars each, two pairs of Indian wrist bands of the value of two Dollars each, one pair of Indian ear wheels made with Silver of the value of one dollar, six pairs of concave broaches of the value of four dollars, one blue calico shirt garnished with Silver broaches of the value of four dollars. One button shawl of the value of one Dollar, one doz. skins . . . of the value of twenty five cents, one Fisher Skin of the value of twenty five

cents, four Muskrat Skins of the Value of One Dollar and fifty cents, three Mink skins of the value of one dollar, three martin Skins of the value of One dollar, one shirt patern [*sic*] of the value of One Dollar, One two and half Point blanket of the value of three Dollars and four yards of Power Loom Shirting of the value of two Dollars.[21]

Oakland County officials prepared for the trial, with the sheriff being directed by Chief Judge William Thompson to subpoena several witnesses. These included men named Thomas Gay, William Warfield, Orison Allen, Lewis Cook, Joseph Almy, Oliver Williams, and Williams' son, Ephraim S. Williams, who was himself interested in trading with the Indians. Some of these men presumably were witnesses for the prosecution, though not all of them were recorded as having been sworn to give testimony. Smith, who was represented by lawyers Henry J. Hunt and Charles Larned, pleaded not guilty at his arraignment on July 17. A few men appear in the court records as sworn witnesses who were not on the sheriff's subpoena list, so it may be that some of these men testified for the defense. These included Oakland County clerk Sidney Dole and men named Olmsted Chamberlain, David Stanard, and Ganet Van der Pool.[22]

No account of the testimony survives, but the record shows a jury of 12 men found Smith not guilty of the burglary of Grant's Saginaw house. There is no indication as to how Smith's attorneys explained the fact Smith was in possession of the stolen merchandise. According to a brief account of the case that appeared in a history of Oakland County, John Grant, the complainant against Smith, was "mulcted" or fined for cost of the case, apparently because the judge or jury believed he had lied or been reckless in his accusation against the fur trader.[23] Though prosecutor LeRoy lost his case against Jacob Smith, he would go on to become Michigan's first state attorney general in the years ahead.

There were more legal difficulties in store for Jacob Smith. Back in the fall, Smith had been released from the Wayne County Jail when David McKinstry and Johnsy McCarthy posted his bond for the judgment he was ordered to pay to the estate of Dennis Campau. But Joseph Campau, administrator of the estate, knew that Smith had left Wayne County after his release. Campau argued that by doing so, Smith violated the terms of his bond. Not only did this mean that his bond was forfeit but, under the law of that time, it also meant that McKinstry and McCarthy (and presumably Smith) owed Campau double the amount of the 1821 judgment, or $646.

Campau brought renewed action in the matter, and he seems to have had all three men arrested, since that summer in Detroit McKinstry, McCarthy, and Smith together pledged a bond "in the penal sum of $646.46½." Unfortunately for Joseph Campau, he was still trying to get his money years later. In fact, his lawyers and those representing McKinstry filed briefs and argued the matter for more than a decade—years after Jacob Smith was dead.[24]

Smith had also filed at least one lawsuit of his own in 1822, and this was against his tenant farmer on the Flint River, David Corbin. Not long after Smith pledged his bond with McKinstry and McCarthy, he ended the lease of his land near the river. In a deal with Corbin, Smith agreed to end his lease and drop a lawsuit he filed against Corbin in Wayne County. In exchange for Smith dropping the suit, Corbin agreed to give Smith "all the wheat, corn, potatoes, barely, peas, beans, and oats and all other crops whatsoever, now growing on said section of land or elsewhere in the county of Oakland."[25] Despite the feud with Smith, Corbin did become an Indian farmer, working for the federal government to teach agriculture to the Chippewa bands of the area.

Only one government payment to Jacob Smith seems to exist for this period, and that was for helping surveyors. Governor Cass's records show a payment of $30 to Smith for "assisting the surveyor in running the line of the tract ceded by the Saginaw treaty. Employment terminated 31st August, 1822." Presumably Smith was able to work at some points that summer helping the surveyors, between the time he spent in jail or the courtrooms of Detroit and Pontiac.[26]

Smith remained in Detroit to face lawsuits and to give a deposition on September 24 in the case filed by Joseph Andre dit Clark against brothers Conrad and Jeremiah V. R. TenEyck, with whom Smith had long been associated. In his statement for that suit, Smith told about how some years earlier he had urged the TenEycks to contract with André for silver work for their Indian trade. His own ability to trade, however, was coming to an end.[27]

By now there was no letup in the legal barrage that resulted from Jacob Smith's debts. Smith and the TenEycks, along with DeGarmo Jones and several other men, some of whom didn't even live in Michigan, were sued by two men, a James S. Craft and one Duncan S. Walker of Pittsburgh, who believed *they* now owned Smith's house and remaining property in Detroit. Though the transactions described in the men's complaint were long, the issue boiled down simply: Jacob Smith owed thousands of dollars in principal and interest on loans he'd taken out on his Detroit home and property. Some of these notes for the loans had been sold or transferred from one purchaser to another before being taken over by Craft and Walker. In short, these men from Pennsylvania expected either that Smith's notes must be paid off or else they should get possession of Smith's property.[28]

What attorneys for Craft and Walker had discovered about Smith's debt on the house angered them. Smith had taken out one mortgage or loan after another on the same piece of property. Yet though months and years had passed, no one to whom Smith was indebted had actually foreclosed on Smith's house. Nor had any of these loans been paid off by Smith. This was fraud, Craft and Walker alleged, and they seemed to suggest that Detroit authorities were complicit, allowing the matter of Smith's indebtedness to drag on and on. Of course, it is likely that Smith wasn't allowed to stay in his house out of the charity of these men to whom he owed money. As with the TenEycks, Smith probably had been working as their agent or employee in the fur trade. But this didn't matter to the angry Pennsylvanians; they wanted to be paid or they wanted the property.

The case, going before the Supreme Court of the territory on September 20, 1822, had an entire cast of defendants: There was Jacob Smith, of course, and De-Garmo Jones, two men who'd already tangled in court. There was Toussaint Dubois of Indiana, a fur trader who had acted in the past as a spy for William Henry Harrison. There were three men named Hill—William Hill, James Hill, and John Hill—all of Pittsburgh; and there was James Boyd Jr. and the TenEyck brothers of Detroit. But Smith and Boyd asked for postponements in the case, and these were granted.[29] Smith wouldn't have to face the music in this suit for some months. By this point, however, he was only forestalling the inevitable.

He Was Dissipated and Bad in His Habits

I n November 1822 Jacob Smith left Detroit and headed back to the Flint River. Perhaps he was glad to return to his post and farm in the wilderness and leave the courtrooms behind him, but it may be that he simply did not care; it is even possible that he enjoyed these legal battles, given his propensity for getting into them.[1] Two of the affairs in which he had been involved that year—the leasing of farmland to a white U.S. citizen, David Corbin, on the Flint River, and the continued surveying of the 1819 Saginaw Treaty cession—were indicative of the changes that were taking place in the territory.

Land was for sale by the U.S. government throughout the Detroit area and parts of southeastern Michigan—land that just a few years earlier would have been considered dangerous locations for new settlers because of the risk of Indian attack. In addition, the ways in which citizens transacted sales in Detroit and Pontiac and the small towns that were popping up became more standardized—something that merchants and businessmen had wanted for some time. For years, local businessmen and individuals had issued their own "due bills" or "change bills"— IOUs—in place of money. There had been cases of counterfeiting and instances of local people issuing their own due bills, only to turn around and refuse to honor them. In addition, commerce in Detroit was complicated by residents' use of many different kinds of coin, some from Europe, and some that had been cut into pieces. Though Cass's administration had issued some scrip or currency for the use of Michigan residents, there was still a general lack of money in the territory.

In September 1822, Jacob Smith was one of many merchants and businessmen who signed a petition putting the public on notice that they would no longer accept the IOUs issued by individuals. There was enough small coin in circulation in the territory that it was no longer necessary to accept these "change bills," these men claimed. Those to whom Smith owed money may have found it ironic that a man who was so deeply in debt was now proclaiming he wanted cash up front in business transactions.[2]

Yet an even more dramatic event took place on the Michigan frontier that year, fulfilling the wishes of territorial officials and settlers alike. While Smith had been fighting his various legal problems, two companies of U.S. Army infantry arrived early in July by lake transports, coming off of the Saginaw Bay and up the river to the place known as Saginaw. There the soldiers pitched their tents and began building a blockhouse and stockade—"a fortress in the heart of the wilderness," one writer called it. Dr. Zina Pitcher, a Detroit physician who went to Saginaw that summer, said the soldiers encamped and began building their fort on the west side of the river—almost directly across from the place where the troublesome Kishkauko had his lodge, the *Detroit Gazette* reported in that summer of 1822.[3]

Of course, fur traders had previously established buildings and animal pens, and even orchards, and U.S. troops had visited Saginaw with Governor Cass back in the fall of 1819 for the treaty. But this was the establishment of a garrison. Lewis Cass had wanted this for months, though he was confident that a fort and garrison wouldn't be required for more than a few years. The commander of the new fort was Major Daniel Baker, who led this detachment of two companies of soldiers from the U.S. Army's 3rd Infantry Regiment at Ft. Howard, Green Bay. As he prepared to leave Detroit to establish his new post, Baker made clear to Governor Cass that he understood his mission: He would take a hard line with Chippewa, he vowed, for he knew of their long-standing hostility toward the United States. He had decided that they were "treacherous insolent and dangerous."

"I consider the principal chief Kishkaukon [*sic*] unworthy of any confidence, and his course and conduct have been turbulent and troublesome," Baker wrote. One of Baker's officers had very close connections to Jacob Smith, and that officer was Captain John Garland, a native Virginian who would make his career as a professional soldier. Garland was married to Smith's eldest daughter, Harriet. The Garlands at some point took over raising her youngest sister, Maria, after their mother had died in 1817, and there is evidence in the historical record that the Garlands also became responsible for Harriet's brother, Albert Smith. By this time, Maria was nine years old, while Albert was 11.[4]

The ships carrying the soldiers arrived at Saginaw Bay in July, and the men moved their supplies and arms by small boats south, up the river, to the site of their fort. In the meantime, Dr. Pitcher of Detroit was appointed assistant surgeon to the detachment. Guided by Capt. Whitmore Knaggs of Cass's Indian department, Pitcher traveled up the Saginaw Trail, through Oakland County by "farmer Williams' mill" (probably that of Alpheus Williams, soon known as Waterford Mills, located near what is today the intersection of Dixie Highway and Andersonville Road in Waterford Township). They continued north to the Grand Traverse and Jacob Smith's trading house at the Flint River and on to Saginaw. Pitcher arrived as the soldiers were putting up their tents.

Captain Garland brought his family with him to Saginaw, as did two other officers, Pitcher said. Besides the military men, other white residents included some traders and their families, and three nonmilitary government employees—an Indian interpreter, a blacksmith, and a farmer to teach the Indians agriculture. There were also four sutlers or merchants catering to the soldiers. With increased traffic on the Saginaw Trail between Detroit and the new fort, and ships moving supplies via Lake Huron, it is possible that Harriet Garland and her young sister Maria and their brother Albert were able to see their father periodically if not regularly. Smith had often traded at Saginaw, though his trading days may have been coming to an end, and he still had a house in Detroit, though it was the subject of litigation.[5]

As 1822 came to a close, Smith seems to have had made a final appearance that year in a Wayne County court. Peter Godfroy, who claimed he hadn't been paid money he'd lent Smith and two other men on a bond, filed suit against them. Smith's portion of the matter would have been only $100—a fairly small sum relative to a fur trader's yearly business transactions. But Smith no longer had any property in Detroit to sell off to raise quick cash.[6]

It was also at this time that the question of the identities of persons named in the Treaty of Saginaw to receive reservations on the Flint River—and whether a fraud had been committed—emerged as a big and perhaps embarrassing matter for federal officials. Sometime in the fall of that year, Gov. Lewis Cass wrote to the

U.S. secretary of the Treasury that he "entertained suspicions of fraud haveing [*sic*] been practised at the Treaty by attributing to certain white persons Indian names & producing Indian children as the persons in whose favour the grants or reservations were made." Cass would later state that he knew what Smith had been up to while the treaty councils had been going on, and now complications were arising. Perhaps this came about because someone who knew what Jacob Smith had done began to complain, but it is also likely that conflicting claims were made over the Flint River reservations.[7]

A copy of the original letter written by Cass couldn't be found years later when compilers published documents dealing with the Michigan Territory, yet details about the issue were contained in some of the surviving correspondence. These show that Cass asked the federal receiver (or treasurer) in Detroit to "endeavor to ascertain the identity of the persons claiming the lands reserved at the Grand Traverse of the Flint River." If fraud had been committed, Cass asked that the federal treasurer and land office director put the land in question up for sale in the fall of 1823.

Treasury officials in Washington agreed that an investigation should be done, but they weren't sure they had the authority to declare that questionable reservations belonged to the U.S. government, even if there had been fraud and deception in the matter of the names and identities of the recipients named in the treaty. Ultimately, this was a boon to Jacob Smith's heirs, for it allowed their claims on the land to remain alive.[8]

Though it was still mostly wilderness, Jacob Smith's region of Michigan—Indian country since long before the arrival of the French in the early 1600s—was now home to a small but growing crowd of newcomers who weren't fur traders who came and went with the seasons, but American farmers, settlers, and soldiers. Only 30 miles or so north of his Flint River trading post was the new Ft. Saginaw; about the same distance to the south were pioneering settlers such as Oliver Williams and his brother-in-law Alpheus Williams, in the area north of the new town of Pontiac.

Decades later, on January 7, 1863, Oliver William's son Ephraim, then nearly 62 years old, would recount how, as a young man, he rode up the Saginaw Trail and crossed the Grand Traverse of the Flint River on horseback in the fall of 1822 with his friends Rufus and Augustus Stevens, young Pontiac area pioneers, to see the new fort. Ephraim S. Williams had been born in Massachusetts and moved to

Detroit shortly after the War of 1812; his father was one of Oakland County's first American pioneers, having built a farm on Silver Lake a short distance off the Saginaw Trail. Both father and son had been subpoenaed as witnesses in the case of the *U.S. vs. Jacob Smith* that summer of 1822, although the record reflects that only Oliver Williams was sworn and presumably testified in the matter.[9]

Ephraim Williams turned 20 that year and he was of a mind to leave the family farm on an adventure with his friends to "explore and see the country" by riding up to Saginaw, where the fort was under construction. "The road from Pontiac followed the Indian trail generally," Williams recalled about the route, comparing the Saginaw Road with its precursor, the Saginaw Trial. Other than the home of young Ephraim Williams's uncle and neighbor in the Waterford Township area in Oakland County, there were "no other houses except the trading post of Smith and others," he said about the journey to Saginaw.

Williams had known Jacob Smith from the days when their family lived in Detroit, but he didn't recollect seeing the fur trader at the Grand Traverse as he made his first trip to Saginaw with his friends in 1822. There the young men "found the work going on for building winter quarters for [the] troops," Williams said. Ft. Saginaw itself was a rectangular stockade, the lumber for which was cut down in the nearby forest. The officers' quarters were along the inside of the north wall, while barracks for the men and their families and a hospital building were constructed along the other walls. The fort was home to about 120 soldiers. Officers, clerks and sutlers, the surgeon and wives and children boosted the population of the fort to about 150, said an old Detroit physician, Dr. John L. Whiting, who also served as the fort's surgeon.[10]

The young explorers soon returned down the trail to the Pontiac area. But not long afterward Ephraim Williams made a trip back to Saginaw during the hard winter of 1822–1823 with three wagons full of provisions and freight for the fort's garrison. Williams and his brother-in-law Schulyer Hodges made this trip with contractors Harvey Williams and Colonel John Hamilton. The fact they could drive teams to Ft. Saginaw was possible because a "wagon track had been cut through upon the Indian trail . . . where the road is now. . . . Then Jacob Smith was at his post at Grand Traverse."[11]

It was soldiers from Ft. Saginaw, under the command of Lieutenants Edward Brooks and Henry Bainbridge, who had cleared the Indian trail to the Flint River so that sledges or sleighs and wagons pulled by horses could bring supplies overland. This was essential, once the waters from Lake Huron to the Detroit River had frozen over and shipping became impossible. But when that first convoy of winter supplies for the fort reached the Flint River, Jacob Smith was not a well man. Ephraim Williams felt that the trading post had become "a hard place."[12]

"His health was poor then," Williams said of Smith. "He was dissipated and bad in his habits." "Dissipated" in the idiom of nineteenth-century America certainly suggested alcoholism, and at a minimum, the sentence implied that Smith had wrecked his own health. The man who wrote down Williams's words, the collector and recorder of the history of the American westward expansion, Lyman C. Draper, indicates that Williams also used the word "flux" in his description of Smith's physical condition, probably meaning that the trader was suffering from diarrhea, perhaps from dysentery. But Smith survived the winter and continued moving between the worlds of Detroit and the Saginaw Valley.[13]

Another Michigan settler who would recount his experiences with Smith during this period was John Todd. Todd was 25 years old in the spring of 1819, when he and his father's family moved from the Mt. Clemens area, the place where the Boyers had been taken captive six years earlier. They built a new farm near Pontiac, on the Saginaw Trail. As an old timer nearly 50 years later, Todd told a Flint newspaper editor that he knew Smith well in the 1820s, and that he considered the fur trader "a gentleman"—a characterization that Smith's enemies in business and lawsuits would have probably disputed. Todd claimed he regularly conveyed the fur trader and his goods between the Flint River and Detroit during these years, after Smith's French-Indian employees would bring his furs down on "Indian ponies" to the Pontiac area.[14]

Todd described Smith as "wealthy." Though the fur trader may have at one time enjoyed a degree of financial success, the evidence is clear that Smith was falling on hard times by the early 1820s. Todd eventually bought property near the Flint River and opened an inn there in the years after Smith's death. As an old man, Todd told a Flint newspaper about his memories of Smith, though the accuracy of his observations is open to question. "He [Smith] always parted with Mr. Todd and his goods at a place called Vinegar Hill, about four miles west of Detroit, where taking a glass of beer at 'Mother Hansomes' he walked to Detroit, leaving Mr. Todd to follow him in the morning," the *Wolverine Citizen* proprietor wrote about Todd's reminiscence. "Mr. Smith's common dress among the Indians being a 'melton' or white blanket coat, with moccasins, &c, was always replaced by an elegant suit of black broadcloth on his appearance in Detroit when Mr. Todd says, 'he looked what he *was*, a gentleman.'"[15]

Whether Smith was being paid to serve as an Indian farmer at the time Ft. Saginaw was established is unclear. But a letter written by Lewis Cass to Major Baker shows that the governor didn't completely trust in the work habits of the men who were being paid by the U.S. government to show the Indians how to farm. He wanted Baker to keep an eye on the four men who were employed as Indian farmers in the Saginaw Valley and make sure they were really doing their jobs.

The president of the United States had determined that $2,000 would be allocated annually for "aiding the Indians in farming," Cass wrote. "Four persons have been employed, all selected by the Indians to assist them." These men, the governor warned Baker, "should be faithful and industrious and put in corn as soon as spring opens." Cass wanted the major to check up on these Indian farmers "as well as every other one employe in the [Indian] Department at Saginaw and at the Flint River. I am at too great a distance to know what they do or how they behave." Cass was particularly distrustful of David Corbin, who had earlier leased land from Jacob Smith there at the Flint River. The governor said nothing about Smith.[16]

Even as Cass was writing and sending this message to Saginaw, Smith's immediate neighborhood saw the arrival of its first settlers from the eastern United States in the spring of 1823. This was the family of a former soldier named Captain Jacob Stevens, who now put down roots along the Saginaw Trail several miles south of the Flint River. The Stevens family had come to the Michigan Territory from Wayne County, New York, in 1822. They were preceded by their son, Rufus, who had convinced his father to move their family to the Pontiac area. Jacob Stevens did so, but he was unsatisfied with the soil and unable to get title to the land he was on. He therefore decided "to try another venture."[17]

With a U.S. Army fort now established at Saginaw, there was more traffic on the road from Detroit than ever before. Jacob Stevens figured that it might be advantageous to locate further up that Saginaw Trail. "In March, 1823, Rufus and I started to explore to the northwest," Jacob Stevens wrote to family back east. "We were much pleased with the country and prospects at this place."[18]

This was the area that the French traders called Grand Blanc, named for the Indian chief described by Louis Campau to have been "white, remarkably so for an Indian." Jacob Stevens and son Rufus built a log cabin on an Indian cornfield. For some time prior to the Stevenses' arrival, traders and Indians themselves had lived and camped in this vicinity and built lodges and shelters. Because of the French pronunciation of the name, settlers who came from the east, like Jacob Stevens, spelling this area's name phonetically as they heard it spoken by the French traders, would refer to this place as "Granblaw" or "Grumlaw."

Stevens noted there were some French families living only "seven miles" to the north. This was a reference to the Grand Traverse of the Flint River, where, according to Ephraim Williams, Barney Campau's son Edouard and brothers George and Archibald Lyon lived (in proximity to Jacob Smith's cabin and farm). Though little is reflected about these people in the historical record, Edouard Campau and the Lyons were almost certainly there to protect the land along the river they believed they or their relatives had been granted in the 1819 treaty.[19]

Jacob Stevens described the location of his own new home in Grand Blanc as an old Indian settlement. But the Indians of Grand Blanc's band were still a strong presence in the area—they had moved their village several miles away to the west to a place they called Copeniconic (also given as Kopeniconick, pronounced "Cope-neh-*con*-ick"). Almost immediately there was a misunderstanding between the Indians and Jacob Stevens, Ephraim Williams would write many years later. For Stevens, as he was finishing his family's home, found the large stone the Indians considered a kind of deity or manitou, Bab-o-quah, on the small rise of ground off the Saginaw Trail. Not knowing the significance of this oddly shaped boulder to the Indians, Stevens loaded it on a cart or sledge and hauled it home to build his fireplace.

"All went well for a time, but at last the Indians missed their idol . . . and were quite excited about the loss," Ephraim Williams claimed. "Searching about, they discovered where it was. They at once appointed a delegation to wait on the captain and insisted upon his returning Bab-o-quah to his original position, saying to him that he had committed almost an unpardonable offense and nothing would answer but returning the stone." Jacob Stevens tried to pay the Indians for the big stone, but they would have none of it. Stevens had to remove it from his fireplace and put it back on the hill. Whatever happened to the boulder-deity after that, Williams didn't know. But from then on, Jacob Stevens was known to the Indians, with sarcastic humor, by the same name as the rock god—Bab-o-quah.[20]

But with his cabin finished, Stevens could now move his family up from Pontiac. "On the 23rd of May, 1823, Eunice, myself, two youngest children, Rufus and Sherman, with a good team and as many goods as would make us comfortable, arrived here," Jake Stevens wrote his kin. "We cleared, plowed and sowed with wheat and oats about ten acres, completing the same June 10th." The Stevenses were likely the first and only white Americans from the east that Jacob Smith knew as neighbors.[21]

Another member of the Stevens family, the youngest son, Sherman, told of having a minor run-in with an Indian when he was sent on an errand up to Jacob Smith's trading post–farm. Sherman Stevens would recount how the family had battled wolves, trying to protect their livestock, and faced other hardships when they came to Grand Blanc. But it was when they broke a critical piece of farm equipment—their yoke—that they were truly in a fix.[22]

Jacob Stevens and his boys could make another yoke of wood, of course, but they would need a suitable auger, or drill. "The nearest possible place to obtain one was at a little trading post kept by Jacob Smith, situated a few rods below [or about 80 feet down river from] the bridge that crosses the river in the now city of Flint," Sherman Stevens wrote in 1884, recalling the circumstances. Young Sherman had never been to the Flint River, but he rode his pony up the trail through the woods, stopping to shoot wild pigeons as he made his way north. He found the banks of the Flint were thronging with Indians—and that was as far as he got. A drunken man accosted him for his pigeons while he was dismounted, Stevens said. Though terrified, the boy pressed his horse forward to get away, but in doing so pushed the Indian down the steep riverbank. The boy quickly got on his horse and rode home without ever getting to Smith's trading post. The Stevens family's fear of Indians soon passed and they got along very well together, according to Jacob Stevens's 1825 letter. Sherman quickly learned their language, and the family happily traded meal, flour, and salt for the Indians' venison, fish, sugar, honey, and other foods.[23]

But if young Sherman Stevens never managed to reach the Grand Traverse during Jacob Smith's lifetime, his eldest brother did: Rufus W. Stevens would later testify that he'd had different conversations with Smith, and that Smith had explained that this land on the north side of the river belonged to his children by virtue of the 1819 treaty. Smith made no secret of this, according to the later testimony of Stevens, Louis Moran, and others. Moran was another of the families of Detroit who, like the Campaus, traveled the trails, lakes, and rivers of Michigan to trade.[24]

If Ephraim Williams's account was accurate—that Jacob Smith had been ill in that winter of 1822–1823—then the fur trader was not the only one who would suffer that year in the Saginaw Valley. "The summer of 1823 proved a very sickly one," Dr. Whiting would recall years later, "a very aggravated form of intermittent fever being the universal disease." The illness, a kind of malaria, hit Ft. Saginaw hard. The detachment's physician, Dr. Zina Pitcher, was sick, and so were the commander, Major Baker, members of Baker's family, and virtually all of the other men. Late in August, Captain John Garland, the fort's acting commander, sent for Whiting in Detroit to relieve Pitcher. Several of the soldiers died during the epidemic, as did an officer and members of Major Baker's family.

John Whiting himself became ill and spent "three of the most harrowing weeks" of his life at the fort before his condition began to improve. Jacob Smith's relatives apparently came through this terrible season of disease alive, but the decision was made to pull all but a handful of the U.S. troops out of Ft. Saginaw. Dr. Whiting later said that on October 25, 1823, most of the command boarded the schooner *Red Jacket* in Saginaw Bay and sailed for Detroit. The five-man garrison that remained would only stay a short time longer before the entire fort was abandoned and sold on the basis it was no longer needed.[25]

Thirty-five miles or so south of Saginaw, settler Jacob Stevens, in the spot called Grand Blanc, was not happy that the soldiers had been pulled out. "At this time we felt morally certain of having neighbors the next spring [1824]," he wrote to his parents. "But here, sir, I must inform you that the government saw fit the winter following to evacuate the post at Saginaw, which measure has, so far, completely paralyzed all settlements to the northwest, turning the tide of immigration, which has been very great, to the south and west."[26]

Even with settlement of the area north of Pontiac slowed and the garrison at Saginaw reduced, the changes in Jacob Smith's region of Michigan must have been remarkable. In clearings and woods where once only Indian campfires burned in Oakland County, now the houses and barns and fences of American settlers were going up. Smith's own trading post–farm on the Flint had been a stopping place for the riders who carried the mail every other week between Detroit and Ft. Saginaw, as well as the vendors who had moved supplies. Around the region, particularly to the south, surveyors continued to do their work, laying out new townships and counties. And across Michigan in areas where white settlers had not yet ventured, American fur traders and their agents were fanning out and taking over trade that had belonged to the British. Of course, settlement would quickly follow these traders.

At the same time, the proud and once-powerful Saginaw Chippewa were fading into a shadow of their former selves. Regions of southeastern Michigan the Indians had ceded by treaty were being cleared for farms and settled. The Indians had come to rely heavily on the whites' goods and services, and they contracted the whites' diseases; some were devastated by alcohol provided them by white traders. When J. L. Cole made his walking trip to Saginaw in the spring of 1822, he had harshly remarked that the Native people appeared to him "filthy, indolent, drunken and wretched." Governor Cass had referred to the Chippewa three years earlier as "these unfortunate people" and "the miserable remanant of those who once occupied our Country."[27]

Individual Indians continued to clash periodically with fur traders or harass the newly arrived settlers, and whites would remain nervous about the Indians for years to come. But in reality, the threat posed by the tribes to the vast majority of settlers in the Michigan Territory was over. The real threat was that of the settlers to the Indians' way of life. Jacob Smith had long recognized what was happening to the Chippewa, and, whether he would have admitted it or not, he had been a direct part of it. He had explained the Indians' situation to the Reverend Morse back in the spring of 1820, when the men had talked of turning the entire Flint River region into an Indian colony. Of course, that would not happen.

Had it all been a sham then, this supposed friendship between Smith and the Chippewa and the Ottawa of the Saginaw Valley? Was it all a cynical matter of expediency for the fur trade, spying on them and manipulating them for the U.S. government and for his family's benefit? Or did Smith really have affection for the Indians, but being a realist, understand that their world was disappearing? Smith's son-in-law John Garland later claimed the friendship between the fur trader and Neome (whom Garland referred to as "Beaume") was real and true, and that was the reason Neome had wanted Smith's children to have land on the Flint River:

> As regards the land given to the children of Mr. Jacob Smith, nothing is more notorious among the old residents (traders) in Michigan than that these lands were given at the instance [insistence] of an old chief (Beaume) [sic], head of the Flint River band, in consideration of Mr. Smith's having supported and taken care of him when old, infirm and blind. I have heard the chiefs speak of it a dozen times when I was stationed at Saganaw [sic] two years after the treaty.[28]

The short historical article about Jacob Smith by lawyer Charles Avery also described relations between Smith and members of the Saginaw Chippewa in the rosy terms of a strong and trusting friendship. This may strike a false note with modern readers, as well it should, given the well-known history of the treatment the Indians received at the hands of the U.S. government and settlers. It is also true that both Avery and Garland directly benefited from the sale of Flint River land, so it is no surprise that they would take the position that Neome and other Chippewa chiefs had wanted Smith's heirs to have it. Avery had no personal knowledge of Jacob Smith's dealings, but represented two of Jacob Smith's sons-in-law, Tom Stockton and Chauncey Payne, in the legal fight over the land in the 1850s.[29]

The contradictions in Smith's relationship with the Chippewa run strong and deep. Smith had understood them and their situation as well as any white man, and Indian witnesses said some of their chiefs had turned to him for his help in the 1819 treaty. Some chiefs would later concede to a government official in the late 1830s that members of their tribe had owed him thousands of dollars when he died. Yet while he had extended them credit and done them favors, he had nonetheless acted as a secret agent of Lewis Cass in the councils of the 1819 treaty for the United States to buy their lands. He had recommended, seemingly in good faith, that the entire basin of the Flint River be turned into a huge Indian colony where, the Reverend Morse had reported, thousands of Indians could live in peace as farmers without the interference of white settlers. To these men, it was the only possible answer for the tribes as their wilderness and their way of life vanished. Of course, as the father of children who Smith believed had been granted thousands of acres of land along the Flint River, Smith may well have figured his family would benefit from the sale of this land to the government in the event an Indian district was actually created here. If not, they would still profit from the sale of land to white settlers, when they came.

Though Smith played various roles as a soldier and spy, man of business, and frontier trader, he ultimately had acted as a provider for his own family by attempting to line up land for them. Certainly he recognized that settlement was coming to the Saginaw Valley and nothing was going to stop that. A town would naturally grow on the Flint River at the crossing of the Saginaw Trail, just as a town was already growing at the crossing of the trail of the Clinton River. If his heirs sold or managed their property and finances wisely—something he himself failed to do—they would never want. As for the Chippewa of Saginaw and the other tribes of Michigan, they would watch the world as they'd known it receding further and further into a distant past.

Only small details about Smith's activities in 1823 can be gleaned from the historical record. He voted at the village of Pontiac on September 4, in the election for delegate from the Michigan Territory to the U.S. Congress, one of nearly 200 Oakland County residents who cast ballots. He also collected a $2 bounty from Wayne County for bringing in the pelt of a wolf during the year. Though it is hard to imagine in the sprawling metropolitan region of southeastern Michigan of today, wolves were a bane to settlers and farmers who lost much livestock to them.[30]

In October, Smith and his attorney James Doty were back before the Territorial Supreme Court in the suit of Craft and Walker, who had sued Smith and the various holders of his notes and mortgages on his Detroit home, including the TenEyck brothers. Smith filed his answer to the accusations, denying that he'd done anything wrong or fraudulent by taking out that series of notes and loans on his Detroit home and store over the previous three years. But as James Abbott had noted in earlier letters and even warned in public notices, Jacob Smith had a controversial reputation and it was well known to the merchants and businessmen of Detroit. Certainly Judges Augustus Woodward and James Witherell knew it; on a motion by the lawyer for Craft and Walker, the judges ordered Jonathan Kearsley, the U.S. Army veteran officer who was now the clerk of the court, to calculate the amount of principal, interest, and costs owed to DeGarmo Jones on his bond and mortgage on Smith's property. The judges also wanted to know the debt owed to the others who had loaned money to Smith or mortgaged his land, including that which he owed on the notes acquired by the plaintiffs and what he owed to his co-defendant, James Boyd Jr.[31]

Though a final total doesn't seem to be a part of the court record, some of Kearsley's calculations showed that between principal and interest on his notes and mortgages on that single piece of property, Smith owed nearly $3,300 to DeGarmo Jones, Toussaint Dubois, and Conrad and Jeremiah TenEyck. That did not include what Smith may have owed others, for Dubois had sold or assigned Smith's bond and mortgage to others and they in turn had assigned it to the plaintiffs, Craft and Walker of Pittsburgh. Nor did that $3,300 figure include what Smith owed James Boyd Jr. for yet another bond and mortgage. Thus it may be that Smith owed significantly more, perhaps thousands more.

Despite Jacob Smith's record of indebtedness and unpaid bills, Judges Woodward and Witherell gave him one last chance: Smith had until May 15, 1824, to pay DeGarmo Jones, James Boyd Jr., James Craft, and Duncan Walker. If he did not, they ruled, he would lose that final piece of property, his Detroit home, and it would go on the public auction block. Proceeds from the sale would pay for court costs, lawyers' fees and taxes, and his debt to Craft and Walker. Any money left over would go to James Boyd Jr.'s lawyer and to Boyd personally.[32]

Smith's son-in-law John Garland later blamed Smith's poverty on the fact that after the fur trader sent thousands of dollars' worth of trade goods into the Saginaw Valley with the Indians, they failed to bring in the furs they were supposed to be getting for him in return. "Some time in the year 1823 when I was stationed at Detroit, Mr. Jacob Smith . . . got me to look over his books and papers connected with the Indian trade in order to show me the true state of his affairs and the cause of his embarrassment," Garland wrote 20 years later. "In making out the statement and deducting the amount of sales of furs, etc. from the amount of the invoices, a heavy loss had evidently been sustained." Smith had provided Indians with several thousand dollars in goods, but they had never paid him, Garland claimed; that had caused the trader's debt. A government official who looked into this claim agreed that Smith "was generally considered poor" when he died in 1825.[33]

Smith's financial problems were so great by now that merchants in Detroit and elsewhere knew better than to extend him credit, and that ended his involvement in the fur trade. More than a decade later, a lawyer from Detroit, appointed by the federal government, examined claims against the Saginaw Chippewa. This was attorney Anthony TenEyck, son of Smith's old business associate, Conrad TenEyck. He learned from testimony and bills and records dating from 1815 and up to 1821 in the hands of Smith's son Albert that the trader was not in the fur business for about the last two years of his life—a period that would have taken in part of 1823 and all of 1824. These bills showed Jacob Smith had debts of $13,000, or what would be roughly $300,000 today. "It would seem that he was a very careless man in his business matters," wrote one of the federal officials about Jacob Smith, "and somewhat extravagant."[34]

It Is the Last Stir of the Dying Wind

Though the Indians had seen their world changing since the end of the War of 1812, the Saginaw chief called Kishkauko remained defiant and violent, not only to the white settlers who came into the territory north of Detroit, but to his own people. In 1823, when settler Eber Ward was away from his home on the Clinton River, the angry Saginaw chief and some of his band demanded whiskey. Indians routinely camped in that vicinity as they made their way down to Detroit, and Ward and his family and neighbors weren't troubled by any of them, except Kishkauko. He "would go into any man's house and take whatever he wanted, no one dared refuse him; he always had a body guard of desperate looking Indians," Ward would later say.

Ward's young daughter Sally explained to Kishkauko that there was no whiskey in the house. In response, Kishkauko stepped over to a barrel of vinegar and opened the tap, allowing the liquid to spill out onto the floor. He grabbed the Wards' bread and as he and his men left, he struck the girl, whipping her with a ramrod and injuring her severely.[1]

As the year came to a close, a Delaware Indian who had married a Chippewa

woman killed another man in a fight at Saginaw. As was often the Chippewa custom, the families of the dead man and the killer met and agreed upon a payment
of furs, goods, and other valuables from the killer and his clan—a kind of traditional reparations negotiation that would prevent further violence between the
families. Kishkauko, however, intruded upon this affair in his own terrible fashion,
according to a Detroit doctor who had served with the U.S. Army at Saginaw. A
tribal council met on the matter of settling the murder at a place on the Saginaw
River called Green Point, located just south of modern-day city of Saginaw where
the Cass, Shiawassee, Tittabawassee, and Flint rivers meet to form the Saginaw
River (now part of the Shiawassee National Wildlife Refuge, a place where Indians
gathered for hundreds of years before the French arrived in the Great Lakes). According to Dr. John Whiting, Kishkauko appeared, walked into the negotiation,
and suddenly smashed the Delaware man in the head with a club, striking him
dead before the stunned onlookers.

"What does this mean?" demanded one of the chiefs, according to Whiting's
account. "It is contrary to Indian law."

"The law is altered," Kishkauko replied.[2]

As fall came on that year, the federal government's land office "register" or receiver
in Detroit, John Biddle, had already come to realize that the matter of who, exactly,
were the rightful claimants to some of the individual reservations of Flint River
land was a veritable can of worms. The names of the recipients, of course, had
been placed on a list by Jacob Smith and handed in to the governor in the treaty
councils back in the fall of 1819, and Cass had complained in 1822 that fraud had
been perpetrated when Indian names were turned in for white individuals. Now
that it was incumbent on Biddle to try to determine the truth of the matter, he had
to tell his superiors in Washington that it wasn't going to be easy. Biddle wrote:

> Considerable difficulty exists in settling the claims of individuals to the eleven
> sections of land reserved at the Grand Traverse of the Flint river—I have to request
> that the issue of patents upon the certificate granted to "Tawcumegoqua" for Sec.
> No. 1 and "Mokitchenoqua" for Sec. No. 8 be suspended—After those certificates
> were issued the right of persons who received them was called in question by other
> claimants.[3]

The problem, Biddle continued, was that "most of the persons named in the Treaty are children; they are designated by names common to many[,] there are conflicting statements as to the individuals to whom the grant was intended to be made." Biddle said he would forward to Washington the statements about the cases, and records show that he and other officials heard testimony from numerous parties, including Indians from Saginaw. He would ultimately testify that he thought the strongest evidence was that Jacob Smith's half-Indian daughter, Nancy, was the girl Mokitchenoqua whom the Saginaw Chippewa wanted to have a reservation on the Flint River. This case and others would drag on for decades.[4]

On May 14, 1824, in Detroit, Jacob Smith's daughter Louisa, then 15 years old, married Chauncey S. Payne, the jeweler and merchant. The ceremony was conducted by Justice of the Peace James Abbott. After his years of service to the community, the war-era controversy over his loyalty to the United States, fueled largely by Jacob Smith, was forgotten. A record of the marriage doesn't reflect whether Smith attended the wedding conducted by his old enemy, but since they had been transacting a certain amount of property business with each other, and since Smith was Louisa's only surviving parent, one would tend to believe that he was there.[5] That was the same month Smith's last piece of property in Detroit—the building and lot at Woodward and Woodbridge that he had purchased in 1807 from Judge James May, his home, rental property, and store—was listed for sale in the *Detroit Gazette* by order of the Territorial Supreme Court. Smith had not paid his debts in the Craft-Walker lawsuit and so lost the property, a lot in Section 4, "No. 59 by the old plan, and No. 63 by the new plan."[6]

"Mr. Smith's *dwelling* house was sold in 1824 under mortgage," John Garland would remember, "for debts contracted by him to carry on his trade with the Indians." While Smith's son-in-law blamed Chippewa for not returning the proceeds of the trade to Smith, his constant borrowing of money and the sheer number of lawsuits against him, some going back 20 years, must have also been major factors. Another surviving record from the mid-1820s left by Smith's heirs shows that Louisa's older sister Caroline, then 18, boarded with a Detroit family for most of that year. Caroline would die sometime within the next decade, unmarried and childless. This record also shows that Jacob Smith still had plenty of legal feuds going on, with as many as seven different civil court actions in which he was suing or being sued.[7]

The last weeks of Smith's life were spent at his trading post and farm on the Flint River, still a faraway place for most Detroit residents. The winter of 1824–1825 was a mild one, and John Todd later told a newspaper editor that Smith stayed overnight with him on his farm in the Pontiac area as Smith made his final trip from Detroit back up to the Flint River. If true, it would have taken place late in 1824 or early in 1825. "On his last visit to this place [Flint] he remained overnight at Mr. Todd's house in Pontiac," a Flint newspaper wrote about Smith, "and being in very poor health, and quite feeble, he said to Mr. Todd that he had not long to live, and that he desired to sleep his last sleep in the quiet neighborhood of his lodge on the banks of the Flint."[8]

Jacob Smith was probably about 52 years old when he died in 1825 at the Grand Traverse of the Saginaw Trail on the Flint River. Though no news of his death seems to have appeared in the *Detroit Gazette,* copies of family documents later filed with the government suggest that Smith died early in the year, perhaps late in March or the first days of April. One account in a Saginaw County history mentioned that Smith was buried "in a rude coffin" at a "secluded spot near the post." Charles Avery would later claim that Smith died "from neglect as much as from disease, at his trading-post, after a lingering and pitiable sickness."

"A good hearted Frenchman, by the name of [Jean Baptiste Cauchois] who was with him upon the trading ground in 1819, and was himself an Indian trader, having his posts upon the Flint and on the Saginaw, performed for the brave but unfortunate man the last sad rites of humanity," that account claimed:

> An Indian lad who had lived with Mr. Smith for several years and who attended him in his sickness, was the only household mourner. . . . A few Indians gathered in mournful groups about the grave as the remains of the unfortunate man were committed to the earth. Ne-ome was there, his trusty and reliable friend, mute with grief. . . . The brave, warm-hearted, generous Indian trader, Jacob Smith, the earliest white pioneer upon the Saginaw and the Flint, lingered and died in a sad condition, and but for the good [Cauchois] and his Indian assistants, would have gone to his grave uncoffined. Within a few days after his decease his son-in-law, C.S. Payne, came from Detroit to the trading house, which had so recently been the scene of such long and unrelieved suffering, and gathered up most carefully and carried away the few poor remnants of the earthly stores left by the noble-hearted Indian trader.[9]

Avery's account also quoted Sagosequa, Neome's youngest daughter. "When Wah-be-sins sick, nobody come; him sicker and sicker, nobody come," Sagosequa is supposed to have said. "Wah-be-sins die, little tinker come and take all him blankets, all him cattle, all him things." "Little tinker" referred to Chauncey Payne, the Detroit jeweler and merchant married to Smith's daughter Louisa a year earlier. Payne's brother-in-law, Capt. John Garland, accompanied him to Jacob Smith's trading post–farm. "I went with the adm[inistrator of Jacob Smith's estate], Mr. Payne to Flint River immediately upon hearing of Mr. Smith's death, and assisted in searching for his books and papers but did not succeed in finding them," Garland wrote later. He wondered if someone who owed Smith money had stolen those papers, to get rid of the evidence and thereby free himself of ever having to reimburse Smith's estate.[10]

On April 4, 1825, Garland, in Detroit, wrote out an authorization for George Lyon to take possession of Smith's house and farm on the Flint River. Lyon, brother of fur trader Archie Lyon and a brother-in-law to trader Jean Baptiste Cauchois, would later say that he spent five years living on the Flint River and knew Smith and area Indians well. Perhaps it was George Lyon who had brought word of Smith's death back to Detroit. In any event, Garland trusted Lyon to take care of Smith's property at the Grand Traverse.

"Mr. George Lyons [sic] is hereby authorized to take possession (in the name of Metawane or Albert Smith, a minor) of the house and farm situated on Flint River, lately occupied by Jacob Smith (deceased)—until some further definite arrangement," Garland wrote. "The horse, cattle, hogs, one wagon, three plows and four sets of harnesses belong to me and Mr. Lyons is hereby authorized to receive them in my name from any person now at the farm."

Garland added a postscript: "All other property on the premises belongs to the estate of Jacob Smith. It is my wish that an inventory be taken of them by Mr. Lyons and Mr. E Campau and be left with Mr. Campau." Campau was Edouard Campau, the half-Indian son of Barnaby Campau. Edouard Campau's Indian name was Nowokeshik, and he had received a reservation by the 1819 treaty on the south side of the Flint River, part of the area across from where Jacob Smith had built his post.[11]

While no notice of Smith's death seems to have appeared in Detroit's newspaper, there was news later that spring that reflected the changing nature of the Michigan

Territory. In June 1825, a small article quoted Major Jonathan Kearsley, receiver at the federal land office in Detroit: "The tide of emigration which poured in upon us in the months of April and May and first weeks of this month, is now sensibly diminishing and will not probably rise to its full vigor again until October," the officer told the paper. Since May, his office had sold more than 47,000 acres of land for just over $60,000. Lots were being sold in Pontiac along the road from Detroit all the way to Saginaw, and the U.S. Congress was approving $3,000 for laying out a road to run from Detroit to Chicago. Even the land at Saginaw where the army's fort had been was going up for sale.

"We have no doubt this will be the site of the largest town which is yet to be on the waters of Lake Huron," wrote the editor of the newspaper late in June. "It is beautifully situated just below the confluence of the Shiawasee [*sic*], Flint, Cass and Tetabawasink [*sic*] rivers." The paper also insisted that health conditions in the Saginaw Valley simply weren't as bad as many believed. "The sickness experienced by the troops at Sagana in 1822 has given an unfavorable character to this section of country," the report continued. "We learn from Mr. [Louis] Campeau, who has resided there for many years, that with the exception of the year alluded to, the place has been comparatively healthy."[12]

Much of the news that year dealt with an ongoing election controversy and the resulting local political feuds. It appears that not until September that year was there any public mention of the death of Jacob Smith, and that was a legal notice:

Estate of Jacob Smith

The subscriber gives notice that he has taken out letter of administration on the estate of Jacob Smith, deceased, and requests all person indebted to said estate, to make immediate payment, and those having claims against the said estate to present the same for settlement.

CHAUNCEY S. PAYNE

Detroit, Sept. 12, 1825[13]

A document regarding Smith's estate survived in family papers. Titled "The Estate of Jacob Smith due to John McDonell," it listed items and services for which the fur trader owed McDonell, a prominent Detroit lawyer. Among the household goods and purchases made on Smith's behalf, tabulated in New York pounds, shillings, and pence and dating from 1816, were 12½ yards of bed tick, two china butter boats, a soup tureen, and two tobacco pipes.[14]

Then there were McDonell's legal fees. Smith also owed him just over £1 for costs incurred in acting as his counsel in the case of *Rathbone vs. Smith,* and other small amounts for cases including *Hastler vs. Smith* (docket number 1644), *Smith vs. Delaney* (docket number 724), and an apparent countersuit against Hastler. Smith owed McDonell a one-pound, four-shilling fee for taking a deposition in the case of *DeGarmo Jones vs. Smith.* Listed last were Smith's 1824 debts to McDonell, including the boarding and lodging of his daughter Caroline for 36 weeks "up to 23 Decr. 1824." For this, Smith's estate owed McDonell £72.

In addition, Smith owed one "T. Palmer" £4 and more than £75 to "McCarty" (probably Johnsy McCarthy) for the balance of a note on money Smith had borrowed. Smith seems to have died expecting a large payment from the U.S. government. The final notation on this document by McDonell claimed the lawyer expected to collect 15 percent of a $470 claim Smith had made on the U.S. government, though the reason for this claim was not explained.[15]

Charles Avery's account of Smith's death also suggested that the fur trader and farmer died in debt and even poor, just as John Garland maintained and as did a federally appointed lawyer later looking into claims against the Saginaw Chippewa. If Smith had been wealthy, as John Todd believed, he presumably would have left a healthy estate for his son and his daughters. But he did not. Garland's more accurate assessment of Smith's situation was that Smith was thousands of dollars in the red when he died. What Smith managed to leave his children, by virtue of his maneuverings at the 1819 Saginaw treaty, was a claim for land along the Flint River—thousands of acres of land allegedly granted to them under Indian names in the treaty. This land wasn't particularly valuable in 1825, but one federal official would note that by the late 1830s and the early 1840s it was extremely valuable.[16] Jacob Smith's heirs would have to lobby and fight a political and legal struggle for it, but ultimately they would win.

The court-appointed bankruptcy commissioners who were named to handle Smith's estate had close connections to Smith's sons-in-law. One was Dr. Whiting, who knew John Garland from their Ft. Saginaw days and earlier, and Levi Brown, a jeweler who had been Chauncey Payne's business partner and who was married to Payne's sister.[17] Whether they were able to settle Smith's estate in a manner favorable to his heirs is unknown, but it would seem doubtful given the number of creditors who must have been in line, hoping to be paid. Despite Smith's financial difficulties in the last years of his life, he had tried to provide for his daughter Caroline. John and Harriet Garland took in and raised her younger siblings Albert and Maria. Smith's daughter Louisa had married a successful merchant who would soon become a very wealthy man through his investments, and wealthier still from the sale and development of her Flint River land and that of her siblings. None of Smith's children, it seems, would suffer privation or want.

In his own small corner of the Michigan Territory, Smith would be remembered simply as the first white man and U.S. citizen to settle on the Flint River, the place that would become the city of Flint. But many prominent Detroiters of his day, some who clashed with Smith in business and in court, like James Abbott and Louis Campau, would not remember him fondly, and for good reason. Others, knowing nothing of the secret work Smith had done for William Hull and Lewis Cass, seem to have forgotten about him quickly. His more controversial legacy— the true role he played in influencing the Chippewa and Ottawa for their approval of the terms of the 1819 Treaty of Saginaw—has been for the most part misunderstood. Yet this would extend far beyond the business debts and lawsuits Smith left in his wake. The claims and legal struggles over those reservations of land on the Flint River made in the 1819 treaty would last until about 1860, dwarfing the business-related lawsuits to which Smith was party in his lifetime.

Yet some of those who had lived on the Michigan frontier in the era of the War of 1812 or who knew of Smith's work did respect him and appreciate his role. Just as Detroit historian B. F. H. Witherell remembered Jacob Smith fondly, so too did Flint pioneer John Todd, as an old man, have kind words for the fur trader. "Mr. Smith was a remarkably brave and intelligent man, and most genial and kind hearted as a companion," the *Wolverine Citizen* said, quoting Todd.[18]

With U.S. soldiers pulled out of Saginaw and the renewed Indian fears stoked by Blackhawk's War in the west, settlement in the Flint River region slowed for several years. The word "secluded" was still an appropriate one to describe that area six years after Smith's death. Alexis de Tocqueville, then a young Frenchman and unknown writer, saw this when he traveled with his friend Beaumont from Detroit up to Saginaw in the summer of 1831. Tocqueville later described this journey in an essay titled "A Fortnight in the Wilderness."

Tocqueville was on a mission to America to discover the differences between U.S. citizens and the French and their respective governments and institutions, and he wanted to see the U.S. frontiers and people firsthand. According to notes left by Tocqueville, when the Frenchmen headed north on the trail from Pontiac on July 24, the only white Americans they met before arriving in Grand Blanc was a "Mr. Williams"—Oliver Williams, the father of fur traders Ephraim and Gardiner Williams—living at his farm on Silver Lake in Oakland County. While traveling north on the Saginaw Trail, the Frenchmen also met an unnamed hunter whose family was encamped with a group of Indians at a place called Little Springs, that source of good drinking water in Springfield Township where the trader Bolieu and his family had lived.[19]

But as they rode over these hills, Tocqueville's horse lost a shoe; a farmer at the place called Grand Blanc shod the animal that evening. The Frenchmen wanted to reach the Flint River by nightfall, and the farmer urged them to hurry since the sun was setting and they still had several miles to go. Unfortunately for the travelers, a cold, moonlit darkness descended over them. The men had a scare when they lost each other after Tocqueville, riding forward alone to make sure there was no danger of an ambush, approached what he described as a couple of unfinished houses. These were located along the Thread River, now called Thread Creek. But no one was home here, and Tocqueville and Beaumont spent some anxious moments before they found one another.[20]

The tired Frenchmen pressed on into the woods and 45 minutes later emerged into a clearing where they saw a light coming from one of "two or three cabins" near the Flint River. A woman who was alone in that unfinished cabin, frightened by the night visitors, pointed them to the nearby home of John Todd, the pioneer who had known Jacob Smith. Tocqueville wrote that he and his friend were surprised to see a chained bear rising on his hind legs to greet them as they approached Todd's cabin.

"What a devil of a country this is," Beaumont said to his friend, "where one has bears for watch dogs." But Todd called his bear away and happily provided accommodations for the men and their horses that night. Ironically, Tocqueville wrote that the next morning, he witnessed Todd shortchange two young Indians he hired to guide the Frenchmen on to Saginaw. Todd, he said, pocketed the two dollars paid by Tocqueville to arrange the guides, and instead gave the Indians a pair of moccasins and a handkerchief worth much less. Then the party left Todd's, forded the Flint River, and went on to Saginaw.[21]

"The road there is only a narrow path, scarcely recognizable to the eye," the Frenchman wrote of the Saginaw Trail once he and Beaumont crossed to the side that had been claimed by Jacob Smith as his white children's land. Though the trail had been widened several years earlier for wagons and sleighs to travel up to Ft.

Saginaw, nature had reclaimed all but a trace of it in the time since the fort was abandoned, according to Tocqueville's description.

As they left the Flint River, riding north, "the last traces of man disappeared." Now the young Frenchmen saw the Michigan wilderness as Jacob Smith had known it for so many years—as it would never be again. "Soon there was nothing even to indicate the presence of savages," Tocqueville wrote, "and we had before us the spectacle which we had been so long pursuing, the depths of a virgin forest." Though it was six years since Jacob Smith's death, the Frenchman's description of the woods on the Saginaw Trail, still wild and unsettled in this final section, was a lonesome epitaph for the fur trader and his life in this part of the Michigan wilderness, with the moan of the wind through an endless lattice of boughs and leaves overhead, an elegy for a time and place that would soon disappear:

> At midday, when the sun darts its beams on the forest, one often hears in its depths something like a long sigh, a plaintive cry lingering in the distance. It is the last stir of the dying wind; Then everything around you falls back into a silence so deep, a stillness so complete, that the soul is invaded by a sort of religious terror; the traveler halts and looks round; pressed one against the other and with their branches interlaced, the forest trees seem to form but one whole, an immense and indestructible edifice, under whose vaults eternal darkness reigns.[22]

No One Was More Anxious to Secure Advantage Than Smith

In the months and years after Jacob Smith's death, a good friend, a rival, and a once-feared character from frontier Michigan came to bad ends—one by illness, one by accident, and one by suicide while in custody for a crime.

The last was Kishkauko, the notorious chief from Saginaw feared by settlers and Indians alike, distrusted by territorial officials and soldiers. Kishkauko outlived Smith by about a year, dying a terrible death in jail in Detroit, reportedly by his own hand. According to a newspaper report, when a Saginaw Indian was found lying in a Detroit street, nearly dead from a tomahawk wound in the back of his head one day in January 1826, Kishkauko, then in town, was immediately the prime suspect. Pursued by residents, Kishkauko fled to the home of the government Indian agent, Colonel Louis Beaufait, for protection. There he was arrested near midnight. The next day, a Sunday, Kishkauko and his son Big Beaver were indicted by a coroner's jury on a charge of murder. One Detroit historian identified the victim as a man named Wauwasson.

In May of that year, after family members were allowed to visit him in jail, Kishkauko was discovered dead of apparent poisoning. Authorities believed one of his wives had brought a toxic concoction for him to drink, at his request, so that he could take his own life rather than live in prison. According to one dramatic account, some of his relatives and followers were allowed to take his body for funeral ceremonies, and buried him by moonlight in an orchard near Detroit.

Big Beaver remained in jail and a delegation of Saginaw Indians came to Detroit early in the summer to ask government officials for him to be pardoned and released, according to a letter on file in the Detroit Public Library. But this was refused and reports say four months later, in early October, Big Beaver escaped from jail. He reportedly died, not long after his escape, drowned in Saginaw Bay.[1] But Big Beaver's escape probably didn't matter much in terms of the public safety of white settlers. With every passing month and year, the threat posed by the Indians to those U.S. citizens coming to southeastern Michigan diminished. In truth, it was the Saginaw Chippewa and other tribes who were witnessing an invasion of settlers into the territory.

Neome, the gentle Saginaw Chippewa chief of the Flint River band, who had been described as Jacob Smith's close friend, with whom the fur trader had such influence, died in 1827, according to accounts by Charles Avery and Ephraim S. Williams. After a long illness, the old chief succumbed at his "tribal home, a few miles above [up river from] Saginaw City," Williams wrote. This was a reference to the Indian village on the Flint River near what became the Genesee-Saginaw county line. On maps and in records of territorial Michigan, Neome's village is usually wrongly labeled "Reaume's Town."[2]

One of Jacob Smith's acquaintances and rivals from the Saginaw Valley trade was Archibald Lyon, the fur trader who had been employed by Louis Campau in the years after the War of 1812. Lyon was described as standing about five feet, ten inches tall and having a "sandy complexion." His Indian name was said to be Wa-she-ba-ga and he was brother-in-law to Jean Baptiste Cauchois, the man who'd helped bury Smith. Lyon was the brother of George Lyon, who had been allowed to operate Smith's farm at the Flint River's Grand Traverse for a time after the fur trader's death. The Lyon brothers were also brothers-in-law to a Joseph Campau of Detroit (in this case, a younger Joseph Campau and not Louis Campau's uncle). This younger Joe Campau had married the Lyons' sister Rose in 1814.

Archie Lyon was well educated and a fine violin player, his friends said. Records show he had worked for merchant-attorney John McDonell during the War of 1812, and helped McDonell purchase from the Indians a number of American soldiers taken prisoner. He had married a half-Indian woman called Catherine and together they'd had a daughter whose English name was Elizabeth. Elizabeth would claim that her Indian name was Mokitchenoqua—the same name that was said to have been given to Jacob Smith's daughter.

Lyon outlived his first wife, married a woman named Elizabeth L. Roy with whom he had several more children, and at some point seems to have had a half-Chippewa wife or companion named Kazheobeonoqua. She described herself in testimony as Lyon's first wife and eventually gave testimony in one of the Smith reservation lawsuits. After working for Louis Campau, Archibald Lyon worked for the Williams brothers, Ephraim and Gardiner, probably for another 11 or 12 years after Jacob Smith's death. But it seems that in the mid-1830s Archie Lyon was working in the trade at an outpost at the "little forks" of the Tittabawassee River, where the city of Midland stands. Lyon, as the story was told, was requested to come and fiddle at a dance being given at Saginaw. Ephraim Willliams and others believed that the fur trader put on his skates and picked up his violin, apparently intending to skate down the frozen Tittabawasee to Saginaw for the party. But Archie Lyon never made it to that dance and his body was never found. The story was told that those who went out looking for him found his tracks on the ice leading directly up to a hole into which he had fallen into the river and drowned.[3]

Jacob Smith's own resting spot, near his old trading post–farm on the Flint River at the crossing of the Saginaw Trail, was not permanent. After the town of Flint had grown and expanded from the 1830s on, cemetery records suggest his heirs had his remains moved from his original grave near the Grand Traverse and reinterred in Flint's Glenwood Cemetery, located at what was then the western edge of town about two miles down the river.[4] By this point in 1866 his old place at the ford had become a neighborhood with homes, shops, and mills, just north of Flint's downtown, with a bridge and a railroad trestle for crossing the river.

The place where Smith's cabin stood is now the site of a State of Michigan historical marker at the corner of West First Avenue and Lyon Avenue in the city of Flint. The individual 640-acre reservation that included this property was originally earmarked, he and his heirs maintained, for his son. Albert Smith eventually transferred it into the hands of his sister and brother-in-law, Louisa and Chauncey Payne. After the Civil War, the Paynes donated a piece of that property, where the ruins of Jacob Smith's log home could be seen for many years, to the First Baptist Church. There a white clapboard-sided chapel was built in 1873, and eventually homes, mills, and businesses covered the property.

No news seems to have appeared about Jacob Smith's second burial. Perhaps after all the controversy and the long legal battle that took place over their Smith Reservation sections, the family made the arrangements quietly, without public notice. But it also may be that, coming just a year after the end of the Civil War with all its death and devastation, an article about another grave was not thought to be of great interest—or at least, not the grave of the controversial trader whose heirs had emerged the winners in the legal fight for the land on which much of Flint was built. Smith's children and their spouses had a large and prominent stone erected to his memory. In time, Smith's son Albert, his daughters Maria and Louisa and their husbands, and other relatives would be buried near him, a location that was then in the countryside and only a few hundred yards from the winding Flint River.

Long before Smith was moved to his final resting place, decades of legal wrangling dragged on over some of those reservations on the Flint River granted in the 1819 Saginaw treaty between the United States and the Saginaw Chippewa and Ottawa. First, there was the matter that, in the early 1820s, Gov. Lewis Cass warned the U.S. Treasury Department that a fraud had been perpetrated at the treaty, and that Indian names for "certain white persons" had been written into it so that they could try to get land near the Grand Traverse of the river. There were immediately questions about how the federal land office in Detroit should handle this. Then there was the matter that more than one person claimed to be Mokitchenoqua, Tawcumegoqua, and other Indian names set down in the treaty. Some of these people were truly Indian or part Indian, while Smith's children in Detroit were white.[5]

Of course, the problem of fraud—that Indian names had been written in for whites—referred to the manipulations of Jacob Smith. Jonathan Kearsley, who had been the federal receiver or treasurer at Detroit during the time after the War of 1812, testified later that Chippewa chiefs were requested to come to Detroit to give their side of the matter; he said he recollected that the Indians agreed they had intended for Jacob Smith's children—his white children as well as his half-Indian daughter—to have land granted to them in the treaty terms. Who these chiefs were Kearsley did not say. Yet the treaty language, approved by Congress in 1820, clearly stated that the people who were to get those reservations of land were of Indian descent. Since Smith's five children with wife Mary were white, government land officials couldn't and wouldn't recognize their claims, even as their husbands or guardians argued that the Chippewa chiefs truly intended this.[6]

In the meantime settlement in Michigan grew west from Detroit, but slower, at first, in Jacob Smith's old stomping grounds in the Saginaw Valley. The question of the rightful ownership of the Flint River reservations was becoming a matter of real money after the last Midwestern Indian uprising and cholera outbreaks passed in the 1830s. The population of Michigan continued growing and residents talked of statehood; land sales exploded. The Smith heirs claimed that development of the town of Flint on the north side of the river—the land they said was theirs—was being inhibited by the conflicting claims. "The Smith heirs had tried in vain to get [President] Gen. [Andrew] Jackson to issue patents to the children," Ephraim S. Williams later said about this time. "He [Jackson] declined on account of the words in the treaty, they [the Smith children] being white. But if they would bring proof from the chiefs that they were intended as the donees [*sic*, recipients], Congress would pass a law perhaps which he would execute."[7]

Ephraim Williams, by now a veteran fur trader, was familiar with the Smith heirs' problem. Slightly more than three years after Jacob Smith died, Williams and his brother Gardiner had gone into the fur trade at Saginaw, living among the Chippewa, learning their language, and becoming agents of the American Fur Company. By the mid-1830s the Williams brothers were experienced businessmen.

The children of Jacob Smith and their spouses understood what they had to do to protect their interest in the land they had been told was meant for them—they needed to change U.S. law. Albert Smith, by now a young man, and his brother-in-law Thomas Stockton, an ex-U.S. Army officer, asked Ephraim and Gardiner Williams for their influence with the Saginaw Chippewa, to get the Indians to make public affidavits or statements that they had truly intended that five of the reservations on the Flint River were for Jacob Smith's white children. Then Congress would have grounds to change the law and allow the Smith heirs to be issued land patents.[8]

Ephraim Williams said later that Lewis Cass, Judge James Abbott, and other influential Detroiters were in favor of bringing the Indians together for a council on this subject. The Williams brothers sent runners to the Indians and got the principal leaders to Saginaw for a council regarding the question. The first meeting was held in the American Fur Company's trading post on the Saginaw River in January 1835—not quite 10 years after the death of Jacob Smith, and shortly before a new Michigan county was laid out around the area where he had established his trading post at the Flint River two decades previously. This new county was called Genesee County, an Indian name or term that was brought by white settlers from the state of New York (which had been Iroquois country), but which had no connection to the Saginaw Chippewa people who still then lived in large numbers near the Flint area and the rest of the Saginaw Valley.

As the Chippewa gathered at the Saginaw trading post known as the Red Store, Williams claimed that Albert Smith was immediately recognized by the chiefs as Metawanene—an obviously positive indication that Jacob Smith's son truly had been the person named in the treaty to receive a section of land. But the council with the Indians did not go quite so easily as that. One of the chiefs of the Chippewa present at the council was Ogemawkeketo, who had been a young and powerful speaker for the Saginaw tribe back in 1819. Ogemawkeketo had reportedly become an alcoholic and his health was poor by 1835, but he understood that the treaty language required the individual Flint River reservations were for people of Indian descent. Since no such person had claimed these sections, Ogemawkeketo argued, the land should revert to the Chippewa. If the U.S. government or any white individuals wanted this land, they could buy it from the Indians, the chief maintained.[9]

This was the last thing Jacob Smith's heirs wanted to hear. Though the number of white Americans building farms and homes at the Flint River was still small, it was growing, and a government land office was to soon open in the vicinity. "The first day's council closed rather dark for the heirs present representing the interests of the Smith children, and they felt it," Williams wrote years later. But significantly, Williams continued: "By certain influences brought to bear upon the chiefs, upon meeting the second morning they changed their minds, and, not having forgotten their good and steadfast friend, [Wabesins or Jacob Smith], they did not hesitate to declare that his white children were the rightful owners of the reservation in the true meaning and intent of the treaty."[10]

What Ephraim Williams did not say in that published account of the 1835 council was that it was he and his brother Gardiner who, "after great exertion," convinced the Indians to give that statement in favor of the Smith heirs. Williams admitted this matter-of-factly to historiographer Lyman Draper, according to Draper's handwritten notes of his interview with Williams on January 7, 1863. But in Williams's own writing—particularly an article that was printed in state and local histories—Williams never admitted that he and his brother "brought influences to bear" on the Chippewa chiefs so they would support the claims of the white Smith heirs.[11]

Thus pressured or influenced by the Williams brothers, 10 chiefs and head men of the Saginaw Chippewa said they had always intended Jacob Smith's white children to have land along the Flint River. On January 22, 1835, the Indian leaders affixed their totems and Xs to a document acknowledging that Metawanene, Messawwakut, Sagosequa, Annokitoqua, and Nondashemau were the Indian names of Jacob Smith's white children. They were the ones, the Chippewa leaders agreed in the statement prepared by the white men, whom the tribe intended to grant five of the Flint River reservations. This statement was notarized by Ephraim Williams, who was then also justice of the peace for Oakland County. Williams and his brother signed the statement as witnesses, as did Thomas Simpson, an employee of the territory's federal Indian Department, and an interpreter named Charles H. Rodd.[12]

That fall, other similar councils were held with Indians, again at Saginaw, at the Big Rock Village on the Shiawassee River and on the Flint River. There the first signer of the statement was Tondogane, who had been one of the chiefs who had ostensibly asked, along with Neome, for Jacob Smith's help in negotiating with Cass back in 1819. Another council was held at a place called the "Grand Saline" reservation, Ketchewaundaugenink (as it was rendered in the Treaty of Saginaw), also on the Shiawassee on October 3, 1835. Indians from the village called Kopeniconick (or Copeniconic, in what would become Genesee County's Mundy Township, just west of Grand Blanc) and from a village on the Red Cedar River in Ingham County also signed that statement. One signer was Ogemos or Okemos, for whom the town of Okemos, near Lansing, is named, and who later testified that he was one of the original signers of the Treaty of Saginaw.[13]

White residents of the Saginaw Valley, both newcomer U.S. citizens who had journeyed to Michigan from the east and longtime Michigan *habitants* of French-Canadian descent, also claimed they understood from the Indians that some of the Flint River reservations were meant for the white children of Jacob Smith, though practically none of these people could have been at the 1819 treaty councils. One signer was George Lyon, who had lived near Smith for at least a few years, and who signed his statement with an X.[14]

Major Robert A. Forsyth, who had been Cass's aide at the treaty, and James Conner, brother of Henry Conner and another of the government's translators, gave depositions in Detroit courts that they had understood that the Chippewa really intended to give Smith's children land as a favor to their father. "Smith was very influential with the Indians," Forsyth stated, "in promoting the objects of the government." James Conner agreed. Smith, he said in his affidavit, "was active in his exertions and very influential in and about the procurement of the treaty stipulations from the Indians."[15]

All these statements, along with petitions signed by residents of Flint and Saginaw, were enough for the U.S. Congress and the Jackson administration, though even a legislative report on the matter was factually incorrect. When Illinois congressman William L. May reported a bill out of the House of Representatives' Committee on Private Land Claims early in 1836, it stated that it had been "an inadvertence," or error, that caused the treaty language to reserve the sections on the Flint River for people of Indian descent. Of course, that was no mistake; Lewis Cass had intentionally placed that language in the treaty and had said so under oath. But the committee reported that its members "were perfectly satisfied from the affidavits of the gentlemen who were present and subscribing witnesses to the treaty, and from the statements of the chiefs and head men of the said tribe, that there were no persons of Indian descent who passed by the names appropriated to said petitioners."[16]

Of course, that last qualifier was not true, either—there *were* people of Indian descent who had those very same names. But the congressmen reported that the heirs of Jacob Smith, though white, were definitely the individuals who were meant to receive these sections of land on the river—why, the Chippewa leaders themselves said so. Of course, Congress and the Jackson administration likely didn't know or care that Ephraim and Gardiner Williams, important agents of the American Fur Company, had influenced the leaders of the Indians of the Saginaw Valley to make the initial statement. As history has recorded, Jackson initiated and supported far harsher measures against Indians elsewhere in the United States.

As summer came on in 1836, Congress passed an act "to authorize the President of the United States to cause to be issued to Albert J. Smith [and his siblings] patents for certain reservations of land in Michigan Territory." The House Committee had noted that Jacob Smith's white children had been adopted as "members" of the Chippewa tribe, and that their Indian names were "theirs alone."[17] Again, that was not the case, since at least two of the names claimed by Smith's children were the names of daughters of Neome. The statement by Congress was also contradicted by Louis Campau, who actually was at the 1819 treaty councils and who later testified that Jacob Smith had "borrowed" the names of Indian children for his own and paid Indian women for the use of their names. But the law was approved and the federal land office issued the land patents, for five sections on the north side of the Flint River to Jacob Smith's white heirs. As far as the heirs were concerned, the question of ownership of the land was settled.

But they were wrong. This legislative "ending" of the matter actually opened an era of legal fighting over the reservations in Michigan courts. Ephraim Williams later explained why, at least in part, he and his brother Gardiner Williams now turned against the Smith heirs and their claim: After influencing the Chippewa to support the claims of Jacob Smith's white children, the Williamses weren't paid for their work. "The council was held at the Red Store," Ephraim Williams said about the American Fur Company's post at Saginaw, where that first meeting had been held with the Indians in 1835, and where Williams and his brother managed to change the Indians' opinion and support the Smith heirs' claim. "At the particular request of the [Smith] family, the Tusseu [brothers] Williams accomplished it too and have never been compensated one cent."[18]

Unhappy at not being paid by the Smith heirs, the Williams brothers switched sides in the battle over the heirs' land claim, charging that the fur traders white children *were not* the intended and rightful recipients after all. Gardiner Williams joined in two of the lawsuits against the claims of the Smith heirs. Ephraim Williams was never an official party to the suits, but he publicly questioned the legitimacy of claims of the Smith heirs, without ever acknowledging the key role he and his brother played in getting the Indians to say they intended for Smith's white children to be granted land.[19]

There may have been another factor contributing to the Williams brothers' unhappiness with the heirs of Jacob Smith. The daughter of their loyal employee, Archibald Lyon, had an application in with the government as early as 1825 for a land patent for Section 8 in the Smith Reservation, which was designated for a person named in the treaty as Mokitchenoqua. Lyon's daughter was Elizabeth or Betsy Lyon, who was reportedly one-quarter Indian. Gardiner Williams and a partner bought out her interest in that section. Of course, they would have to prove Betsy Lyon was Mokitchenoqua, and that brought them into a direct legal conflict with Jacob Smith's white heirs, who maintained Mokitchenoqua was Smith's half-Indian daughter Nancy.

Why did Smith's white heirs fight this particular case? Before Congress decided in 1836 that land patents could be granted for the sections they claimed on the north side of the Flint River, they were faced with the possibility that they might just be left with no land whatsoever. The eldest Smith son-in-law, the professional soldier John Garland, insisted that Jacob Smith's half-Indian daughter was the real Mokitchenoqua. The governor's men would testify that Nancy had been raised in Meadville, Pennsylvania, but she returned to Michigan and in 1830 married a blacksmith from upstate New York named Alexander D. Crane, who had come to the territory three years earlier. Nancy and Alexander Crane were wed in Redford, Michigan, and moved to the Ann Arbor area, where he soon became a lawyer; they settled in Dexter. Garland and his brothers-in-law bought the Cranes' interest in Section 8, which lay on the south side of the Flint River, across from the area where Jacob Smith had his trading post.[20]

A third woman, named Marie Lavoy, also put her claim in for the land, saying that she was the intended Mokitchenoqua, but she never joined in the resulting legal battle. Of course, the conflicting claims could only be settled in court. Some witnesses testified that Jacob Smith had openly talked about how one of the reservations on the south side of the Flint River was Betsy Lyon's. But Louis Campau testified that Smith had actually complained that Archie Lyon "stole" Nancy's Indian name to put in Betsy's application for that section of land. Some witnesses testified they heard Smith say he got sections of land on the north side of the river for his children at the treaty talks in Saginaw, but not on the south side, where the section for Mokitchenoqua had been laid out.[21]

Which claimant was the real Mokitchenoqua? At the request of the Smith heirs, Lewis Cass was deposed in Wayne County Circuit Court on November 26, 1835, about the generalities of the Treaty of Saginaw and Jacob Smith. Cass, the former territorial governor and now the U.S. secretary of war, did not mention that Smith had been working for him as a secret agent, but merely noted with considerable understatement that the fur trader "was present at the treaty." Cass stressed that the Indians had asked "for grants of land for some of their half-breeds." He said that he agreed this should be done, but was soon informed by one of the Indian subagents—"I think it was Capt. Knaggs"—that a plot was being hatched so that land was to be "granted to the white children of Jacob Smith under their Indian names." Cass noted on cross-examination that he knew Smith's white family in Detroit personally. Two federal officials in Detroit who gave depositions in the case in 1840, John Biddle and Jonathan Kearsley, testified that they believed that of the two conflicting Mokitchenoqua claims, Nancy Smith Crane's was the strongest.[22]

The case went before Michigan's chancery court in February of 1843. Ironically, it was Jacob Smith's words, living on in the form of hearsay evidence, that defeated the claim of his heirs that Nancy Smith Crane was the true Mokitchenoqua. The chancellor, or chancery court judge, Randolph Manning, said that testimony regarding Smith's statements about the Flint River land—statements Smith had made to friends and acquaintances—was key to his ruling in favor of Elizabeth Lyon's claim. She was the true Mokitchenoqua, the judge ruled. "The repeated declarations of Smith after the treaty that there was a section reserved at the Flint for Lyons' daughter is almost conclusive of itself," Manning said. "No one, perhaps, was more anxious to secure personal advantage by the treaty, or knew better for whom reservations were made, than Smith himself."[23]

Thus Gardiner Williams and his partner had won the case, but only temporarily. The Smith heirs appealed and lost again in the state Supreme Court in 1845. Yet this loss in court did not cost them the section of the south side of the Flint River. Though the state Supreme Court also ruled for Williams and his partner—that Betsy Lyon was Mokitchenoqua—Jacob Smith's sons-in-law ultimately held onto the land when a local court in Flint refused to eject them from the contested property. Incredible as this may seem, the local court, ignoring the state Supreme Court's decision, ruled that there was insufficient evidence to prove that Elizabeth Lyon was the real Mokitchenoqua. The Smith heirs, Stockton and Payne, thus kept possession of that section despite the fact that the highest courts in Michigan had ruled against them.[24]

Even though they fought a legal battle acknowledging Jacob Smith's half-Chippewa daughter, it appears that his white children and their spouses otherwise avoided discussion of Nancy Crane, who died in 1842 at the age of 35. When Albert Smith was asked in a deposition whether his father had any children with an Indian woman, Smith only answered that he had "heard" he had an Indian sister. In the accounts about Jacob Smith that appeared in local Flint area histories, only brief mentions of the case of Nancy Crane, the Indian daughter of Jacob Smith, can be found.[25]

Gardiner Williams and other partners kept fighting the Smith heirs. Probably at the urging of Williams and his allies, an Indian named Jack, who as a lad had lived with and worked for Jacob Smith for several years, put in a claim that he was the real Metawanene, and that Section 2 of the Smith Reservation was meant for him. This section was where Smith had his trading post and farm on the Flint River at the Grand Traverse. In addition, Saginaw Chippewa women, including

Chief Neome's daughters Sagosequa and Annoketoqua, also put in claims that they were the individuals who were supposed to have been granted nearby Sections 3 and 4. Of course, the Smith heirs maintained that Metawanene was the name the Chippewa had given Albert J. Smith, while Louisa Payne was Annoketeoqua and Caroline Smith, who died sometime after her father's death, was Sagosequa. Legal maneuvering over these competing claims dragged on for years before going to trial in the circuit court of Genesee County in 1856 and in Oakland County in 1860, but the Smith heirs won these cases in the battle for these sections of land they claimed along the north side of the river, with white juries ruling in their favor.[26] In the meantime, a town had long since grown up around the place where once Jacob Smith had been the territorial governer's man on the Saginaw Valley frontier. Within another generation, Flint would become one of the most important industrial centers in the world and the second largest city in the state of Michigan.

—————— ╬═╳═╬ ——————

The White Man Takes Away
What He Bought of the Indians

—————— ╬═╳═╬ ——————

There were no legal battles over the remaining four sections of land in the original Smith Reservation on the south side of the Flint River as set aside under the terms of the 1819 treaty. These went to the heirs of a woman named Catharine Mene (Kitchegeequa); Phyllis Beaufait (Petabonequa), the daughter of Colonel Louis Beaufait, longtime U.S. Indian agent and interpreter; a man named John Fisher, or alternately, Jean Visger (Checbalk); and Francis Edouard Campau (Nowokeshik), the son of Barney Campau. Each of these persons was described in the historical record as offspring of white men and Indian women. Nor does it appear there were lawsuits over the other two sections on the north side of the river claimed by Jacob Smith's daughters Maria Stockton and Harriet Garland.

The final section in the Smith Reservation was Section 1—the only reservation on the north side of the river not claimed by Jacob Smith's heirs. Earmarked in the 1819 treaty for an individual named Tawcumegoqua, it was also at the center of a long lawsuit. This case boiled down to whether the intended Tawcumegoqua was the part-Indian daughter of fur trader Bolieu (the man who reportedly first brought Jacob Smith to the Flint River), or a full-blooded Chippewa of the same name, the daughter of the chief named Mixenene. Mixenene, some witnesses said, had been advised by Smith at the treaty councils with Lewis Cass.

The land claim of Bolieu's daughter, which passed to her children with the last names of Coutant and Chauvin, was eventually sold to Joseph Campau of Detroit, uncle of Louis Campau. A daughter of the "mixed blood" Tawcumegoqua, Angelique Chauvin, testified in Wayne County in 1857 that two Saginaw Valley Indian leaders had come to see her mother before the treaty councils were held in the fall of 1819, advising her to attend. "The chief they call Grand Blanc & also Kishcauco [*sic*] came & asked her to go [to the Saginaw treaty council to get a reservation of land]," she said. "Both these chiefs were relatives of my mother."

On the other side of this case was the full-blooded Chippewa woman who said she was the real Tawcumegoqua; she reportedly sold her interest in the section, which ultimately came into the possession of business partners named George Dewey and Rufus Hamilton. By the time this case ended in their favor after trial in the state Supreme Court, the Civil War was under way. That land earmarked for Tawcumegoqua turned out to be the one contested section in the Smith Reservation where the courts of white men determined it had been intended to go to a full-blooded Chippewa individual. Of course, by the time the case was over Tawcumegoqua and her husband had long since sold their interest to white men. Tawcumegoqua, who had been a child at the time of the Treaty of Saginaw, died in 1848. She was then around 35 years old.

One of the witnesses at the trial in the Tawcumegoqua case, held in Saginaw, was a Chippewa man named Naugunnee, who said he was a grandson of Neome. Naugunnee testified that even as a child at the treaty, he had not expected his people to fare well as they agreed to land cessions in the talks with Governor Cass. Naugunnee also said it was Jacob Smith who'd advised Neome to get special reservations for his (Neome's) children. "When the children came into the council room I was standing [by the] side of Neome; Gen. Cass was nearby," Naugunnee testified. "I stood so near Neome because I had by past experience learned that the white man generally takes away what he bought of the Indians, and I was anxious to see what this would lead to."

Land sales and development, towns and farms, sprawled west from the Detroit area along the routes to Chicago in the years after Jacob Smith's death. By this point Lewis Cass, considered one of the nation's leading experts on Indians, changed his mind about them; he had previously thought that they could and would learn how to farm as did white men, that they must become "civilized." But now he wrote that they were unable to do so, that they were by nature "wild" and violent, despite the efforts of whites to reform them. Little wonder, then, in the mid-to-late 1830s, as the pace of the settlement of the Saginaw Valley increased and Michigan became a state, that the U.S. government pressed the Saginaw Chippewa chiefs to give up most of their large remaining tribal reservations.

Jacob Smith's sons-in-law, John Garland of the U.S. Army and Thomas B. W. Stockton, a former officer, and Smith's son Albert, who was employed as an aide to Garland, were witnesses to one such treaty signed at the Flint River, where farms, businesses, and settlers' homes were growing around this place where Smith had traded with the Chippewa. The influx was now an irreversible tide. Albert Smith would act as a government agent, trying to get Chippewa leaders in Michigan to move their people west. Cass, in the meantime, had become Andrew Jackson's secretary of war in 1831, and Garland was commissioned major. He would escort the famous Sauk chief Black Hawk to Washington, D.C., after a brief, bloody, but unsuccessful uprising against whites taking over their lands in Illinois and Wisconsin, which was at that point still part of the Michigan Territory. This marked the end of Indian armed resistance to the coming of the settlers in what had once been called the Old Northwest.

Ephraim and Gardiner Williams, the men who had helped the Jacob Smith heirs secure federal patents for the Flint River land by pressuring Chippewa leaders in 1835, regretted what they had done, but there is no suggestion in available records they admitted this while the court battles dragged on. Another man who had helped in that effort was Thomas Simpson, an Indian agent who had "acted in concert" with the Williamses "and got no pay" for his work. "Simpson shot himself at Saginaw, depressed and discouraged," Ephraim Williams told historian Lyman Draper. Ironically, Williams later wrote in a published paper that the U.S. government's granting of land to Smith's white children was "a betrayal" of the Indians' trust. He also rejected the notion that the five Indian names claimed by the white children of Smith for the Flint River reservations were accurate, implying that their claims on this land were improper and even fraudulent, even though he had had a direct hand in the government's acceptance of these claims.

The name "Nondashomau," supposedly given Maria, the youngest daughter, was a man's name, Williams wrote; so was "Messawwakut," the name supposedly given to Harriet, the oldest daughter. Other names given in the treaty article,

Annoketoqua and Sagosequa (names the Smith heirs claimed were for Louisa Payne and Caroline Smith) were the names of real Chippewa women, daughters of Neome, he pointed out. "How inconsistent and ridiculous to suppose for a moment that Jacob Smith would have done so inconsistent a thing as to have presented, at the treaty of 1819, the names of three Indians for the names of his daughters as given in the treaty; not at all probable," Williams claimed. "I knew Mr. Smith, and I never believed he did any such thing."

Of course, there was plenty of information to dispute Williams on that point, for testimony had been given by people present at the treaty that Smith did "borrow" Indian children and even paid Indians for the use of their names—all so Chippewa names for his white children would be placed in the treaty as people receiving sections of land. Williams also neglected to point out that he and his brother helped the Smith heirs get the federal land patents to the reservations by pressuring Chippewa chiefs. In truth, Ephraim and Gardiner Williams had helped pave the way for the "betrayal" by a Congress that didn't have all the facts and may not have been interested in them in any case.

One other claim was made in relation to Jacob Smith in the years after his death, and that was by his son Albert J. Smith. In a treaty signed with the United States in 1837, the Saginaw Chippewa agreed to set up a fund from the sale of some of their land. This fund would be used to pay U.S. citizens of Michigan whose property they had damaged or destroyed after Detroit was surrendered to the British in the War of 1812.

Albert Smith eventually learned from his brother-in-law, Lt. Col. John Garland, that his father Jacob Smith was owed several thousand dollars for trade goods by members of the Saginaw Chippewa tribe at the time of his death. In general, the practice of fur traders was to keep a record of what goods individual Indians bought on credit or were taken on consignment by individuals who acted as a trader's agent or employee, to trade to other Indians. Though Smith's account books were never found, several chiefs of the tribe admitted that members of the Saginaw Chippewa were indeed indebted to him at the time of his death for goods they had been advanced.

No one, however, could say just how much they had owed the fur trader. Albert Smith, in the name of his father's estate, asked for $8,000 from the tribe. But the Chippewa chiefs and U.S. commissioner, a Detroit-based lawyer named Anthony

TenEyck, met in the fall of 1839 and decided that Albert Smith should get $1,600. Unfortunately for Smith, War Department officials rejected his claim against the Chippewa in part because they reasoned that Jacob Smith had been "given" so much land on the Flint River by the Indians—land that had become valuable as the years passed by. John Garland protested that the matter of the reservations on the Flint River was separate from the debts that members of the tribe owed Smith. Perhaps even more surprising was that several Chippewa chiefs, unnamed in TenEyck's report, agreed with Garland in the late 1830s—they had indeed wanted the fur trader's children to have this land, not because they owed Smith, but "on account of their friendship for Smith, out of his kindness to them, and particularly for one of the principal chiefs of their tribe."

Whether the chiefs were still being influenced or pressured as they had been by the Williams brothers nearly five years earlier is impossible to say. But the War Department was unmoved and Albert Smith's claim against the Chippewa for payment of their trade debts was rejected. Albert Smith introduced notes from various Detroit merchants and businessmen that Jacob Smith had owed them a total of $13,000 and he appealed his claim to the Congress and the administration of President John Tyler Jr. But the earlier decision was upheld. The land that Smith's children had received along the Flint River was payment enough, federal officials decided.

The complicated trail of Jacob Smith's maneuverings at the 1819 Saginaw treaty talks and the subsequent lawsuits over the Flint River reservations left a crowd of witnesses who gave a variety of statements and opinions, some of them contradictory, some of them flatly wrong. Yet there was a record of evidence showing Jacob Smith's manipulation at the councils; of controversy about the treaty terms, charges of fraud and deception about the indenties of the individuals who were to receive sections of land along the Flint River. There was the assertion that most of the Indians present in Saginaw in 1819 didn't really understand the provisions of the treaty to which they agreed. There was the testimony of men who had served Governor Cass at the Saginaw treaty talks that Jacob Smith had taken control of the list of the individuals who were to receive sections of land. And there was the statement by Ephraim Williams of the influence later brought to bear by himself and his brother on Saginaw chiefs to support the claims of Smith's white heirs for individual reserves.

Yet from the 1820s on to the middle of the nineteenth century, there was also the testimony of a number of men, white men, and the report of Anthony TenEyck—all who had spoken directly with the Chippewa chiefs—reaffirming the sections were indeed the tribe's gift to Smith's children. Is it possible that all these witnesses lied, or that they succumbed to outside pressure each time, in order to protect the claims of the white children of the controversial fur trader? Certainly that is possible; it is also likely that Chippewa who opposed the Smith heirs were ignored, at least until or unless white men purchased Indian claims.

Cass himself had tried to head off the ability of Smith's white heirs to make claims to Flint River land when he was warned about what Smith was trying to do at the treaty councils. The governor's aides and interpreters knew it, too. But they, like Cass, testified years later that Smith had great influence over the Saginaw Chippewa, general statements that were frustratingly devoid of any detail about the hows and whys. Yet these sufficed as explanation for what had happened at the treaty. The statement Ephraim Williams made in 1863 makes clear the Smith heirs weren't willing to pay him and his brother for their influence with the Chippewa—they were convinced the sections had been meant for them.

Of course, the heirs ultimately won their suits on the Flint River land in courts that were disposed to look favorably on the claims of Chauncey Payne and Thomas B. W. Stockton, white men who resided in Flint in the 1830s, who claimed ownership of the sections through their spouses, and who sold and developed the property. If possession is indeed nine-tenths of the law, the judges and jurors who decided the Smith reservation lawsuits likely saw the Jacob Smith sons-in-law as the rightful owners of the land in question. Their opponents in the courtroom battles for this land, who purchased interest in the property from Indian claimants, certainly faced an uphill struggle. Perhaps one of the most ironic aspects of these Flint River reservation cases was an argument by attorneys for Smith's sons-in-law that "Indian testimony is not entitled to much if any weight at all."

A Flint magazine article from 1930, without specifically citing racism as a factor, touched on this when it described how the "Metawanenee" case was covered in a local newspaper back in the 1850s. The case, of course, centered on whether Albert Smith was the real Metawanenee, as the defendants maintained, or whether it was really the name belonged to an Indian man, as the plaintiffs claimed. The *Genesee Democrat*, writing about the case in 1856, came down squarely on the side of the Smith heirs, who produced four Christian Indians as witnesses to support their claim, while the plaintiff brought in 12 Indian witnesses who had not converted. "The Genesee Democrat comments on the fact that the defendant's witnesses were Christianized, enlightened ones," according to a summation of the reporting, "while the plaintiff's were unenlightened savages."

Perhaps Neome was one of a handful of Chippewa chiefs who knew what really happened with Jacob Smith and the Flint River reservations during those September days and nights at Saginaw in 1819. But if the chief had been tricked or manipulated, even he may not have understood what Smith had done. Thus it is possible only the fur trader himself knew the truth of the matter, and that Smith took it with him when he died at his frontier farm and trading post early in 1825.

As the vexing, complicated, and contradictory details of the testimony and statements about Smith's actions at the 1819 Saginaw treaty were forgotten over the years, certain simple but false assumptions and myths grew up in the Flint area and became part of its popular history. These myths went along the following lines: "Jacob Smith lived among the Indians; therefore his children were part Indian." Or: "The 1819 Treaty of Saginaw specified that the reservations along the Flint River were for people of Indian descent; therefore Jacob Smith's children were part Indian." This was not at all true, but by about 1930, many people of the Flint area had read misinterpretations of Smith's actions at the treaty councils, and accepted as true the assertion that Smith's wife was an Indian and his children were of mixed blood. To this day, for example, in the Genesee County Court House in Flint, a plaque states that Smith resided with his Indian wife at a trading post at the Grand Traverse—something for which there is no evidence. The truth was that the mother of Smith's Indian daughter had resided in the vicinity of what is today Mt. Clemens, on Lake St. Clair, in the years before the War of 1812.

Even some of the descendants of Jacob Smith's white children mistakenly came to believe that they have an American Indian genealogy when in reality only the descendants of Smith's mixed-blood daughter Nancy Smith Crane could make such a claim. Take the example of one of Jacob Smith's grandchildren, Louisa Garland. The daughter of John and Harriet Garland, Louisa would marry a young U.S. Army officer named James Longstreet, who went on to become a hero of the Mexican War and one of the Confederacy's most important generals. In modern times, Longstreet biographers and descendents have wrongly believed that Louisa Longstreet's mother, Harriet Garland, was half Indian. This is based on the incorrect assumption by biographers that Jacob Smith's wife was Indian or part Indian;

therefore their daughter Harriet was also of Indian heritage. Of course, records show that Harriet's mother, Mary Reed Smith, was the product of the marriage of an Irish woman and an Anglo/British Canadian innkeeper. There was nothing "Indian" about Mary Smith or her daughters.

Jacob Smith's descendants didn't always encourage the notion that they were part Indian. In 1930, a great-grandson of Smith, Thomas F. Stockton, a Flint lawyer, presented family papers to a local magazine to show conclusively Jacob Smith's wife, Mary, was white and not Indian after a historically incorrect article about Smith's heirs was published. "Jacob Smith's Children Not Indian, Documents a Century Old Indicate," read the headline on the follow-up article. But this article failed to mention the strong evidence that Jacob Smith had indeed fathered a mixed-blood daughter, Nancy Smith Crane, with a Chippewa woman.

Other stories about Jacob Smith that fell short of the truth appeared in histories of Genesee and Saginaw counties in the mid-to-late nineteenth century. Charles Avery, a lawyer who came to Michigan and represented the Smith heirs in court, wrote an article on the treaty that maintained the Indians had insisted up front to the governor's men that they wanted to grant land to Jacob Smith's white children. But the author could find no primary source evidence that anything like that took place at the Saginaw treaty councils. Avery did not mention in the article that he purchased some of the disputed land in Flint from Smith's heirs. Clearly, it was in his interest, just as it was for the Smith heirs, to maintain that leaders of the Saginaw Chippewa demanded the fur trader's white children receive section-sized reservations on the Flint River.

Then there was the writing of Ephraim Williams, who had changed his position on the question of the legitimacy of the Smith heirs' claim. He knew the Saginaw Chippewa, camping and trading with them and listening to their stories and legends for many years. He had known Jacob Smith and he knew Indians and traders who had known Smith. After he and his brother pressured the Indians to support the Smith heirs' claim for sections of Flint River land, the Williamses turned around and attacked the legitimacy of that claim when they didn't get paid. By playing both sides, Williams truly helped to muddy the waters regarding the truth of the matter in a historical sense.

In time, Williams also appropriated Charles Avery's account of the Treaty of Saginaw, and that account has been misunderstood and misinterpreted by some historians. In a standard reference history of Michigan, Willis Dunbar and George May stated that Cass had to allow treaty provisions that granted Smith's children land in order to get Smith and the Indians to support the treaty. Of course, that was not correct; the governor's own records showed Smith had been working on the Indians to look favorably on a land-ceding treaty with the United States for weeks before Cass and the Chippewa met at Saginaw in the fall of 1819.

Other frontier tales about Smith were exaggerated. Williams or another of the American pioneers in the Saginaw Valley contributed an incorrect story that was printed in Saginaw County histories under the dramatic heading "The White Captives." This tale had blacksmith David Henderson being sent by Governor Cass into the Saginaw Valley to work for the Indians around 1820 (in reality, Henderson had been employed by the government's Indian Department and sent to Saginaw in the early 1800s, during the tenure of Governor William Hull). The story continued that Henderson had gone to Detroit on business, when Kishkauko, the erratic and violent Indian leader, took Henderson's family prisoner and "made known his intention to kill them." It was Smith who came to the rescue, according to the tale:

> Jacob Smith, of Flint, hearing of the capture and threat, mounted his horse and came with all possible speed to Saginaw. Hastening to the old chief, he demanded to know what were his designs regarding the wife and children of Henderson. 'I am going to kill them," answered the chief.
>
> "What!" said Smith. "Will you kill those little children who have never done you or any other any harm?" Nervously the chief replied, "Take them away quick." "But," said Smith, "it is of no use for me to take the woman and her children through the woods. I shall meet some other Indians, and they will take them away from me and kill them. You must give me some men to go with me to Detroit."

Kishkauko agreed, the story went, giving Smith six braves to accompany him and the Hendersons to Detroit. These Indians were arrested and taken into the fort when the party arrived there, "but through the influence of Smith, they were released." The Indians were also given food and escorted back to safety beyond the reach of angry white settlers, according to this tale. Thus peace was kept and violence averted due to the intervention of the clever fur trader.

Of course, this story of "The White Captives" was wrong on several points. The Hendersons had been taken captive at Saginaw at the beginning of the outbreak of hostilities in the War of 1812, and they were aided by friendly Indians to get back to Detroit. Though it's quite possible Smith had a hand in their rescue, no proof of anything like "The White Captives" can be found in the historical record. Similarly, stories of Smith's 1812 spying mission for General Hull—and its subsequent discovery by Indians and wild escape—seem to have gotten taller with the telling. By the late 1800s, it was claimed that one of Smith's comrades on this supposed intelligence mission was captured and killed on the spot by the Indians as Smith and his assistants galloped back to Detroit from Saginaw. Thus the real story of Smith's escape from the Indians on his mission to Ft. Michilimackinac in July 1812 was forgotten, essentially lost for 200 years.

The tale of Smith's nameless compatriot being caught and killed may have been the result of the joining together of one historical fiction with another. Some Genesee County pioneers found a pit of fire-blackened stones at a place on the banks of the Thread Creek in Grand Blanc in the 1830s, and they were told that this was a spot where a white man, taken prisoner by the Indians, had been burned to death. Local residents accepted this, so much so the spot was actually marked on an 1873 plat map of Grand Blanc Township in a Genesee County atlas. But was this story true?

Certainly Indians sometimes practiced ritualistic torture and murder of their enemies, and there are accounts that captured U.S. soldiers met such terrible ends near Detroit, Chicago, and elsewhere during the War of 1812. One white prisoner of the Saginaw Chippewa, a man named James Hardan, was said to have been saved from such a tortuous death at the hands of the chief Mixenene in 1813 when businessman-trader Joseph Campau paid a ransom for his release. Yet there is no suggestion in the historical record of a white man being killed by the Indians in the Flint or Grand Blanc area during the War of 1812. While that certainly doesn't mean it didn't happen, Ephraim Williams, who knew as much about the Saginaw Chippewa as any white man of his time, doubted that the blackened stones found by settlers in Grand Blanc had anything to do with a man being burned at a stake. Instead, he said that the pit or well of stones were probably the remains of a kind of smothered fire in which certain kinds of roots were cooked in hot ashes, and that the Indians who said that it was a place of execution were telling tall tales to impress the whites. Though there was no historical evidence, statement, or report of a comrade of Jacob Smith's being captured and killed, that story was also recorded in an 1879 history of Genesee County and became an accepted part of the local lore.

A State of Michigan's Historical Commission marker that stands at the southeast corner of First Avenue and Lyon Street in the city of Flint is typical of the misunderstandings that lived on about Jacob Smith and his role. While this plaque accurately gives the location of Smith's trading post, just a block or so north of the

Flint River, it inaccurately describes him as a representative of the Indians at the 1819 treaty councils at Saginaw, just as Smith claimed to the Reverend Jedidiah Morse. While it was true that certain chiefs did turn to Smith for help and Smith willingly advised them, the larger truth was he was a secret agent for Governor Lewis Cass and had no official role at the treaty councils.

The historical picture that has existed of Jacob Smith, small as it is where he was remembered in Michigan in the Flint and Saginaw area, has been obscure, romanticized, and not always accurate. In Detroit, where Smith angered businessmen and civic leaders like James Abbott and the Campaus, men with important connections and influential families, he was hardly remembered at all. To them, Smith had been a rascal and man of dubious character, though B. F. H. Witherell indicated that some remembered him as brave and heroic, a good man to know in the Michigan wilderness. Perhaps the only aspect of Smith that was not open to question is the matter of his enormous influence with Saginaw Chippewa leaders.

Smith won no battles or blazed no new trails; he was not even an official party, signatory, or witness to the 1819 treaty he helped the federal government win from the Indian leaders. Yet no other fur trader in the Michigan Territory had the sort of influence he did. Smith certainly knew that the Michigan Territory was changing and settlement was coming to the Saginaw Valley after the War of 1812—he lived to see the Saginaw Trail become the Saginaw Road, and to witness the sale of land along that road in the years before his death. He had been the first white U.S. citizen to farm on the Flint River, able to do so because of his close relationships with the Saginaw Chippewa, though others of French and Indian descent seem to have done the same, raising crops there just as the Indians had done before them.

There can be no sugar-coating of his actions as a spy and secret agent of influence, nor of his roguish conduct in business, which were part and parcel of his identity and role in the Michigan Territory. Michigan's Bruce Catton, author, historian, and editor, once noted there was an old saying on the American frontier: "It's good to be shifty in a new country." It meant that one had to be ready to grab and run with whatever advantages and opportunities presented themselves in order to survive, get ahead, and hopefully prosper on the frontier, however questionable these actions may be. Certainly Smith's role in the Treaty of Saginaw can be viewed as that of a scheming confidence man teamed with U.S. government officials to relieve the Indians of millions of acres of land, though Chippewa

Indians were said to have spoken of their regard for him and even testified about this. Perhaps it was only a matter of indebtedness—the fact that members of the tribe allegedly owed Smith thousands of dollars—that allowed Smith to influence the Saginaw Chippewa leaders to agree to the treaty.

By the early American period in the Great Lakes region in the 1800s, it was policy and practice of the federal government to get more land by treaty. The result of the Saginaw councils in 1819 was little different from the scores of others U.S. commissioners had signed and would continue to sign with tribes across the American frontier. Given that the fledgling United States had been involved in two major wars with Great Britain and her Indian allies in the span of little more than 30 years—and that Michigan and the Great Lakes were not only a geopolitical frontier but an important fur trade region for the rival nations—it is almost surprising that U.S.-Indian relations weren't even more violent in southeastern Michigan. Yet after the War of 1812, war and bloodshed between the Indians and the Americans in what would become the state of Michigan was basically over.

Smith's part in this was not small, though it wouldn't be until the 1830s and 1840s that white settlers came in significant numbers to the Saginaw Valley. The system of U.S. government Indian interpreters, agents, and subagents set up by Lewis Cass before the end of the War of 1812—a network of men who were essentially fur traders—helped to open Michigan to settlement by co-opting the Indians from engaging in resistance and raids, to get them to accept land cessions to the U.S. government and promote the American notions of debt and credit for the goods they wanted and needed. This allowed farmers and builders to move into areas that had only recently been Indian lands with confidence that the threat of attack and confrontation was fading, at the same time depriving the Chippewa of their previous way of life in the Saginaw Valley, as well as other tribes elsewhere in Michigan.

To help to accomplish this, Cass, as did William Hull, utilized the wily Jacob Smith as an unofficial and confidential agent. While checking anti-U.S. hostility and gaining land for the government through Smith and others, Cass and other government officials encouraged favorable publicity about Michigan in the eastern United States to promote settlement, something they believed would ensure that the Old Northwest would never again be threatened by the British in Canada and would force the Indians to move or give up their traditional ways. The decades after Jacob Smith's death represented the end of Michigan's golden age of the fur trade. By the time he died, there was strong evidence the Indians of the region were dependent on white men's goods and had suffered the terrible effects of white men's disease and alcohol. Through the fur trade, their world had long since been altered, their way of life compromised.

One Michigan fur trade historian noted, in what is now considered a dated work, that by their work among the Indians, traders "were making civilized society in these sections possible, and by their influence saved many a future infant colony from the tomahawk and the scalping knife." While this view of Indians is considered outdated and insensitive today, the underlying point was essentially correct. Jacob Smith had played a major part in the early years of the Michigan Territory through trade and treaty, helping to co-opt, neutralize, and overcome Saginaw Chippewa antipathy toward the United States and the threat they had once posed to American settlement in the lands that lay north of Detroit.

Outside of the Flint area, where some of his heirs settled, Smith's name would not be remembered with the soldiers, leaders, and Indian-fighting scouts associated with the popular and romanticized versions of the "winning" of the American frontier in battle and bloodshed, though the risks he took on behalf of the United States and for himself were great. The real story of Smith in the Michigan Territory exemplifies how, in powerful but quieter ways, the fur trader was a force for change, ushering in the time of the white settler and farmer in Michigan, and marking the passing of the day of the Indian warrior and hunter, and of the daring trader himself.

NOTES

Introduction

1. Cass to Dallas, Feb. 16, 1816, Cass Letterbook, Record Group 56-26, Department of State, Archives of Michigan.
2. *American State Papers*, 2:318.
3. Morse, *Report to the Secretary of War*, page 19 of the appendix.
4. Conner affidavit, Jan. 15, 1835, in Claim of the Children of Jacob Smith, HR 24A-G81, Record Group 233 (House of Representatives), National Archives.
5. Avery, "Indian and Pioneer History," 9; Abbott to Sibley, May 27, 1813, Sibley Papers, Burton Historical Collection, Detroit Public Library.
6. Massie, "Jacob Smith in the Saginaw Valley," 117.
7. Ibid.; Tanner, "The Chippewa of Eastern Lower Michigan," 359.

Chapter One. Witness to Murder

1. Smith's age and parents are in his marriage record, July 25, 1798, Register of Holy Trinity Anglican Church, 1786–1800, Quebec, Canada, 2:501, microfilm roll C-2898, National Archives of Canada. Smith butchers in Quebec are listed in 1792, 1795, and 1798 censuses transcribed in *Rapport de l' Archiviste de Québec*, 14, 22, 32, 82, 104, 131, and 146. According to biographical notes on Smith written by son-in-law Thomas B. W. Stockton and held in the Alfred P. Sloan Museum's Perry Archive in Flint, Smith was born in Quebec, his parents

were German, and he had two brothers, Charles and William.

2. Quebec census records for 1798 are in *Rapport de l' Archiviste de Québec*, 131, 146. Charles P. Avery, an amateur historian and lawyer who later represented Smith's sons-in-law in court, wrote that Smith was a slight but athletic man skilled in Indian ways. This description appeared in his "Indian and Pioneer History of the Saginaw Valley," an article published in the *Detroit Free Press* in the early 1860s and later in a directory called *Indian and Pioneer History of the Saginaw Valley . . . and Business Advertiser for 1866 and 1867.* Smith's description tion appears on pages 11, 12, and 15. Avery's article was essentially copied later by Ephraim S. Williams and appeared as "The Treaty of Saginaw in the Year 1819." Here Smith's description is on pages 266 and 268. Campau described Smith as "smart as steel," words that appeared in Avery's article and also in a statement Campau gave Lyman C. Draper, dated May 19, 1864, Wisconsin Historical Society Archives, Madison. Louis Campau, of course, knew Smith personally, as did Ephraim Williams.

3. Birthplaces of Mary Reed Smith's mother and stepfather, Mary McMasters Reed and Andrew Doe, are given in a motion filed in *Jacob and Mary Smith vs. Andrew Doe and His Wife Marguerite McMaster,* the King's Bench, Oct. 15, 1798, file 5096 of 1798, TL 1980-09-024/6, Archives nationales Québec. An extract from the Parish Register of the Protestant Congregation of Christ Church (Montreal), made on Oct. 4, 1798, gives the marriage of "Thomas Reid" and Margaret McMaster. Information about Mary Reed's family also comes from an extract of records made by the "former rector of the English Church at Quebec," dated Oct. 2, 1798, showing burials of Thomas Reed and his children Thomas and Ann years earlier. Both of these extracts, marked as evidence in Smith's lawsuit in Quebec, are in Stockton Papers, Perry Archive, Sloan Museum. The Andrew Doe-Margaret Reed 1784 marriage record is in *Lost in Canada?* 8, no. 3 (1982): 138.

4. Register of Holy Trinity Anglican Church, 1786–1800, Quebec, Canada, 2:501. The lawsuit against Does is documented in pleadings in *Jacob and Mary Smith vs. Andrew Doe and His Wife,* the King's Bench, Oct. 15, 1798, Archives nationales Québec. Mary Smith referred to the estrangement of her father (stepfather) in a letter to her half-sister Peggy, Aug. 22, 1815, Stockton Papers, Perry Archive.

5. The birth and baptismal record of the first daughter of Jacob and Mary, Harriet M. Smith, is in the Register of Holy Trinity Anglican Church, 1786–1800, Quebec, Canada, 2:542.

6. Though Canada was ruled by the British in 1798, Quebec and Montreal were of course French cities, and it seems Smith had to speak French to be in business there; he was born there and even his lawyer was French. In Detroit Smith signed petitions and deeds written in English and French. This is evidenced in Carter, *Territorial Papers*, vol. 10 (*Michigan Territory, 1805–1820*) and in various deeds and records on file in the Burton Historical Collection, Detroit Public Library. Examples of Jacob Smith writing in English are Smith to Isaac Morris, Feb. 10, 1814, Woodbridge Papers, Burton Historical Collection; and Smith to Cass, Dec. 5, 1815, Cass Letterbook, Record Group 56-26, Department of State, Archives of Michigan.

7. Information about the fur trade and Detroit around 1800 is from Bald, *Detroit's First American Decade*, 73–80; Gilpin, *Territory of Michigan*; Haeger, *John Jacob Astor*, 47, 53–54, 74; Johnson, *The Michigan Fur Trade*.

8. Bald, *Detroit's First American Decade*, 38, 61, 74.

9. Gilpin, *Territory of Michigan*, 39; Wheeler-Voegelin, "Anthropological Report," 26; Tanner, "Chippewa of Eastern Lower Michigan," 351; Hickerson, *Chippewa and Their Neighbors*, 10.

10. Smith linked to the North West Company is from biographical notes by Thomas Stockton, Perry Archive, Sloan Museum; Smith having creditors in Montreal is from Smith to Cass, Dec. 5 1815, Cass Letterbook, Archives of Michigan.

11. William Smith, brother of Jacob, is listed in the biographical notes, Stockton Papers, Perry Archive; a man named William Smith, seemingly a Canadian, is mentioned by Mrs. Jacob Smith in her letter to her half-sister Peggy, Aug. 22, 1815, Stockton Papers. A William Smith who is described as a "hatter" was living in Detroit around 1802 according to Bald, *Detroit's First American Decade*, 196, 197. Other historical references note that a man named William Smith was partner in business with a Robert Forsyth during this time in *John Askin Papers*, 2:280 n. 10.

12. The Detroit area settlement is from Report of Charles Jouett, *American State Papers*, 1:757–760. For the few Americans residing, see Gilpin, *Territory of Michigan*, 9. Information on more American traders coming is from Johnson, *The Michigan Fur Trade*, 108. For British-Canadian traders reluctant to see Detroit in American hands, see Bald, *Detroit's First American Decade*, 8–9, 30, 139. The Indian population is given in Gilpin, *Territory of Michigan*, 39.

13. See Haeger, *John Jacob Astor*, 49.

14. Tanner, "Chippewa of Eastern Lower Michigan," 356–357. The example of Saginaw Indians attacking Americans in Ohio is from McKee to Maj. Smith, July 20, 1791, *Miscellaneous Intercepted Correspondence*.

15. Murder indictment of "Kiskacon," in Blume, *Transactions of the Supreme Court of Michigan*, 2:17–18. Other documents make clear that "Kiskacon" was the Chippewa man called Kishkauko.

16. Angus Mackintosh letter, April 7, 1802, Mackintosh Letterbook (photostatic copy), 347–348, Burton Historical Collection, Detroit Public Library.

17. Bald, *Detroit's First American Decade*, 195–196; there is a description of Kishkauko in Witherell, "Kish-kaw-ko and Big Beaver," 333–334; witnesses on indictment are listed in Blume, *Transactions of the Supreme Court of Michigan*, 2:17. Retired trader Louis Campau would testify decades later that Kishkauko claimed to "have white blood" (see Cooley, *Michigan Reports*, 391–392), but John Tanner's account indicates Kishkauko was the son of Indian parents who resided at Saginaw.

18. Bald, *Detroit's First American Decade*, nn. 195–196; Blume, *Transactions of the Supreme Court of Michigan*, 2:19. Kishkauko had already taken part in at least one raid on American settlers, traveling hundreds of miles to do so. In 1789, nine-year-old John Tanner was abducted by Saginaw Chippewa warriors from near his father's home near the Ohio River about 20 miles west of Cincinnati. Tanner identified his captors as Kishkauko and Kishkauko's father, "Manito-o-geezhik" (given more accurately in documents as Meuetugesheck, or Little Cedar). Months later, these same Chippewa also abducted one of Tanner's brothers, but that boy was able to escape back to his family. See Tanner, *The Falcon*, 3–4, 12–13. Tanner

spent two years among the Saginaw Indians before he was sold to Chippewa who lived in Minnesota.

19. Carter, *Territorial Papers,* vol. 7 (*Indiana Territory*). A petition protesting the attachment of Detroit to Indiana, in both English and French, along with the names of the signers, is on pages 99–106; Smith's name appears on 104; Smith's "twenty years" among the Chippewa is recorded in Morse, *Report to the Secretary of War,* 19.

20. *Smith vs. Swart,* box 5, file 958 (Wayne County Court of Common Pleas) and *Smith vs. Chene,* box 6, file 1051, Burton Historical Collection.

21. For Jacob Smith going into business and constructing a building with James Dodemead, see Burton, *Proceedings of Land Board,* 241–242. Smith's name doesn't appear in records listing those who received donation lots, yet there is evidence that Smith was considered a resident of Detroit in 1803 and presumably met the requirement to receive a lot. While Smith would in time own land and buildings on donation lots, these seem to have been purchased or acquired in business dealings.

22. General Orders for militia by William Hull, Sept. 17, 1805, in *Michigan Pioneer and Historical Collections* (hereafter *MPHC*), 36:138.

23. Louis Campau statement, May 19, 1864, Wisconsin Historical Society.

24. Grand jury indictment of Kishkauko, Sept. 19, 1805, Blume, *Transactions of the Supreme Court of Michigan,* 1:349 and 2:17; Smith's resignation from ensign post is in Orders of Oct. 3, 1805, in *MPHC,* 36:148.

25. Bald, *Detroit's First American Decade,* 74–78. Bald indicates that beaver had been practically trapped out of existence by this time in southeastern Michigan, but there was still trade for deer skins and raccoon pelts.

26. Record Book of Licenses Issued Indian Traders 1806–1817 (Michigan Territory), Burton Collection.

27. The springs in the vicinity of the Saginaw Trail are mentioned in Drake, "History of Oakland County," 415.

28. Petition of Albert J. Smith (Jacob Smith's son), HR 28A-G8, Record Group 233 (House of Representatives), National Archives, a claim made in the late 1830s against the Saginaw Chippewa for money he said they owed Smith. In his claim, Albert Smith noted his father traded at places on the Flint, Saginaw, and Cass rivers.

29. 1840 depositions of Henry Conner and Louis Beaufait, men who had been U.S. government Indian agents and interpreters, in land records about Smith's Indian daughter, Liber A, Genesee County Register of Deeds office, Flint, 323–324. Smith's daughter, whose English name was Nancy, is discussed in the next chapter.

30. British control of fur trade is described in Bald, *Detroit's First American Decade,* 246; for the Indian speech about alcohol from traders delivered on behalf of several different nations, see Miami (Maumee) Country to Capt. Elliott of the British Indian Department at the Glaize (river), March 7, 1792, in *Miscellaneous Intercepted Correspondence.*

31. Bald, *Detroit's First American Decade,* 172.

32. Mackintosh to Tavish, Forshbier, Jan. 31, 1801, Macintosh Letterbook, 219, Burton Collection.

33. Record Book of Licenses Issued Indian Traders 1806–1817, Burton Collection; Louis Campau statement, Wisconsin Historical Society. An Indian named Okemos, an Ottawa-Chippewa chief who lived in the Lansing area, later testified that "Big Rock" was Chesaning; see Webber, "Treaty of Saginaw," 524. Where did the name Owosso come from? History shows that a Saginaw war leader named Wasson had taken part in the attacks on the British fort in Detroit during Pontiac's Uprising in 1763, some 50 years before, and he may be the source of the name. In retaliation for the death of his nephew in the fighting, Wasson gruesomely tortured to death a British officer, Captain Campbell, seized by Pontiac when he came out of the fort under a flag of truce. Henry R. Schoolcraft, longtime Indian agent for the U.S. among the Chippewa of northern Michigan, recorded the name of "Owasso," in his recounting of a Saginaw Chippewa legend. See Williams, *Schoolcraft's Indian Legends*, 215. The story "Owosso and Wayoond" is in various other books and collections about Schoolcraft and his research.

34. The locations called "Big Rock" and "Ketchewandangenink" (yet another variation on the Indian name for the Grand Saline) are both mentioned in a treaty the U.S. government and Saginaw Chippewa agreed to in the fall of 1819, in *American State Papers,* 2:195; Bolieu and the belief he traded at Owosso and the Grand Saline is from the Campau statement, Wisconsin Historical Society, and Ellis, *History of Shiawassee and Clinton Counties*, 11; Bolieu and the Grand Saline are mentioned in Gould, "Four Papers," 248–249, 250, 253, 264.

35. The claim that Bolieu brought Smith to the Grand Traverse, or the crossing of the Saginaw Trail at the Flint River, is in Gould, "Four Papers," 248–249.

36. Court testimony about Bolieu is in Cooley, *Michigan Reports,* 386–389. Chippewa culture ethnographer Frances Densmore recorded that the word for flint, a hard stone for striking sparks to start a fire, was "biwa' nug," with the first syllable pronounced "bee," denoting smallness. In Michigan and elsewhere in the Midwest, the term was said to be pronounced with a "p," like "pe-wa-nug" or "pe-wa-nuk." Other translators wrote that "siba" or "seebah" meant river. For Bolieu alleged to be married to Neome's kin, see Cooley, *Michigan Reports,* 386; Ellis, *History of Shiawassee and Clinton Counties,* 11; Angelique Chauvin, daughter of Bolieu's half-Chippewa daughter, testified that Kishkauko and Grand Blanc were related to her mother in a statement dated May 27, 1857, Campau Family Papers, Burton Historical Collections, Detroit Public Library.

37. Cooley, *Michigan Reports,* 386–389; Campau statement, Wisconsin Historical Society.

38. Tanner, "Chippewa of Eastern Lower Michigan," 351–352; Johnson, *The Michigan Fur Trade,* 93; John V. Ryley wrote that he last wintered with the Saginaw Chippewa and Ottawa in 1799 or 1800, Ryley to Woodbridge, Oct. 22, 1819, Woodbridge Papers, Burton Collection. The Ryleys' name is often given as "Riley" in documents and records written by others in Michigan in the early 1800s, but the signatures of both the father and the sons show they spelled the name "Ryley."

39. Tanner, "Chippewa of Eastern Lower Michigan," 354; the visit of "Tromble" to Saginaw is reported in Leeman, *History of Saginaw County,* 597. The violence involving Saginaw Chippewas and others is also mentioned in White, *The Middle Ground,* 203–205.

40. Records indicate that Smith was working for Governor Hull at least as a courier of messages

to the Saginaw Chippewa, if not also as an agent of influence, by 1807: Hull, "Estimate of Expenses," 232. Evidence Smith was working in the summer of 1807 among the Indians is in a deposition given by Abijah Hull, reproduced in Carter, *Territorial Papers*, 10:112. For Knaggs, see Bald, *Detroit's First American Decade*, 64. Early settlers in Shiawassee County seemed to have confused the son of Whitmore Knaggs with his father, but a family genealogy makes clear that it was the son, Whitmore Peter Knaggs, who traded at the Grand Saline, seemingly after the War of 1812.

Chapter Two. The Saginaw Trail

1. For example, Louis Campau told of moving goods in during the winter months, early in 1815, by pony, from what is now the Mt. Clemens area, going northwest into the Saginaw Valley: Campau statement, Wisconsin Historical Society. John Todd, an American settler who came to the Flint River after the death of Jacob Smith, told a newspaper that he remembered Smith bringing fur pelts down the Saginaw Trail from the Flint to the Pontiac area, also by ponies: *Flint Wolverine Citizen*, Dec. 21, 1867.
2. Cole, "J. L. Cole's Journal," 470. When Alexis de Tocqueville made this trip years later, he, too, described the area outside of Detroit as flat and marshy, and said that he was in the woods shortly after leaving town on the road to Pontiac, which had by then been built. Louis Campau, telling Lyman C. Draper about this area, would describe the Cranberry Marsh as lying between Detroit and Royal Oak, Campau statement, Wisconsin Historical Society.
3. Williams, "Indians and an Indian Trail," 137; For Pine Knob see Cole, "J. L. Cole's Journal," 471. Tocqueville, making the trip in 1831, remarked on the hills and valleys after passing through Oakland County's Waterford Township.
4. Williams, "Indians and an Indian Trail," 138. For a good account of a trip by horseback on the Saginaw Trail circa 1830, see Tocqueville, *Journey to America*. This particular edition of Tocqueville's writings contains his "Pocket Notebook No. 2" and his finished article "A Fortnight in the Wilds." By that time some settlers in northern Oakland County were clearing land, but the area between Pontiac and Grand Blanc was barely settled, if at all, and mainly wooded between Grand Blanc and the Flint River. Good descriptions of the land along the trail from Detroit to Saginaw also appeared in letters and articles printed in the *Detroit Gazette* from about 1817 on through the 1820s.
5. Louis Campau statement, Wisconsin Historical Society. Grand Blanc's Indian names can be seen on a treaty he signed in 1807 with the United States in Kappler, *Indian Treaties, 1778–1883*, 94. Another rendering of his name, "Apeche-caur-boway," appears in a transcription of some of Governor Hull's papers, *MPHC*, 36:361. This is on an invoice from September 1809 of presents to Indians of Michigan, and shows names of other leaders, including Walk-in-the-Water and the Saginaw Chippewa chief Little Cedar. Also shown are the men's totems, picture-signatures depicting various birds or animals that represented a chief's individual clan. Whether a typographical error or a mistake by the translator, Grand Blanc's French name was given as "Grand Bland" in the transcription.
6. Williams, "Indians and an Indian Trail," 139–140.
7. Leah Beach Garner, "Historical Sketch," 1, and "Early History of the City of Flint, Genesee

County," 16, both in "The Writing of Leah Beach Garner." The Chippewa name of the Flint River is in Miller, "Rivers of the Saginaw Valley," 506. This is a poem by Miller, who had worked as a young man in the early 1830s for an early white settler at the Flint River named John Todd. Miller said he had quickly learned to converse in the language of the Chippewa. Louis Campau used the term "Grand Traverse" in 1864 when he described crossing the Flint River early in 1815 in his statement to Lyman Draper, Wisconsin Historical Society. Garner and others, writing in the 1920s and 1930s, put the Grand Traverse near today's Beach Street in downtown Flint, and noting that the river was much wider in Smith's era than in modern times.

8. Garner, "Historical Sketch," 1–2. Franklin Ellis, author of a Genesee County history published in 1879, wrote that Muscatawing, the open fields, were contiguous to the crossing place (*History of Genesee County*, 14); Louis Campau, in his statement to Lyman C. Draper in the Wisconsin Historical Society, agreed that the location of Muscatawing was where the city of Flint grew; Flint amateur historians writing in the 1930s put this on the north side of the river where Atwood Stadium was built on W. Third Avenue, west of the Grand Traverse and Smith's trading post there.

9. Smith's claim about the size of Indian villages on the Flint, Saginaw, and elsewhere is given in Morse, *Report to the Secretary of War*, 19. John Tanner said that village or settlement of "Sauge-nong" around 1789 "consisted of several scattered houses." Tanner, *The Falcon*, 9. Though Tanner only spent about two years in Saginaw, his brief account of that period provides a look at the culture and customs of the Chippewa there in the late eighteenth century.

10. J. L. Cole mentioned the luxuriant grasses of the river flats at Saginaw and points along the Flint, as well as the high, rolling, and uneven land between Smith's trading post and Neome's village, "J. L. Cole's Journal," 474. A Chippewa translator named Louis M. Moran advised the proper rendering or phonetic spelling of the word meaning "a flinty place" was "pee-wau-naw-kee." But because certain syllables were typically dropped in the Indian pronunciation, or were inaudible to those unfamiliar with the language, the spoken word would sound like "pee-wau-kee," he said: See Draper, *Wisconsin Historical Collections*, 3:337. Kiskabawee, on the Flint River, is marked on survey maps north of Neome's Town (which was in Genesee County's Montrose Township) in 1820s surveyor records in the Archives of Michigan, and Kishkabawee is also mentioned in the 1819 Treaty of Saginaw.

11. Mills, *History of Saginaw County*, 47.

12. Louis Campau, for example, said that Smith traded on both the north and the south sides of the Flint River, at Neome's Village and also at Saginaw: Campau statement, Wisconsin Historical Society. The Record Book of Licenses Issued Indian Traders 1806–1817, Burton Historical Collection, indicates Smith also traded at the Grand River and other locations, including a location in Indiana.

13. Johnson, *The Michigan Fur Trade*, 56, 83, 86–87, 151. Several anecdotes about the trading of alcohol to Indians can be found in the memoir of a French-Canadian contemporary of Jacob Smith's who worked for the North West Company after 1803. These appear in "Memoir of Thomas Verchères de Boucherville." Boucherville's examples include Ottawa Indians from the Saginaw area who came to Amherstburg on the Detroit River in the spring of 1812 for

trade and rum.

14. Though unsigned, the wording of this first-person account, dated Feb. 16, 1815, in the Duncan McArthur Papers of the Burton Historical Collection, indicates Jacob Smith was the author, since the man who wrote it was asked by a Detroit officer, George McDougall, to consult with McArthur about the Indian villages of the Saginaw Valley. Smith, then a captain, was the ranking militia officer on this particular mission, after McDougall. The document, titled "Expedition Under General McArthur," was later published in *MPHC*, 8:652–653. Smith did command a local militia company late in the war. In an affidavit sworn before a Detroit justice of the peace in February 1819 on behalf of Joseph LePlante, Smith stated he commanded a company of volunteers and that LePlante was a member. This is in the Charles Larned Papers, also in the Burton Collection.

15. *American State Papers,* 1:745.

16. Burton, *Proceedings of Land Board,* 241–242. A handwritten document listing the dates of the births of the children of Jacob and Mary Smith, excluding the oldest daughter Harriet and Smith's half-Chippewa daughter Nancy, is in the Stockton Papers at the Perry Archive, Sloan Museum.

17. Burton, *Proceedings of Land Board,* 241–242.

18. Depositions by Beaufait, Conner, and Robert A. Forsyth in Liber A, Genesee County Register of Deeds' office, Flint, 320–327. Genealogical records for the family of the man who married Nancy Smith Crane give for her a birthdate of June 9, 1807. This record, however, doesn't identify Nancy's parents, who Henry Conner said were Jacob Smith and Nowabeshekoqua; it also gives her birthplace as Meadville, Pennsylvania.

     In reality, Nancy was born in Michigan among her mother's people near the mouth of the Clinton River and sent as a child by Smith to Meadville, indentured to a man who raised her there, according to the testimony of Michigan Indian agents and interpreters. The chief called The Wing appears in a British military communication in August 1812; a letter by a former American fur trader written after the 1819 Treaty of Saginaw; and in a pioneer memoir of St. Clair County. This last reference is in Stewart, "St. Clair County," 345.

19. Louis Campau statement, Wisconsin Historical Society; Stewart, "St. Clair County," 345.

20. Gilpin, *War of 1812,* 3–7; Gilpin, *Territory of Michigan,* 39–40. see also Sugden, *Tecumseh: A Life.*

21. Gilpin, *Territory of Michigan,* 42. The account of Indians from Saginaw attacking an American party in Ohio is in a letter, McKee to Maj. Smith, July 20, 1791, *Miscellaneous Intercepted Correspondence.*

22. Gilpin, *Territory of Michigan,* 38–39; Bald, *Detroit's First American Decade,* 246; Wallace, *Jefferson and the Indians,* 275.

23. For example, Detroit area Canadian trader John Askin complained about fallen fur prices in 1800, Bald, *Detroit's First American Decade,* 165. Smith's claim of large Indian towns is in Morse, *Report to the Secretary of War,* 19.

24. Territorial documents in *MPHC,* 40:144–145.

25. Ibid.

26. *MPHC*, 40:151–153.
27. Ibid.; Gilpin, *Territory of Michigan*, 43.

Chapter Three. Trouble in Detroit

1. Gilpin, *Territory of Michigan*, 6, 16, 28; Burton, *Proceedings of Land Board*, 164.
2. Affidavit of Abijah Hull (July 30, 1807), Carter, *Territorial Papers*, 10:112.
3. Territorial documents, *MPHC*, 36:165; affidavits of Smith, Griswold, and Abbott, in Carter, *Territorial Papers*, 10:112–114, and petition by Detroit residents, 109.
4. See Carter, *Territorial Papers*, 10:111 n. 82; Gilpin, *Territory of Michigan*, 14–18.
5. Territorial documents, *MPHC*, 40:232.
6. For Smith's purchase of Detroit property that was his family's home for nearly two decades see "Deed: James May Esquire to Jacob Smith . . .," Detroit Land Records (microfilm), BHC 656, reel 30, Burton Historical Collection, Detroit Public Library. The house and location are described in Zug, "Detroit in 1815–16," 498, and Trowbridge, "Detroit in 1819," 477.
7. Trowbridge, "Detroit in 1819," 477; Pattinson mortgage on Smith's property in Detroit Land Records (microfilm), BHC 656, reel 30. The Eli Bond lawsuit, Michigan Territorial Supreme Court records, box 8, file 294, Bentley Historical Library, University of Michigan.
8. Bond lawsuit, Michigan Territorial Supreme Court records, box 8, file 294, Bentley Library, University of Michigan.
9. Receipt for the fine Jacob Smith paid, signed by Elijah Brush, treasurer, Sept. 11, 1807; and a letter, W. Park to Sibley, Nov. 23, 1807, both in Solomon Sibley Papers, Burton Historical Collection. For Wilkinson, see Burton, *Proceedings of Land Board*, 198.
10. Woodford and Hyma, *Gabriel Richard, Frontier Ambassador*, 67.
11. Hull's worries about the Saginaw Chippewa are reflected in report by a British Indian agent in the *MPHC*, 23:42–43.
12. Hull, "Estimate of Expenses," 232; *American State Papers*, 1:747; Kappler, *Indian Treaties, 1778–1883*, 2:94–95. Some Indians later disagreed with the cession as described, saying they didn't understand that the treaty terms included so large an area, stretching through southern mid-Michigan to Lake Huron. The cession included some of the southern portion of the Saginaw Valley, where Smith was trading.
13. *American State Papers*, 1:746.
14. Hull to Dearborn, Dec. 28, 1807, *MPHC*, 40:240–241.
15. Carter, *Territorial Papers*, 10:138–142.
16. DesForge insanity case, Blume, *Transactions of the Supreme Court of Michigan*, 1:410 and 2:184. Wiggins, Emerson & Little case, Michigan Territorial Supreme Court records, box 7, file 280, dated Sept. 5, 1811, Bentley Library.
17. Hull's problems regarding the controversial militia uniforms are discussed in the *MPHC*, 40:35; Gilpin, *Territory of Michigan*, 17.
18. Carter, *Territorial Papers*, 10:186.
19. Ibid.
20. Gilpin, *Territory of Michigan*, 17–18; Jefferson to Duane, Feb. 7, 1808, in Carter, *Territorial*

Papers, 10:196.

21. Gilpin, *Territory of Michigan,* 18. Documents dealing with the court of inquiry in the Griswold case appear in Carter, *Territorial Papers,* 10:179–194.

Chapter Four. War Clouds

1. The story of Grand Blanc rejecting Governor Hull's medal offer and showing the governor his medal from the British king is in Claus to Prideaux Selby, Feb. 15, 1808, Claus Papers (microfilm) reel C-1480, National Archives of Canada.

2. Wells to Secretary of War, April 2, 1808, Carter, *Territorial Papers,* 7:540–541.

3. Smith serves as juror, Blume, *Transactions of the Supreme Court of Michigan,* 2:232, 431, 438, 444, 445, 447.

4. Hull message to the chiefs of the Chippewa at Saginaw, Oct. 11, 1808, "Territorial Records," *MPHC,* 36:357.

5. Partial list of the births of Jacob and Mary Smith children, part of a larger genealogy, in Stockton Papers, Perry Archive, Sloan Museum.

6. The Smart case is listed in Solomon Sibley Papers, May–June 1809, Burton Historical Collection, Detroit Public Library, page titled "May term"; the Forsyth & Smith case is listed on another page, same file, under "new entries." The order for Smith's arrest in the complaint in district court for $1,300 by Forsyth and Smith is in the October 1809 file, Sibley Papers. For Smith on the jury acquitting Richard Smyth, see Blume, *Transactions of the Supreme Court of Michigan,* 1:476.

7. Gilpin, *Territory of Michigan,* 31–32.

8. Blume, *Transactions of the Supreme Court of Michigan,* 1:328, 333, and 2:427, 430, 496.

9. *Roi vs. Pomeroy and Conner* in Michigan Territorial Supreme Court Records, box 8, file 245, Bentley Historical Library. Statements of David Henderson and Jacob Smith are in the Sibley Papers, May 1810, Burton Collection.

10. Blume, *Transactions of the Supreme Court of Michigan,* 1:533, 541.

11. Ibid., 1:530.

12. Ibid., 1:216, 549, 554, 559. Robert Forsyth should not be confused with his son, Robert A. Forsyth, who would soon attend West Point and serve as an aide to Governor Lewis Cass in the years ahead.

13. Albert Smith's birth is in the list of Smith children, Stockton Papers, Perry Archive, Sloan Museum. For Mary Smith's sugar order see M. Smith to J. Campau, March 28, 1811, Campau Family Papers, Burton Collection.

14. Biographical information about the TenEyck brothers is in Burton, *Proceedings of Land Board,* 205–206; Thompson, "History of Judge Bunce," 437, refers to Detroit, TenEyck, Payne, and Smith. For Conrad TenEyck and James McCloskey's bond see the Lewis Cass Papers, Clements Library, University of Michigan. TenEyck's losses are mentioned in the supplementary article in the 1819 Treaty of Saginaw, which appears in *American State Papers,* 2:195.

15. That Smith was transacting business with Indians and Detroit men months after the War of 1812 began is reflected on a page in Michigan Territorial Supreme Court records, box 10, file 587, Bentley Historical Library. This lists the account of Richard Jones with Jacob Smith,

as well as a deposition of Pierre Matura De Parinto regarding deliveries he made at Smith's direction for Jones, "a frequent customer."

16. Depositions of Conner and Forsyth, in Liber A, Genesee County Register of Deeds' office, Flint, 320, 322–324, 327. Indexes of records and articles at the Crawford County Historical Society of Meadville, Pennsylvania, show that a former Hessian soldier, Henry Reichard, bought property in that area in 1794 and resided there for years after.

17. The message from Indians complaining about fur traders from "Miamis, Potawatomies, Chippewas and Wyandots" to James Madison, Nov. 13, 1811 (photostat) is in the Cass Papers, Clements Library, University of Michigan.

18. Dwight H. Kelton, "Mackinac County," *MPHC*, 6:242; Schoolcraft, "Memoir of John Johnston," 73–74.

19. This period is briefly summarized in Gilpin, *Territory of Michigan,* 56–57. For a more detailed account, see Gilpin's *The War of 1812 in the Old Northwest.*

20. Gilpin, *War of 1812,* 16–18.

21. Jefferson to My Children, Chiefs of the Ottaways, Chippeways, Poutewotomties, Wyandotts and Shawanese, Jan. 1809, National Archives, Records of the Office of the Secretary of War, letters sent, Indian Affairs, 8:418–419 (photocopy) in the files of the Ziibiwing Cultural Society of the Saginaw Chippewa, Mt. Pleasant, Michigan.

22. For Michigan Detached Militia, see Gilpin, *War of 1812,* 65; Jacob Smith's muster and payroll record is with Maj. Witherell's Detachment, Michigan Volunteers and Militia, Capt. Richard Smyth's Company of Volunteer Cavalry (dragoons), National Archives.

23. The misbehavior of militia soldiers is in "Miscellaneous Documents," *MPHC,* 8:622–626.

24. The rescue of the Hendersons from Saginaw by sympathetic Indians is described in McCloskey to Cass, Sept. 13, 1819, Michigan Superintendency of Indian Affairs, 1819–1931 (microfilm reel no. 32) Bentley Library, University of Michigan. In this letter, McCloskey wrote on behalf of Henderson in hopes that the government would take steps during treaty negotiations to make the Indians pay the family for its losses from seven years before. He made no mention of Smith in the letter.

25. The fanciful version of the Hendersons' story is "The White Captives," in Leeman, *History of Saginaw County,* 124–125. Its proximity to other stories of Chippewa Indians told by former fur trader Ephraim Williams suggests that he could have been a source, though other pioneers heard and repeated such stories. Williams, as a boy, lived in Detroit after the War of 1812 and became a fur trade agent in the late 1820s. As noted previously, Williams actually knew Jacob Smith.

Chapter Five. War in the Michigan Territory

1. Gilpin, *War of 1812,* 50–52. Another excellent book dealing with the Detroit area in the war is Sandy Antal's *A Wampum Denied.*

2. Gilpin, *War of 1812,* 29, 33, 35. That Smith was still in the fur trade at the start of the war is in Michigan Territorial Supreme Court Records, box 10, file 587, *J. Bellows, D. Stone, surviving partners of R. H. Jones, vs. Smith,* Bentley Historical Library.

3. Gilpin, *War of 1812,* 52–53; the deposition of Charles Girard dit Lavisite about Smith's mission

to Michilimackinac is in *Smith vs. Abbott,* Michigan Supreme Court Records, box 9, file 507, Bentley Historical Library. Hull's orders to the frontier U.S. forts appear in Quaife, *War on the Detroit,* 218–219. This book contains two memoirs of the War of 1812, one Canadian by Thomas Verchères des Boucherville and one from an Ohio officer who may have been James Foster, called "The Capitulation, or a History of the Expedition Conducted by William Hull, Brigadier-General of the Northwestern Army."

4. The meeting between Hull and the chiefs from around the Detroit region is in Gilpin, *War of 1812,* 71, and is also in diary entries of an American officer on July 6 and 7, 1812: Lucas, *Robert Lucas Journal,* 24, 25.

5. For British forces getting word of the U.S. declaration of war, see Cruikshank, *Documents Relating to Invasion of Canada,* 37, 38. According to a communication to the British commander of the fort at St. Joseph's Island, not far from Mackinac, the British Adjutant General's office in Quebec received word of the declaration of war from one of the proprietors of the North West Company on June 25, 1812. References to this affair also appear in Cruikshank's "General Hull's Invasion of Canada in 1812" in the *Proceedings and Transactions of the Royal Society of Canada,* vol. 1, section 2, 232 (1907). Another account is in *War, 1812,* 11. And it is discussed in Axel Madsen's *John Jacob Astor,* though John Haeger argues in his Astor biography that Astor "was not intentionally unpatriotic." See Haeger, *John Jacob Astor,* 146–147.

6. Cruikshank, *Documents Relating to Invasion of Canada,* 17n.2, 37–38; Gilpin, *War of 1812,* 89.

7. Gilpin, *War of 1812,* 89–90.

8. Charles Girard dit Lavisite deposition, *Smith vs. Abbott,* Michigan Supreme Court Records, box 9, file 507, Bentley Library; Capt. Roberts to (unaddressed—Capt. J. B. Glegg?), Aug. 16, 1812 in Cruikshank, *Documents Relating to Invasion of Canada,* 150–151.

9. Girard dit Lavisite deposition, *Smith vs. Abbott,* Michigan Supreme Court Records, Bentley Library. The Wing is mentioned by Captain Roberts as advising Indian neutrality in the war; American settlers who later came remembered him as being pro-U.S. at the time of the War of 1812. See Stewart, "St. Clair County," 345.

10. Girard dit Lavisite deposition, *Smith vs. Abbott,* Michigan Supreme Court Records, Bentley Library.

11. Ibid. Roberts to (Glegg?), Aug. 16, 1812 in Cruikshank, *Documents Relating to Invasion of Canada,* 150–151.

12. Girard dit Lavisite deposition, *Smith vs. Abbott,* Michigan Supreme Court Records; Roberts to Glegg, July 29, 1812, in Cruikshank, *Documents Relating to Invasion of Canada,* 101.

13. Girard dit Lavisite deposition, *Smith vs. Abbott,* Michigan Supreme Court Records, Bentley Library.

14. Ibid. Captain Roberts's letter of July 29, 1812, states that Smith was to be taken to Ft. Malden, Cruikshank, *Documents Relating to Invasion of Canada,* 101.

15. Girard dit Lavisite deposition, *Smith vs. Abbott,* Michigan Supreme Court Records.

16. Ibid., Roberts to (Glegg?) Aug. 16, 1812, Cruikshank, *Documents Relating to Invasion of Canada,* 150–151.

17. Girard dit Lavisite deposition, *Smith vs. Abbott;* Roberts to (Glegg?) Aug. 16, 1812,

Cruikshank, *Documents Relating to Invasion of Canada,* 150–151. According to an account in Richardson, *Richardson's War of 1812,* a party of 270 British-allied warriors rapidly canoed from Michilimackinac to Amhertsburg in six days late in July, something that is confirmed by letters in Robert Dickson's papers. These Indians took the direct but dangerous route by crossing Saginaw Bay, rather than the longer, safer route hugging the shoreline. Was this the express from which Jacob Smith and Girard escaped? Did these warriors cut across Saginaw Bay trying to recapture Smith? Perhaps, though there is no reference to the Smith affair in the account.

18. Girard dit Lavisite deposition, *Smith vs. Abbott,* Michigan Supreme Court Records, Bentley Library. The fact that Smith returned the messages to Detroit postmaster James Abbott is in Carter, *Territorial Papers,* 10:447, in a transcription of an 1813 letter from the U.S. postmaster general to the former governor, William Hull.

19. As noted previously, the story called "The White Captives," which credits Jacob Smith with rescuing Mrs. David Henderson and her children, was printed in Mills, *History of Saginaw County,* 48, 49. The story also appears in the earlier *The History of Saginaw County* by Michael A. Leeman.

20. The story about Smith escaping from the Saginaw Chippewa on horseback after an intelligence-gathering mission early in the war appears in Ellis, *History of Genesee County,* 13. A very brief (and almost illegible) version of the story is also in biographical notes about Smith by son-in-law Thomas B. W. Stockton, Perry Archive, Sloan Museum.

21. Stewart, "St. Clair County," 345.

22. Gilpin, *War of 1812,* 91–92; John Askin Jr.'s declaration that the inhabitants of Mackinac Island would have all been killed had the Americans resisted is in a letter, July 18, 1812, in *MPHC,* 15:113.

Chapter Six. The Arrest of Jacob Smith

1. The complaint by Captain LaCroix of the Michigan Militia to Maj. Witherell about the bad conduct of some of Smyth's company is dated July 17, 1812, B. F. H. Witherell Papers, Burton Historical Collection, Detroit Public Library.

2. Gilpin, *War of 1812,* 81. Oddly enough, witness Robert Lucas, *Robert Lucas Journal,* noted in his diary that a ship bearing the Americans captured on Mackinac Island, and then paroled, arrived at Detroit on July 26—three days earlier. Why Hull didn't immediately write a letter that day reporting the terrible news to the U.S. government is unknown, unless the date of his letter was a mistake or simply misread.

3. Gilpin, *War of 1812,* 96–97.

4. Ibid., 99–100; Smith service record, National Archives.

5. Gilpin, *War of 1812,* 106, 108 n. 38, 111–112.

6. Ibid., 113, 115–116.

7. Benjamin F. H. Witherell ("Hamtramck"), "Incidents of the War of 1812," in the Mary Ruth Lacey Papers, Burton Collection.

8. John E. Hunt statement, Lyman C. Draper Papers (Draper's notes), series S, vol. 21S, 62, Wisconsin Historical Society.

9. Summaries of Smith's company payroll and muster roll from the National Archives end on Aug. 16, 1812, "the date of surrender as prisoners of war by Brig. Gen. Hull, then commanding the army at Detroit." Smith is also listed in the Aug. 15, 1812, "morning report," a kind of military attendance record, for the "Detachment of Militia in the Service of the United States Under the Command of Maj. J. Witherell." This is in the Woodbridge Papers, Burton Historical Collection. Smith later gave a deposition before Justice of the Peace Thomas Rowland in Detroit on the loss of his horse, saddle, and bridle; this is part of Smith's service record in the National Archives.

10. Loyal British residents on the Canadian side of the river also complained about Indians taking their horses, and British officers said it was impossible for them to control this conduct. See Antal, *A Wampum Denied,* 113–115.

11. In the spring of 1813 James Abbott wrote that he had been directed by Gov. William Hull, in the previous summer, to store property and supplies confiscated from British-Canadians by U.S. forces in their brief invasion of Canada. Some of this material was apparently placed in Jacob Smith's building, which was across the street from Abbott. A reference to this appears in Carter, *Territorial Papers,* 10:447. Smith claimed that the British knew about the losses he suffered when Detroit surrendered, and this appears in a statement he made for Secretary of War John Armstrong on March 8, 1813, in Knopf, *Document Transcriptions of the War of 1812,* 7:161.

12. British policy and declaration that the Michigan Territory was forfeit to the United States are discussed in Antal's *A Wampum Denied,* 104–105, 156–157. A British paper about the Michigan Territory and its implications for the Indians appears in the *Miscellaneous Intercepted Correspondence.* Antal attributes this paper to Procter.

13. British policy and declaration about Michigan Territory, Antal, *A Wampum Denied,* 104–105, 156–157.

14. Muir quoted in a deposition by Lyon, Jan. 9, 1817, John McDonell Papers, Burton Collection. Lyon and McDonell purchased white prisoners taken by the Indians during the war, according to Lyon's statement.

15. List of children of Jacob and Mary Smith / genealogical papers, Stockton Papers, Sloan Museum archive.

16. Gen. William Henry Harrison received reports from spies in the Detroit region: Harrison to Eustis and Harrison to Meigs, Sept. 5, 1812, *Papers of William Henry Harrison,* reel 6, 105–108. Of course, these spies for the United States are not named.

17. Jacob Smith told of his arrest in statement to U.S. Secretary of War, March 8, 1813, in Knopf, *Document Transcriptions of the War of 1812,* 7:161.

18. Walker's arrest by the British is in the Lyman Draper Papers, U-11, Wisconsin Historical Society, cited by Ralph Naveaux in *Invaded on All Sides,* 63–64 nn. 128–129; 316–317.

19. Procter's complaining about American spies in Detroit is in a letter to an unknown officer (probably one of the British generals in Canada), Dec. 23, 1812, and again to Gen. Sheaffe, Feb. 1, 1813. Both of these letters are in the *Miscellaneous Intercepted Correspondence.*

20. Smith statement to Secretary of War, March 8, 1813, in Knopf, *Document Transcriptions of the War of 1812,* 7:161.

21. Proctor to Sheaffe, Feb. 1, 1813, *Miscellaneous Intercepted Correspondence.*

22. The accuracy of Smith's report about the plans of Robert Dickson to raise an Indian force can be seen in Dickson's own letter to his "Commander in Chief," Dec. 23, 1812, *MPHC,* 15:208–209. Other papers and biographies of Dickson in the Wisconsin Historical Society show that he was in Montreal, where Smith was being held in prison, late that year. Of course, history shows that Dickson did indeed recruit a huge force of hundreds of warriors to fight the Americans in 1813.

Chapter Seven. I Pray You Inform Me . . . the Character of Jacob Smith

1. Smith biographical notes by Thomas B. W. Stockton, Perry Archive, Sloan Museum.

2. Gilpin, *War of 1812,* 163–165, 166–168, 170.

3. Smith biographical notes, Thomas Stockton, Perry Archive, Sloan Museum.

4. Ellis, *History of Genesee County,* 13–14. This version has been repeated in a subsequent history of Flint and Genesee County published in the early twentieth century, Wood, *History of Genesee County.*

5. Col. Anthony Butler's bragging to British officers about how he knew what their Indian agents were up to in Michigan late in 1813 appears in *MPHC,* 15:514–515.

6. Gilpin, *War of 1812,* 170; Smith statement to the Secretary of War, March 8, 1813, Knopf, *Document Transcriptions of the War of 1812,* 7:161. Similarly, Stockton's notes show that Smith's family wrongly believed he was arrested and imprisoned in Montreal at the beginning of the war after he crossed the Detroit River to visit his brother on the other side, only to be released later in a prisoner exchange. Of course, Smith actually went on the mission to Ft. Michilimackinac after the war began, and he himself reported he was arrested by Procter in Detroit in the fall of 1812, four months after the war began. Again, the Stockton notes about Smith seem to reflect his family's imperfect understanding of Smith's activities.

7. Smith to Cass, Dec. 5, 1815, in the Cass Letterbook, Record Group 56-26, Department of State, Archives of Michigan, Lansing.

8. Cass to U.S. Treasury Secretary A. J. Dallas, Feb. 16, 1816, Cass Letterbook, Archives of Michigan.

9. References to people in the Detroit area, who like fur trader John Kinzie, were spying for the United States during the War of 1812 are in Antal, *A Wampum Denied,* 264, 272 n. 59, and Sugden, *Tecumseh: A Life,* 342. Of these suspected Detroit spies arrested by Procter, it seems that only Kinzie was identified by name.

10. Procter's complaint about Whitmore Knaggs is in a letter dated July 13, 1813, *MPHC,* 15:338–339. The fact Knaggs had truly been a scout for the army of U.S. volunteers under General Winchester appears in Hubbard, "Early Colonization of Detroit," 362. This quotes an article by Detroit historian B. F. H. Witherell, probably one that originally appeared in the *Detroit Free Press* in the 1850s.

11. Smith's showing up at Ft. Meigs after his release from prison in Canada is in a letter, Smyth to Brady, March 20, 1813, Josiah Brady Papers, Burton Historical Collection, Detroit Public Library.

12. For William Henry Harrison's receiving intelligence on British and Indian plans around the

same time of Jacob Smith's return from Canada see Harrison to Meigs, Feb. 16, 1813, *Papers of William Henry Harrison*, reel 7, 528; and Knopf, *Document Transcriptions of the War of 1812*, 7:179–181.

13. Smyth to Brady, March 20, 1813, Josiah Brady Papers, Burton Collection.

14. Ibid. Black Rock, New York, was just a few miles from Buffalo on the Niagara River, just across from the British-Canadian military post, Ft. Erie.

15. Smith statement to the Secretary of War, March 8, 1814, Knopf, *Document Transcriptions of the War of 1812*, 7:161.

16. Gilpin, *War of 1812*, 181–182.

17. Ibid., 182–187.

18. Smith's friend and former militia captain, Richard Smyth, becoming an officer in Ohio in the war effort is in *Papers of William Henry Harrison*, reel 7, 667.

19. Abbott's appointment to handle mail for the U.S. Army in Ohio is in Granger to Harrison, Feb. 13, 1813, *Papers of William Henry Harrison*, reel 7, 501.

20. Gideon Granger, postmaster general, to James Witherell, May 11, 1813, Carter, *Territorial Papers*, 10:442–443; Abbott to Solomon Sibley, May 27, 1813, Sibley Papers, Burton Collection.

21. Carter, *Territorial Papers*, 10:442–443.

22. Ibid., Granger to Abbott, May 12, 1813, 444–445.

23. Abbott to Sibley, May 27, 1813, Sibley Papers, Burton Collection.

24. Ibid. Sibley wrote a statement that Abbott was a loyal U.S. citizen, June 20, 1813, Sibley Papers, Burton Collection.

25. The reference to Abbott opening army mail is in Granger to Abbott, May 11, 1813, in Carter, *Territorial Papers*, 10:444.

26. The postmaster general tells of Smith's charges, Granger to Abbott, June 23, 1813, ibid., 445–446. Granger also outlined the charges in a letter to William Hull, the former Michigan governor, on July 7, 1813, ibid., 447.

27. Ibid., 447; Abbott to Sibley, May 27, 1813, Sibley Papers, Burton Collection.

28. Carter, *Territorial Papers*, 10:447; Abbott to Sibley, May 27, 1813, Sibley Papers, Burton Collection.

29. Carter, *Territorial Papers*, 10:445, 446.

30. Ibid., 446–447; Sibley to Abbott, June 20, 1813, Sibley Papers, Burton Collection.

31. Carter, *Territorial Papers*, 10:447; Sibley to Abbott, June 20, 1813, Sibley Papers, Burton Collection.

32. Caitlin, *The Story of Detroit*, 207–208.

33. Granger to Hull, July 7, 1813, Carter, *Territorial Papers*, 10:447. Hull wrote two books after the war, the first in 1814 specifically about his own court-martial, and another in 1824 about his role in the war, but neither mentioned the matter of John Jacob Astor's letter or Jacob Smith's attempt to reach Michilimackinac. As far as Hull was concerned, the fact that the British had control of the Great Lakes meant that U.S. forts at Chicago and the Mackinac Island were doomed to fall, since they could not be supplied or reinforced.

34. Abbott to the Grand Jury, Oct. 16, 1814, Duncan McArthur Papers, 3:517–519 (photostat),

Burton Historical Collection. This letter also appears in the Carter, *Territorial Papers*, 10:493–495.

Chapter Eight. Abduction to Saginaw

1. Lindley, *Fort Meigs*, 49–50.
2. Jacob Smith's deposition about Loranger's destroyed house is in Loranger's claim, Nov. 18, 1819, part of the August 1812 folder of the Solomon Sibley Papers, Burton Historical Collection, Detroit Public Library.
3. The incorrect assertion Smith came to Detroit in 1810 is in Mills, *History of Saginaw County*, 48. William Henry Harrison's use of spies in *Papers of William Henry Harrison*, reel 7, 696. That spies and men from Detroit were coming and going from the Ohio fort is in Lindley, *Fort Meigs*, 99, 102, 103, 104, 111, 112, 127, 129, 137.
4. List of the births of the children of Jacob and Mary Smith, genealogy record, Stockon Papers, Perry Archive, Sloan Museum.
5. John Askin Jr.'s statement is in a letter, Askin to Cameron, June 3,1813, *MPHC*, 15:310–311.
6. The story of the young Kentucky soldier who escaped from Saginaw and made it back to Ft. Meigs with the help of Detroit area residents is in a letter, Clay to Meigs, June 20, 1813, in Knopf, *Document Transcriptions of the War of 1812*, 2:232.
7. Gilpin, *War of 1812*, 208–212.
8. Ibid., 223–226. A detailed account of the Battle of the Thames, also called the Battle of Moraviantown, and the death of Tecumseh, may be found in *Tecumseh's Last Stand* by John Sugden.
9. Hunt, *John Hunt Memoirs*, 22, 49. Hunt wrote that as the British set fire to the fort and got in their boats to cross back to Canada, his brother ordered him and a black man named Guss to hurry to the warehouse and destroy 10 barrels of whiskey stored there, so that the remaining Indians didn't get it. "I did so and just as it was done, about twenty Saganaw Indians came running down the hill hunting for whiskey," he wrote. Hunt was convinced Detroit would have suffered much violence, if not destruction, if he had failed in his mission. After the British were gone, Hunt saw three Saginaw Indians standing on Detroit's dock, watching as some American soldiers rowed back to reclaim the town. These Indians waited until the Americans were halfway across the river before fleeing.
10. Smith's new commission in the reorganized Territorial Michigan Militia is in Robertson, *Michigan in the War*, 1021; Sibley petition, Carter, *Territorial Papers*, 10:457.
11. The death of John Rudolph Smith is recorded in Registers of the St. Andrews Presbyterian Church in Quebec City, National Archives of Canada, folio 53, microfilm reel M-138.14.
12. Harrison to Meigs, Oct. 18, 1813, *Papers of William Henry Harrison*, reel 9, 443.
13. Witherell, "Perils of the Border." Louis Campau, who lived in that area and knew the Boyers, later hired Nick Boyer's half-Chippewa son as a guide early in 1815 when he took his first, legally questionable trade expedition to the Saginaw Valley: Campau statement, Wisconsin Historical Society.
14. Campau statement, Wisconsin Historical Society; Witherell, "Perils of the Border." That the principal Indians in Cecilia's account were real individuals—Kishkauko, Tickesho, and

Chemokamun—is beyond doubt. Kishkauko is mentioned in many reports and letters of territorial Michigan. Tickesho appears in the postwar business records of Detroit merchant David Mack Cooper in the Detroit Public Library's Burton Collection. Chemokamun or Chemkokemun was a Chippewa chief who signed a treaty with the United States in 1817. In a copy of that treaty, which appeared in the *Detroit Gazette* of Feb. 19, 1819, Chemokemun's name was translated as "American" though it literally meant "Big Knife"—the term Indians used for white men because of the swords they carried. Witherell wrote that the French called him "Le Grand Couteau."

15. Witherell, "Perils of the Border."
16. Ibid. Nicholas Boyer would, in the 1830s, file a claim against the Chippewa Indians for holding him and his family captive, but he would not succeed in collecting damages. Louis Campau confirmed in his Civil War–era statement to Lyman Draper, in the Wisconsin Historical Society, that the Boyers were taken hostage for ransom.
17. Cass mentioned sending out a party to get American prisoners released from Indian captivity in Cass to War Department, Dec. 4, 1813, U.S. War Department Papers, vol. 17, W195, Burton Collection.

Chapter Nine. The Return of the Boyer Children

1. Conditions in Detroit and the creation of a group of U.S. "interpreters" to spy on the Indians are described in Cass to Armstrong, Oct. 21, 1813 and Dec. 4, 1813, in U.S. War Department Papers, vol. 27, June 1813–August 1814 (photostat copies), in the Burton Historical Collection, Detroit Public Library.
2. Cass again stressed the need for interpreter-spies in Cass to Armstrong, July 25, 1814, "Correspondence with the War Department regarding Indian Affairs," Cass Papers, also in the Burton Historical Collection. In a few years time, he would explain his expenditures in Michigan to Secretary of War John C. Calhoun in *American State Papers*, 2:314.
3. If Cass didn't make Smith an officer in the local militia, then William Henry Harrison may have: Harrison to Armstrong, Oct. 10, 1813, *Papers of William Henry Harrison*, reel 9, 345. "I shall take it upon myself to arm and organize their Militia for their temporary defense," Harrison wrote about the Michigan men. This was shortly before Cass was given command of U.S. forces in the area and before he was named territorial governor of Michigan.
4. Smith's contract for stones for the federal government is in Settled Account 4448, Jacob Smith due $50, Rec'd March 5, 1819, Treasury Dept., 3rd Auditor's Office. This document comes from Record Group 217, Third Auditor, National Archives.
5. Smith to I. Morris, Feb. 10, 1814, Woodbridge Papers, Burton Historical Collection.
6. Blume, *Transactions of the Supreme Court of Michigan*, 2:397.
7. Captain Bullock's report that most Indians except for a few Saginaw Indians still sided with Britain is from his Feb. 26, 1814, letter to Captain Loring, an aide to British commanders in York (Toronto) in "Papers from the Canadian Archives," *Wisconsin Historical Collection*, 12:113.
8. The report about British-allied Indians at Saginaw who wanted to renew the attacks on Detroit is from William Claus, May 14, 1814, in *MPHC*, 15:553–554. Information on the Saginaw

chiefs and warrior at a council on Mackinac Island asking for ammunition and supplies to keep the war against the Americans going is in *MPHC*, 23:455.

9. Claus letter, May 14, 1814, *MPHC*, 14:553–554.

10. Continuing attacks on Detroit settlers in 1814 are mentioned in an article by B. F. H. Witherell ("Hamtramck"), "1814," in the Mary Ruth Lacey Papers, Burton Collection. In this article, Witherell quoted his father James Witherell's letter of July 4, 1814, to a friend in Vermont. Cass discussed this situation in a letter to the War Department (no date, filed in August, 1814), Cass Papers, Burton Collection.

11. *Rodgers vs. Jacob Smith*, file G-43, box 4, Wayne County Clerk's Office (miscellaneous papers), 1819–1820, Burton Collection.

12. Witherell, "Perils of the Border."

13. James Witherell to ——, July 4, 1814, quoted by B. F. H. Witherell ("Hamtramck"), in "1814," Mary Ruth Lacey Papers, Burton Collection.

14. Witherell, "Perils of the Border."

15. A lawyer and amateur historian, Charles Avery mentioned Smith's rescue of the Boyer children in his article "Indian and Pioneer History."

16. The claim by Nicholas Boyer against the Saginaw Chippewa tribe for capturing him and his family is reflected in a letter from Hartley Crawford, War Department Office of Indian Affairs, to Secretary of War J. R. Poinsett, Oct. 16, 1839. A copy of this letter appears in the Petition of Albert J. Smith, HR 28A-G8, Record Group 233 (House of Representatives), National Archives.

17. The attack in which McMillan was killed in Detroit and his son Archie abducted by Indians is in Witherell, "Incidents, 1807–1814."

Chapter Ten. Jacob Smith versus Louis Campau, 1815

1. Jacob Smith's jury service is in Blume, *Transactions of the Supreme Court of Michigan*, 4:7–8, 10–11. The death of his mother is in Records of St. Andrew's Presbyterian Church, register for 1814, folio 48, Archives nationales Québec, microfilm M-138.14.

2. The McArthur raid is in Gilpin, *War of 1812*, 255–257, and Brown, *Authentic History of the Second War for Independence*, 210.

3. Capt. Jacob Smith is listed in a "Mememoradum of our Expedition under Gen'l. McArthur," *MPHC*, 8:654, which names the Michigan men who took part.

4. The report about the McArthur raid, necessarily written or narrated by Jacob Smith, **is** "Expedition Under General McArthur." The original document is in the Duncan McArthur Papers, Burton Historical Collection. An archivist in the Burton, or perhaps Clarence Burton himself, noted that this document is in the handwriting of McDougall and must have been written by him. Certainly the statement may have been written out by McDougall, but it is clear that McDougall didn't "call upon" himself and he is clearly not the person relating the story. The narrator of this account is Jacob Smith, who was called upon by McDougall for advice on McArthur's raid into the Saginaw Valley, which of course was strictly a fiction.

5. McAfee, *History of the Late War*, 447. John Askin's witnessing the American raiders passing by his home is in "Diary of John Askin," 473.

6. "Expedition Under General McArthur," 652–653.

7. Ibid. Dr. William Turner was a U.S. Army surgeon.

8. Ibid.

9. Askin, "Diary of John Askin," 473.

10. An extensive report on the raid for the U.S. War Department is in McArthur Papers, Burton Collection.

11. Carter, *Territorial Papers*, 10:477.

12. Arrest order for a man who owed Jacob Smith money, Dec. 8, 1814; the "Soyer" case notification, and note of the loan to Francois Gobeille, are in the Solomon Sibley Papers, December 1814 file and Jan.–Feb. 1815 file, Burton Collection.

13. The warning by Woodbridge of possible Indian attacks is in Carter, *Territorial Papers*, 10:535–537.

14. Ibid. The fact Smith was already back at the Grand Traverse of the Flint River early that year was reflected in Louis Campau statement, Wisconsin Historical Society.

15. Cass wrote about his Indian spies to the War Department, March 1815 in "Correspondence with the War Department regarding Indian Affairs," Cass Papers, Burton Collection.

16. Campau statement, Wisconsin Historical Society.

17. Ibid. British Indian Department records do show that a Canadian-born man named Louis Campau, who had lived in the Michigan Territory, became an Indian interpreter for the British on the recommendation of Colonel Procter in February 1813. Records indicate, however, that this was not the same Louis Campau who was Jacob Smith's fur trade rival. It was very likely one of his relatives, however. John Askin Jr. wrote that "Lewis Campau," the interpreter for the British Indian Department, was killed in the fighting near Moravian Town in the fall of 1813, where Tecumseh was also killed. *Wisconsin Historical Collections*, 10:99–100.

18. Campau statement, Wisconsin Historical Society.

19. Ibid. James Abbott was identified as the American Fur Company agent in Detroit in 1815 in Little, "Life of Uncle Harvey Williams," 24.

20. Campau statement, Wisconsin Historical Society.

21. Writer Gustavus Myers charged in his book *Great American Fortunes*, vol. 1, that a 1909 newspaper article reported an American Fur Company ledger showed a transfer of $35,000 to Governor Cass in 1817, but others, notably John D. Haeger, point out that no other researcher has been able to find this entry. The article cited by Myers described the money transfer as a bribe so that Cass would allow Astor's company the fur-trading licenses his company wanted. While Myers claimed to have seen the actual ledger, no historian has since located it. Author Axel Madsen, in his biography of Astor, claims the page showing the money transfer to Cass was removed from a ledger held by the Detroit Public Library. For Haeger's view of the matter, see his *John Jacob Astor*, 26. While Haeger doubts a bribe took place, he admits that Astor routinely met, consulted with, loaned money to, and contracted with the federal government and officials in regard to foreign trade, foreign policy, the war, finance, banking, etc., and that James Monroe and Henry Clay borrowed money from him; Astor also handled investments for his friend, Albert Gallatin.

22. Record Book of Licenses Issued Indian Traders 1806–1817 (Michigan Territory), Burton

Collection; Louis Campau statement, Wisconsin Historical Society.

23. *Smith vs. Abbott*, over his being owed for his expenses on the trip he made to Mackinac, in Records of the Michigan Territorial Supreme Court, box 9, file 507, Bentley Historical Library, University of Michigan.

24. Smith's signature on the petition memorializing Puthuff is in *MPHC*, 8:655–656.

25. M. Smith to Peggy, Aug. 22, 1815, Perry Archive, Sloan Museum. Peggy's last name doesn't appear in the letter. Her given name was probably Margaret or Marguerite, after her mother, and her maiden name was almost certainly Doe.

26. A copy of the McNeal/McNeil 1815 transfer or deed of Detroit property and power to collect for the estate to Jacob Smith is part of the recording of the sale of that property, in turn, on Dec. 18, 1818 by Smith to James Abbott and Robert Smart, Abbott Papers, Burton Historical Collection. It is also recorded in Detroit Land Records (microfilm), BHC 656, reel 12, also at the Burton.

27. Jacob Smith wrote about taking on the mission to get the Saginaw chiefs to attend the peace treaty in the late summer of 1815 in a letter to Lewis Cass, dated Dec. 5, 1815, Letterbook, Record Group 56-26, Department of State, Archives of Michigan, Lansing. This was clearly a matter of Smith acting as an unofficial agent for the United States, though again, Smith was not on Cass's list of Indian "interpreters" or spies. Cass confirmed Smith's important role in a subsequent letter recorded in that same letter book.

28. Kappler, *Indian Treaties*, 2:117–119. The desperate condition of Michigan Indians is reflected in a British letter, Caldwell to Claus, Aug. 2, 1815 (continuation of a July 30 letter), Indian Affairs, Deputy Superintendent General's Office Correspondence, National Archives of Canada, microfilm reel C-1109.

Chapter Eleven. Peace

1. Witherell, "Perils of the Border."

2. That Smith got still-hostile Saginaw Chippewa chiefs to attend the treaty is in Cass to Secretary of Treasury Dallas, Feb. 16, 1816, Cass Letterbook, Archives of Michigan.

3. Statement of Smith's account with Dennis Campau from *Joseph Campau, administrator for the estate of Dennis Campau, vs. Jacob Smith*, file J-189, box 4, Wayne County Clerk's Office (miscellaneous records) 1819–1820, Burton Historical Collection of the Detroit Public Library.

4. Smith to Cass, Dec.5, 1815, Cass Letterbook, Archives of Michigan.

5. Ibid.

6. Ibid.

7. Cass to Dallas, Feb. 16, 1816, Cass Letterbook, Archives of Michigan.

8. Lawyer A. H. Tracy complained about Smith in a letter to William Woodbridge, June 1, 1820, William Woodbridge Papers, Burton Collection.

9. Record Book of Licenses Issued Indian Traders 1806–1817, Burton Collection.

10. Detroit Land Records / Wayne County Notarial Records (microfilm) BHC 656, reel 12, Burton Collection.

11. DeGarmo Jones's letter to Sibley is in Sibley Papers, Feb.–March 1816 file, Burton Collection.

12. Jones's suit against Smith in Blume, *Transactions of the Supreme Court of Michigan*, 4:54; and in Records of the Michigan Territorial Supreme Court, box 9, file 534, Bentley Historical Library, University of Michigan; Record Book of Licenses Issued Indian Traders 1806–1817, Burton Collection. The third place Smith listed in the territorial license book seems to simply say "Lakes."

13. Harriet Smith and John Garland's wedding date is given in Garland Family File, Jones Memorial Library, Lynchburg, Va.; the description of Harriet Smith Garland is in a letter by Thomas C. Sheldon to Eliza Sheldon, Oct. 16, 1819, John P. Sheldon Papers, Burton Collection. Maria Smith Stockton is described in "Early History of the City of Flint," 6, in "Writings of Leah Beach Garner," in the Flint Public Library. This description of Maria is also given in "Early History of Flint," 3, in "Pioneer Recollections of Genesee County," another book of amateur historian articles from the 1920s and 1930s published by the Flint library.

14. Death of Mrs. Jacob (Mary) Smith in *Register of St. John's Church of England* (compiled by the Kent and Essex branches of the Ontario Genealogical Society, 1990), 48. This gives Mary Smith's first name as "Harriet," but it is apparently an error reflecting the name of her oldest daughter, since no other document gives this for Mrs. Jacob Smith's first name. Judge Woodward's invitation to Mary Smith's funeral is in the Stockton Papers, Perry Archive, Sloan Museum.

15. The assertion that Jacob Smith lived for the most part at Flint River after the death of his wife was published in Ellis, *History of Genesee County*, 14; Smith's son, Albert J. Smith also stated this in a deposition, part of the filings in the suit *Williams et al. vs. Payne*, Record Group 81-44, box 31, file 27 (Genesee County courts), State Archives of Michigan, Lansing. Yet records show that Smith had his house in Detroit until a year or so before his death and was routinely in Detroit.

16. Harriet Garland's death is from the *(Flint) Wolverine Citizen*, Sept. 8, 1860, 3; John Garland's death is from Crawford, *The 16th Michigan Infantry*, 13–14.

17. Garner, "Writings of Leah Beach Garner," 6; marriage record of Louisa Smith and Chauncey Payne, Stockton Papers, Sloan Museum.

18. The reminiscence of Benjamin O. Williams about the school held in Smith's house in Detroit is from "My Recollections," 548–549.

19. Smith's resignation from the Michigan Militia is reflected in Cass to Smith, July 3, 1817, Cass Letterbook, State Archives of Michigan. Cass had claimed this authority to make officers earlier in the war: "The power of appoint[ing] the captaincies and subalterns is entrusted to me," Cass wrote to an unidentified correspondent as he was being placed in command of new regiments recruited in Ohio. This was in a March 25, 1813, letter in "Correspondence with the War Department Regarding Indian Affairs," Cass Papers, Burton Historical Collection. As noted previously, Smith was listed as one of six men to receive lieutenants' commissions from Cass on Dec. 18, 1813. See Robertson, *Michigan in the War*, 1021.

20. Smith's reimbursement for his lost horse, saddle, etc., is in federal claim/compensation documents, no. 1993, Jacob Smith, April 4, 1817, signed by Richard Bland Lee, National Archives. His failure to show up at court is in Blume, *Transactions of the Supreme Court of Michigan*, 4:69–70.

21. Gilpin, *Territory of Michigan*, 72–73. The accusation that Cass accepted a bribe from Astor in 1817 is in Myers, *History of the Great American Fortunes,* part 2, chapter 2, titled "The Inception of the Astor Fortune," in note 89. As noted previously, John D. Haeger, in *John Jacob Astor,* states that the "bribe" or transfer cannot be documented. Astor biographer Axel Madsen maintained that the page from of the American Fur Company ledger that showed the transfer of $35,000 to Cass was torn from the book, which was kept in the Detroit Public Library's Burton Collection. See Madsen, *John Jacob Astor,* 173n.
22. Campau statement, Wisconsin Historical Society.
23. The description of Neome is from Charles Avery's "Indian and Pioneer History," 11. Avery's account was appropriated by Ephraim Williams in a paper published years later. Though Williams as a young man actually knew Smith, and Avery did not, Williams apparently accepted Avery's account as accurate. Williams's version of this article was published with the title "The Treaty of Saginaw in the Year 1819." The description of Neome and his friendship with Smith is on page 266.
24. Campau's own description of Neome is in Webber, "Treaty of Saginaw," 526. Webber, one of the attorneys in the lawsuit *Dewey vs. Campau,* published transcripts and extracts of testimony from the case in this article.
25. Albert Smith told of being adopted by Neome in a kind of ceremony in his deposition, *Williams et al. vs. Payne,* Record Group 81-44, box 31, file 27 (Genesee County courts), Archives of Michigan.
26. Avery, "Indian and Pioneer History," 11–12.
27. As noted previously, the most important references to Smith having a daughter with a Chippewa woman living at the mount of the Clinton River on Lake St. Clair appear in depositions of former aides and agents of Governor Cass, transcribed in Liber A, 320–327, Genesee County Register of Deeds office, Flint, Michigan. Other references are in Williams, "Treaty of Saginaw," 266; and in Henry N. Walker, *Reports of Cases Argued*a, 140. Again, this daughter of Smith's was called Nancy. She married a man named Alexander Crane in Redford, Michigan, in 1830. Local histories published in and about Flint, Michigan, assumed that Smith's Indian wife was from Neome's band on the Flint River, but this is wrong; the evidence is clear from men who knew her that she was from the Mt. Clemens area and their relationship was before the war.

Chapter Twelve. Conclude a Treaty for the Country upon the Saginac Bay

1. Gilpin, *Territory of Michigan,* 117.
2. Correspondence between Major Puthuff at Mackinac Island and Cass in Detroit appears in Carter, *Territorial Papers,* vol. 10 and other manuscript collections, but the issue of Astor's influence on these matters is summed up in Gilpin, *Territory of Michigan,* 119–120, and more pointedly in Madsen, *John Jacob Astor,* 173–174.
3. The complaint about Jacob Smith introducing alcohol to the Indians at Saginaw is in Crooks and Stewart's letter to Astor, Jan. 24, 1818, in Draper and Thwaites, *Wisconsin Historical Collections,* 20:21.
4. Gilpin, *Territory of Michigan,* 119–120. Another detailed explanation of the matter is in

Haeger, *John Jacob Astor,* 191–199.

5. The notice mentioning the delivery of stone to "Jacob Smith's wharf" is in the *Detroit Gazette,* Aug. 21, 1818.

6. The Bellows-Stone suit against Smith is in Blume, *Transactions of the Supreme Court of Michigan,* 3:94.

7. The matter of this silver work, which was ultimately provided in part by a metalworker named Andre dit Clark, and the resulting lawsuit by the TenEycks in which Jacob Smith was deposed, is in Records of the Michigan Territorial Supreme Court, box 13, file 911, *Andre vs. TenEyck,* Bentley Historical Library. The Smith deposition, in the file, is dated Sept. 20, 1823.

8. Ibid.

9. James Abbott's notice warning people against purchasing a note he and Robert Smart had issued to Jacob Smith is in the *Detroit Gazette,* Dec. 24, 1818.

10. The notice that the newspaper's proprietor wanted to sublet rooms rented from Smith is in the *Detroit Gazette,* Jan. 8, 1819.

11. The affidavit Smith made on behalf of J. Laplante is dated Feb. 15, 1819, Charles Larned Papers, Burton Historical Collection.

12. Record of payment made to Smith on Jan. 1, 1820, along with other payments for Smith's services to Lewis Cass in the preceding year, in *American State Papers,* 2:307.

13. "Account of monies received by the treasurer of Wayne County . . .," *Detroit Gazette,* Feb. 25, 1820.

14. The fact new Indian agent George Boyd opened an investigation into Smith is in Boyd to Cass, July 27, 1819, Cass Papers (microfilm copy of documents in the National Archives), reel 32, Bentley Historical Library.

15. Letters by Lewis Cass and William Woodbridge to U.S. officials urging them to ask for a treaty with the Saginaw Chippewa are in Carter, *Territorial Papers,* 10:808, 816–817.

16. Ibid.

17. March 6, 1819, Cass Papers, reel 32, Bentley Library.

18. Secretary of War to Cass with instructions, March 27, 1819, Schoolcraft, *Narrative Journal,* appendix A, 285.

19. A. Wendell to Cass, April 10, 1819, Cass Papers, reel 32, Bentley Library.

20. A. Macomb to Cass, Aug. 7, 1819, Cass Papers, reel 32, Bentley Library.

21. John Ryley to Cass, May 31, 1819, Cass Papers, reel 32, Bentley Library; his father, Judge James V. S. Ryley, wrote to William Woodbridge about his involvement in the treaty councils in a letter he called "A statement of facts relative to a treaty held in the month of September last in the Michigan Territory . . . ," [Dec. 24,] 1819, Woodbridge Papers, Burton Collection; Judge Ryley also wrote to Cass on May 1, 1820, Cass Papers, reel 33, Bentley Library.

22. Cass told of Judge Ryley's involvement in the treaty in a letter to William Woodbridge, March 3, 1820, Woodbridge Papers, Burton Collection.

23. Louis Campau statement, Wisconsin Historical Society.

24. Ibid.

25. The names of Henry Conner, Whitmore Knaggs, and other interpreters can be seen on a transcription of the treaty in Kappler, *Indian Treaties,* 187.

26. Avery, "Indian and Pioneer History," 12. His words are also in Williams, "Treaty of Saginaw," 266–267.

27. Wood, *History of Genesee County*, 152; Campau's statement that the U.S. government had confidential agents at the treaty who were not sworn interpreters is from Webber, "Treaty of Saginaw," 527.

Chapter Thirteen. The Treaty Councils Begin

1. Letters by Lewis Cass to the Secretary of War about his preparations for the Saginaw treaty councils are dated May, 1819 and Aug. 1, 1819, Carter, *Territorial Papers*, 10:827 and 848. Campau's preparations are from the Campau statement, Wisconsin Historical Society, and from his testimony as reflected in Webber, "Treaty of Saginaw," 525. This extract-transcript quotes Campau and other witnesses who gave evidence in a trial, *Dewey vs. Campau*, a dispute over the ownership of a section of land granted as a reservation in the Saginaw treaty.

2. Charles Avery addressed the treaty preparations in "Indian and Pioneer History," 4–5, or alternately, in Williams, "Treaty of Saginaw," 263, Avery's account was essentially copied by Williams. Payments by Cass to Jacob Smith for his efforts before the treaty are in *American State Papers*, 2:305, 310. These pages show expenses incurred by Cass and under the heading "Accounts of Superintendents of Indian Affairs." Campau described Cranberry Marsh in Campau statement, Wisconsin Historical Society.

3. Campau statement, Wisconsin Historical Society.

4. Woodbridge to Keiff, Sept. 9, 1819, Woodbridge Papers, Burton Historical Collection, Detroit Public Library.

5. McClosky to Cass, Sept. 13, 1819, Cass Papers, microfilm reel 32, Bentley Historical Library, University of Michigan.

6. Cass wrote to Secretary of War John C. Calhoun on Saturday, Sept. 11, 1819, that he was leaving Detroit on "Monday next" for Saginaw. Judge James Ryley wrote that they left on Sept. 13; see his letter, Dec. 24, 1819, titled "A Statement of facts relative to a Treaty held in the month of September last in the Michigan Territory . . .," Woodbridge Papers, Burton Collection; Webber, "Treaty of Saginaw," 520–521, 525; Ryley to Cass, May 1, 1820, Cass Papers, reel 33, Bentley Library. The fact Ottawa were also present was mentioned by Ryley in his "statement of facts" to Woodbridge and was echoed in Avery, "Indian and Pioneer History," 5. The name of the Chippewa woman Menawcumgoqua, mother to John, James, and Peter Ryley (spelled "Riley" in the terms of the Saginaw treaty) is given in the treaty; see Article 3 of the treaty in Kappler, *Indian Treaties*, 185–186.

7. Ryley to Cass, May 1,1820, Cass Papers, reel 33, Bentley Library.

8. Campau testimony, "The Treaty of Saginaw, 1819," *MPHC*, 26:526; Ryley to Cass, May 1, 1820, Cass Papers, reel 33, Bentley Library.

9. Campau statement, Wisconsin Historical Society.

10. Ibid.

11. Ibid.

12. Avery quoted this answer in his "Indian and Pioneer History," 8, though where he got the wording of the statement is not clear. Ephraim Williams, who came to Saginaw as a trader

in the late 1820s, described Ogemawkeketo in his statement to Lyman Draper, Wisconsin Historical Society.

13. The report about the progress in the talks and the appearance of the land along the Saginaw Trail is in *Detroit Gazette,* Sept. 24, 1819.

14. Cass wrote to William Woodbridge about the opening talks on Sept. 19, 1819, Woodbridge Papers, Burton Collection.

15. The two slightly different transcriptions of Louis Campau's description of the events at Saginaw are in the Campau testimony in Webber's "Treaty of Saginaw," 526; and in Cooley, *Michigan Reports,* 390.

16. Ryley to Cass, May 1,1820, Cass Papers, reel 33, Bentley Library.

17. Avery, "Indian and Pioneer History," 12. The truth was, of course, that Jacob Smith was a secret agent of Cass and the U.S. government, and was paid for his work.

18. Campau statement, Wisconsin Historical Society; Col. Caldwell (British Army) to Claus, July 20, 1815, Indian Affairs, Deputy Superintendent General's Office (microfilm) C-1109, group 3, roll 14, National Archives of Canada.

19. Avery, "Indian and Pioneer History," 11. James V. S. Ryley claimed credit for convincing the Indians to cede land to the U.S. government, though he admitted that Cass's agents believed that "my services were but of little use at that treaty." Cass agreed with his men; he felt that Ryley didn't play an important role. See Cass to Woodbridge, March 3, 1820, Woodbridge Papers, Burton Collection.

20. Testimony in Webber, "Treaty of Saginaw," 527–529.

21. Ibid., 522; Kaukokesik testimony, Dec. 17, 1853, *Dewey vs. Campau,* Record Group 81-44, box 31, file 10, Archives of Michigan, Lansing.

22. Testimony in Webber, "Treaty of Saginaw," 527; and *Dewey vs. Campau.*

23. Testimony in Webber, "Treaty of Saginaw," 528.

24. Avery, "Indian and Pioneer History," 12–13.

25. Depositions of Robert A. Forsyth, Aug. 5, 1840, and Louis Beaufait, Aug. 6, 1840, in Liber A, 321, 324–325, Genesee County Register of Deeds, Flint, Michigan.

26. Beaufait deposition, Liber A, 323–324, and Forsyth deposition, 321, Genesee County Register of Deeds; Marsac testimony, *Dewey vs. Campau*, Archives of Michigan.

27. Marsac's statement about Smith's list of individuals who were to receive land is in *Dewey vs. Campau*, Archives of Michigan.

28. Ibid.

29. Walker, *Reports of Cases Argued,* 134–135.

30. Testimony in *Dewey vs. Campau,* Archives of Michigan; and Webber, "Treaty of Saginaw," 522.

31. Cass to Secretary of War John C. Calhoun, Sept. 30, 1819, Carter, *Territorial Papers,* 10:865; Campau testimony in Webber, "Treaty of Saginaw," 526; Judge Ryley to Cass, May 1, 1820, Cass Papers, reel 33, Bentley Historical Library. Cass wrote to Calhoun: "Reservations have been made for a few half-breeds. It was absolutely necessary to our success, that these should be admitted into the treaty." Though the Ryley brothers received a section of land, their father was dissatisfied with this. He apparently wanted them to get land on the Tittabawassee

River at the "Salt Spring" (near modern-day Midland) and complained he should have also been paid in land or funds for his work at the treaty.

32. John Truedell testimony, April 4, 1856, in *Gardiner D. Williams & David Dewey vs. Campau,* Archives of Michigan.

33. Testimony in Webber, "Treaty of Saginaw," 522–23. Kaukokesik's testimony and that of other witnesses also appear in *Dewey vs. Campau,* Archives of Michigan.

34. Webber, "Treaty of Saginaw," 528.

35. Cass's denial that Indian children were brought forward so that he could see the intended recipients of the individual sections was accepted as gospel by a writer of a local history of the Flint area name Franklin Ellis, despite the multiplicity of Chippewa witnesses who testified they saw it happen. Their testimony was dismissed by Ellis as "wholly incorrect"; see Ellis, *History of Genesee County,* 30. Cass testified in a deposition on Nov. 26, 1835, that he "had no recollection of any Indian children being brought to me" at the treaty: Cass deposition, *Williams vs. Chauncey Payne,* Record Group 81-44, box 31, file 27, Archives of Michigan.

Yet an 1822 letter by John Biddle, head of the government register's office in Detroit, states that Cass suspected fraud had been perpetrated at the treaty talks by someone "attributing to certain white persons Indian names & producing Indian children as the persons in whose favour the grants or reservations were made." Cass had written a letter to that effect to the U.S. Treasury secretary, Biddle wrote, but government archivists were unable to find that letter decades later. See Biddle to the Commissioner of the General Land Office, Washington, D.C., Nov. 22, 1822, in Carter, *Territorial Papers,* 11:295–296.

36. Testimony in Webber, "Treaty of Saginaw," 524.

37. Ibid.; deposition of Now-chig-o-ma, Dec. 17, 1853, *Dewey vs. Campau,* Record Group 81-44, box 31, file 10, Archives of Michigan; Cooley, *Michigan Reports,* 384–385.

38. Cooley, *Michigan Reports,* 383–384, 391.

Chapter Fourteen. He Was Smart as Steel

1. A statement from a letter by Lewis Cass, dated June 22, 1831, that Jacob Smith intended to have Indian names for his white children written into the treaty language so that they could claim land on the Flint River, is in a War Department communication quoted in Ellis, *History of Genesee County,* 27. I was not able to locate this particular letter in its original form. However, the wording as quoted by Ellis is very similar to that given by Cass in a deposition in Michigan on Nov. 26, 1835, in *Williams et al vs. Payne,* Record Group 81-44 (Genesee County court records), box 31, file 27, Archives of Michigan, Lansing.

2. Cass letter extract, June 22, 1831, Ellis, *History of Genesee County,* 27; Cass deposition, *Williams vs. Payne,* Archives of Michigan.

3. The fact that Lewis Cass believed fraud had been committed at the Saginaw treaty councils when Indian children were represented as the persons named to receive reservations of land, when in fact the Indian names were actually for white individuals, is from a letter by John Biddle, Nov. 14, 1822, in Carter, *Territorial Papers,* 11:295–296. In this letter, Biddle quotes Cass. There can be no doubt Cass was referring to the introduction of Chippewa children and names for Smith's white children, since Cass, in other records and letters, states he was

concerned about Smith's attempt at the treaty to do this.

4. Cass letter extract, June 22, 1831, Ellis, *History of Genesee County,* 27.

5. Louis Campau's statement about Smith paying Indian women for the use of their names, even though the sections of land were intended for mixed-blood individuals, is in Cooley, *Michigan Reports,* 5:391.

6. Cass letter extract, June 22, 1831, in Ellis, *History of Genesee County,* 27. Law and policy going back to the mid-1780s that Indians could sell or grant land only to the United States and not to individuals is in Prucha, *American Indian Policy,* 45.

7. See Kappler, *Indian Treaties,* 185–186.

8. Testimony about Smith's statements that he'd gotten land for his children at the Saginaw treaty is in Henry N. Walker, *Reports of Cases Argued,* 135.

9. Claim of the Children of Jacob Smith, HR 24A-G81, Record Group 233 (House of Representatives), National Archives.

10. Copies of petitions signed by various Chippewa chiefs are part of the record of the Claim of the Children of Jacob Smith, National Archives. Ephraim Williams, in a statement to Lyman Draper on Jan. 7, 1863, Wisconsin Historical Society, said that "after great exertion" on the part of himself and his brother Gardiner Williams, assembled Chippewa chiefs in Saginaw agreed to a sworn statement that they intended Smith's white children to be "donees" or recipients of Flint River reservations. This was in 1835. The Smith heirs came to the brothers Williams, he wrote, for "their influence & exertion with the [Chippewa] nation."

11. Judge Ryley's complaint that the vast majority of the Indians present at the treaty didn't understand the provisions is in Ryley to Cass, May 1, 1820, Cass Papers, reel 33, Bentley Historical Library.

12. Marsac testimony in *Dewey vs. Campau,* Archives of Michigan.

13. Biddle to McLean, commissioner of the General Land Office, Nov. 14, 1822, in Carter, *Territorial Papers,* 11:295–296.

14. Paper titled "No. 68 Albert J. Smith claim," part of the Petition of Albert J. Smith, HR 28A-G8, Record Group 233 (House of Representatives), National Archives. This recommendation to settle the claim of the son of Jacob Smith against the Saginaw Chippewa seems to have been written in the summer of 1839, by a Detroit lawyer, Anthony TenEyck.

15. The estimate that the cession of Indian land to the United States in the Saginaw treaty amounted to slightly more than 4 million acres is in Stout, "Ethnological Report," 89. According to a map on page 164 in Stout, the cession included all of the present counties of Saginaw, Bay, Midland, Eaton, Alcona, Iosco, Arenac, Gratiot, Clinton, Huron, Ogemaw, and Gladwin; more than half of the counties of Ingham, Barry, Tuscola, Alpena, Oscoda, Ionia, Isabella, and Montcalm; and parts of the counties of Montmorency, Sanilac, Genesee, Shiawassee, Jackson, Calhoun, Kalamazoo, Roscommon, and Clare.

16. The costs of supplying the Indians with services and payments for the treaty cession was estimated in Cass to Calhoun, Sept. 30, 1819, Carter, *Territorial Papers,* 10:864–865.

17. Cass to Calhoun, Sept. 30, 1819, Carter, *Territorial Papers,* 10:865; Kappler, *Indian Treaties, 1778–1883,* 186.

18. Webber, "Treaty of Saginaw," 521–522. The spelling of Neome's name as Reaume is a matter

of routine in records of Cass's Indian Department.

19. Campau statement, Wisconsin Historical Society; also, Campau testimony in Webber, "Treaty of Saginaw," 526.

20. Campau statement, Wisconsin Historical Society. In this statement, written out by Lyman Draper on May 19, 1864, Truedell's name was not included, but the name of Detroit merchant Tunis Wendell was, along with Godfroy and TenEyck.

21. Campau statement, Wisconsin Historical Society.

22. Ibid. His account of opening barrels of whiskey because he was angry with Cass and Smith is also in Avery, "Indian and Pioneer History," 14, 15 and Williams, "Treaty of Saginaw," 268.

23. Campau statement, Wisconsin Historical Society; Avery, "Indian and Pioneer History," 15. Campau is quoted in the Avery article as using language that is substantially the same as he uses in 1864 statement in the Wisconsin Historical Society he gave Lyman Draper. The words attributed to Campau, spoken to Lewis Cass—"you let Smith plunder and rob me"—appear in Avery, but they are not in Draper's notes. Avery was an attorney in lawsuits about the Flint River reservations and heard Campau's testimony.

24. Campau statement, Wisconsin Historical Society; Ryley to Woodbridge, Dec. 24, 1819, "A Statement of facts relative to a Treaty held in the month of September last in the Michigan Territory . . .," Woodbridge Papers, Burton Collection, Detroit Public Library.

25. Cass to the Secretary of War, Sept. 30, 1819, Carter, *Territorial Papers*, 10:863–865.

26. The supplemental articles desired by the Indians, which were rejected by Congress, are in *American State Papers*, 2:195.

27. Cass's payments to Jacob Smith and others appear in *American State Papers*, 2:305, 306, 309, 310, and 318. Other payments to Smith for later work not directly tied to the treaty also show up in these pages

28. Ibid., 2:318. Using Ephraim Williams's account, "Treaty of Saginaw," Willis Dunbar and George May concluded, wrongly, that Smith used his influence against Cass and the treaty until the names of his children were written into the treaty provisions to get sections of land. The error appears in the 1995 third edition of their book, *Michigan: A History of the Wolverine State*, 148–149.

29. *American State Papers*, 2:310.

30. Cass to Woodbridge, March 3, 1820, Woodbridge Papers, Burton Collection.

31. Avery, "Indian and Pioneer History," 12.

32. Cass to Calhoun, Sept. 30, 1819, in Carter, *Territorial Papers*, 10:865–866.

33. Barney Campau claim, *MPHC*, 36:596–598.

34. *American State Papers*, 2:310.

35. Ibid., 2:309.

36. Cass to Woodbridge, March 3, 1820, Woodbridge Papers, Burton Collection.

37. Cass deposition, Nov. 26, 1835, in *Gardiner Williams vs. Chauncey Payne*, Archives of Michigan.

Chapter Fifteen. Mounting Trouble, Mounting Debt

1. Gilpin, *Territory of Michigan*, 80; Carter, *Territorial Papers*, 11:7–11.

2. The 1812 losses of TenEyck to the Saginaw Chippewa are in *American State Papers*, 2:195;

Claim and reimbursement for the loss of Smith's horse and saddle, part of his service record, National Archives.

3. The settlement of Smith's case against Abbott for payment of his unsuccessful mission to Michilimackinac in the war is in records of the Territorial Supreme Court, *Smith vs. Abbott,* box 9, file 507, Bentley Historical Library, University of Michigan.

4. Blume, *Transactions of the Supreme Court of Michigan,* 4:161, 166, 185–186, 221; "Detroit, Michigan, 1814–1863," an index compiled by Clarence Burton, 199, Burton Historical Collection, Detroit Public Library.

5. Loranger claim, August 1812 file, Solomon Sibley Papers, Burton Collection.

6. Smith's trouble with his unpaid mortgages and notes is in the records of the Territorial Supreme Court, *Craft & Walker vs. Smith, D. Jones, T. Dubois, William Hill, John Hill, James Hill, James Boyd Jr., Conrad TenEyck and J.V.R. TenEyck,* box 12, file 904, Bentley Library.

7. Ibid.

8. *Rogers vs. Smith,* case G-43, box 4, Records of the Wayne County Clerk's Office (miscellaneous), 1819–1820, Burton Collection. On different documents, the name of the plaintiff is given as Rogers and Rodgers.

9. The seizure of Smith's household goods, livestock, and items at both the Flint River and in Detroit, and the intervention on his behalf by Conrad TenEyck, are in the Records of the Territorial Supreme Court, *Bellows and Stone, surviving partners of R. H. Jones, vs. Smith,* box 10, file 587, Bentley Library.

10. Garland to Hartley Crawford, Dec. 5, 1843, part of the Petition of Albert J. Smith, HR 28A-G8, Record Group 233 (House of Representatives), National Archives.

11. Various 1819–1820 letters by and reports to Lewis Cass and entries in the digest/index of the *Detroit Gazette,* Burton Collection.

12. Gilpin, *Territory of Michigan,* 76–78.

13. Use of canoes made by Saginaw Chippewa in the Cass-Schoolcraft expedition is in Mentor L. Williams in his introduction to Schoolcraft's *Narrative Journal,* 12 and 403 (appendix F, Journal of James D. Doty). Smith's role as middleman is reflected in payments for the canoes in *American State Papers,* 2:309. The involvement of interpreters Ryley and Parks is also in Schoolcraft's *Narrative Journal,* 61n.

14. Cass's business with Smith's future son-in-law, Chauncey Payne, for Indian silverwork, is in *American State Papers,* 2:309.

15. Tracy's complaint about Jacob Smith's legal bill, Tracy to Woodbridge, June 1, 1820, William Woodbridge Papers, Burton Collection.

16. Jedidiah Morse's belief in the need for the Indians to become Christian farmers and his mission to assess their condition in the continental United States and its territories of the time are in Morse, *Report to the Secretary of War,* 9–12.

17. Ibid., 13,14, 16; *Detroit Gazette,* June 9, 1820.

18. Morse, Report to the Secretary of War, page 19 of the appendix.

19. Ibid.

20. Ibid., pages 19–20 of the appendix.

21. Ibid., page 20 of the appendix.

22. Ibid., pages 20–21 of the appendix.

23. Ibid.

24. Ibid., appendix, 23.

25. Calhoun to Cass, March 27, 1819, quoted in Schoolcraft, *Narrative Journal,* appendix A, 285.

26. Description of Morse is from Dr. John J. Bigsby, a British physician who traveled widely in Canada and the Great Lakes; Bigsby's description is quoted in Landon, *Lake Huron,* 297. Smith's affidavit against Campau, Aug. 16, 1820, is in Woodbridge Papers, Burton Collection.

27. Smith's bond to Godfroy is in *Godfroy vs. Howard, McKinstry and Smith,* file O-51, box 3, Wayne County Clerk's Office (miscellaneous papers), 1821–1822, Burton Collection; *Smith vs. John Connelly,* file M-212, and *Smith vs. I. Solomon,* file K-272, are in box 4, 1819–1820, Burton Collection.

28. Smith's sale of Detroit property to Abbott is reflected in deeds dated Sept. 8 and Sept. 15, 1820, Abbott Papers, Burton Collection.

29. Carter, *Territorial Papers,* 11:83; Blume, *Transactions of the Supreme Court of Michigan,* 4:237.

30. Smith is mentioned as a witness to the Indians' taking Oliver Williams's crops in Williams to Cass, Nov. 21, 1820, Cass Papers, microfilm reel 33, Bentley Library.

Chapter Sixteen. *U.S. vs. Jacob Smith*

1. An Internet-published transcription by Josie Reed Garzelloni and Carole Mohney Carr shows two men in Smith's household who fell within the category for white males aged 45 and up. Yet *Michigan Censuses 1710–1830* shows there was one white male in this age group at Smith's house, but two boys between the ages of 16 and 18. "Doane" is mentioned as working with Smith at the Flint River in Parke, "Recollections of First Tour," 575.

2. Blume, *Transactions of the Supreme Court of Michigan,* 4:310; *Joseph Campau, administrator for the estate of Dennis Campau, vs. Jacob Smith,* file J-189, box 4, Wayne County Clerk's Office (miscellaneous records) 1819–1820, Burton Historical Collection.

3. *American State Papers,* 2:312.

4. Parke, "Recollections of First Tour," 576. The railroad bridge to which Parke referred crossed the Flint River at roughly a 45-degree angle from Saginaw Street on the south bank. The northern end of the trestle was several hundred feet from the site of Smith's trading post. Cass to Capt. Smith, May 4, 1821, Records of the Michigan Superintendency of Indian Affairs, letters sent, 1818–1823, vol. 3 (microfilm, roll 4), National Archives.

5. Ibid.; The surveyor's field note booklet dealing with the Flint River reservations and other reservations is marked "Indian Reservations," contained in box 53, file 10 (Survey Notes of Indian Reservations 1818–1822), Record Group 60-8-A, Archives of Michigan.

6. The Camapu lawsuit appeal and subsequent suit over the bond posted for Smith are in Blume, *Transactions of the Supreme Court of Michigan,* 4:310 and 5:385–395, 417–426.

7. Parke, "Recollections of First Tour," 576.

8. Wampler to Woodbridge, Nov. 7, 1821, Woodbridge Papers, Burton Collection. Wampler to Tiffin, Nov. 7, 1821, in Carter, *Territorial Papers,* 11:169; Wampler to Cass, Dec. 13, 1821, Records of the Michigan Superintendency of Indian Affairs, letters received, July–December 1821 (microfilm, roll 9), National Archives; and Cass to Wampler, Dec. 24, 1824, Records of

the Michigan Superintendency of Indian Affairs, letters sent, 1818-1823, vol. 3, (microfilm, roll 4), National Archives.

9. Woodbridge to Calhoun, Nov. 24, 1821, and Woodbridge to Kearsley, Dec. 6, 1821, in Woodbridge Papers, Burton Collection.

10. Forsyth testimony in Liber A, 321, Genesee County Register of Deeds Office. Henry Reichard, an early Meadville settler, property owner, and family man, appears in the records of the Crawford County (Pennsylvania) Historical Society, and is the only individual with this name during this time frame, except for similar references to "Henry Richard." These appear to be one and the same man.

11. Government payments to Smith, "Territory Records," *MPHC*, 36:453.

12. That David Corbin signed a lease to use Smith's land on the Flint River is reflected in a document canceling that lease. This so-called "bill of sale," dated Aug. 5, 1822, is part of the Heirs of Jacob Smith file, Petitions & Memorials referred to the House of Representatives Committee on Private Land Claims, Record Group 233, National Archives. The fact Corbin was one of the "Indian farmers" for the Saginaw Chippewa is in a letter from Cass to Maj. Daniel Baker, March 18, 1822, Baker Papers, Burton Collection.

13. Albert J. Smith deposition in *Williams et al. vs. Payne,* Archives of Michigan, Lansing.

14. Brainerd, *Pioneer History of Grand Blanc,* 16. The remnants of the cabin survived for decades: Fox, *History of Saginaw County* (a business directory), 6n.

15. Information about the other whites (French or mixed blood) people living at the Flint River in the early 1820s come from a letter, Jacob Stevens to parents, July 1825, quoted in Smith, *Account of Flint and Genesee County,* 26; and Ephraim S. Williams statement, Jan. 7, 1863, Wisconsin Historical Society, Madison.

16. The notion that fur traders were exaggerating adverse conditions such as flooding in the Saginaw Valley rivers, to keep settlers from moving in, is from the *Detroit Gazette,* June 7, 1822. This article is cited in a paper by Stout, "Ethnohistorical Report," 198–201.

17. *U.S. vs. Jacob Smith,* file dated July 1822, Oakland County Legal Records Division, Oakland County Clerk's Office. Two records in the file—a statement by Grant to a justice of the peace and Grant's "recognizance" or pledge to appear—appear to have been misdated April 11, 1822. Because the alleged burglary of Grant's Saginaw trading post didn't happen until April 22 or later, these "April 11" documents must have been misdated, with May 11 likely being the correct date.

18. Cole, "J. L. Cole's Journal," 470–472. This account was printed in the *Detroit Free Press,* March 11, 1877.

19. Ibid., 2:472–475.

20. The spring 1822 letter of Lewis Cass about the need for a fort at Saginaw to encourage settlement and to counter Chippewa hostility is in Carter, *Territorial Papers,* 11:236.

21. *U.S. vs. Jacob Smith,* Oakland County Legal Records Division. "Point blankets" were commonly used goods in the fur trade. The term "points" referred to the number of thin black lines woven or embroidered into the edges of these woolen blankets to indicate their weight and size.

22. Ibid.

23. That Smith was not convicted in case—and that the complainant, Grant, was fined—is in Durant, *History of Oakland County*, 40.

24. Smith's bond, releasing him from the Wayne County Jail, is in Blume, *Transactions of the Supreme Court of Michigan*, 5:423. A copy of the bond, dated July 22, 1822, appears in the Territorial Supreme Court's "Selected Papers" in the same volume on page 422. Campau's lawyers noted that Smith again left Wayne County, in violation of his bond, on Nov. 22, 1822, 424.

25. Smith-Corbin "bill of sale," Aug. 5, 1822, in Heirs of Jacob Smith petition/claim file, National Archives.

26. The government payment to Smith for helping surveyors is in *American State Papers*, 2:404

27. Smith deposition in Records of the Territorial Supreme Court, *André dit Clark vs. C. TenEyck and J. V. R. TenEyck*, box 13, file 911, Bentley Library.

28. Blume, *Transactions of the Supreme Court of Michigan*, 3:347.

29. Ibid.

Chapter Seventeen. He Was Dissipated and Bad in His Habits

1. That Smith left Wayne County that fall is in pleadings on the matter of the bond that was posted for his release from jail in the Campau case, Blume, *Transactions of the Supreme Court of Michigan*, 5:424.

2. Smith's signing the petition along with other merchants saying they would no longer accept change bills is in the *Detroit Gazette*, Oct. 18, 1822.

3. The arrival of U.S. troops at Saginaw in the summer of 1822 is from Leeman, *History of Saginaw County*, 164; Dr. Pitcher's account was quoted by Fox in *History of Saginaw County*, 5, 6; *Detroit Gazette*, Aug. 2, 1822.

4. Baker to Cass, July 7, 1822, Baker Papers, Burton Historical Collection. Historical documents and accounts show that Garland and his wife Harriet raised her youngest sister, Maria, at some point after their mother Mary Smith died in 1817. Garland, as a U.S. Army officer, eventually made his young brother-in-law, Albert Smith, an aide in the years ahead.

5. Fox, *History of Saginaw County*, 5, 6.

6. *Godfroy vs. Howard, McKinstry and Jacob Smith*, file O-51, box 3, Wayne County Clerk's Office (miscellaneous papers), 1821–1822, Burton Collection. The case is dated Dec. 28, 1822.

7. Cass was quoted by John Biddle in a letter to the U.S. federal land office in Washington, D.C., Biddle to McLean, Nov. 14, 1822; Carter, *Territorial Papers*, 11:295–296. Cass's deposition, Nov. 26, 1835, is in *Gardiner D. Williams et al vs. Chauncey Payne*, Archives of Michigan.

8. McLean to Biddle, Jan. 6, 1823; and Biddle to Graham, Sept. 2, 1824, both in Carter, *Territorial Papers*, 11:323 and 584–585.

9. Ephraim Williams statement, Wisconsin Historical Society; *U.S. vs. Jacob Smith*, Oakland County Clerk's Office, Legal Division.

10. Williams statement, Wisconsin Historical Society. Parts of this statement by Williams would later be published under the title "Personal Reminiscences" in 1886 in the *Michigan Pioneer and Historical Collection*, but in that version the reference to "the trading posts of Smith and others" was left out (see *MPHC*, 8:240). Williams had his reasons for not including

those references to Jacob Smith, since he changed his position from supporting the claims of Smith's heirs for land on the Flint River to opposing them. This is discussed later. Whiting, "Whiting's Historic Sketch," 461.

11. Ephraim Williams statement, Wisconsin Historical Society.
12. Ibid.
13. Ibid.
14. *(Flint) Wolverine Citizen*, Dec. 21, 1867.
15. Ibid. "Mother Hansome" or "Mother Handsome" was actually a woman named Mrs. Chappel, who seems to have been a former camp follower, or prostitute, who had catered to Detroit's soldiers. Other accounts say her home/inn was several miles from Detroit. For years, the inn of Mother Hansome seems to have been the first such establishment a person would reach as he came down the Saginaw Trail into Detroit.
16. Cass to Baker, March 18, 1823, Baker Papers, Burton Collection.
17. The letter of Jacob Stevens to his parents, written from the area called Grand Blanc to his parents in July 1825, was reproduced in Wood, *History of Genesee County,* 1:204–205.
18. Ibid.
19. Campau's description of Grand Blanc is in his statement to Lyman C. Draper, Wisconsin Historical Society; Stevens to parents, July 1825, Wood, *History of Genesee County,* 1:204–205; Ephraim Williams statement, Wisconsin Historical Society.
20. Ephraim Willams told the story of Jacob Stevens's misunderstanding with the Indians over the large rock on the hill in "Indians and an Indian Trail," 140.
21. Stevens to parents, July 1825, Wood, *History of Genesee County,* 1:204–205.
22. Sherman Stevens told of riding to the Flint River as a boy in "Sketch of Early Pioneer Life," 94.
23. Ibid. The Saginaw Street bridge mentioned by Stevens was about two blocks from the site of Smith's trading post.
24. Summaries of testimony in Ellis, *History of Genesee County,* 1:28–29. Other summaries are in Walker, *Reports of Cases Argued,* 138–39.
25. Whiting "Whiting's Historic Sketch," 461.
26. Stevens to parents, July 1825, in Wood, *History of Genesee County,* 1:205.
27. Cole, "J. L. Cole's Journal," 473; Cass to Calhoun, Sept. 30, 1819, in Carter, *Territorial Papers,* 10: 864.
28. Smith's son-in-law John Garland insisted that Neome ("Beaume") intended land for Smith's children in his letter to Hartley Crawford of the War Department, Dec. 5, 1843, in Petition of Albert J. Smith, HR 28A-G8, Record Group 233 (House of Representatives), National Archives.
29. Avery, "Indian and Pioneer History," 11, 12, 13. Avery, a lawyer who came to Flint in the 1850s, purchased an interest in the land the Smith heirs maintained had been granted to Smith's son, Albert, in the 1819 treaty language; Garland acquired title to Flint River land that had allegedly been granted in the treaty to Jacob Smith's part-Chippewa daughter, Nancy Smith Crane, whose name was supposedly Mokitchenoqua, even earlier, in the mid-1830s. See Ellis, *History of Genesee County,* 26, 28.

30. Carter, *Territorial Papers*, 11:473–474; Smith's $2 payment of bounty for "a wolf scalp" in 1823 was reported in the expenses of Wayne County in the *Detroit Gazette*, March 12, 1824.

31. Blume, *Transactions of the Supreme Court of Michigan*, 4:482–483; Records of the Territorial Supreme Court, *Craft and Walker vs. Smith et al*, file 904, box 12, Bentley Historical Library.

32. Blume, *Transactions of the Supreme Court of Michigan*, 4:482–483; *Craft and Walker vs. Smith et al*, Bentley Library.

33. *Craft and Walker vs. Smith et al*, Bentley Library.

34. The document is part of the Petition of Albert J. Smith, Record Group 233 (House of Representatives), HR 28A-G8. It is a handwritten copy of TenEyck's findings attached to a letter dated Oct. 16, 1839, from Hartley Crawford of the War Department's Office of Indian Affairs to Secretary of War J. R. Poinsett.

Chapter Eighteen. It Is the Last Stir of the Dying Wind

1. "Incidents in the Life of Eber Ward," 473.

2. *Detroit Gazette,* Dec. 5, 1823; Whiting, "Whiting's Historic Sketch," 461–462.

3. Biddle's Sept. 2, 1824, letter to the government land commissioner is in Carter, *Territorial Papers*, 11:584–585.

4. Ibid.; Biddle deposition, Aug. 6, 1840 in Liber A, 325, Genesee County Register of Deeds, Flint.

5. The certificate of marriage between Louisa L. Smith and Chauncey S. Payne, July 16, 1824, by Judge Abbott, is in the Jacob Smith Papers, Perry Archive, Sloan Museum. News of the wedding is in *Detroit Gazette*, May 21, 1824.

6. The advertisement of sale of Smith's Detroit house and property is in Clarence Burton (ed.), *Detroit Gazette* Digest, vol. 3, July 18, 1823–Feb. 21, 1828 (Detroit: typescript, n.d.), Burton Historical Collection, Detroit Public Library.

7. Garland to Crawford, Dec. 5, 1843, in Petition of Albert J. Smith, HR 28A-G8, Record Group 233 (House of Representatives), National Archives. That Smith still had lawsuits pending and that daughter Caroline was boarding with a family is in a document, "Estate of Jacob Smith due to John McDonell," in the Smith Papers, Perry Archive, Sloan Museum.

8. *(Flint) Wolverine Citizen,* Dec. 21, 1867.

9. Smith's grave is given in Leeman, *History of Saginaw County*, 160; Avery's account of Smith's death is in Avery, "Indian and Pioneer History," 17. This was copied by Ephraim S. Williams in "Treaty of Saginaw," 269–270. Clarence Burton's thumbnail biographical sketch of Smith in the Detroit Public Library states that Smith died in June, 1825, but family papers make it clear he died before April 4. Jean Baptiste Cauchois (sometimes spelled "Cachois" and routinely misspelled as "Cochios" in Genesee County histories) was the son of a trader of the same name. The elder Cauchois was born in Montreal in 1732 and died at Mackinac in 1778. The younger Cauchois, who seems to have been based in Detroit, was married to trader Archibald Lyon's sister Catherine.

10. Avery, "Indian and Pioneer History," 18. Garland told of going with his brother-in-law Chauncey Payne to the Flint River after Smith had died in his letter to Hartley Crawford, Dec. 5, 1843, in Petition of Albert J. Smith, National Archives. The name "Sagosequa" was

claimed by the Smith heirs to have been given by Indians to Caroline Smith. Of course, one of the Smith Reservations on the Flint River was earmarked by the 1819 Saginaw treaty for Sagosequa. Unfortunately for the Neome's daughter, her claim for that section was unsuccessful.

11. Garland's note about the use and return of Smith's property at the Flint River was submitted to Congress years later as proof of Albert Smith's ownership of a section of land there by virtue of the 1819 Treaty of Saginaw. It is part of the Claim of the Children of Jacob Smith, HR 24A-G81, Record Group 233 (House of Representatives), National Archives.

12. *Detroit Gazette*, May 10, May 17, and June 28, 1825. Stories in these issues told of the land sales and road projects that were extending settlement far to the north and west of the Detroit area.

13. *Detroit Gazette*, Sept. 13, 1825.

14. "Estate of Jacob Smith due to John McDonell," in the Smith Papers, Perry Archive, Sloan Museum.

15. Ibid.

16. This document, titled "No. 68 Albert J. Smith claim," is part of the Petition of Albert J. Smith, HR 28A-G8, Record Group 233 (House of Representatives), National Archives. It is attached to an 1839 letter by Hartley Crawford of the Indian Affairs office of the War Department to Secretary of War J. R. Poinsett, and appears to have been written by Crawford or Detroit attorney Anthony TenEyck, who met with Saginaw Chippewa leaders about claims made against the tribe.

17. *Detroit Gazette*, March 28, 1826.

18. *(Flint) Wolverine Citizen*, Dec. 21, 1867.

19. Tocqueville's trip up the Saginaw Trail is described in his *Journey to America*, 134–135, 371–372, 375–376. Pages 134–135 are part of Tocqueville's "Pocket Notebook No. 2," while the subsequent pages are from the finished article "A Fortnight in the Wilds."

20. Ibid., 135, 376–378. Beaumont also wrote about the trip to the Flint River in a letter to one Chabrol, cited in Pierson, *Tocqueville in America*, 258–259n.

21. Tocqueville, *Journey to America*, 136, 378–380. For the record, no other account of John Todd's tavern-inn near the Flint River mentions a pet bear.

22. Tocqueville's description of the wind through the trees on the Saginaw Trail is from *Journey to America*, 383; also in *MPHC*, 2:461–462.

Chapter Nineteen. No One Was More Anxious to Secure Advantage Than Smith

1. A news account about the arrest of Kishkauko is in the *Detroit Gazette*, Jan. 10, 1826. Additional stories about his death and the escape of his son appeared in the paper on May 23 and Oct. 10, 1826. His burial and the subsequent death of Big Beaver are in Palmer, *Early Days in Detroit*, 141–142; the account that named Kishkauko's victim, Wauwasson, is in Caitlin's *The Story of Detroit*, 278; the appeal by Saginaw Chippewa for the release of Big Beaver is in William Woodbridge to Barbor, June 20, 1826, Woodbridge Papers, Burton Historical Collection, Detroit Public Library.

2. Avery, "Indian and Pioneer History," 18; also in Williams, "Treaty of Saginaw," 270. For an example of "Reaume's Town," see John Farmer's published 1825 map of the territory, Detroit Public Library.

3. Deposition of Archibald Lyon, Jan. 8, 1817, John McDonell Papers, Burton Collection, Detroit Public Library; Ephraim Williams statement, Wisconsin Historical Society; and Burton, *Proceedings of Land Board,* 194–195. The name is given as both Lyon and Lyons in the historical record. When Lyon signed an affidavit about his activities with John McDonell in purchasing the freedom of U.S. soldiers taken prisoner by the Indians, he finished with a flourish that makes it uncertain whether or not if the last character of his name was an "s."

4. The reburial of Jacob Smith is from Record Book I, Glenwood Cemetery, Flint. It states Smith was reinterred on Sept. 6, 1866, and that Smith was 48 years old at the time of his death. But Smith's relatives were wrong on that point; he was actually about 52 when he died, since the Quebec census clearly indicates that 1773 was the year of his birth. The large stone marker on his grave gives the correct year, 1773.

5. The fact that Governor Cass and federal officials in Detroit warned the General Land Office in Washington, D.C., of the fraud that had been committed at the treaty councils in Saginaw in 1819 by the entry of Indian names for white persons to be issued sections of land on the Flint River is reflected in 1820s letters in Carter, *Territorial Papers,* 11:295–296, 323, 371–372, 389–390, 584–585.

6. Kearsley deposition, Aug. 6, 1840, Liber A, 326, Genesee County Register of Deeds; Ephraim Williams statement, Wisconsin Historical Society. It should be noted that Kearsley's testimony came five years after Ephraim Williams said he and his brother pressured Chippewa chiefs to endorse a statement to Congress that they intended Smith's white children to get sections of land in the 1819 treaty, and after the Congress, during the administration of Andrew Jackson in 1836, approved the claims of Smith's white children, adapting the treaty terms.

7. Ephraim Williams statement, Wisconsin Historical Society.

8. Ibid.; also Williams, "Certificate or Statement," 142.

9. Ephraim Williams statement, Wisconsin Historical Society.

10. Williams, "Certificate or Statement," 142.

11. Ephraim Williams statement, Wisconsin Historical Society.

12. Statements endorsed by the Chippewa are part of the Claim of the Children of Jacob Smith, HR 24A-G8.1, Record Group 233 (House of Representatives), National Archives.

13. Ibid.

14. Ibid.

15. Ibid.

16. Committee on Private Land Claims, 24th Congress, 1st session, Report No. 101, House of Representatives, "Heirs of Jacob Smith," Jan. 12, 1836 (Washington: Blair & Rives); a copy is in the Burton Historical Collections. The document is also part of the committee's record of the Smith heirs' claim in the National Archives.

17. Ellis, *History of Genesee County,* 26. The legislation appears in various records of the 24th Congress, including *American State Papers,* 8:339. Congressional records show the measure

was approved on June 23, 1836.

18. Ephraim Williams statement, Wisconsin Historical Society.

19. Gardiner Williams was a party to lawsuits for Section 2 of the Smith Reservation, intended for "Metawanene," who the Smith heirs maintained was Albert Smith; and Section 8, which was intended for "Mokitechenoqua," who the Smith heirs said was Jacob Smith's Chippewa daughter. See Ellis, *History of Genesee County,* 26, 28. Ephraim Williams's attack on the legitimacy of the Smith heirs' claim for reservations on the river is in "Certificate or Statement," 140–144.

20. Ellis, *History of Genesee County,* 28; Alexander D. Crane marriage to Nancy Smith is in Crane, *Genealogy of the Crane Family,* 2:330–331.

21. Ellis, *History of Genesee County,* 28–29; Walker, *Reports of Cases Argued,* 139.

22. Cass deposition, *Williams vs. Payne,* Archives of Michigan; Biddle and Kearsley depositions, Liber A, 323–327, Genesee County Register of Deeds.

23. Walker, *Reports of Cases Argued,* 141.

24. Ellis, *History of Genesee County,* 28–29.

25. Albert Smith deposition, *Williams et al. vs. Payne,* Archives of Michigan.

26. Ellis, *History of Genesee County,* 26–28. For example, a brief reference to Nancy Smith Crane and the Mokitchenoqua section lawsuit appears in an anonymous paper in "Pioneer Recollections of Genesee County," a typescript compilation of speeches presented by amateur Flint-area historians in the 1920s and 1930s, 2, Flint Public Library.

Chapter Twenty. The White Man Takes Away What He Bought of the Indians

1. Ellis, *History of Genesee County,* 31.

2. Ibid., 29.

3. Chauvin statement, May 27, 1857, Campau Family Papers, Burton Historical Collections, Detroit Public Library; Ellis, *History of Genesee County,* 30–31.

4. Testimony in Webber, "Treaty of Saginaw," 528.

5. Ellis, *History of Genesee County,* 22–24. Cass's opinion about the Indians is in Trask, *Black Hawk,* 18–19; Garland escorting Black Hawk and surviving Sauk to the eastern United States is on page 304.

6. Ephraim Williams statement, Wisconsin Historical Society; Williams, "Certificate or Statement," 142–144.

7. The claim by Albert Smith, the decisions of the War Department about it, and letters by John Garland about the claim are part of the Petition of Albert J. Smith, HR 28A-G8, Record Group 233 (House of Representatives), National Archives.

8. Walker, *Reports of Cases Argued,* 125.

9. "Jacob Smith's Children Not Indian, Documents a Century Old Indicate," *Flint Saturday Night* 3, no. 52 (May 3, 1930): 20, Perry Archive, Sloan Museum.

10. For example, author Jeffry D. Wert notes in his biography of Longstreet that John Garland's wife, Harriet Smith, was one-half or one-quarter Indian. See Wert, *General James Longstreet,* 34. Of course, that would require that Mary Smith was Indian or half Indian, something

that records show was not true; Wert's incorrect information about Jacob Smith's "Indian wife" being the mother of Harriet and the other Smith children appears to have come from a doctoral dissertation about Longstreet written in South Carolina.

An article in a twentieth-century Flint magazine exemplified how this mistaken notion that Smith's children were Indian had taken root locally. This appeared in an unsigned article, "Jacob Smith First Settler Here, Outwitted Gov. Cass, Started Woe," *Flint Saturday Night*, April 12, 1930, 17–18. That article, in turn, prompted a great-grandson of Smith's to show Canadian church records proving that Mary Reid Smith was white, born of an Irish mother and an Anglo father. Just weeks later, the magazine ran a story headlined "Jacob Smith's Children Not Indian, Documents a Century Old Indicate," *Flint Saturday Night*, May 3, 1930, 20.

11. "Jacob Smith's Children Not Indian, Documents a Century Old Indicate," *Flint Saturday Night*, May 3, 1930, 20.

12. See Avery, "Indian and Pioneer History," 12–13; for Avery's purchase of an interest in Smith Reservation land, see Ellis, *History of Genesee County*, 26.

13. Dunbar and May, *Michigan*, 177–178.

14. Mills, *History of Saginaw County*, 48, 49. The story also appears in the earlier *History of Saginaw County* by Leeman.

15. Ellis, *History of Genesee County*, 13. In his undated biographical notes on Jacob Smith in the Sloan Museum archive, son-in-law Thomas B. W. Stockton also wrote that Smith and all but one of his "engages" (employees) escaped from the pursuing Indians.

16. The story of the supposed Indian burning-torture site was told by a Grand Blanc area settler named Alvah Brainerd in his book, *Pioneer History of Grand Blanc*, 40.

17. The story of a real U.S. soldier whose life was purchased by Joseph Campau is mentioned in Ellis, *History of Genesee County*, 16–17.

18. Ephraim Williams dismissed the Grand Blanc torture-murder in his article, "Indians and an Indian Trail," 138. Williams said the Chippewa had an excellent sense of humor and enjoyed awing their white neighbors with shocking tales of violence.

19. The language of the Michigan historical marker for site of Jacob Smith's house and hundreds of other state markers can be read at www.michmarkers.com.

20. The quote appears in Catton, *Glory Road*, 3. For more about the saying, an Internet search reveals various articles, research, and citations.

21. Johnson, *The Michigan Fur Trade*, 161.

BIBLIOGRAPHY

Unpublished Sources

Archives nationales Québec: *Jacob and Mary Smith vs. Andrew Doe* (court file), King's Bench, 1798–1799.

Archives of Michigan, Michigan Historical Society, Lansing: Lewis Cass Letterbook; Genesee County Court records; Plats of Genesee County (map), 1821 Indian reservations; Survey Notes of Indian Reservations.

Bentley Historical Library, University of Michigan, Ann Arbor: Lewis Cass Papers (documents and correspondence of the Office of Indian Affairs and the Michigan Superintendency of Indian Affairs); Records of the Supreme Court of the Michigan Territory; records of the courts of Wayne County and Detroit.

Burton Historical Collection, Detroit Public Library: James Abbott Papers; Daniel Baker Papers; Josiah Brady Papers; Campau Family Papers; Silas Farmer Papers; William Henry Harrison Papers; Mary Ruth Lacey Papers, including typescript articles "1814" and "Incidents of the War of 1812" by B. F. H. Witherell (under the pseudonym "Hamtramck"); Charles Larned Papers; Angus Mackintosh Letterbook; Duncan McArthur Papers; John McDonell Papers; Record Book of Licenses Issued Indian Traders 1806–1817 (Michigan Territory); U.S. War Department Papers; John P. Sheldon Papers; Solomon Sibley Papers; B. F. H. Witherell Papers; William Woodbridge Papers; *Detroit Gazette*; *Detroit Free Press*; court and land (notarial) records of Wayne County and Detroit.

Clements Library, University of Michigan: Lewis Cass Papers; War of 1812 Papers.

Flint Public Library: Leah Beach Garner, "The Writing of Leah Beach Garner," articles or talks written and presented in the 1930s; "Pioneer Recollections of Genesee County."

Genesee County (Flint, Michigan) Register of Deeds: Liber A (320–328), 1840 depositions regarding "Mokitchenoqua" / Nancy Smith Crane / Elizabeth Lyon and Jacob Smith.

Hatcher Graduate Library, University of Michigan: "Letters of the Secretary of War 1800–1816" (a hand-transcribed booklet of letters dealing with War Department affairs in Michigan).

Jones Memorial Library, Lynchburg, Virginia: Garland Family File.

Minnesota Historical Society: Robert Dickson Papers.

National Archives and Records Administration, Washington, D.C.: Jacob Smith's payroll and muster record from Michigan (Detached) Militia; record of claims of loss of horse at the surrender of Detroit; claim of Albert Smith regarding Chippewa debts to Jacob Smith; petition of heirs of Jacob Smith relating to Flint River reservations.

National Archives of Canada: Records of the Holy Trinity Anglican Church, Quebec; Registers of St. Andrews Presbyterian Church in Quebec City; Records of the British Indian Department, Deputy Superintendent General's Office; William Claus Papers.

Oakland County (Pontiac Michigan), Legal Records Division, Clerk's Office. *U.S. vs. Jacob Smith* (court file).

Sloan Museum, Merle Perry Archive, Flint, Michigan: T. B. W. Stockton Papers, including biographical notes about Jacob Smith; 1798 extracts of church records regarding the parents of Mrs. Jacob Smith (Mary Reid); 1815 letter by Mary Smith to Peggy; invitation to Judge A. Woodward to the funeral of Mary Smith; Jacob Smith's account/debts to John McDonell; *(Flint) Wolverine Citizen.*

Wisconsin Historical Society: Ephraim S. Williams biographical statement; Louis Campau biographical statement; Lyman C. Draper Papers, Draper's notebooks, series 3, vol. S21.

Ziibiwing Cultural Society Center of the Saginaw Chippewa, Mt. Pleasant, Michigan: Transcripts and photocopies of Indian Affairs Department/Bureau records and communications from the War Department, in "Calendar of Research for the Saginaw Chippewa, Primary Documents Part 1, 1792–1836."

Published Sources

American State Papers: Documents, Legislative and Executive, of the Congress of the United States, Indian Affairs, vols. 1 and 2, Private Land Claims, vol. 8. Washington, D.C.: Gales and Seaton, 1832, 1834, 1861.

Antal, Sandy. *A Wampum Denied: Procter's War of 1812.* East Lansing: Michigan State University Press, 1997.

Askin, John. "The Diary of John Askin." In *Michigan Pioneer and Historical Collections,* vol. 32, 1903.

———. *The John Askin Papers,* 2 vols. Milo Quaife, ed. Detroit: Detroit Library Commission, 1931.

Avery, Charles P. "Indian and Pioneer History of the Saginaw Valley." In *Indian and Pioneer History of the Saginaw Valley . . . and Business Advertiser for 1866 and 1867.* East Saginaw: Lewis and Lyon, 1866.

Bald, F. Clever. *Detroit's First American Decade, 1796–1805.* Ann Arbor: University of Michigan Press, 1948.

Blume, William Wirt, ed. *Transactions of the Supreme Court of Michigan 1805–1814.* 6 vols. Ann Arbor: University of Michigan Press, 1935–1940.

Boucherville, Thomas Verchères des. *Memoir of Thomas Verchères des Boucherville.* In *War on the Detroit,* ed. Milo Quaife. Chicago: Lakeside Press, R. R. Donnelley & Sons, 1940.

Brainerd, Alvah. *A Pioneer History of the Township of Grand Blanc.* Flint: Globe Press, 1878.

Brown, Samuel R. *An Authentic History of the Second War for Independence, Comprising Details of Military and Naval Operations.* Vol. 2. New York: J. G. Anthony, 1815.

Burton, Agnes M., ed. *Proceedings of the Land Board of Detroit.* Detroit, 1915.

Caitlin, George B. *The Story of Detroit.* Detroit: Evening News Association, 1923.

Carter, Clarence, ed. *The Territorial Papers of the United States.* 28 vols. Washington, D.C.: U.S. Government Printing Office, 1934–1975.

Catton, Bruce. *Glory Road.* Garden City, N.Y.: Doubleday, 1952.

Cole, J. L. "J. L. Cole's Journal of a Pedestrian Tour from Detroit to Sagana (Saginaw) River in 1822." In *Michigan Pioneer and Historical Collections,* vol. 2, 1880.

Cooley, Thomas M. *Michigan Reports: Reports of Cases Heard and Decided in the Supreme Court of Michigan from November 14, 1860 to the End of January Term, 1862.* Vol. 5. Chicago: Callaghan, 1879.

Crane, Ellery Bicknell. *Genealogy of the Crane Family,* vol. 2. Worcester, Mass.: Press of Charles Hamilton, 1900.

Crawford, Kim. *The 16th Michigan Infantry.* Dayton, Ohio: Morningside Books, 2002.

Cruikshank, E. A., ed. *Documents Relating to the Invasion of Canada and the Surrender of Detroit, 1812.* Ottawa: Government Printing Bureau, 1913.

———. "General Hull's Invasion of Canada in 1812." *Proceedings and Transactions of the Royal Society of Canada* 1, sec. 2 (1907): 211–290.

Densmore, Frances. *Chippewa Customs.* Reprint, St. Paul: Minneapolis Historical Society Press, 1979.

Drake, Thomas J. "History of Oakland County." In *Michigan Pioneer and Historical Collections,* vol. 22, 1894.

Dunbar, Willis F., and George S. May. *Michigan: A History of the Wolverine State.* 3rd ed. Grand Rapids: W. B. Eerdmans, 1995.

Durant, Samuel W. *History of Oakland County, Michigan.* Philadelphia: L. H. Everts, 1877.

Ellis, Franklin. *History of Genesee County.* Philadelphia: Everts and Abbott, 1879.

———. *History of Shiawassee and Clinton Counties.* Philadelphia: D. W. Ensign, 1880.

"Expedition Under General McArthur." In *Michigan Pioneer and Historical Collections,* vol. 8, 1886.

Fitting, James E. *The Archaeology of Michigan.* Bloomfield Hills, Mich.: Cranbrook Institute of Science, 1975.

Fox, Truman B. *History of Saginaw County.* Saginaw: Enterprise Print, 1858.

Gilpin, Alec R. *The Territory of Michigan 1805–1837.* East Lansing: Michigan State University Press, 1970.

————. *The War of 1812 in the Old Northwest*. East Lansing: Michigan State University Press, 1958.

Gould, Lucius E. "Four Papers on the Early History of Shiawassee County." In *Michigan Pioneer and Historical Collections,* vol. 32, 1903.

Haeger, John D. *John Jacob Astor: Business and Finance in the Early Republic.* Detroit: Wayne State University Press, 1991.

Harrison, William Henry. *The Papers of William Henry Harrison 1805–1815.* Ed. Douglas Clanin. Microfilm, 10 reels. Indianapolis: Indiana Historical Society, 1999.

Hickerson, Harold. *The Chippewa and Their Neighbors: A Study in Ethnohistory.* Prospect Heights, Ill.: Waveland Press.

Horr, David A., ed. *Chippewa Indians V.* New York: Garland, 1974.

Hubbard, Bela. "The Early Colonization of Detroit." In *Michigan Pioneer and Historical Collections,* vol. 1, 1877.

Hull, William. "An Estimate of the Expenses Incurd [*sic*] by the Treaty of Detroit." In *Michigan Pioneer and Historical Collections,* vol. 40, 1929.

————. "Message to the Chiefs of the Chippewa at Saginaw, Oct. 11, 1808." In *Michigan Pioneer and Historical Collections,* vol. 36, 1908.

Hunt, John. *The John Hunt Memoirs: Early Years of the Maumee Basin, 1812–1833.* Ed. Richard J. Wright. Maumee, Ohio: Maumee Valley Historical Society, n.d.

"Incidents in the Life of Mr. Eber Ward, Father of Capt. E. B. Ward of Steamboat Fame as Related to Mrs. E. M. S. Stewart in the Summer of 1852." In *Michigan Pioneer and Historical Collections,* vol. 6, 1884.

Johnson, Ida Amanda. *The Michigan Fur Trade.* Lansing: Michigan Historical Commission, 1919.

Kappler, Charles J., ed. *Indian Treaties, 1778–1883.* New York: Interland, 1972.

Kelton, Dwight H. "Mackinac County." In *Michigan Pioneer and Historical Collections,* vol. 6, 1884.

Knopf, Richard, ed. *Document Transcriptions of the War of 1812.* 10 vols. Columbus: Ohio State Museum, 1957–1962.

Landon, Fred. *Lake Huron.* New York: Bobbs-Merrill, 1944.

Leeman, Michael A. *History of Saginaw County.* Chicago: Charles C. Chapman, 1881.

Lindly, Harlow, ed. *Fort Meigs and the War of 1812: Orderly Book of Cushing's Company, 2nd U.S. Artillery, April 1813–February 1814 and Personal Diary of Captain Daniel Cushing, October 1812–July 1813.* Columbus: Ohio Historical Society, 1975.

Little, C. D. "Sketch of the Life of Uncle Harvey Williams." In *Michigan Pioneer and Historical Collections,* vol. 1, 1877.

Lucas, Robert. *The Robert Lucas Journal of the War of 1812 During the Campaign under General William Hull.* Ed. John C. Parish. Iowa City: State Historical Society of Iowa, 1906.

Madsen, Axel. *John Jacob Astor: America's First Multimillionaire.* New York: John Wiley & Sons, 2001.

Massie, Dennis. "Jacob Smith in the Saginaw Valley." *Michigan History* (Summer 1967): 116–129.

May, George S. *War, 1812.* Lansing: Mackinac Island State Park Commission, 1962.

McAfee, Robert Breckinridge. *History of the Late War in the Western Country.* University of Michigan Microfilms, 1966 reprint.

"Memorandum of our Expedition under Gen'l. McArthur." In *Michigan Pioneer and Historical Collections,* vol. 8, 1886.

Michigan Censuses 1710–1830, under the French, British, and Americans. Detroit: Detroit Society for Genealogical Research, 1982.

Michigan Historical Commission / Pioneer Society of Michigan. *Michigan Pioneer and Historical Collections.* 40 vols. Lansing: Michigan Historical Commission / Pioneer Society of Michigan, 1877–1929.

Miller, Albert. "Rivers of the Saginaw Valley Sixty Years Ago." In *Michigan Pioneer and Historical Collections,* vol. 14, 1889.

Mills, James Cooke. *History of Saginaw County, Michigan.* Saginaw: Seeman & Peters, 1918.

"Miscellaneous Documents." In *Michigan Pioneer and Historical Collections,* vol. 8, 1886.

Miscellaneous Intercepted Correspondence, 1789–1915. War of 1812 Papers of the Department of State, National Archives Microfilm Publications, microcopy 588, roll 7.

Morse, Jedidiah. *Report to the Secretary of War of the United States, on Indian Affairs* . . . New Haven: S. Converse, 1822.

Myers, Gustavus. *History of the Great American Fortunes.* Vol. 1. Chicago: C. H. Kerr, 1910.

Naveaux, Ralph. *Invaded on all Sides.* Marceline, Mo.: Walsworth, 2008.

Palmer, Friend. *Early Days in Detroit.* Detroit: Hunt & June, 1906.

"Papers from the Canadian Archives, 1767–1814." In *Wisconsin Historical Collection,* vol. 12 Madison: Democrat Printing, 1892.

Parke, Hervey. "Recollections of my First Tour in Michigan in 1821." In *Michigan Pioneer and Historical Collections,* vol. 3, 1881.

Pierson, George Wilson. *Tocqueville in America.* Baltimore: John Hopkins University Press, 1996.

Prucha, Francis Paul. *American Indian Policy in the Formative Years.* Cambridge: Harvard University Press, 1962.

Quaife, Milo, ed. *War on the Detroit.* Chicago: Lakeside Press, R. R. Donnelley & Sons, 1940.

Rapport de l'Archiviste de la Province de Québec 1948–49. Quebec: Queen's Printer, 1949.

Register of St. John's Church of England at Sandwich in the Western District of the Province of Upper Canada 1802–1827. Chatam: Kent and Essex branches of Ontario Genealogical Society, 1990.

Richardson, John. *Richardson's War of 1812.* Toronto: Historical Publishing, 1902.

Robertson, John. *Michigan in the War.* Lansing: W. S. George, 1882.

Schoolcraft, Henry R. "Memoir of John Johnston." *Michigan Pioneer and Historical Collections,* vol. 36, 1908.

———. *Narrative Journal of Travels Through the Northwestern Regions of the United States.* . . . Ed. Mentor L. Williams. Reprint, East Lansing: Michigan State College Press, 1953.

Smith, William V. *An Account of Flint and Genesee County from Their Organization.* Dayton, Ohio: National Historical Association, 1925.

Stevens, Sherman. "Sketch of Early Pioneer Life." In *Michigan Pioneer and Historical Collections,* vol. 7, 1886.

Stewart, Aura P. "St. Clair County: Recollections of Aura P. Stewart of St. Clair County of Things Relation to the Early Settlement of Michigan." In *Michigan Pioneer and Historical Collections,* vol. 4, 1883.

Stout, David B., "Ethnohistorical Report on the Saginaw Chippewa." In *Chippewa Indians V*, ed. David A. Horr. New York: Garland, 1974.

Sugden, John. *Tecumseh: A Life*. New York: Henry Holt, 1997.

———. *Tecumseh's Last Stand*. Norman: University of Oklahoma Press, 1985.

Tanner, Helen Hornbeck. "The Chippewa of Eastern Lower Michigan." In *Chippewa Indians V*, ed. David A. Horr. New York: Garland, 1974.

Tanner, John. *The Falcon: A Narrative of the Captivity and Adventures of John Tanner*. New York: Penguin, 1994.

Thompson, O. C. "History of Judge Zephaniah W. Bunce." In *Michigan Pioneer and Historical Collections*, vol. 1, 1877.

Thwaites, R. G., ed. *Wisconsin Historical Collections*. Vol. 20, *The Fur Trade in Wisconsin: 1812–1825*. Madison: Wisconsin Historical Society, 1911.

Tocqueville, Alexis de. *Journey to America*. Ed. J. P. Mayer. Trans. George Lawrence. New York: Anchor, 1971.

Trask, Kerry A. *Black Hawk: The Battle for the Heart of America*. New York: Henry Holt, 2006.

Trowbridge, C. C. "Detroit in 1819." In *Michigan Pioneer and Historical Collections*, vol. 4, 1883.

Walker, Henry N. *Reports of Cases Argued and Determined in the Court of Chancery of the State of Michigan*. Detroit: Harsha & Willcox, 1845.

Wallace, Anthony F. C. *Jefferson and the Indians: The Tragic Fate of the First Americans*. Cambridge: Harvard University Press, 1999.

Webber, William. "The Treaty of Saginaw in the Year 1819." In *Michigan Pioneer and Historical Collections*, vol. 26, 1896.

Wert, Jeffry D. *General James Longstreet: The Confederacy's Most Controversial Soldier*. New York: Simon and Schuster, 1993.

Wheeler-Voegelin, Erminie. "An Anthropological Report on Indian Use and Occupancy of Northern Michigan." In *Chippewa Indians V*, ed. David A. Horr. New York: Garland, 1974.

White, Richard. *The Middle Ground*. New York: Cambridge University Press, 1991.

Whiting, John L. "Dr. J. L. Whiting's Historic Sketch." In *Michigan Pioneer and Historical Collections*, vol. 2, 1880.

Williams, Benjamin O. "My Recollections of the Early Schools of Detroit That I Attended from the Year 1816 to 1819." In *Michigan Pioneer and Historical Collections*, vol. 5, 1884.

Williams, Ephraim S. "A Certificate or Statement Made by the Chippewa Chiefs, Signers of the Treaty of 1819." In *Michigan Pioneer and Historical Collections*, vol. 7, 1886.

———. "Indians and an Indian Trail: A Trip from Pontiac to Grand Blanc and the Saginaws." In *Michigan Pioneer and Historical Collections*, vol. 10, 1908.

———. "The Treaty of Saginaw in the Year 1819." In *Michigan Pioneer and Historical Collections*, vol. 7, 1886.

Williams, Mentor L., ed. *Schoolcraft's Indian Legends*. East Lansing: Michigan State University Press, 1956.

Wisconsin Historical Collections. Madison: State Historical Society of Wisconsin, vol. 3., 1904; vol. 10, 1888; vol. 20, 1911.

Witherell, B. F. H. "Incidents, 1807–1814." In *Wisconsin Historical Collections*, vol. 3, ed. Lyman C.

Draper. Madison: State Historical Society, 1904.

―――. "Kishkauko and Big Beaver." In *Wisconsin Historical Collections*, vol. 3, ed. Lyman C. Draper. Madison: State Historical Society, 1904.

――― (under the pseudonym "Hamtramck"). "Perils of the Border." *Detroit Free Press*, Feb. 17, 1856.

Wood, Edwin O. *History of Genesee County, Michigan*, 2 vols. Indianapolis: Federal Publishing, 1916.

Woodford, Frank, and Albert Hyma. *Gabriel Richard, Frontier Ambassador.* Detroit: Wayne State University Press, 1958.

Zug, Samuel. "Detroit in 1815–16." In *Michigan Pioneer and Historical Collections*, vol. 1, 1877.

INDEX